NOWHERE TO BE HOME

*We dedicate this collection to our mothers, Sue and Lisa,
and their mothers, Betty and Evelyn.*

NOWHERE TO BE HOME

NARRATIVES FROM SURVIVORS OF
BURMA'S MILITARY REGIME

EDITED BY

MAGGIE LEMERE AND ZOË WEST

WITH A FOREWORD BY

MARY ROBINSON

Associate editor
K'PRU TAW

Assistant editors
EMILY HONG, DEBBIE LANDIS,
THELMA YOUNG, CINDY CHOUNG

Additional assistance
SOE LIN AUNG, SAI ZOM HSENG, KIRK ACEVEDO, SALAI CUNG CUNG,
AUNG AUNG OO, TOBEY WARD, WILLIAM LLOYD GEORGE

Research editor   *Assistant research editor*
MICHAEL HAACK   ARIANNA KANDELL

VOICE OF WITNESS

VOICE OF WITNESS

MᶜSWEENEY'S BOOKS
SAN FRANCISCO

For more information about McSweeney's, see *mcsweeneys.net*
For more information about Voice of Witness, see *voiceofwitness.org*

ISBN (Hardcover): 978-1-934781-95-1
ISBN (Paperback): 978-1-936365-02-9

VOICE OF WITNESS

The books in the Voice of Witness series seek to illuminate human rights crises by humanizing the victims. Using oral history as a foundation, the series explores social justice issues through the stories of the men and women who experience them. These books are designed for readers of all levels—from high school and college students to policymakers—interested in a reality-based understanding of ongoing injustices in the United States and around the world. Visit *voiceofwitness.org* for more information.

VOICE OF WITNESS BOARD OF DIRECTORS

CONTENTS

THERE IS ENORMOUS POWER IN LISTENING

by Mary Robinson

Growing up in the west of Ireland, I would watch my father, a doctor, go on rounds through the countryside to visit sick families, families too poor to pay doctors' fees. My father spent long days traveling from home to home, sincerely and patiently listening to the stories of these families and administering care. Though I would often impatiently wonder when he'd be done, I gradually came to appreciate the time he gave and the sense he had of the dignity of each person.

When he would return, my father would recount the stories his patients told him. The stories were filled with suffering and sadness, yet many of them were also defined by courage and resilience in the face of great hardship. That courage inspires and guides my work to this day. Those stories first compelled me to pursue a lifetime of working for human rights, and since then my belief in the power of stories to foster compassion and guide us as a society has only grown stronger.

The narratives in *Nowhere to Be Home* speak strongly to the power and importance of storytelling, and its role in cultivating the respect and nuanced understandings that are crucial to creating progressive change. The twenty-two people who share their intimate accounts of life under Burma's military regime have shown exceptional courage in telling their stories.

Burma held my attention and elicited my deep concern during my time as the United Nations High Commissioner for Human Rights. It remains paramount in my mind as a member of The Elders, a group of world leaders brought together by Nelson Mandela to support peace building, address major causes of human suffering, and promote the shared interests of humanity.

Burma has been ruled by a military regime since 1962, and the current regime's oppressive economic and political policies leave the people of Burma in a constant struggle for essentials like basic healthcare and a living wage. Instability is entrenched by endemic poverty and oppressive rule, with bitter tensions dividing the government and Burma's many ethnic groups. It is a country with a deeply fractured society. Civil war between the government army and armed opposition groups has continued for decades in some border areas. Millions of Burmese have fled or been displaced from their homes.

Displacement is at the center of the stories in this book. There are instances of physical displacement—like the story of the young boy whose family spent years secretly moving from one makeshift jungle village to another to escape military attacks—but there are also symbolic displacements, such as the experience of political prisoners who felt unwelcome in their communities after being released. Military rule in Burma has created a society marked by fear and distrust, putting home out of reach for both those who are physically displaced outside of Burma and those who remain in Burma.

On November 7, 2010, elections were held in Burma for the first time since 1990. The main opposition party, the National League for Democracy (NLD), refused to participate because of unfair election laws and a new constitution that enshrines military rule. Political participation in the elections was severely restricted, and observers were not surprised when the party linked to the national military claimed a landslide victory amid reports of vote manipulation, intimidation, and ballot rigging. The election presented a difficult situation for political activists and politicians in Burma, who were faced with the choice between participating in the election or boycotting as the NLD did. I am sympathetic to all of the difficult decisions faced by people living under the current military regime.

The leader of the NLD, Nobel Peace Prize winner Daw Aung San Suu Kyi, is a leading advocate for democracy and human rights in Burma. When The Elders joined together to form our organization in 2007, we appointed Daw Aung San Suu Kyi as an honorary Elder. And while her military-imposed house arrest has prevented her from joining our meetings, we always keep an empty chair to honor her and Burma's political prisoners.

Thankfully, on November 13, 2010, Daw Aung San Suu Kyi was released from house arrest. While her release is a very important step, we must not allow ourselves to forget the plight of the more than two thousand other political prisoners who remain incarcerated. The Elders call for all political prisoners in Burma to be released, and for a peaceful transition to a more open society.

My fellow Elders and I also urge the international community to assist in opening a dialogue between the government, the opposition, ethnic minorities, and religious groups of Burma in order to begin a process of reconciliation. It is essential that a plurality of voices is heard if Burma is ever to see peace and social justice.

It is in that spirit of inclusion and giving that I also urge you to listen to and honor the courageous voices in this volume. The intricacies of the life stories here shed light on the complex challenges the Burmese people face, and therefore inform the ways we might all act to support human rights in Burma.

---

*Mary Robinson is a member of The Elders (*www.theelders.org*). She was the first female president of Ireland and is the former United Nations High Commissioner for Human Rights.*

INTRODUCTION

IF WE FEAR THEM, WE ARE USELESS

by Maggie Lemere and Zoë West

As we write this, Burma finds itself in a defining moment.

A country of more than 55 million people, marked by oppressive military rule and civil war, Burma has been ruled by successive military regimes for the past five decades. The current regime, the State Peace and Development Council (SPDC)—led by Commander-in-Chief of the Tatmadaw (Burma's military), Than Shwe—is among the most notorious human rights violators in the world.

The military regime held the first national elections in twenty years on November 7, 2010, in what was widely viewed as an attempt to consolidate and legitimize its rule under the veil of "disciplined democracy." Citing deeply flawed election rules, the main democratic opposition party, the National League for Democracy, boycotted the election, refusing to enter a candidate. As many analysts predicted, the junta-backed Union Solidarity and Development Party (USDP)—headed by the SPDC prime minister and other SPDC ministers—won approximately 75 percent of parliamentary seats.

One week *after* the election, NLD leader Daw Aung San Suu Kyi—Burma's widely respected and beloved democratic voice—was released from house arrest after being confined for fifteen of the past twenty-one years. Meanwhile, new rounds of fighting erupted between armed opposition groups and the Tatmadaw along Burma's eastern border with Thailand.

Nineteen armed opposition groups have signed tenuous ceasefire agreements with the ruling SPDC regime, while others have refused, and still actively oppose the regime. In its campaign to crush armed resistance to their rule, the Tatmadaw has committed widespread human rights abuses, eliciting grave concern from the international community. The Tatmadaw has tortured and imprisoned thousands of nonviolent democratic opposition members; at press time, there were 2,203 political prisoners,[1] including activists, journalists, politicians, artists, and Buddhist monks. With brutal and calculated tactics, Burma's military regime has successfully imposed a deeply embedded fear of dissent across the country.

No matter how you interpret recent events, Burma remains in the same protracted crisis it has been in since colonialism began in the late 1800s and since a military coup d'état thwarted the progress of the newly independent state in 1962. The people of Burma continue to suffer the far-ranging and severe impacts of oppressive military rule and ongoing violent conflict; the civil war between the Karen National Liberation Army and the Burmese government is considered the longest-running civil war in the post–World War II era.

Across the country, the military junta's abuses have included forced labor; arbitrary arrest and detention; physical and sexual violence; torture; severe restriction of speech, assembly, and movement; the destruction of homes, property, and villages; forced military conscription, including the conscription of child soldiers; and severe persecution against religious and ethnic minorities. As a result, between 2 and 4 million Burmese are

---

[1] The Assistance Association for Political Prisoners (Burma); as of November 3rd, 2010.

displaced both internally and across Burma's borders. Since just 1996, more than 3,500 villages have been destroyed in eastern Burma alone.[2]

Nowhere to Be Home delves into the diverse lives of twenty-two people from Burma, who describe life under the military regime in their own words. The narratives in this book are based on interviews conducted with people inside Burma, as well as people who fled and are now living in Thailand, Malaysia, Bangladesh, and the United States. The narrators encompass a wide range of intersecting and constantly evolving identities. Stories of persecuted ethnic minorities stand beside the story of a child soldier forced to become persecutor; the words of political prisoners stand beside that of a fisherman with HIV.

Though the narratives in this collection were gathered in the year leading up to Burma's November 2010 election, the stories depict full spans of life experience, and the persistence of the human rights crisis over decades.

Though slightly smaller than Texas, Burma is a diverse, multiethnic country. While two-thirds of the country are ethnic Burmans, there are more than 135 other ethnic nationalities, and more than 100 distinct languages.

Many of Burma's current challenges stem from divisions—both of land and of people—fostered under the British colonial regime, which gained complete control in 1884 over territories that were previously independently ruled.

Toward the end of World War II, Burmese nationalists led by General Aung San fought the British for independence. In 1947, the British ceded to the demands of the independence movement, and Aung San became the leader of an interim government. Aung San and representatives of a few of Burma's ethnic nationalities signed the Panglong Agreement in 1947, in which they agreed to form a Federal Union of Burma and grant ethnic minorities some autonomy. Independence was officially granted in Janu-

---

[2] From "Protracted Displacement and Militarization in eastern Burma," a report by the Thai–Burma Border Consortium, 2009.

ary 1948, but General Aung San was assassinated with most of his cabinet before the constitution went into effect. It is believed that a group of paramilitaries connected to a political rival carried out the assassinations.

The assassination of Aung San and his cabinet members became a major obstacle to the formation of the new union. The years between 1947 and 1962 were marked by instability as ethnic nationalities felt increasingly threatened by the directions the new leadership was taking. New armed groups were formed along ethnic lines, and the union of Burma collapsed.

In 1962, a Burman general named Ne Win led a military coup d'état, which would set in motion nearly five decades of military rule and armed conflict in Burma. Economic reforms were enacted that largely isolated the country and created a precipitous downward spiral. By 1987, the economy was in ruins and protests had erupted all over the country. The largest demonstrations in Burma's history occurred on August 8, 1988, and saw the emergence of Daw Aung San Suu Kyi as an important proponent of democracy. The current ruling junta, the State Peace and Development Council, or SPDC (formerly known as the State Law and Order Restoration Council), seized power in 1988 after the protests. When Daw Aung Suu Kyi's party, the National League for Democracy, won national elections in 1990, the SPDC refused to hand over power. They imprisoned Suu Kyi and other opposition leaders. Suu Kyi remained under house arrest for the majority of the subsequent two decades, but she continued to call for a tripartite dialogue between ethnic minorities, the military, and the democracy movement.

Despite ongoing resistance to its rule—including the monk-led "Saffron Revolution" in 2007, which was brutally suppressed—the SPDC military junta maintains its oppresive power. The regime profits greatly and reinforces its strength with the sale of natural resources, earning around $3 billion annually through trade with countries such as Thailand, Singapore, China, and India.[3] While the regime and its

---

[3] Earthrights International, Revenue Transparency in Burma Campaign.

business cronies are extremely wealthy, they only invest 1.4 percent of Burma's GDP in health care and education, leaving most Burmese citizens with substandard options on both fronts.

In 2005, the SPDC moved Burma's capital to a gleaming new city, Naypyidaw, built to the tune of around $2 billion. Naypyidaw, built in secrecy, is effectively an isolated city largely reserved for military officials and civil servants. As the only city in Burma with twenty-four hour electricity, the disparities between Naypyidaw and the rest of the country are stark—and revealing.

"Imagining what it is like to be someone other than oneself is at the core of our humanity. It is the essence of compassion, and it is the beginning of morality."
—*Ian McEwan*

With a country like Burma, where news reports emphasize millions of displaced and affected peoples and a conflict stretching over decades, it can be hard to connect to the people who face this reality every day. The individual lives of the Burmese people become buried under a pile of issues, abuses, and statistics.

Oral history creates a space for those "faraway stories"—the experiences of people whose realities seem starkly different from our own—to enter the realm of our awareness through their own voices. It offers the chance for those stories to be heard in delicate nuance, rather than sweeping generalizations.

Just as any person does not fit into neat categories, the people who shared their stories in this book are multidimensional and not easily categorized. The narrators highlight not only the incredible challenges of life under the military regime, but also what they love—what they are fighting for. Every person we interviewed took pleasure in describing his or her best memories, in highlighting a side of life in Burma that reveals hope and dignity. Nge Nge, a teacher, recounted how blessed she felt every time she walked into school and was greeted by a flock of students hoping for the privilege of carrying a book for her or holding her hand.

Khine Su transported us to the lush rice fields where she worked as a girl, singing with her friends as the rain fell around them. In honoring the fullness and fluidity of their lives, the narrators demonstrate the humanity that is missing in simple labels like "migrant worker" or "refugee."

Each narrator reveals complex truths and realities, cast upon the backdrop of perpetual instability in Burma—a son or a daughter, a migrant worker one day, an underground activist the next, or both at the same time.

Understanding the complexity and richness of people's life experiences in Burma is paramount to understanding the current political and social landscape in the country itself. As you read these stories, the interconnections between different narrators' experiences will begin to surface. Each narrative builds another layer in the larger picture, with intersecting experiences that reveal a loose web of causes and effects, actions and reactions.

You'll read the story of Knoo Know, whose father was a general in the Kachin Independence Army (the KIA, an ethnic opposition army), alongside the story of Saw Moe, who fought in Burma's military against the KIA. You'll hear from U Agga, a monk who recounts his experience escaping the SPDC's crackdown on the Saffron Revolution, as well as from Philip, a monk who became a soldier in the Shan State Army-South. Though this book is by no means exhaustive or representative of every Burmese person's experiences, these stories, viewed collectively, form a multifaceted portrait of the crisis in Burma.

As editors, we strove to create a unique collection of narratives, balancing an array of important issues and demographic factors. Choosing which narratives to include was a difficult task, and is inevitably an imperfect process. Those more familiar with Burma will immediately realize what *wasn't* included.

We'd also like to note that this book does not represent a comprehensive view of Burma's border regions; because of various constraints, interviews were not collected on the China–Burma or India–Burma borders. Border areas inside Burma were also mostly inaccessible to us. We point you to the work of Human Rights Watch, EarthRights International, and the Network for Human Rights Documentation – Burma, for a more quantitative overview of the human rights situation inside Burma and in its border regions.

The sociopolitical landscape in Burma is constantly changing, and will no doubt have evolved in the time it takes for this book to reach your hands. Right now, the SPDC claims to be ceding power to democratic rule through the recent elections, yet the ruling generals have carefully enacted measures to ensure their continued authority.

The elections were widely condemned as a sham by the international community. Political prisoners were barred from participating, and substantial voter fraud and voter intimidation was reported. The new political landscape overtly privileges the military, as the new constitution drafted in 2008 reserves one-quarter of the seats in the lower-house and one-third in the upper-house of Parliament for military officials. Further, many military officials resigned from their posts earlier in the year in anticipation of taking power in the civilian government.

Most argue that the election was a definitive setback, allowing the regime to cast itself as "reforming" and therefore gain more lucrative business deals, while consolidating its power. However, some contend that small steps in the right direction will potentially open the door for more civil participation. But no matter how you look at it, profound change is imperative, because Burma is crumbling. Long-neglected infrastructure is reflected in the dilapidated streets of Rangoon, Burma's former capital city. The din of generators is a constant soundtrack where electricity is fickle and sometimes limited to six hours per day. The internet is heavily censored, and short-wave radios are the primary means for secretly accessing news from outside the country.

Around 70 percent of the population lives in rural areas, relying on farming for their livelihood.[4] One-third of the population lives below

---

[4] CIA World Factbook: Burma.

the poverty line, and the GDP per capita is reported to be the thirteenth lowest in the world.[5] Many of the people we interviewed, such as Khine Su and Ko Mg Mg, described forced labor as a normal part of life in their villages. For a family that lives from hand to mouth, months, weeks, or even days of unpaid forced labor can be crippling. Such abuses are embedded in the everyday lives of much of Burma's population, creating an unforgiving set of circumstances where daily survival is a challenge. This system leaves people to face tough choices, as many of our narrators describe—decisions like leaving your family and your country for years on end in an attempt to find a better livelihood.

The day Daw Aung San Suu Kyi was released, thousands of well-wishers gathered in front of the gates of her home in anticipation of hearing her speak publicly for the first time in seven years. One of Aung San Suu Kyi's first statements reported after her release was simple and powerful: "I want to listen to the people of Burma's voices." We hope that in reading this collection, you'll listen to the voices of people from Burma, and feel an enduring connection that motivates continued interest, reflection, and, when appropriate, action.

The severity of the abuses in Burma is undeniable, but as many narrators revealed in their stories, there is also hope for transformation. While living and working on the Thailand–Burma border, we were consistently impressed and inspired by the impact of education and training programs through which the people of Burma are devoting enormous effort to working with their communities.

Beyond providing skills and knowledge, these educational initiatives open new spaces for people from Burma to move beyond the deep divisions enacted by geography, ethnic nationalism, and class, among other factors. This dynamic environment seems especially crucial for the youth living in border areas, many of whom are dedicated to better-

[5] Refugees International, Burma: "Current Humanitarian Situation."

ing themselves through education despite the challenges they face daily. These organizations and efforts deserve the continued support of the international community. For a poignant reflection on the importance of education—particularly for youth from Burma, where the education system is in shambles—we hope you will read the epilogue written by the associate editor of this book, K'pru Taw. K'pru is a young Karen man from rural Mon State, Burma, who persevered through a long bout of tuberculosis and his family's entrenched poverty (compounded by forced labor) to continually seek education. When he was sixteen, he left his home and went to a refugee camp on the Thailand–Burma border so he could study. In the past six years, he's made remarkable strides in his education and work—as part of Voice of Witness, as well as with other organizations and projects. His tireless commitment to this book was vital to its completion.

It is our intent that these stories demonstrate the humanity we all share, through our histories and in our present moment. What may seem beyond our comprehension is worth listening to with the hope of gaining small but important insights into the human condition, and thus, ourselves—such reflection is vital to our ability to promote the progressive and lasting change we wish to see. As they shed light on the crisis in Burma, the narrators in this book are also testifying to the value inherent in telling and remembering.

—*Maggie Lemere and Zoë West*

METHODOLOGY

We conducted seventy interviews for this book over the course of twelve months in 2009 and 2010. The interviews ranged from several hours to several days in length, and more than 400 hours of audio were recorded.

When we began working on this book, both of us were based near the Thailand–Burma border, working separately on projects with local Burma organizations. We met our interviewees through our networks of friends, colleagues, and the local leaders of community-based and human-rights organizations. We would like to acknowledge and thank a small core group of colleagues who helped shape the scope of this project from its initial conception. Throughout the process of compiling this volume, they continued to offer their guidance and feedback in structuring the book. They were instrumental to our process of identifying interviewees, arranging logistics, and undertaking additional research.

We worked with interpreters to conduct the majority of the interviews in this book; the interpreters, who were often working with community organizations, generously volunteered their time. The narrators have a range of native languages through which interviews and interpretation were done. Follow-up interviews were done in every case possible—in most cases, several follow-ups were made. Of the seventy individuals who told us their life stories, twenty-two were chosen to be included here. Although we could include only a limited number of the interviews, it was truly an honor and an integral part of the process to listen to and learn from each person we met.

The book is divided into five sections, by country: Thailand, Malaysia, Bangladesh, Burma, and the United States. The book follows the geographical order where interviews were first conducted and how the project took form. The variety of locales where we held our interviews reflects the wide range of circumstances in which the narrators live.

In Thailand, interviews took place in Bangkok, Chiang Mai, Mae Sot, and Khao Lak. We met Ma Su Mon, for example, at a Starbucks café in a bustling modern shopping mall in Bangkok, where she works and studies—a world away from the Burmese prison where she was held in solitary confinement. In fact, Ma Su Mon confessed that every time she drinks a cappuccino or dines at a nice restaurant, she cannot help feeling guilty as she thinks of her friends who remain behind bars. Other interviews in Thailand were conducted in venues ranging from a home in the middle of a rubbish dump, to the office of an organization of exiled monks, to the house of a group of underground youth activists. Thailand is known to be the reluctant host to thousands of Burmese migrant workers and refugees, and as the central hub of Burmese political activists in exile.

A few months after we began interviews in Thailand, we traveled to Malaysia, where interviews took place in Kuala Lumpur and Puchong. One day we drove to the outskirts of Kuala Lumpur, the capital city, and took a short hike through the jungle to meet a group of refugees living in what had become known as a "jungle camp." When we arrived at the wooden hut that marked the entrance to the settlement, a group of dogs surrounded us, snarling and advancing until a man hurried over and warmly greeted us. Only a handful of men were there; the residents had gotten news that the camp would soon be raided by Malaysian law enforcement officials. All of the refugees had fled farther into the jungle to escape arrest, and these men had returned to assess the situation. Everyone sat nervously during the interview, listening for law enforcement to possibly arrive on the hillside. After a phone call of warning was received, we had to cut the interview short. Other interviews in Malaysia were held in hidden community refugee centers bustling with people recently arrived from Burma, and the single-room apartments where refugee families—sometimes twenty people or more—lived together. The interviews featured the stories of urban migrants and refugees who are perpetually vulnerable to the high rates of human trafficking, the absence of refugee camps, and the presence of multiple detention centers, within which more than 1,300 people have died since 2006.

In Bangladesh, interviews were conducted in Dhaka and Cox's Bazar, as well as inside two large unofficial refugee camps, Kutupalong makeshift camp and Leda. We walked through the sprawling Kutupalong makeshift camp, home to more than 20,000 Rohingya refugees. The refugees had built simple huts with walls of mud, sticks, and sheets of plastic. The Burma–Bangladesh border is home to thousands of stateless Rohingya refugees who fled severe religious and ethnic persecution and are now living in both official and unofficial refugee camps with scant resources, as well as living as migrant workers without security. This border area also hosts refugees from other ethnic nationalities who have fled from western parts of Burma. The people of the camp generously accepted us into their homes, where they told us the stories of why they had to leave Burma, and about the current challenges they face in Bangladesh.

In Burma, interviews were conducted in the country's two biggest cities, Rangoon and Mandalay, as well as at the Loi Tai Leng army base of the Shan State Army-South. We cannot share the precise details of where and how we conducted interviews inside Burma, as it would compromise the security of those who must still resort to largely secretive methods in order to share important information with foreign visitors and journalists.

In the United States, interviews took place in Utica, Brooklyn and Buffalo, New York, where thousands of refugees from Burma have been resettled. One can only imagine the monk U Agga's initial arrival in upstate New York in the dead of winter, never before having seen snow. Yet despite the vast adjustments required of them, the people we met—monks, students, a journalist—were steadily and successfully building their new lives. Their households were filled with English, Burmese, and Karen language, Burmese curry and cans of Pepsi, computers and *longyis*, the traditional sarongs worn in Burma by both men and women.

We have taken many measures to protect the security of the narrators in this book; most names of narrators and the people they discussed have been changed. In addition, many place names have been omitted, and other identifying details have been left out. In most cases, the final edited versions of the stories were sent to the narrators for their review and approval. In the few cases where it wasn't possible to contact the narrators again, they had given us approval in the initial interview to edit and publish their narratives at our discretion, following their requests for security.

We conducted the majority of the interviews outside of Burma, mainly for the plain fact that anyone caught doing an interview with us inside the country would stand a real risk of arrest, torture, or imprisonment. We therefore limited the number of interviews we did inside Burma and took great measures to protect our narrators' security while working inside the country. However, the majority of our narrators interviewed outside of Burma had only recently left the country, and spoke mainly about their lives before leaving.

Those who spoke to us from neighboring countries also experience little security. Often living without documentation, there is a constant anxiety in the awareness that they could be arrested at any time, exploited, and possibly even forced back to Burma. Even our narrators who have been resettled to the United States must still consider the security of their family and friends in Burma, as the military is known to threaten and harass the families of anyone they perceive to be tied to the opposition.

The act of speaking was for some narrators an act of resistance; for others, a plea for help; for others, catharsis. Many narrators were committed to sharing their stories in order to help others avoid facing similar traumatic situations. But for every narrator, the risk of speaking out was and is very real—the act of speaking demanded great courage.

The ubiquitous presence of informants and military intelligence (now called Military Affairs Security) has led to a prevalent sense of distrust among the people of Burma. And though one of the military junta's most successful strategies has been to capitalize on division and a culture of fear, they have not succeeded in diminishing the deep warmth and hospitality shown by many people we interviewed.

THAILAND

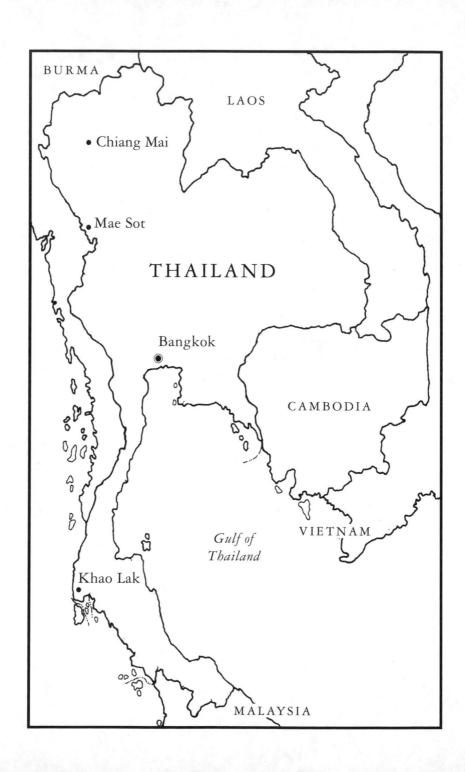

KYAW ZWAR

40, political activist

ETHNICITY: *Burman*

BIRTHPLACE: *Rangoon Division, Burma*

INTERVIEWED IN: *Mae Sot, Thailand*

We met with Kyaw Zwar in a compound where he works with youth activists. The walls of the compound are covered in graffiti sporting the group's logo, a thumbs-up symbol. Activists strategize for revolution and practice beat-boxing and guitar around the compound (the group also releases music videos and albums). Kyaw Zwar had been released from his second internment as a political prisoner in Burma just weeks before we interviewed him. According to the Assistance Association for Political Prisoners (Burma), as of November 3, 2010, there were 2,203 political prisoners detained in Burma. They include monks, students, musicians, comedians, elected members of parliament, and lawyers.

If I explained how I became a political organizer, I would have to tell you my whole life story. Ever since 1988, I feel like the military regime took me, put me in a pot, and has been shaking me around. I'd say it's getting worse.

I was born in Rangoon in 1970. I am the youngest person in my family—I have three brothers and four sisters. When I was young, I didn't know about politics, and I was not interested. I felt that I had freedom.

Rangoon is not developed but it is crowded. I would say the place where I lived is beautiful. There are different kinds and classes of people in Rangoon. There are those who are struggling for basic needs, and those working as government personnel in different government departments. My family was middle class. My father sold car parts, my brother sold building supplies for homes, and my sisters sold betel nut.

I went to school in Rangoon. I went from twelve o'clock noon to four in the afternoon, and the teachers would take turns instructing us. But sometimes I would run away from school. On those days when my friends and I had some money, we would go to Inya Lake to swim and spend our time there.[1] At the time when school was supposed to end, we would go back home.

My favorite subject in school was history. I didn't like world history when I was young, but I liked learning about Burma's history. We had to learn about Burmese dynasties in the past as well as the English and Japanese eras in Burma. I learned a little bit about the different ethnic groups of Burma in school, but if I wanted to learn more about different ethnicities, I had to read books from outside the country.

When we listened to adults speak about history, they would tell us conflicting things. I didn't know what was true and what wasn't. I was certain that the history about the kings was true, but when I learned the history of different ethnic groups of Burma, I realized that their stories were different than the ones I'd heard. I didn't know what the truth was about different events that had happened throughout history. I wanted to learn what the truth really was.

OUR SOCIALISM WAS NOT LIKE REAL SOCIALISM

When I was eighteen years old, the uprising happened. I still wasn't that interested in politics, but my enthusiasm grew from the anger I felt when

---

[1] Inya Lake is in Rangoon. On its banks are the elite neighborhoods that contain Daw Aung San Suu Kyi's compound and the late general General Ne Win's residence.

I saw the military kill university students.

In 1988, Ne Win was the head of state and he was using the Burmese Way to Socialism to control the country.[2] There was only one party in the whole country and he was the head of it. He ruled the country as a dictatorship—our socialism was not like real socialism.

There are many reasons that the protests happened in 1988. One of these is that the Ne Win government put everything under state ownership. They later declared the abolishment of some banknotes. They made an announcement that they would abolish the 35-kyat and 75-kyat notes. At the time, the 75-kyat note was the biggest note in Burma. The government had previously abolished the 100-kyat notes and replaced them with the 35-kyat and 75-kyat notes. But after the government gave out these replacement notes to the public, they declared the notes illegal and they didn't produce anything new. We weren't given any compensation or any new notes.[3]

People were angry. We faced problems, because although we had money, we could not use it any more. If you had that money, you could just boil it in water—it had no use. Some families and university students just burned it.

My family had quite a lot of money at the time, but after the government declared that we couldn't use it any more, we just gave it to children to play with. To survive, my family could sell off our materials, like car parts and building supplies, but we could not sell a lot. For six months, we struggled. Like everyone, my parents said the government was really bad.

I believe the government abolished the money because of inflation. The government itself was not affected, because they gave out all those

---

[2] The Burmese Way to Socialism was Ne Win's plan to build the Burmese nation post-independence. For more, see pages 461-463 of the "A Brief History of Burma" in the appendix.

[3] On September 5, 1987, Ne Win announced Burma's second demonetization, taking 25, 35, and 75 bank notes out of circulation. The official reason for the demonetization was to fight inflation and black market activities. For more about Burma's demonetization, see appendix pages 463-464.

banknotes to the people before they abolished them—only the people were affected. Some were starving.

Discontent grew among the university students, because they no longer had enough money for tuition, transportation, or food. At the end of every month, their parents would send them money for tuition and daily expenses, but the students could no longer use it. Their discontent became the spark for the '88 uprising.

THEY COULD CHALLENGE HIS POWER

I didn't see the demonstrations in March, but I heard about what was happening because I was near Rangoon. The demonstrations started on March 13. The fighting actually started the day before, when students from the RIT—Rangoon Institute of Technology—got into a big fight with one of the sons of a BSPP official.[4] The students were angry because one of them got injured in the fight, but the son of the party official was only detained for a moment by the police and then released. Because of this, the students went to protest on March 13. A clash broke out that night, and a student named Maung Phone Maw was killed.[5]

After those incidents, the students were angry. On March 16, students from both the RIT and Rangoon University marched together. The students were protesting government oppression, demanding that they investigate the death of the student and take action against the people who killed him.

Ne Win knew that if he didn't oppress the students, they would be able to challenge his power. That day, the students started marching through Rangoon. When the students were at the bank of Inya Lake, riot

---

[4] The Burma Socialist Programme Party was the only legal political party in Burma from 1962 to 1988. The party congress met periodically and repeatedly "elected" Ne Win as its chairman. For more on the Burma Socialist Programme Party, see appendix pages 462-463.

[5] Ko Maung Phone Maw was murdered by the military on his school's campus while participating in pro-democracy protests. His death was the catalyst for the 1988 popular uprising.

police came and aggressively started cracking down on the protest. A lot of students started running into the lake to escape the brutal crackdown, and some of them drowned. The riot police also beat and killed some of the students.

Both male and female students were put inside extremely crowded trucks and transported away. I was in Insein Township and I heard one of the trucks as they went through the city to Insein Prison. The people inside were shouting, "We're all dying inside the truck! We are students—we were unjustly arrested!" I heard they overcrowded that prison truck so much that some people could not breathe and they died of suffocation.[6]

After the March 16 protest, the government closed all of the universities and made all of the students return to their homes. The government didn't want the students to assemble and form organizations.

Although it happened so long ago, we can still feel what happened that day, especially when we are standing at the banks of Inya Lake.

THE '88 UPRISING

The protests continued throughout March, but everyone stayed quiet in April and May.

The university students left Rangoon and went back to their hometowns to spread news about what had happened. They talked to high school students about how the government had oppressed them. The students' feelings were growing even stronger.

When the schools opened again in June, the students formed a demonstration camp at Rangoon University. Young people, including high school students and workers, joined the university students at the demonstration camp and went out on the streets together to protest. They were really angry at the police and wanted action to be taken against those who'd killed the students.

---

[6] Forty-one students suffocated to death in the van. This incident became a lightning rod for the student democracy movement.

Some students didn't go back to their hometowns and stayed in Rangoon so they could organize protests to bring down the Burma Socialist Programme Party. This was the start of the '88 uprising.

Groups of students were marching, and people joined them. On June 18, 19, and 20 they were marching in the streets, but they were shot at on June 21 in Myaynigone. Some students were killed. More and more groups joined the uprising until everyone was involved. With the force of so many people, combined with their dissatisfaction, the '88 demonstrations became a fight to bring down Ne Win's government.

THE MILITARY SHOT DIRECTLY AT US

In August of 1988, the government started to really crack down.

I marched in Rangoon on August 9 and 10. At the front of the crowd there were monks and students giving speeches. The army and riot police were cracking down on the protesters. The army used guns and the riot police used batons and shields. The police marched and hit the students with the batons at close distance. When using the batons didn't seem to be successful anymore—because some students were able to resist by throwing stones—the government switched the soldiers who were on duty. Then the army soldiers came close and shot at the students. The soldiers marched forward step by step, firing their guns.

Even though people were really angry, they became very afraid of the consequences for marching, because Ne Win had told the military not to shoot in the air, but to shoot directly at the people.

At the time of the demonstrations, I just helped in general with everything. For example, I took responsibility for providing water and food to demonstrators, and I looked for medicine if it was necessary.

We marched to the sections of the township that were not actively involved in politics yet. We marched in big crowds so that we could encourage the young people to be brave and come join the protests. If the number of people who were marching was small, I'd go around and organize other people to join with us. We also persuaded the women, and eventually they went on to form the women's union and other organizations. Our forces became stronger.

In a lot of places around Rangoon, the soldiers shot and cracked down on the demonstrators. There was also shooting in other states, but it was the worst in Rangoon, because that's where the government was located. Students were shot in front of everyone.

MY OWN DISCONTENT BEGAN THERE

The military coup happened on September 18, 1988. On that morning, the students were marching on the streets. The government cracked down and there were more casualties. We couldn't go out on to the streets anymore. The army was deployed onto streets everywhere, and martial law and a curfew were declared. During the crackdown, General Saw Maung from the State Law and Order Restoration Council announced that the government would prepare for a multi-party democratic system, and that it would allow parties to register. Everyone was waiting to see what would happen, and eventually we saw political parties come out to register. But while organizing the parties, some of the party leaders were arrested.

I don't know how other people felt at the time, but I was very angry—I felt like I was one of the students. My own discontent began there.

I DID NOT FEAR ANYTHING

You could say that the first time I started to have real political views and knowledge was during the uprising in 1988, when I started to listen to speeches by Min Ko Naing, the current leader of student groups in Burma.[7] The All Burma Federation of Student Unions leaders elected Min Ko

---

[7] Min Ko Naing is a well-known political dissident who entered Burma's political arena as a prominent leader of the student uprising in the late 1980s. He was formerly chairman of the All Burma Federation of Student Unions (ABFSU), and is currently being held in prison for his role in the 2007 Saffron Revolution.

Naing unanimously as their leader because of his enthusiasm and strong spirit, his speeches and his capacity to lead.[8] In the '88 demonstrations, his persuasion, organization, and the firm path he took made him a really worthy leader.

The ABFSU has a long history. It was originally formed by General Aung San, and was involved in the struggle against colonialism.[9] Under Ne Win's regime, the ABFSU became active again, and the students were the first ones to fight against the government. Then Ne Win abolished the ABFSU and bombed their office. He targeted the student groups because they produced all of the educated people and politicians who resisted him.

After the military coup, there was no more marching and I had to become involved in the democracy movement in different ways. After high school, I could not continue my education and go on to university because all of the schools and universities were closed by the government in response to the uprising. I thought about what to do next. Many of the people who were involved in the protests were NLD members, so I contacted the party.[10] Older party members gave me books to read, so I began to have more ideas about politics.

I decided that I wanted to work with the NLD youth. I submitted an application to the NLD and I was accepted as a member and an organizer. After the coup, we needed to be part of organizations in order to increase our political power.

I started going to Daw Aung San Suu Kyi's compound on January 1,

---

[8] The All Burma Federation of Student Unions traces its roots back to the 1930s struggle for independence, but reemerged during the 1988 uprising under the leadership of Min Ko Naing. For more on the ABSFU and students' role in Burmese politics, see the appendix pages 463-467.

[9] General Aung San is Burma's independence hero who led the fight against British rule. He is the father of Nobel Peace Prize winner Daw Aung San Suu Kyi. For more on Aung San, see the "A Brief History of Burma" section of the appendix, pages 459-460.

[10] The National League for Democracy is the party of Nobel Prize winner Daw Aung San Suu Kyi and former Tatmadaw Commander-in-Chief U Tin Oo. The NLD won Burma's 1990 elections. For more on the NLD see the appendix pages 465-468 and 473.

1989. We met at her compound every week and discussed young people's issues and the political situation in Burma. When she had free time, she would tell the students to choose a discussion topic. At the time, there were about twenty or thirty students going there. Sometimes she told the young students about international and Burmese politics.

Sometimes I went to her compound once or twice in a week, and sometimes I slept there for two or three nights. I visited the compound for a few months and then I left in July, but I have many memories from there. What I cannot forget is how Daw Aung San Suu Kyi gave encouragement to the young people when we felt unhappy. She always steered us the right way.

Daw Aung San Suu Kyi has influenced me more than anyone else. She does what she believes in, and she never gives up. She always told us that the young people must take leadership roles and that other people must open a door for young people to bring changes in the country. That is my best memory.

At the time, my family was worried for me, because if you are involved in politics in Burma, if you work with the ABSFU or if you meet with Daw Aung San Suu Kyi, you will very likely be imprisoned. The more active you are, the more you're at risk. They didn't want me to be involved in politics. When I returned home in the evenings, my mother would say, "Come and stay with the family. Stop your political work." She cried and explained her feelings to me, but I didn't want to listen to her. I continued participating because I had hope and enthusiasm.

I did not fear anything at the time. Everyone has their own personal problems, right? I didn't care about mine. I just wanted to be involved in politics because I wanted there to be change.

I THOUGHT THEY WOULD DESTROY MY FUTURE

Daw Aung San Suu Kyi was put under house arrest on July 20, 1989. At the time I was working at the NLD office in Insein Township, and I was responsible for youth and information. In August, I was arrested because I'd organized people to ask for Daw Aung San Suu Kyi's and U Tin Oo's release.[11] When they arrested me, I felt like the government destroyed my enthusiasm.

On that day, there were seventy young people in the office. We heard that the army would come to arrest us and we didn't want everyone to get arrested, so we asked many of them to leave. But when the army surrounded our office, there were eight leaders still inside.

Four trucks full of soldiers came to the office. There were about thirty or forty soldiers. They came in the office and destroyed our signboards that asked for Daw Aung San Suu Kyi and U Tin Oo's release. They also broke the NLD flagpole, they broke the windows, and they threw our papers on the floor. They insulted us and called us names like "motherfuckers." They said, "Who are you? What are you doing? Even if I kill you, I won't lose my position—I'll get promoted."

We replied, "We have an agreement with the government that we can have this office, so you cannot come in here violently and destroy it. If you want to arrest people, you must have the order to arrest, and then you can come in and make the arrests." They closed the office and arrested all eight of us and put us in a truck.

At nineteen years old, I was the youngest activist. The other arrested NLD members were in their twenties, up to about forty years old. When they put me in the truck I wondered, *What will happen to me? Maybe they will take me to interrogation, and then they will beat me or kill me.* I was very worried—I was sweating, you know. I'd never talked about torture and punishment with other people before, but I knew that if I was arrested, I would be tortured and beaten.

I thought that I would face a worse situation than the other NLD members because I was the youngest. I thought I might be killed, or become crazy. I thought they would torture me until I became handicapped and destroy my future. I was also very worried about my mother, because

---

[11] U Tin Oo is the deputy leader of the NLD and the former Commander-in-Chief of the Burmese military.

I thought she would feel bad about my arrest and that the condition of her heart would deteriorate.

It was only forty-five minutes in the truck to the interrogation center at Insein Prison. The rest of the NLD members encouraged me at the time, saying, "Don't worry, they will not kill us. They cannot kill us." They tried to make me feel better. I felt encouraged when they said those words.

When we first arrived at the interrogation camp at Insein Prison, we were separated. Each person was handcuffed and taken to a separate room. My body and my head were tied to a post with a rubber rope. I had to squat down with my knees apart and my bottom in the air. Then they put a water container over my head. It had very little holes in it that water dripped through. The water dripped and dripped and dripped, hitting my head. After five minutes it felt like bricks were falling into my head—it was very painful, and hard to endure.

Under my feet there were two needles, so I had to squat down and put my feet out a little bit. If I put my feet down under my body, the needles could pierce my feet and go into my muscle. My thighs became very rigid and very hot because I had to squat down for so long. Sometimes I fell down to the floor and they kicked me.

They would ask me things like, "Did someone tell you to call for Daw Aung San Suu Kyi and U Tin Oo's release, or was this your own idea?" I responded that our eight leaders decided by ourselves and that we implemented it. I didn't mention the other seventy people involved so they wouldn't be beaten. The eight of us took full responsibility. Other people may think that we were very courageous for answering their questions in this way, but we had to do it. We had to accept the difficulties we would experience. If we answered in any other way, other people would also have gotten in trouble.

I had to stay in the squatting position while they interrogated me. If I responded that I didn't know or if I lied to them, they would ask me the questions over and over again until I gave them an answer.

I was in the interrogation camp for eight days.

SIX YEARS WITH HARD LABOR

After they finished with us at the interrogation camp, we were sent to the military court. I saw the other leaders there, and we were so happy to see that nobody had died.

When we arrived at the military courtroom, all the jury members were in military uniform. I was not able to speak at my trial, and we weren't allowed to hire lawyers. I knew I had no hope of escape, no hope of being released. I had some friends who had faced trial in a military court, but they couldn't ask questions or appeal and they weren't allowed to have a lawyer. They just had to accept the sentence and go to jail. Because of this, I knew that I would be imprisoned.

The trial took only half an hour. After fifteen minutes, the judge stopped the trial for another fifteen minutes and then came out and opened the envelopes. He read everyone's names. Then the judge said, "Under emergency law, you are charged with destroying the state." Everyone was sentenced to six years with hard labor.

My mother came to the trial. As I was being taken away she came out to see me on the street. I was in the military truck and my mother was only two meters away. She mouthed to me, "How many years?" I raised six fingers. She seemed fine, and she asked, "Is that six months?" But when I said, "It's six years," she was so shocked she fell down. That is my most unforgettable memory of that day.

But I made myself calm down because I am working for change in my country, not for my personal benefit. If something happened to my mother, it would be devastating for me, but I would have to stay calm because I am working for other people. Other people are also suffering.

IT WAS LIKE MY MOUTH WAS SEWN SHUT

When I was put in prison, the officers said to us, "If you are in prison, you become a prisoner. No one is a *political* prisoner here. Every prisoner has to work. You have to do the work that we order you to do." We replied, "We are here for our country. We didn't commit any crimes or steal anything. We have our dignity and we cannot do this kind of work."

When they tried to force us to work, we went on a hunger strike. There were forty-nine political prisoners. At first they told us that if we didn't do the work, they would take us somewhere to meet with higher prison officials. But instead they put us in an isolated room that was dark and dirty, and they beat us.

One and a half months after our isolation started, we were allowed to see our families. When my family came, I went out of the room to see them. But there were two sets of iron bars separating me from my family. I had fifteen minutes to meet with them. I was allowed to talk about family, but not politics—if I talked about prison conditions then I would be put into the dark room again, or my family visits would be canceled. A prison worker accompanied my family during the visit and recorded what we were saying on a piece of paper. They do that for every political prisoner, but not for the other prisoners. I really wanted to say more to my family, but it was like my mouth was sewn shut.

When prison staff or officers got drunk, they would verbally abuse prisoners like me. We asked the other prison staff to take action against these abusive officers. We did another hunger strike, refusing to accept our meals if they didn't take action against them. The hunger strike lasted four days. They put us in the dark room and kept telling us, "We will take action against those people who are not cooperating!" We talked to each other and decided not to oppose them any longer because people would die. The prison staff didn't care what happened to us, so it would have been useless if one of us died in prison.

After twenty days in the dark room, we were taken to Tharrawaddy Prison in Pegu Division. We had spent over a month in Insein Prison.

WE HAVE TO RESIST THE TORTURE TOGETHER

Tharrawaddy Prison was strange to me. When I arrived there, they asked us to do hard labor in the prison compound. They made the prisoners smash stones, dig the earth, or carry waste from their toilets. There were two hundred political prisoners there, including older people who could not do hard labor. The prison officers said they would punish us if we did not do it, so all the younger political prisoners got together and ninety-seven of us decided to resist their orders. We knew that we could be beaten to death. I didn't think about my family or my country at the time; I just thought, *We have to work together. We have to resist the torture together.*

When the prison worker came and told us to do the hard labor, we said we wouldn't do it. We told him we wanted to meet the prison officer. Then the prison officer came to us and said, "Whoever is not willing to do hard labor, leave the room." Ninety-seven of us left the room, and the prison officer said he would send a senior prison officer to meet with us.

We were separated into groups of five, and they put each group in a different cell. They asked us to sit with our hands on top of our heads. After more than an hour, around seventy prison staff came into the compound and poured water into our cells. It was December and it was very cold. They didn't give us blankets—we would have to sleep on the cold, wet floor.

About half an hour after they poured the water into the cells, they took us outside and told us to sit on the ground with our hands on our heads again. The five of us sat in a line and three prison staff stood behind us and started beating and kicking us. They used canes and rubber sticks, and they beat our waists, our backs, and the back of our necks. Tharrawaddy Prison is in a field, so no one can hear when you scream or shout.

They beat us so much, and then they made us walk on our knees and elbows back to our rooms. When we got back to the room, ten of the prison staff came into our room and beat us again, for two or three hours. They said it was because we refused their orders. The prison officer told us, "It doesn't matter if we beat you to death."

They came and poured water into our rooms three times a day, morning, noon, and night. They beat us a lot—I had bruises on my body, and my waist was in pain as the weather got colder. People had other kinds of injuries, and some people were vomiting blood. One of my friends was disabled and used a cane to walk, but they tortured him just as badly as the rest of us. Another friend of mine was paralyzed from the waist down because of the beatings. Two months after they beat me, my lungs became swollen.

After beating us for the first two weeks, they lessened the punishment and forced us to stay in squatting positions for the rest of the month. They made us squat with our bottoms in the air and our hands on our heads for a long time. It was very hard—our legs got tired, and we had to keep our hands very straight on our heads so that our arms were straight over our shoulders. If we got tired and moved at all, they would say, "Which hand or leg is tired? Give me your hand or leg." Then they would beat that hand or leg. Sometimes we would move around if we didn't hear the guards' footsteps outside, but sometimes we got caught. We had to sit in that position from 7 a.m. until we ate lunch at 11 a.m., then from 1 p.m. until 4 p.m., then again after dinner from 6 p.m. until 9 p.m. We weren't allowed to talk to anyone.

The senior-level government people are responsible for this torture, because the prison staff has to follow their orders. The prison staff get promoted if they treat us badly, so sometimes they torture us even more seriously than they were ordered to. But we have continued to oppose the SPDC, because we want justice and freedom. The SPDC took power without laws and without a constitution. If we fear them, we are useless.

WE WROTE POEMS

When we were in the prison, we were not allowed to read or to write. All we could do every day was sit in the positions they told us to, eat, and sleep. We became so tired of our lives.

Sometimes we would talk about politics with our friends, and sometimes we would debate why we weren't successful in '88, but we were really tired every day. We wanted to read, and we wanted to know about what was happening in the country. Whenever my family or other families came to visit, they brought us cheroots, a kind of Burmese cigarette. The cigarettes were rolled into pieces of newspaper, so we would unroll the cigarettes and take out the newspaper pieces. Then we'd soak them in water to be able to see the letters and the words in the news. We'd read the clippings and discuss them with our friends. It was our only chance to read. But we could never know exactly what the real news was because the pieces were very small.

Sometimes we wanted to write poems, but we didn't have any pens or paper, so we tried to make clay boards. During the day we were allowed to go out at bathing time for two hours. We'd take clay from next to the bathing area and make it flat. The walls inside the prison were painted with limestone, so we soaked the powder off the limestone with water and then we applied it to the clay. After that, we used nails to write on it.

My friends and I made a patrol for the security staff. If the security staff was coming, the patrol person would raise the alarm so we would all know, and we'd hide the clay boards.

We wrote poems, but if they saw that we were writing, they'd put us in the dark room and punish us. I wrote about my life experience. For example, I wrote about when I had to depart from my mother. Or sometimes if I remembered my girlfriends, I would write songs. After we wrote something, we'd share with our friends. We'd read our poems and songs to each other, but then we had to erase them.

MY FRIENDS STARTED TO WATCH ME

When I was in prison I heard my mother had been hospitalized. I felt very bad when I heard that, like I wanted to do something to myself. I thought that my mother's health condition was because of me, and I felt I didn't deserve to live any more. At that time, we were given blankets—I had plans to use mine to hang myself.

I told one of my friends about my feelings and asked him to do some things for me if I died. My friend felt very bad about what I wanted to do. I asked him not to tell other people, but he did. My friends started to watch me. Even when I was sleeping, some of them would stay awake to watch me. They told me that I had to think about how I was working for our country, how it was not bad to do political work. One of my friends came and encouraged me, "You didn't do anything bad to your mother, so calm down. Killing yourself is against our religion. You are doing a good thing for the country." All those things encouraged me and made me calm. Then my mother got better.

We all had a common problem while we were in prison. We suffered mental problems. we had to think a lot. Sometimes we felt happy, smiling and joking around with our friends or while remembering our past. But sometimes we would remember our mothers, and then we would cry. We thought a lot about our families and friends. We thought about the times when we were in school. So it created mental problems for us, you know?

THE WARMEST PLACE

I was released from prison in 1994. In Burmese we have a saying: "The day you are released from prison and the day you get married are the happiest times in your life." But I was not happy when I was released from prison because I knew that a lot of my friends would still be in there.

When I was released from prison I could not sleep alone any more. At night, I would go and sleep with my mother, because being with her feels like the warmest and safest place in my life.

When I slept, I'd dream about my experience in the prison. Sometimes I would wake up suddenly and I would shout a lot. My family would come and say, "What happened to you?"

I also had problems when people shut doors loudly, because the prison staff usually slammed the doors of the cells when they locked them. When I was in my house and my nephew slammed the door very loudly, it would upset something in my mind. I would go and beat my nephew, even though he was very small. I can see how my mind was affected.

When I came out from prison, sometimes I didn't want to talk to my friends. I would go and sit in an isolated or quiet place and I would think about my time in school, my friends, and my family. If we compare ourselves to ordinary people it's not obvious, but we former prisoners suffer from mental problems. Some of us become addicted to drugs and alcohol.

Sometimes I thought about changing my enthusiasm for politics and just relaxing. I saw my friends who were fairly successful in business, and I thought about becoming like them. But it was only thoughts; I still had the passion to fight for change in my country.

I FELT FURTHER AND FURTHER OUTSIDE OF SOCIETY

In Burma, people discriminate against those who have been in prison. They talk about "the kind of people" who have been in there. When I walked around, my neighbors and anybody who wasn't involved in politics would not talk to me. I thought, *Why do they treat me this way? I went to prison for these people.* It was very, very painful. Even now I always think about this.

I had one friend I'd been close with since we were kids. We went to school together and I would visit his home. His mother was very friendly, and his home felt like my home—I have very good memories of that. But when I got out of prison and went to visit him, his mother told me that even though I used to be friends with her son, I couldn't visit her house because I had done something against the government. The military intelligence was following me and keeping track of what I did, so if I talked to her son, her son might get in trouble and could be arrested.

Sometimes I would think about my place in life. I was working for these people, but as time passed by I felt further and further outside of society. The main reason people act like this is fear. Fear is also the main reason we can't get democracy—that's why Daw Aung San Suu Kyi tells people to be free from fear. The young people in Burma are afraid of the government, and they dare not oppose it. But the government should be afraid of the young people, because throughout history young people have been a very powerful force. Young people should not be afraid.

All real thinking has been taken out from the youths' brains. They only think, "We have to struggle, we have to get money, we have to eat." If you go to Burma, you will see that a lot of children are illiterate. Children work as waiters, young boys sell lottery tickets and work as agents in soccer gambling. In Thailand, I've witnessed children from Burma working on construction sites; I've seen small girls sewing. I think these children should be going to school. But they don't have opportunities to learn.

If the young people become educated, I believe that the new generation has the power to change the government—but it will take time. I've been working with young activists, and I know they have power and they care.

I RAN AWAY TO ANOTHER PLACE

I began to talk to my other friends who had been released from prison. We discussed doing something about politics, because the political situation at the time was very quiet, very calm. We wanted to hold a literature discussion so that people would read about politics.

As we were working to organize the literature discussion in December that year, two new activists that worked with us got arrested. Because of this, some of my friends also got arrested and the police went to my house and asked my mother about me. My mother told me not to come back home because I could be arrested too. My family gave me money to run away.

I ran away to Kawthaung, a town in the Tenasserim Division in southern Burma. I had no money left so I had to do some manual labor there. I wasn't able to work as hard as the owner wanted, so he forced me to quit after the first day. This place was new for me and not like Rangoon; I felt very depressed. Then I went to Thailand to try and survive. It felt like a different world to me. In the beginning I got trafficked in Chumphon—I was sold to a manager of a pig farm, but I managed to escape after three weeks.

I spent thirteen years there, staying in many places—Ranong, Chumphon, Phuket, Nakhon, Phang Nga, and then Bangkok. I took jobs as they came because I had to survive.

I did some work in restaurants, hotels, fishing boats, and construction. I even started a business with a friend, making steel buckles, but we didn't always make a profit. I did all those things just to be able to survive, but they didn't give me any satisfaction.

I HAD MY COUNTRY,
BUT I WAS NOT ALLOWED TO STAY THERE

I was drinking a lot throughout my time in Thailand. At the time I was very depressed. I missed home and I thought my life was useless. Now I've stopped drinking completely, but in the past my body needed the alcohol—it stimulated me.

Sometimes when I drank, I would remember my family and my colleagues in prison. In 2005, my father passed away. My auntie told me on the phone when I was in Bangkok, but it wasn't possible for me to see my family. I had my family, my community, my country—but I wasn't allowed to stay there. Living in Thailand, I felt like I was outside society.

The whole time I was in Thailand, I was very depressed by the situation in Burma. I was very disappointed with politics. Even though I had done a lot of political work, it hadn't been successful. I wasn't in contact with any of my former political colleagues from Burma who were staying in Thailand. I didn't believe that change could come to Burma unless it was done by people who were inside the country, in direct contact with the government.

But in 2007, the Saffron Revolution was a big push; it revived my urge to join politics.[12]

I was at a restaurant in Bangkok when I ran into one of my close friends from prison. The UNHCR had resettled him to the U.S. after he'd lived in the refugee camps, and he was visiting on his U.S. passport.[13] I had tried to avoid seeing him in Bangkok because I didn't want to be asked, "What are you doing now? Are you working for your country?" But we started talking and he encouraged me to do political work again. We discussed politics over three days, and we talked about the politics inside and outside Burma. He said, "The young people are working for politics in Burma. They are trying their best, so we shouldn't avoid this—we should cooperate."

My friend had an office in Mae Sot, on the Thailand–Burma border, and he told me to go there and start working in politics again. When I arrived in Mae Sot I saw some of my other activist friends and I felt very encouraged. The Saffron Revolution was happening at that time—it was the biggest demonstration in Burma since '88. We discussed the revolution, and since we shared so many ideas, we decided that we would help set some activities in motion.

Even though it was very dangerous for me to go to Burma, I wanted change in my country. I had hope that the Saffron Revolution marches would bring change, so I decided to go back and join the protest.

WE WOULD TRY AGAIN

When I was at the border checkpoint between Mae Sot and Myawaddy,

---

[12] The Saffron Revolution was a large, monk-led uprising that took place in August and September of 2007. For more on the Saffron Revolution, see appendix page 468.

[13] The Office of the UN High Commissioner for Refugees is a United Nations organization with headquarters in Geneva, Switzerland. The primary mandate of UNHCR is the protection of refugees and finding durable solutions for refugees, including assisting in the voluntary repatriation of refugees to their home country, integration into the country of asylum, or resettling refugees to a third country.

51

I tore my passport apart and then I crossed the water into Burma.[14] It was my first time returning to Burma in thirteen years. Although I expected the worst, I decided I would just face whatever happened to me.

I left Thailand on September 24 and I arrived in Rangoon on September 26. I didn't go and see my family because my name was on the government blacklist. The blacklist has all the names of people the government considers to be destroyers of the state, guilty of causing riots and unrest. I could have been arrested if I went back to my home.

I had contacted my friends to get involved in the uprising, but the military was already cracking down heavily and arresting people. People couldn't go out in the street. I was sad that people were not in the streets any more, but I was not disappointed. I thought if we could not do it this time, then we would try again. I couldn't join in the protest movement above ground then, because I knew some of my friends had been arrested, and information threatening my security would leak from them. So I retreated. Some of my friends were in hiding too. We discussed how to reorganize the scattered democracy groups.

I helped organize with the people I knew from before. I helped people avoid arrest and suggested places for people to hide. I was also trying to connect the people I knew with other activist networks, to make sure they all worked together. Then I set up my own network with our young people.

When I went back to Rangoon, it took me one month to look for and join my friends who had gone into hiding. I rented an apartment there because I wanted to see if the situation would change, but nothing did, so I spent three months figuring out how to travel around Rangoon safely. I also rented three or four apartments that my friends and I could stay in to avoid arrest. I stayed in Rangoon from September until December.

I returned to Thailand in December for a training about leadership and nonviolence. I saw some of my old friends again and we discussed some of the next activities that we would launch inside Burma.

---

[14] Myawaddy is a town on the Burma side of the Moei River, which divides Thailand and Burma. It is one of several official border-crossing points between the two countries.

I continued to work with other activists to help politically active youth have the opportunity to join the revolution. We helped with food and rented safe houses and phones for them. We wanted the momentum of the Saffron Revolution to continue. We didn't start another organization to do this, we were just organizing people and supporting people in our networks.

A NEW WAVE

I went back to Burma in the first week of January 2008 to plan some special events for Independence Day and to do campaigns on Union Day with Generation Wave.[15] Generation Wave is an organization of young activists that had initially been set up after the Saffron Revolution. I wasn't involved with them when the organization first formed, but one of my old activist friends told me I should work with them because I was young. The name is Generation Wave because we already had the '88 generation, and we wanted to create a new wave, a new generation with powerful force. We decided to organize a protest that would happen in March, so we contacted our friends in Rangoon to organize with them.

But when we were ready for the protest, some of our friends got arrested, so we had to go into hiding in Rangoon Division. Zayar Thaw, a hip-hop singer in Burma, was arrested, and a lot of the Generation Wave members were arrested too. So I had to avoid arrest and went into hiding. When my friends got arrested, our force was brought down.

My friend whom I lived with got arrested when he went to meet with the ABFSU. He wasn't known as a Generation Wave member, but when he was tortured at the detention camp, he leaked some informa-

---

[15] Union Day is celebrated on the anniversary of the signing of the Panglong Agreement, an agreement between General Aung San and a number of Burma's ethnic groups that they would work together in an independent, federated Burma. For more on the Panglong agreement see page 460 of the "A Brief History of Burma" in the appendix.

tion. My friend couldn't resist the torture and revealed information about the protest and where we were living.

When we got the news about this, we had to leave our apartments. The plan for a protest in March was cancelled. We called all our friends and sent them to stay in places very far from Rangoon; we couldn't tell anyone where we sent them. I ran away to Pegu Division and stayed there for a month.

During that time, I had to move around. In the morning, I might be in one place, but that night I would sleep in another place. I contacted some friends I had worked with before. The Saffron Revolution anniversary was approaching, so my friends and I discussed what we should do to prepare. I couldn't go to see my friends, so I contacted them on the phone. I also talked to groups like the ABFSU so that we could cooperate with each other. I was very careful not to be arrested, because I knew that if I ended up in prison I would face the worst possible situation.

Then I returned to Rangoon in April, and the members of Generation Wave came together. In May, Cyclone Nargis happened, and we went to help the Nargis victims with food, water, and accommodations. We continued helping until July, and then we started to plan a demonstration for September 2008. In July, I went back to Thailand for a training with some other Generation Wave members. After it finished, we returned to Burma, held trainings locally, and increased our membership.

I work with Generation Wave because I want young people to have new ways of thinking and taking action. I came into politics when I was young; sometimes young people want to do something, but adults become a barrier for them. Our country's situation has become worse; it is not like other countries. Everything is very restricted, even if you just want to go from here to there. I was nineteen when I went to prison and twenty-four when I got out, but I still had to promise my mother that I would be home by 7 p.m.

Our young generation has new ideas that should be carried out without the control of older people. We want to move our lives and our country forward with new ideas and freedom.

"ARE YOU KYAW ZWAR FROM GENERATION WAVE?"

We discussed our plans for a September demonstration with monks and with the ABFSU; we needed to join together to have more force. At around 9 or 10 p.m. in early September, I got a phone call from a man whom I had already met about the demonstration. His group had a lot of members, and we needed their help in launching the event. He wanted to meet the next day. Even though I was feeling uncomfortable, the next morning I went to meet him at a tea shop.

I told three Generation Wave members to come and watch our meeting from a distance. The man was already there when I arrived. When I ordered a coffee, three people came up to me from behind, and four people approached me from the front. They asked, "Are you Kyaw Zwar from Generation Wave?" They already knew who I was; I couldn't lie. They were plainclothes police who had been sitting at the coffee shop, pretending to sell newspapers and pretending to be waiters. My friends saw me get arrested. The man who called me to arrange the meeting must have been tortured a lot in prison—the police made him do it.

I was arrested the next day, and then I was sent to an interrogation center for a month. When I was in the interrogation center, the prison staff tortured me to get information on Generation Wave, and on who was involved in the protest. I didn't tell them anything important. I was beaten, and I endured the pain. They didn't give me any food or water. I had to drink water from the toilets.

Now we train the young people in Generation Wave how to escape at the last minute, and how to avoid the police. Even if we are very friendly, we don't tell each other where we live because then somebody could leak that information if they were arrested.

I was taken to court for my trial. I was charged with crossing the border illegally, having contact with illegal organizations, and forming a group, through establishing Generation Wave. It wasn't a military courtroom and I was allowed to have a lawyer and witnesses, but the prosecution also had a lawyer and witnesses, and I lost.

In October, I was sent to Insein Prison again. On the day when I was brought to the prison, my family came to meet me. "We don't know what you are doing," said my mother. "Son, I am only able to see you when you're in prison."

I got sick during my second time in prison. It was like malaria, but it was just a really high fever. If I asked for medicine in the prison, they only gave paracetamol, so I had to ask my family to send medicine. There were some political prisoners who were doctors, so they told me what medicine I needed.

My second time in prison, I wasn't asked to do forced labor and I was allowed to go out of isolation for an hour every day. The political prisoners were still very united. We read books and we discussed Burma's current political situation.

SOMETIMES WE THINK WE'RE CRAZY

I was released in September 2009. I saw that my friends all had happy families. I felt really discouraged, and I thought, *I don't have a family. I have nothing now.* But I tried to calm myself by remembering that I was doing this work for my country. If I want to do this kind of work, I need to forget other things. Even if there is someone I love, I have to stay far away. I need to make sacrifices.

If Burma gained democracy, I would not stay away from my family and live in another country. I would establish my life, do things for myself personally. But it is difficult to think about how I would do this. Ever since I got involved in politics, I haven't been able to think about anything else—it has changed me. I can't think about the future any more.

Sometimes we think we're crazy. But we have hope, and we continue working toward our goal. I've met other politicians, our brothers, who have forgotten their goals and are living a relaxing life. But I cannot leave this work because I want my friends to be free like the young people in Singapore, for example. Young people there have freedom, they can pursue their education. But not my friends. My friends are in the prisons. Now I sit here, in Thailand—I am free, and I want my friends to be free as well. That's why I cannot leave this work. I want to fight for my friends.

Since I am forty years old, I cannot be a member of Generation Wave any more—the age limit is actually thirty-five years old. But I have plans to continue working as an activist. We don't accept the constitution, so we will continue to fight against it. The government will do what it wants in the 2010 elections, so we need to fight against it all the time.

I haven't had a chance to see my family, and when my father died I could not go to his funeral. I have been away from my family for so long that I am not sure what my mother is like any more. People like me, who are more active and want change, we suffer the most—the government shakes our lives the most.

BYIN PU

23, student

ETHNICITY: *Kachin*

BIRTHPLACE: *Kutkai Township, Burma*

INTERVIEWED IN: *Mae Sot, Thailand*

Byin Pu met us in a tall wooden house that a half dozen American NGO workers rent on the Thailand–Burma border. The interpreter for our interview picked her up on the back of his motorbike and brought her to meet us, as a spinal injury prevents Byin Pu from being able to drive. As a child, Byin Pu dreamed of one day becoming a school teacher, but instead of pursuing her education, she quit attending school and went to China to work when she was just fifteen. In China, Byin Pu met a difficult set of circumstances, including exploitation and an attempted assault, and found herself fighting for her freedom. After a serious injury incurred during one harrowing incident, Byin Pu came to the Thailand–Burma border for medical care.

I have prayed for two years to be able to tell my story.

I was born in Northern Shan State, in Kutkai Township. Kutkai is a wonderful place. The township is flat, but it is surrounded by mountains that we call Loi Sam Sip, the Thirty Mountains. When you open the door in the early morning or in the evening, you can see the mountains clearly—even in the nighttime, we can see lights on the mountains coming from monasteries and pagodas. It's very comforting. When traveling home, we always see the mountains and the pagodas long before we reach Kutkai. It touches our hearts when we see them, and we really feel like we're home.

Growing up, I had eight brothers and sisters, and our family was very poor and faced a lot of difficulty. Our situation was very depressing, but when I looked around at the mountains, I felt comforted and it became clear in my mind that no matter how hard our family situation was, God would help us at the right time.

The first time I became conscious of my family's economic situation was when I was eight, and my family realized that even with both of my parents selling vegetables in the Kutkai market, it was not enough for our survival. So my parents started to do some business buying pigs from a remote mountain area and selling them in Kutkai. They would cycle for six hours from our home to the mountain and then back again to pick up the pigs each morning. Still, they'd only make a couple of thousand kyats in profit.[1]

MY DREAM WAS TO BE A SCHOOLTEACHER

In our village we had Kachin people, Chinese people, and Palaung people. There were a few ethnic Shan people too, and maybe one or two Burman and Indian people. There wasn't ethnic discrimination against the Kachin, because we were the majority. There was more discrimination against people who were poor.

When I was five years old and in primary school, I would wake up early in the morning and then I would run to school. In the rainy season, I had to find a banana leaf to carry over my head to keep dry. Later, in middle school, most of the students had a bicycle to ride to school, but I still had to run.

---

[1] Approximately US$2.

My dream was to become a schoolteacher, but the reality was that my family could not even pay the school fees until the middle of the semester or until the final examinations. That's why the students and teachers discriminated against us.

It didn't matter who was the most intelligent or who got high marks in school—the teachers just cared about who was paying the tuition fees. They didn't have enough income either, so they told us, "If you want to pass the examination you have to pay the tuition fee every month." People would talk about how our family was eating the same curry every day and about how our parents couldn't give any donations to pay for school materials. I was very thin, and the other students would push me to the ground when I tried to sit in a chair.

I cried a lot on the way to school, because I felt so ashamed.

Our school uniforms were very thin because they got passed down from our older brother to the next brother and so on. We never had new clothes, so the other students would say that our uniforms were very old and thin.

Five or six students would wait for me on the way to school and they would bully me. They would say, "You have to say that you love this boy or else we'll take your *bukrong*.[2] Do you love him?" I said no, and they took my *bukrong*. I would try to run after them, but they would all stand around me and throw it back and forth like they were playing ball. I was seven or eight years old at the time.

KACHIN STATE IS JUST A NAME

I cannot explain the history of Kachin people. Even though we have an area called Kachin State, it's just a name—we don't have equal rights because the military regime does whatever it wants in our area.

The governing body in charge of our village was the SPDC, the military regime. But the heads of our villages were Chinese or sometimes

---

[2] *Bukrong* is the Kachin word for the sarong (*longyi*) typically worn throughout Burma.

Kachin. Usually the Chinese were in charge because they had more money than the Kachin and could offer donations to the people, as well as give payments to the military to gain their favor. The Chinese did illegal business, such as transporting drugs, so they paid the local SPDC authorities bribes as a way of shutting the local SPDC authorities' mouths. Then they could transport their goods freely and have security.

The people in our village were very, very poor. But the authorities ordered that a regular tax had to be paid, no matter how poor you were. There was also forced labor.[3] If you couldn't do the forced labor, they would make you pay a fine. I think there were generally three types of forced labor: road construction, making canals, and cutting grass. They requested strong men to make the canals and do construction. Families without a strong man to send for forced labor would be fined 3,000 to 5,000 kyats, so they'd try to find another man who could do the forced labor in their place for one day.[4]

I have three elder brothers, and one brother was away serving in the KDA—the Kachin Defense Army—so he could not do forced labor.[5] The other two brothers were working in farming in a different area, so they could not do forced labor either. We had to hire someone to take our family's place, and it was usually easiest to hire a drug addict; other people had jobs and things to do. We would pay the drug addict 2,000 kyats and give him food for the day.[6] We'd also hire them because they would not steal things from our houses if we gave them some money.

---

[3] Forced labor is compulsory, unpaid labor. The SPDC imposes forced labor on citizens throughout Burma, in areas such as cultivation, infrastructure projects (including building roads, railways, and dams), municipal work, and in war zones. Portering is a specific type of forced labor that entails carrying rations, supplies, and weaponry for the military; porters are frequently used as minesweepers as well.

[4] 3,000 to 5,000 kyats is approximately US$3 to US$5.

[5] The Kachin Defense Army is an armed organization formed in 1990 after the Kachin Independence Army's 4th brigade surrendered to the government army in the midst of a major offensive.

[6] Approximately US$2.

Our village was near the KDA base. The KDA say their goal is to support and protect the people because they love their nationality, but they don't actually do anything for the Kachin people. They take taxes from the farmers, and when the SPDC comes they just follow along with them. If the military asked the KDA to destroy the village church, for example, the KDA would do it. Also, to multiply the number of KDA soldiers, they would collect the names of the young people in each family and force whichever young men they wanted to go to military training.

When I was three years old, I witnessed my eldest brother being forcibly abducted by KDA—he was very young at the time.

But another armed group, the Kachin Independence Army—part of the Kachin Independence Organization—organizes group discussions about national and international politics so people are educated and aware.[7] The KIA also taxes people in the areas under their control. In the Kutkai area, the taxes are charged by the government, through the head of the village.

Palaung, Shan, and Kachin people in my area felt that the military regime wasn't doing much for any of the ethnic people in Burma. But then they saw the KIO and Kachin leaders discussing the ceasefire with the military regime.[8] I think it's important for the Kachin leaders to talk to the military regime and take a stand for the Kachin people. It's better to discuss and solve problems together instead of fighting each other with weapons.

SELLING OPIUM LIKE POTATOES

I remember working in the opium poppy fields when I was eight or nine

---

[7] The Kachin Independence Organization was formed in 1961 and subsequently launched an armed rebellion, through the Kachin Independence Army.

[8] In the 1990s and 2000s, the military regime signed ceasefire agreements with the majority of the armed ethnic opposition groups. The KDA signed one in 1990 and the KIA in 1994. See the "Ceasefire Agreements" section of the "A Brief History of Burma" in the appendix for more details.

years old. We were allowed to grow opium then, but we had to pay taxes on it to the KIA, the KDA, and the government. There was a lot of taxation by the different authorities, but our family was able to keep a small amount of money. When people were working in the opium fields, they had nothing else to do, so they would use a little bit of the drug.

The bosses gave opium or heroin to the workers so they would do more work in the field. In the same way that regular people need rice to survive, the drug addicts needed the drugs. It was like their food, and they were too weak to work without it. People could choose whether to get paid in opium or money.

Selling opium was legal, so it could be sold freely in the markets like potatoes or tomatoes. Opium was sold near Kutkai in Kongkha, Loikang, and Mongnye Townships, all areas under control of the KDA. Almost every house had one or two drug addicts.

Then in 2002 and 2003, the SPDC banned the cultivation and sale of opium. People had no right to discuss the decision with the local government. They threatened that if you had opium fields, they would burn down your house and put you in prison for ten years, or they would give you the death penalty. Just before harvest time, the authorities came to destroy the opium. The villages that grew opium suffered from excessive loss and faced many difficulties. Some villagers had taken out loans with interest to grow the opium, so they ended up hungry and in debt.

Many young men in Kutkai were addicted to drugs because they worked in the opium fields. They began using when they were schoolboys, only twelve or thirteen years old. The worst age was around twenty-one or twenty-two; that's when the situation got bad and most of them would die. We were very sad and worried; like most families in our township, our family had drug addicts. We eventually lost two of my brothers due to addiction. Naw died in 2007 and La died in early 2008. They were very young.

The bosses also gave young people opium and money if they transported the packages of opium from Kongkha, Mongnye, and Kutkai to China. Transporting the opium was very dangerous, because if they met with armed groups like the SPDC military, they could be killed on the spot.

The local SPDC authorities arrest drug addicts and then tell their family members to pay a fine for their release. Then they just arrest them again, and the family has to pay money again. They are making a business of it—they aren't rehabilitating the drugs users.

Even if the SPDC doesn't allow us to sell opium, they don't prevent drug addiction either—I believe they encourage it. They allow ethnic people to be addicted to drugs, because then it is difficult for them to become more educated and improve their standard of living. They also allow the drug dealers to pay bribes to the police and the courts for their release.

My perspective is that they banned opium growing because they want to destroy the ethnic people; I believe they were afraid of the Kachin people becoming educated. Before the ban, Kachin and Chinese people had a better standard of living. We could go to university, or build a small new house. With the money we earned from opium, some Kachin people saved money, studied, got a diploma, and became educated.

After they banned growing opium in 2003, people faced a difficult situation. Before 2003, nobody was working in China as housemaids, laborers, or midwives.[9] But after the opium ban, there was a lot of trafficking and business inside China in the border area. A lot of people who were trafficked faced rape and torture.[10] There were no jobs to do in our township, and most people were going to China.

THERE WAS NOTHING LEFT IN OUR HOUSE

When he was young, my father became a communist leader and a soldier

---

[9] Immigration from Burma to China has steadily increased since 1988, when the Burmese government began negotiating official border crossings and trade agreements with China and Thailand.

[10] According to a 2008 survey by the Kachin Women's Association Thailand (KWAT), about 37 percent of trafficked women from Burma end up as wives of Chinese men, while about 4 percent are sold into the sex industry or as housemaids.

in the Communist Party of Burma.[11] The Communist Party was very strong at the time. The Kachin community tradition is to give alcohol to a leader if you want to discuss something with them. The soldiers were leaders in the community, so he would have discussions about social activities or about the village activities, and they would just drink and discuss. Little by little, he became an alcoholic.

Early in the morning, he would start drinking rice alcohol before eating any breakfast. It's a very alcoholic drink—if you run out of petrol in your motorbike, you can pour some rice alcohol in your tank and go. He always had a bottle of alcohol hidden somewhere on his body.

In 1992, he stopped serving in the Communist Party of Burma because my mother couldn't take care of or feed all of the children without his help.

I can't remember exactly, but I think my father was around fifty-seven years old when he had to go to the hospital. I don't know the word for the medical condition he got from drinking, but it caused fluid to build up in his stomach and his legs, and they became very swollen. When the doctor told us how much it would cost to treat the disease, I overheard my father say that he would not spend that amount of money on himself because he had to take care of his children. I was really sad that he did not get treatment. I wanted to look after my father and comfort him.

My father's friend had been a medical assistant in the Communist Party of Burma, and he treated my father at his small clinic. Every week for a year, they used a syringe to take the fluid from his stomach. Those were very long and unhappy days. My mother had to do all of the work on her own, and my father still drank a little bit, even though everyone told him not to.

After one year, we took my father to the Kutkai hospital again and

---

[11] The Communist Party of Burma (CPB) is one of Burma's oldest political parties, and it was also an armed opposition group.

they said we had to send him to a bigger hospital, like Lashio Hospital,[12] where the treatment would cost 500,000 kyats.[13] My mother sold her small gold necklace that my father bought for her and that she adored, but it wasn't enough money so she had to borrow from other people. Getting the medical treatment created a lot of debt for the family.

The people who'd loaned us the money kept coming to the house asking to be paid. Later, they started coming to the house and just taking whatever they thought was useful, like a pig or something inside the house. Eventually there was nothing left in our house.

My father was treated for fifteen days at the Lashio Hospital, and then a car brought him home. When we saw the headlights outside, my brothers and sisters and I were all clapping our hands and shouting "Wa Wa!" or "father, father" because we were very happy that our father was home. My mother looked very sad and she said, "Children, be quiet—otherwise I won't hear anything your father says." That's when we knew something was wrong. Our father said nothing; he could only take his final breaths.

After my father passed away, my two elder brothers were married and had their own families; they were also both drug addicts. My mother couldn't depend on her sons, so she thought it would be better to get married again and have a loving family.

When her new husband arrived in our home, I could not accept him as my new father. I didn't understand that my mother made the decision for the good of our family. I couldn't sit down for meals with them, and I also couldn't study any more because there was so much chaos in my mind.

I FELT LIKE SHE WAS MY CHILD

When I was fifteen, I decided that I really wanted to help my family

---

[12] Lashio is the largest town in Northern Shan State and is located approximately 125 miles northeast of Mandalay. It includes a mix of Shan, Chinese, and Burman citizens.

[13] Approximately US$500.

and support my younger brother to go to school. I had worked as a house servant in Kutkai for two months, but I only earned 5,000 kyats each month.[14]

My friends told me that I could go to China and work as a house-maid—I could take care of a baby and do housework and earn 30,000 kyats in one month.[15] Then my elder brother Naw told me that his wife's aunt in Shweli, China needed someone to help with her children.[16]

In December of 2002, I left Kutkai and went to China. Naw accompanied me. The journey from Kutkai to Shweli is about 100 miles. First we took a bus from Kutkai to Muse, passing the 105-mile checkpoint gate. Since we didn't have ID cards, we took a ten-minute boat ride from Muse to cross the river into Shweli. After we reached Shweli, it took us over an hour to walk to the house.

By this time, I had already used all my money to travel.

The house owner's name was Awng Li and his wife's name was Seng Nu, and they were Kachin. In the beginning, they said that my only job was to take care of their six-month-old baby girl, Lu Mai, and their son, Brang Aung. But there were guests coming all the time, so I had to prepare the guest room; I would sleep on the chairs in the dining room.

We would usually all eat together in the house, but most of the time the baby was crying while everyone was eating breakfast or lunch, so I had to take care of her. When I came back from caring for the baby and looked at the table, there was usually very little food remaining.

The baby's parents were never home. The father was always traveling for business, and the mother also spent all her time traveling or playing dominoes. That made me angry.

Whenever the baby slept during the day, I had to clean the whole house, wash all the clothes, and do all of the cooking. I had no chance to

---

[14] Approximately US$5.

[15] Approximately US$30.

[16] Shweli is the Burmese name for Ruili, a town in China on the China–Burma border. Shweli serves as a vital trading ground in both legal and illegal goods and services.

rest. Whenever she cried during the night, I had to get up and prepare more formula. Sometimes I would collapse from exhaustion.

My whole body smelled like the baby and I felt like it was really my child. At the time I was so young and I didn't have a boyfriend, but I felt like I was a mother.

THEY WANTED ME TO BE FAMILY

At the beginning, I felt like helping them because I thought we were part of one family. But after I had been working for six months, I still had not been paid. I asked the house owners many times to please pay me, but they gave me nothing. They just ordered me around: "You have to do this. You must do that." They'd say, "We have a problem and we cannot pay you, but we are all the same family, so you should help us." When it came to working, they treated me like a slave. When it came to paying me, they wanted me to be family.

Around that same time, my family in Burma called me and told me that my grandfather had passed away. I wanted to go back to Burma to visit my relatives and to give them comfort, but the house owners would not let me go.

I HAD NO CHOICE

I was never beaten or physically tortured by the house owners, but I had one problem when the mother went for a week to visit her native place in Xinjiang.

While she was away, the baby slept in her bedroom and I had to sing her songs to help her fall asleep; sometimes I would fall asleep too. One morning when I opened my eyes, I saw that Awng Li, the baby's father, was lying beside me and looking at me. I didn't know if he had touched me or not, but I was so afraid I just got up and left the room. One of our neighbors was staying as a guest at the house, and when she saw me she said, "What's the problem?" I felt very ashamed and scared, so I said,

"Oh, nothing's wrong."

When Awng Li gave me 20 yuan to buy vegetables at the market, I put the money in my pocket and decided that maybe on my way to buy food, I would run away.[17] I left the house and then realized that if I went back to Burma at that moment, I wouldn't have any money for my family. I would have nothing. I kept thinking about what I should do.

Then I looked behind me toward the house and Awng Li was coming toward me on a bicycle, watching to see if I would try to run away or not. I had no choice but to go back to the house. Awng Li never said anything to me about what happened.

I JUST WALKED OUT

After more than a year had passed, I still had not been paid. I pleaded to the house owners, "Please, now it's been one year and four months and you haven't paid me anything. Please allow me to work somewhere else in Shweli." But they still refused to pay me.

I decided to leave the house. In the end, I wasn't helping my family, and I was also abandoning my education. I felt like I had no freedom.

I decided to go and work in a restaurant owned by a couple I knew, a Kachin man and his Chinese wife. Early one morning, I just put my clothes in a plastic bag and I told Awng Li and Seng Nu that I was leaving. They didn't want me to leave the house, but I just walked out. They did not say anything when I left. I met the Kachin man and followed him to his restaurant.

I think the house owners didn't pay me because they looked down on me. My family was not wealthy or educated or very strong in the Kachin community. They thought that if anything happened to me, no one would come to protect me. This is also one of the underlying reasons I was later trafficked.

---

[17] Approximately US$3.

MY BITTER EXPERIENCE

After I stopped working as a housemaid, I went to work in the restaurant owned by the Kachin man I had followed. I did not have any education, so I wanted to learn how to cook. I thought it would give me a skill to use into the future so I could survive when I got older. My plan was to borrow a little bit of money and then open up a small restaurant.

In 2007, I started working at a Chinese restaurant. I was very happy to work there, even though I got a small salary. I was asked to work as a receptionist because I could speak Chinese, Burmese, and Kachin, and I'm polite. I woke up very early every morning and worked really hard. The first month I got 120 yuan, and the second month I got 150.[18] The owners really appreciated my work, but the other workers in the restaurant did not like me. One of the owners was Roman Catholic and she allowed me time off to go to church, so the other workers were jealous, I think.

My co-workers were nine women. They were from Lashio, in Burma, and they were all ethnic Chinese. I was the only Kachin and the only Christian of the workers. One of my co-workers, a woman called Ah Ying, would speak very sweetly to me and call me honey, and we would eat together sometimes. We were just acquaintances, but we'd talk every day.

The women all knew that I didn't have an ID or passport from Burma. Because they hated me, they decided to sell my body.

I TOLD THEM THAT I DIDN'T WANT TO DRINK

The date was August 20, 2007. That night, I took my bicycle and started going toward my friend's house to stay with her for the night.

On the way, Ah Ying called to say that her cousin wanted to join her at a party but didn't know how to find it, so she wanted to use my bicycle to go and meet him. I told her that I was using my bicycle, but that I could go with her to meet her cousin and take him to the party.

---

[18] 120 yuan is approximately US$18; 150 yuan is approximately US$22.

After walking for about five minutes, we reached a big restaurant and nightclub. I waited outside on my bicycle while Ah Ying went inside to get her cousin, Li Qiang. I didn't know it at the time, but they were talking about me in there. When they came out of the restaurant, they pressured me to go inside the nightclub and enjoy the party with them. I was very tired and wanted to rest that night. Also, I had heard that the clubs could be dangerous. But Ah Ying was a friend from the restaurant, so I didn't think she would do anything bad to me.

I told them, "You can enjoy the nightclub and so on, but I have relatives who live near the club so I will leave soon and visit them." So they took me into the nightclub, but then they said, "Oh, this nightclub is full of people and there is no place to sit. We'll go to a different club."

We took a taxi to another place, but I didn't really feel like going there. At the next club, we met with five women from the restaurant where I worked, and two men. Everyone was singing karaoke. I told them that I didn't want to drink any alcohol because I had to get up early to work the next morning. They got a little bit angry and said I asked to go home too many times.

Then Ah Ying told me that Li Qiang wanted to talk to me, and that he was waiting for me outside the karaoke room. I said that I didn't want to go outside to see him, and asked what was going on. As a woman, I was afraid to go outside alone.

Then Li Qiang came back into the karaoke room. He sat beside me and smoked a cigarette. My co-workers started grabbing my hands and pouring shots of alcohol into my mouth, even though I didn't want it. At that time, it was really noisy in the room. Everyone was singing and drinking and smoking.

It was the first time I'd had alcohol, and my head started to hurt. I wanted to rest. Li Qiang was outside the room again and another woman said to me, "If you are afraid to go outside alone, the two of us can go outside to meet him together." The woman just took me and we went.

Li Qiang was sitting by the door smoking a cigarette. He said that he wanted to talk to me, but that he was a little bit shy. The woman I went outside with said, "I will let the two of you talk," and then she just left. Li Qiang said, "You can sit beside me and we'll talk." He started telling me his feelings about his family, and I told him that after he finished talking, I would go back inside the room.

"No please just sit, and I will share," he said. "I haven't finished sharing my personal feelings yet." So he just continued talking nonstop about his feelings. When he told me that he didn't have his father as a child, I sympathized with him because I had the same experience. I think at that time he may have thought that I was soft, and easy to persuade. After a while, he looked at me very seriously and told me that he fell in love with me the first time he saw me. I just lied to him and said, "You're too late. I already have a boyfriend."

Just after he told me that he was in love with me, a car arrived in front of the restaurant. Three young man came out and grabbed me and pushed me into the car. I was holding on to the car window and I kept shouting, "Please, save me! Save me!" Li Qiang got into the car. Three waiters from the restaurant saw what was happening, but they just thought it was a fight between a girlfriend and a boyfriend, because they saw that we'd already been talking together for about an hour.

I pleaded with the driver not to drive away. Li Qiang pushed me and said to the driver, "I paid to use this car. You have to drive."

We drove away and Li Qiang was grabbing my hands. We were driving for about fifteen minutes and I continuously tried to resist, but I couldn't. I realized that I was really in trouble. Finally we reached a guesthouse with a small gate. An old man who worked at the guesthouse opened the gate for us. Just as he opened the door, I shouted to him, "They've abducted me! This is not my choice!" But Li Qiang told the old man to do what he said. The gate was locked behind us, and I was brought into the guesthouse.

I tried to hold on to the side of the stairs and refuse to go up, but Li Qiang was very strong. His face was red, and he looked angry. I think he was very drunk or had done a lot of drugs. He grabbed my body and pushed my back very forcibly until I was in pain. He pushed me up the stairs, and when we reached the third floor, he opened the door to one room, pushed me in, and then closed the door behind us.

I asked him, "What are you doing?" He said, "Oh, we'll call your friends again and tell them we'll sleep here tonight." He held his phone and pressed the numbers as though he was calling, but he was just pretending. I grabbed his phone, but he just took it back.

I went to the bathroom and closed the door, but he kept knocking on the door and trying to force it open, saying, "Please open the door. I love you." I tried to look for a stick or a knife or anything that I could defend myself with, but I couldn't find anything. As I was thinking about how to escape, I saw there was another door in the bathroom. It was a little bit open and I saw there was another room with three or four men sleeping without their clothes on. I was so afraid when I saw them. I thought that it was more men who could rape me, so I closed the door in the bathroom and then I went back to the other room.

I said to Li Qiang, "There is only one sleeping cot and only one room. Do you think I am a prostitute? Did you negotiate for this?"

I was thinking about how I could find an excuse to leave, so I told him that I wanted to eat noodles. But he said that he would phone the front desk and that they would bring the food to me. So then I told him that I wanted to drink some tea, so that he would have to leave to get hot water. So he left the room, but he made sure that he locked the door behind him so I could not leave.

He came back with the hot water, but I didn't actually want to drink it. I ran to the door and tried to open it. Then Li Qiang realized that I was trying to run away, and he pushed me onto the cot.

I was worried that if I tried anything else that he would get angrier and that he might torture me. So I sat with him on the cot. He said, "Oh, I love you so much," and then he put his arms around me and started trying to rape me.

I thought about how hard I had worked during my life. Ever since I was a child, I had been trying very hard for myself and for my family, and I didn't want to have an incident like this in my life. So when he tried to kiss me, I just bit his tongue. He was in a lot of pain. He grabbed my clothes and tried to hit my face. I prayed to God, *Please save me. Let me survive.*

Li Qiang missed my face when he tried to hit me. He had glasses so I grabbed them and threw them to the ground. I was afraid, but I was also angry. He was looking for his glasses and finally he found them and put them back on. When he put them on, his eyes were very sharp and angry.

He could not speak because of the pain in his tongue, so he pointed at my face and looked into my eyes, and I understood that he would rape me or do whatever he wanted. He was very angry.

At that time I prayed to God, *Please, what should I do?* I looked around the room and saw that the window was not closed, and there was a screen to keep the mosquitoes out. I was three floors up. If I jumped, I would die. But if I died, it would at least be in an accident. I prayed again to God. If I died, I would not be able to support my family. But I did not want to live if I was raped.

I didn't know if the screen would be locked or not, but it just opened. I took the screen out of the window and I jumped. I tried to grab the roof of the house next door, but I was falling too fast, and then my back hit the ground.

My whole body was covered in blood, but at the time I felt no pain. All I could think about was trying to escape. With all of my energy, I tried to stand up to run, but my legs wouldn't move. The whole lower part of my body wouldn't move. I could only move my hand.

The accident happened at about four-thirty in the morning. The family in the house next door had woken up when I fell to the ground. The house members and other neighbors came out and were looking at me. I was shouting in Chinese, "Please save me! If you help me, I will never forget it and I will find some way to pay you back, however I can!"

But at the same time Li Qiang was shouting from up above on the third floor of the hotel, "Why did you do this? I love you. Why did you jump?" He was speaking very sweetly. Then he came down to where I was, and although everyone was looking at me, no one helped.

I thought that if I kept shouting it might cause more problems for me, so I decided to pretend that I was dead. He took my body and carried me to the street. He tried to stop a taxi, but my whole body was covered in blood, and none of the drivers wanted to take me.

After another taxi passed, he decided to try blocking the road to force a taxi to take me to the hospital. He tried to push my body into a taxi and told the driver, "Please go to the Shweli Hospital. This is my wife." But the driver did not want to go. Then he told the driver, "If my wife dies, the responsibility will be yours, so please go." The driver took us.

While we were going to the hospital, Li Qiang told me, "Oh Byin Pu, please answer me. If you die, I will also die." He spoke to me very sweetly, but I remembered what he had done, what he had said. I was very afraid and I still pretended to be dead. Finally we arrived at Shweli Hospital.

I WILL NEVER BE YOUR WIFE

When we arrived at the hospital, Li Qiang asked me to be his wife. I could not move from the waist down, so I could only think about seeing a doctor. When I saw the doctor, I begged him to save my life.

While we were waiting for the results of the X-rays, Li Qiang kept telling me that if I agreed to be his wife, he would pay for all of my medical costs. At that moment, the hospital made an announcement that all of the patients' caretakers needed to register and pay the fees.

I said to him, "This happened to me because I don't want to be your wife. I will never, ever want to be your wife." Then he left the room. Since I could not pay the hospital fees, one of the nurses agreed to let me use her mobile phone to call my friends.

I decided to make my first call to Awng Li and Seng Nu, the house owners I had worked for. Awng Li told me not to feel downhearted, and he said they would come right away. They came to see me at the hospital, and they gave me a phone to use while I was there.

It had been over thirty minutes since the hospital requested that caretakers pay for the patients, and Li Qiang was still gone. I realized he must have run away from the hospital. I called the nurse over and told her that he had tried to rape me, and to tell the guards to detain him if they saw him running away from the hospital. Then I saw two policemen passing the room I was in, and I started calling out to them, "Police! Police!"

They came to me and asked, "Is your name Byin Pu?" I found out from them that the man who tried to rape me was at the police station, and had admitted that the incident was his fault. He told the police that the whole incident, that our "fighting," happened because he loves me. I'm sure he reported it in a way that would make the punishment less severe. I told the police that was just his excuse. Another man, I don't know who, had also filed a report of the incident.

The police wanted to check whether or not the report was real. They asked me to tell them about the case three times—once in Chinese, once in Kachin language, and once in Burmese.

SHE THOUGHT I WAS DEAD

I didn't want my family in Burma to know about the accident; I didn't want to burden them. But Awng Li told them, and my relatives and friends and members of my church came to the hospital to pray for me.

In Burma, my mother thought that I was about to die—the information had spread from person to person and she'd heard incorrectly. She came to Shweli and brought the pastor with her so that he could pray during my funeral service.

At that time, my younger brother, who was about seventeen, was working in construction in Shweli. He and all of his friends came to the hospital and surrounded me to make jokes and to comfort me. When my mother arrived at the hospital, she just opened the door and there I was, smiling and laughing. Most of her sorrow went away when she saw that. She came over to me and grabbed my leg, but it was as heavy as iron; it still had blood on it, and I couldn't move it.

The doctor came and showed me my X-ray results, which showed that my spine had been seriously injured from the fall. I was in shock—it was broken. The doctor said my spine had to be fixed within seven days or I would never be able to move my legs again. He also said that we needed to go to a bigger hospital in Kunming. The cost would be 90,000 yuan.[19]

When I told my mother, she said, "How we can get 90,000 yuan if we don't even have 90,000 kyats?[20] If we had 90,000 yuan, we could touch the sky or the moon."

SEARCHING FOR SUPPORT

After seven days passed, the doctors came every morning to ask about payment. They didn't say directly that they wouldn't treat me, but we know their system—they will not treat without money.

A local pastor organized members of his church to give some donations to me. We also had some support from our relatives and our friends, including food and some monetary donations to help pay for the daily treatment. We were able to stay in the hospital for about fifteen days with the people's support.

Because I didn't have any money to treat my spine at the time, the hospital was just giving me small treatments. I could no longer afford to stay in my room, so the staff arranged for me to stay at the hospital in the area behind the toilets. It smelled really bad and was really dirty.

After fifteen days, we were still unable to find 90,000 yuan. The doctors came every day and said that if I could not find the money that I should leave and go to a different hospital.

The whole time I was in the hospital, it just felt like the accident had been a dream. Sometimes I didn't know whether it was real or not, and I didn't believe that I really couldn't walk.

I also felt very ashamed. Many people in the community were gossiping about my situation and spreading false information—Awng Li was telling

---

[19] Approximately US$13,500.

[20] Approximately US$90.

people it happened to me because I ran away from their house to find a boy-friend and to go to nightclubs. I wanted to explain what really happened, about the attempted rape and the torture, but I could not tell everyone.

A lot of people are told that they will have a job in China, but when they are brought there, they are forced to sleep with someone the first day and made to believe that it's not rape or torture, that they have to do it in order to work.[21] They don't know how to distinguish that these are viola-tions of their rights. The women are afraid to have a bad name, and so they keep silent. Some women have accepted some money and remained silent about this issue, but I did not. I told people that there are many rape cases happening in our community, but no one was saying anything about it—no one was challenging it.

A LIFE CAN NEVER BE MEASURED IN MONEY

I was only able to raise 2,600 of the 90,000 yuan needed to pay for sur-gery.[22] A Kachin family who also had a family member staying by the toi-lets recommended that we go see a traditional healer, so my mother went to the mountains to see this healer and brought him back to the hospital. He just touched my spine and said, "Oh, I can fix this up." Then he left.

Many people believed that going to a traditional healer was risky, but it was my best option. We paid the hospital 2,200 yuan and then we went to the healer on the mountain. I still couldn't move by myself so my friends and family carried me when necessary.

The healer used traditional plants and herbs as medicine. I was in so much pain. It felt like someone was hitting my bones with nails. I could not move my body from left to right when laying down, and I could not sit up normally.

---

[21] The US State Department's 2010 Trafficking in Persons Report estimates that from 2006 to 2009, Burmese officials arrested 1,251 traffickers and 265 smugglers, who were linked to 2,000 trafficking survivors and smuggled migrants.

[22] Approximately US$400.

After almost three weeks of treatment, I could sit up for the first time. The healer told me that I would not be able to walk normally or run for three years. To this day, I still cannot run.

The healer told me I had to go back to my house. But the problem was, I didn't have a home. I didn't want to go to Burma injured and be a burden to my family, and I still wanted to learn a skill that would provide me with future opportunities, so I decided to stay in China.

While I was still on the mountain getting treatment, the two policemen who were responsible for my case came to see me. They took pictures of my injuries, including my back and my leg, and asked me how I wanted to process my case—if I wanted the man to be jailed or if I'd prefer to solve the problem by compromising with some money for the medical costs.

Then Li Qiang called me and asked how much money I wanted for the "accident." I replied, "The life of one human being can never be measured in money." He and Ah Ying both called me and tried to offer me money, but I didn't want money. I wanted the truth.

I had two different feelings during this time. On the one hand, I felt like I didn't want to see anyone. I felt like this early in the morning, while my younger brother was cooking my breakfast and I would open the window and see the sunshine—I wanted to stay in a very silent place and live alone. But on the other hand, I felt like I had to give testimony about my experiences, to be an example for other people in our community who had been through this kind of incident.

I could not decide between these two different feelings in my heart, so I prayed to God. At last God answered me and told me that many people who had never seen my face gave donations while I was in the hospital, and they wanted to meet me. I also wanted to testify in court, so I decided to rent an apartment in Shweli and stay there.

My brother and I stayed at a house in Shweli for about five months until we ran out of money. I would walk around a little with my cane, and sometimes I took a taxi and visited some of the people who had helped me while I was in the hospital. Some of those people shared with me that their children had also had incidents like mine. I said that we had to stand for the truth and that we had to speak up for it.

ANYONE WITHOUT AN ID IS LIKE DUST

I didn't have an ID or a passport, and anyone in Shweli without an ID is like dust, you know. It is really difficult to start a court case without an ID, and I didn't have the money to hire a lawyer either.

It was a long process. After the court did more investigating, they told us that without the legal documents, we could not move our case forward. In order to solve the case in a Chinese court, I needed a passport and more money to obtain legal documents. I didn't want to persecute the man—I just thought he should receive a fair punishment.

The other option was Kachin customary law. There is a missionary group in Shweli called the Kachin Customary Committee (KCC), which is led by local Kachin elders. They make decisions about cases of stealing, rape, divorce, or murder in the Kachin community. The Kachin Customary Committee's system is not for bringing a lawsuit to court, but they could at least help me with my medical costs and help me reveal the truth. I applied for them to review my case.

At the beginning, the KCC went to see the owners of the Chinese restaurant for some help, and the owners gave them 2,000 yuan to help cover my medical costs.[23] The KCC later requested that one of the police officers responsible for my case come to mediate, and I told him that I wanted at least 60,000 yuan to support my treatment.[24] The police officer spoke with my attacker and his family, and then said I had to reduce the amount. They acted like I was just selling vegetables, trying to bargain for 21,000 or 20,000 and so on.[25]

---

[23] Approximately US$300.

[24] Approximately US$9,000.

[25] 21,000 yuan is approximately US$3,100; 20,000 yuan is approximately US$3,000.

The group of guys who abducted me that night were really afraid of going to jail, so they asked me to consider their offer again; we finally agreed on 25,000 yuan and the case was over.[26]

I didn't really want to accept the 25,000 yuan from them, but at that time I had no money to eat or to wash my clothes. I didn't want to become the enemy of those guys and their families. I didn't want any more problems in my life.

I ARRIVED IN THAILAND

After five months in Shweli, I ran out of money. When I was almost twenty-one, a network called the Kachin Women's Association Thailand (KWAT) contacted me about my case and asked me to join them in Kachin State. KWAT specializes in helping women who are trafficked from Burma into other countries. They told me they could provide lessons on how to make traditional Kachin clothing, and that while I was studying with them, they would take care of all of my expenses. I went to KWAT and became a student at their office.

While I was there, I requested KWAT's help in getting medical treatment because the muscles on my left side were still weak and my left leg was still a bit lame. KWAT supported me to get treatment three times in Janghkong—the Kachin name for Jinghong, China—and then they suggested that I go to Mae Sot, in Thailand, to get treatment.

I returned to Kutkai, but I couldn't leave again without an ID—it would be very difficult to travel without one since I was over eighteen. I got the ID from the immigration office after one month, and then I traveled all the way to Mae Sot, Thailand in a van. Some friends traveled with me for part of the journey. The whole trip took one month and ten days; I arrived in Thailand on November 15, 2008.

---

[26] Approximately US$3,700.

I BELIEVE I WILL GET BETTER

When I arrived at the Mae Tao Clinic in Mae Sot, Thailand, they checked my body and told me that I was very badly injured. They treated me with needles, which made me a little better. They said they weren't able to fully treat me at their clinic, and that I should go to Mae Sot Hospital.

My health situation now is that I cannot walk for more than five minutes. I cannot run or jump, and I cannot sit for a long time because my muscles become so swollen I can't even touch them.

Sometimes my muscles stop working and go numb, and it's very painful for me. I get hot pains in my back, but I just stay calm. I have no feeling in my right calf, no strength in my fingers, and I cannot stand up straight. I want to get treatment so that I can recover from this condition very soon. I believe that I will get better; I pray to get better.

KNOWLEDGE CAN BE MULTIPLIED

I've been living in my house in Mae Sot for five months now, receiving medical treatments at the Mae Tao Clinic and going to human rights trainings. My only source of income is when I attend trainings, where sometimes the trainers give me 500 baht.[27]

I am going around without documents or a work permit, so I worry about going to the Mae Tao Clinic. The police can charge 5,000 baht[28] if you're caught without documents, but the total amount for a work permit is 10,000 baht.[29] I used to have a work permit, but it expired after six months. There are many risks. Mae Sot is a very small community, so if the police get you one time, they will recognize you.

My main goal in coming to Mae Sot, other than medical treatment, was to get an education. There are many political organizations in Mae

---

[27] Approximately US$15.

[28] Approximately US$150.

[29] Approximately US$300.

NOWHERE TO BE HOME

Sot that do training sessions.[30] I'm not sure if I could go back to Burma now, because now they may suspect that I was involved in politics. I have learned about human rights, the history of Burma, democracy—about what the government of Burma does to the people. Now I can see more clearly and oppose these things in my mind. I would like to do something more for my people.

I am encouraging my younger brother to save his money and come to Mae Sot to get an education. But sometimes he says he just wants to become a KIA soldier.

IT IS MY COUNTRY

I don't have any motivation to go back to Burma right now; I can only help my community if I become educated. So I will do as much as I can here, and I will go back to Burma one day because it is my country.

My dream for the future is to have a new beginning. In my previous life, people would mock me and talk about the bad things that happened to me. Back then, I just wanted to work to get money to support myself, but I never felt satisfied just searching for money. Now I feel satisfied with my life because the knowledge in my mind can be multiplied.

Now my goal is to help other people. By sharing my story, I hope that I can prevent this kind of experience from happening to another woman in the future. I want the whole world to know what happened to me.

---

[30] Mae Sot is known as a hub for political and social organizations working for change in Burma as well as working to help refugees and migrant workers in Thailand.

NGE NGE

40, migrant worker
ETHNICITY: *Mon/Karen/Hindu*
BIRTHPLACE: *Hinthada, Irrawaddy Division, Burma*
INTERVIEWED IN: *Khao Lak, Thailand*

Nge Nge was eager to share her story, in the hope that it would help other women avoid the painful experiences forced upon her. While working as a teacher in her early twenties, Nge Nge was raped and then forced into an abusive marriage. As her situation worsened, Nge Nge turned to the police, the courts, and to the Myanmar Women's Affairs Federation for help, all of whom were bribed out of helping her. Nge Nge's story illustrates the deep corruption that is endemic in Burma's government and justice system, as well as the vulnerability of women in this system. Nge Nge now works for a women's income generation project in southern Thailand. She has attended many women's rights trainings, and is working to make a better life for herself and her son.

I was born in Hinthada, in the Irrawaddy Division.[1] My father was a government worker, and we had to move when he was reassigned to

---

[1] Hinthada is a city located in central Burma on the banks of the Irrawaddy (also transliterated Ayeyarwady) River.

Mopalin in Mon State, and later to Mottama.[2] My mother is a mix of Mon and other ethnicities, and my father is Karen and Hindu. I have one elder brother, two elder sisters, and one younger sister. I'm not close with my elder siblings, because it is Burmese tradition that I have to accept whatever my elders say and I was afraid of them, but I was close with my younger sister.

My mother and father are very traditional people. When I was a girl, I wasn't allowed to speak with boys. It's quite funny—I wasn't even allowed to sit next to boys, because they told me I could get pregnant. When I bathed in the stream, I was not allowed to be downstream from any boys. My parents said I could also get pregnant that way, and I believed them.

I wasn't allowed to play like other children, because my family didn't want me to get dirty. If I got dirty, my whole family would become angry with me. I was scared of that. They just wanted me to read books. If I just stayed home and read books or practiced math calculations, that was okay with them.

THE MAN LOOKED AT ME AND GAVE ME HIS JACKET

I finished university when I was twenty-five and I started teaching that same year. The first teaching job I had was in a Karen village ten miles away from my village. There was no transportation, so I had to walk the ten miles on Monday mornings and stay there during the week. The villagers had a house for teachers, so I stayed in that house. Every evening, some children would come to my house and do their homework with my help and then sleep over in my home.

One evening, I was walking back to my village from the school. It was a bit dark, and I didn't see anyone else on the path. Then a man came up to me and asked me how to walk to my village. I had never seen him

---

[2] Mottama is a small town in the Thaton District of Mon State (Southeastern Burma), located on the Thanlwin River.

before. I told him, "This is the way to the village," and then I kept walking. But he followed me as I walked on the path through the forest that went to my home. The path was narrow and meant for just one person, as there were bushes and trees on both sides. I almost always used this path, as did many other people.

Then the man suddenly grabbed my hands and tried to take off my clothes. My clothes ripped and I tried to escape from him, but he started punching me. First he punched me in the cheek, and then in the breast, and then in the belly. When he fought me like that, I couldn't stop him and I couldn't escape. You know how the situation can be—I was so scared of him. Then he raped me. We were on the path the entire time. Afterward, as I sat in the same place where he raped me, the man told me that he did not have a wife or children, and that he would marry me.

My clothes were torn apart and so I was very ashamed to return to my home like that. I was still quite far from home—when the incident happened, I still hadn't gotten halfway to my village. The man looked at me and gave me his jacket to put over my body and told me again that he would marry me.

I was scared and I could not reply to anything the man said because he had punched me in the chest, all around my right ear, and in the stomach. I was so scared, and I didn't dare resist him anymore at that point.

I didn't have much confidence or experience in dealing with different people in my life, and I was too shy to say anything back to him. I had no courage to speak back to strangers. Moreover, because of the way my parents had always controlled me my entire life, I was scared of doing anything to fight back. When the man hurt me, I was just more afraid of him.

I was afraid to escape from him, but I was also afraid to face my parents. According to our tradition, sexual relations should only happen between a wife and a husband. I was so afraid of him, but if I denied him, what would he do to me? So I kept silent and followed him. I was scared that he would do something else to me. I would have been so ashamed to become pregnant and live my life without a husband, so I had to follow him. His name was Win Nyut.

Win Nyut took me to his sister's house in Nyaunglaybin Township in Pegu Division. I stayed with him there for one week. During that week, I was both physically and emotionally hurt. He sexually assaulted me again and again—I couldn't stand it.

I was so scared to sleep while next him; I felt like I didn't dare breathe or move. If I moved then he would wake up, and he would hurt my body again. He tried to get whatever he wanted from me. If I refused, then he would slap my face many times and hurt me. Because of his abuse, one morning I couldn't even walk normally anymore.

I felt so terrible while that was happening to me that I wanted to commit suicide.

NOBODY BELIEVED ME

After that week, I went to inform my school why I had been absent for a week. I told them exactly what had happened to me—that a man had raped me and then said he would marry me. I said I was afraid to escape from him, so I had to follow him. But some people didn't believe me because the man had already gone to the school and told them that I would take leave for a week. No matter what I said, they didn't believe me. I reported the rape case to the Education Department and I also told my friends about what happened, but no one believed what I told them. I didn't get any suggestions or advice about what to do. I felt like Win Nyut was the black ink stain that had destroyed all the bright colors in my life.

I went back to work after having disappeared for a week. Next, I went to tell my family. It was 8 p.m. when I arrived at the village. I told my parents exactly what had happened to me, but they did not believe me. My father hit me in the chest and back. My parents had planned for me to marry another man before and I had agreed, but they thought I was lying to them because I wanted to marry a different man. They said, "We have never had a situation like this in the history of our family." My father said, "I'm ashamed. You are not our daughter anymore. You are already dead to us. Leave by yourself, or I will kill you." They didn't even let me stay one hour.

The next day, my father told their next-door neighbor that I had passed away in a car accident. He asked him to make a coffin. He said that I'd been disfigured by the accident, so my body should not be seen. My father put some of my things into the coffin, as well as any photos they had of me, and they cremated the coffin. They put a gravestone in the cemetery.

At the time, I really did want to die. I felt lonely, and I couldn't contact my family anymore. But I was afraid to commit suicide because I had a lot of sympathy for my students—if I left, there would be no one to teach them. I also thought about how the people and the students' parents in the village were very friendly to me and treated me well. I decided that I shouldn't die because of this bad man. Indeed, he should have been the one to die because he was of no use to anyone. But if I died, the children would suffer. That's why I chose to stay alive.

I went back to the school and tried to stay at the house nearby. I was only there two or three days, and then Win Nyut came and took me. I was afraid to deny him again, in case he physically hurt me. I was also afraid to tell other people about my situation. In Burmese tradition, if something like this happens to a lady, she is too ashamed to tell anyone. As far as I know, I was the only person to have been raped in the area where I lived, so I didn't know if people would look down upon and discriminate against someone who had been sexually assaulted. Almost no one knew about what happened to me, except for my parents. They'd already publicly announced that I'd died in car accident and even held a funeral so that everyone would believe the story. So I didn't know how the community would treat a victim like me.

After I went to see my parents, I reported the incident to the police. They just recommended that I wait and solve the case in court. So I stayed with Win Nyut at his sister's house, and I met his mother, his father, and his sister. He only stayed there with me two or three days each week. I don't know where he would go the rest of the time.

JUSTICE IS ABOUT MONEY

Soon after that, I went to court with him. I was still afraid of him.

The judge asked me, "Do you agree to this marriage? Did he ask you to marry him, or did he force you?" I said, "I do not agree. I do not love him. He's forcing me to marry him." I said it in front of Win Nyut, and he looked at me and touched me to signal that I shouldn't say that in front of the court. The judge asked me three times, and I answered three times. Then I saw Win Nyut hand an envelope to the judge. It was stuffed with a significant amount of money. The judge then forced me to sign the marriage document. The court didn't do anything to my husband, and so now we had a legal marriage at the court.

This kind of corruption affects women in Burma negatively throughout their entire lives. Justice is about money. In the area where I am from, if you can give a big enough bribe, you will surely win any court case you're in. Money determines the results. I reported what had happened to me to my school, but no one believed me; they just watched me talk. No one helped me to report the case to the police or to go to court against the man.

After we got married, I continued working at the same school for another year. When I worked at that school, my husband couldn't get angry with me so often; the villagers there loved me, and some of them were from the Karen army. Sometimes, if he punched me or yelled at me, they would go and tell him, "Don't do that again."

I stayed with the Karen people for a long time. They were kind to me and they told me not to worry about anything or be afraid if I needed something or had a problem. They said they would help me. They even told me that if anyone hurt me or caused me problems, that they would kill that person. But I didn't want anyone to die because of me. I believe in karma. I believe that someone will face bad luck and eventually die because of bad things they do in their lifetime.

Then my husband pushed me to transfer to a school in his village in Kyaikkami Township, where his job was. It's very far from where I had been teaching—it takes an entire night to get there, traveling by both train and bus. He knew that if I kept working at the same school, he couldn't hit me or yell at me. For a teacher to transfer to another place, the requirement is an informed agreement and a signature, but I didn't know anything about it until a letter arrived confirming my transfer—it said that I would be moving to my husband's village.

I asked my husband how he'd arranged my transfer and I found out that he'd reported to the Education Department that the Karen village was not suitable for me. He told them that I was not in good health living there. I wanted to stay in that village, but it was impossible after he told them there was a problem with my health. He had already bribed them, so I had no choice.

HE NEVER TOLD ME, AND I DIDN'T ASK

We moved on a regular day. I woke up in the early morning, at four-thirty. I cooked some food, and then around five or five-thirty, the monks came to collect alms and I offered them some rice and some food. When Win Nyut got up, I had to prepare a towel for him to wash his face.

Our regular breakfast was fried rice and tea. I had to prepare breakfast nicely for him. If he didn't like the tea I made for him, I had to go to the shop to buy him tea. After that, I took a shower and handwashed our clothes. Before I left for school, I had to prepare a lunch for him and have it ready on the table for him to eat.

Sometimes he came to the school and said, "Why didn't you do this? Why did you forget that?" When I finished work, I went to the market to buy food. When I got home, I prepared dinner. Win Nyut came home around that time, and he would ask me to do things for him. I had to prepare soap, toothpaste, and a toothbrush for him to take a shower. Then I went to shower and wash clothes.

My home was high up on stilts, and the posts were very high—at least the height of a man with his arms stretched out above him—so I had to walk down nine steps and then walk to the well at the end of the street. It was a normal man-made well that was covered with wood. I had to carry water from the well for cooking and drinking, and there was a compound beside the well with a big piece of wood where we could wash our clothes.

Even if I was hungry and wanted to have dinner a bit earlier than my husband, he said I had to wait for him. Even if he came home late or had gone out somewhere, I had to wait for him. I felt unhappy to sit with him for dinner, only the two of us. He would just talk about himself while we were eating. Then he would ask if I had to go somewhere, and if I did, he would go there with me. I was not allowed to go out of the house if my husband was not at home. If I did so, he would beat and torture me.

After dinner, I had to do grading or other work from school. He went to bed at that time. Sometimes he wanted to have sexual relations with me before bed, and I had to do whatever he wanted. At first, I was worried about getting pregnant; I didn't want him as the father of my baby. But I couldn't protect myself from pregnancy because I couldn't get that kind of medicine. After we had sexual relations, I had to finish my work. So I went to sleep after my husband, but I'd wake up before him the next day.

I didn't know what his job was—he never told me, and I didn't ask. He gave me money sometimes, but I never asked him for it. When he didn't give me money, I bought things with my salary. But it wasn't enough. Sometimes I couldn't buy enough food and I'd tell him, "We don't have enough food. We only have dinner for one person." So he would just eat by himself, and not invite me to eat with him. He would just eat and then go out.

One time, one of my students wasn't feeling well. I went to his home to check on him because he was so young. When I came back home, Win Nyut said, "Where did you go?" But he knew exactly what time I'd gone to my student's home, because he always kept track of the exact number of the trishaw I took, and what time I came home.[3] So he and I were arguing, and then he went outside and locked me inside the house and went

---

[3] A trishaw is a bicycle rickshaw. It is one of the cheapest ways to travel short distances in Burma.

out to drink alcohol. Then he came home drunk, hitting me and saying, "Why did you go to that student's home?"

If I had meetings at school, he would wait outside the door during the meeting, from start to end. Anywhere I wanted to go, I had to go with him. I think maybe it was because he had another girlfriend, and he didn't want me to be around other people and hear things about him. He was protecting himself.

I was never happy when I was living with him. I had friends, but I couldn't talk openly with them. The only times I felt happy were when he wasn't home or when I was at school teaching the students. During those times, I felt so happy.

I HAD NO TRUST IN THE GOVERNMENT

I was so happy to be a teacher. Many of the students would come to welcome me when I arrived at the school, and they all wanted to carry my bag. But if I only gave my bag to one child, then only that student would be proud, while the other children would be so sad. So I had to take out whatever I had in my bag and give each student one thing to carry. If I didn't have enough things for all the students, I would hold hands with the children who weren't carrying anything. I was so happy with them.

I worked at a school that had a primary and middle school, and my students were between five and fifteen years old. I taught them Burmese literature and science. We also had sports and activities at the school. Sometimes we had to go to another village to have a competition with another school, and I would stay overnight with the students at a big monastery. I would cook for them. During exam time, we had to drive to a big school because our village was so small and didn't have testing halls. When we went to that school, we also stayed at a monastery, so I had to teach the students at the monastery during exam time. I also cooked for them and washed their clothes; it was such a happy life with them. Win Nyut would request to go with me on those trips, but I didn't agree to it. So he followed me and he would find a place to stay near the monastery or maybe even in a different building of the monastery where I stayed. He wouldn't come over to me; he would just watch me.

After my husband and I had been married for three years, the government transferred me to teach in another village, and then I lived there. Win Nyut would stay with me there for one or two days during the week, but then would disappear the rest of the time. I didn't know where he was going and I didn't ask any questions about where he went. He would just say he was going on a trip. I was happy when he wasn't home, so I didn't care where he was going. But at the new school where I worked, my colleagues said to me, "Do you know that your husband has another wife and six other children?"

I felt sad to find out I was his second wife, and I also felt sad for his six children. But on the other hand, I was also happy that he had another wife and six children, because it meant he couldn't stay with me for his whole life. My colleagues weren't nice to me when they told me—they blamed me and said, "Why did you marry this man? Why would you become a second wife?" I explained to them what had happened, but they didn't believe me. I felt humiliated in front of many people because they were all talking about it. People talked all the time about how he was such a terrible womanizer, and I was accused of destroying his family and stealing his other wife's husband. I cried almost every day after I heard this. I cried because I was married to this man.

This isn't traditional, but a lot of men have two or three wives. For example, I heard about a doctor who has four wives staying together in one home. Some men will find another wife or a girlfriend when they're traveling. They don't marry them in the legal, formal way.

Win Nyut hadn't told me where he was going because he wanted to protect himself. He didn't want me, or his first wife and children, to know about each other. I requested a divorce, but he did not accept it. So I went to the court to request a divorce, but they said that the wife couldn't divorce her husband unless he accepted. So I tried to find another way to get help.

In Burma, we have a government organization called the Myanmar Women's Affairs Federation that is supposed to help women with domestic violence.[4] A woman I knew suggested I contact this organization. When I went there, the people at the organization asked me details about my situation. When they called my husband in to meet with them, he bribed them—he gave them 5,000 kyats and prepared a table of food for them.[5] The group was happy about the presents, so they told me that I should stay with him and try to be husband and wife again. Nothing happened for me. I was forced to stay with my husband.

I think corruption is the big problem in our country. The Myanmar Women's Affairs Federation is composed of the wives of generals and other high officials—the women act just like their husbands, they don't do anything different. Women who don't have a high status background can't participate. They just follow the money. The police and courts also cannot be trusted because corruption is everywhere.

By this time, I had sought help from the government—from the police and the court—and also from the Myanmar Women's Affairs Federation. But, each time the government failed to take action against my husband. I had no trust in them, and I had no more energy or ability to seek help.

FREEDOM IN MY LIFE

A while after that incident, I became pregnant. I was happy to be pregnant, because in my new baby I would have a partner, a friend. When I was three months pregnant, I found out my husband was planning to marry another girl—the parent of one of my students told me about my husband's plan. The parent told me that the wife-to-be had a shop selling rice and curry. I took a bus from my school and headed to the shop as directed by the parent. I arrived just as it was turning into night.

---

[4] Myanmar Women's Affairs Federation is a nongovernmental organization formed in December of 2003, with the goal of providing greater resources to women while advocating for more significant involvement in Burmese government. It has close connections to the government and employs the wives of prominent junta members.

[5] Approximately US$5.

I entered the shop and asked the girl to speak with her for a moment. She agreed to my request. Then I told her all about the man she was going to marry. I told her that it was up to her wishes and she could do as she wanted. At first, she got angry because she thought I was trying to shame her. But then I explained to her, "I am sympathetic to you because we are both women."

I asked the girl to help me with the divorce and I promised that I would not ruin her wedding ceremony. I told her that I would come after the ceremony was finished in order to get an official divorce agreement between my husband and me, and that I would also use my lawyers to help arrange their marriage documents.

But then the girl noticed that I was pregnant, and at that point she decided she didn't want to marry Win Nyut anymore. But I worried that she could be shamed in front of the whole community because everything for the wedding had already been arranged, and she would have to face her parents. I felt that the community would treat her badly and say bad things about her and her family if they canceled the wedding. So I persuaded the girl that she should not cancel the wedding, and that she should invite the village leaders to her wedding

At that time, I had saved up some money. On the day of the ceremony, I went to the home of a lawyer in the girl's village. I gave him 5,000 kyats and he agreed to help me.

I went to the ceremony with the lawyer and two other officials—the lawyer had arranged for them to go to the ceremony with us; I'm not exactly sure who they were. At the ceremony, Win Nyut and his new wife were making offerings to the monks and to other people. All of the guests were there. I arrived with the documents for divorce.

When Win Nyut understood what was happening, he grabbed my hand to take me away from the wedding ceremony, but I told him I could not go. I told him that the officials present knew all about the situation and knew what I wanted to do. I explained everything to everyone involved, including the girl's mother. I gave him the divorce documents and then I gave his new wife our marriage documents.

Everyone was calm while I was explaining things because I was with the lawyer and the officials, but Win Nyut still didn't agree to divorce me. But then I told him that the lawyer was on my side and that I had already paid him 5,000 kyats for the divorce. I said that I was a government staff person as a teacher, and that the girl was asking him for an official marriage; if he was going to marry her, he had to divorce me. Eventually, Win Nyut agreed and signed the divorce papers, and then the marriage papers for the girl. After he signed the documents, we were officially divorced.

After that, I went to live near the school where I worked. I was pregnant at the time, so I was struggling. But I was so happy—I had freedom in my life. Also, I was going to be a mother. When I was five months pregnant, I wasn't doing well, so I took leave from my job. Since I was only five months pregnant, I had to take leave without pay to get medical treatment. The government is supposed to provide salary and support for six weeks before and six weeks after giving birth, but I only got half of what they promised at that time.[6]

I TRY TO FORGET THE PAST

During the time I stayed with my husband, I couldn't stand my life—sometimes I wanted to commit suicide. I looked so skinny and serious. But when I had my baby, I became really happy. I wanted to live for this baby. I was happy to have freedom after I divorced Win Nyut.

I gave birth to my son in 1999, at Moulmein Hospital in Mon State. Moulmein is the capital city of Mon State. One and a half months after I gave birth, I went back to work at the school and brought my son with me. In Burma, we make a cradle for our babies with some cloth and some

---

[6] According to Burmese law, women are allowed a compulsory six-week maternity leave before and after they give birth, as long as their work fits within the scope of legal, compensated labor as defined by the Social Security Act of 1954. Those who have contributed to social security for at least six months of the year preceding their pregnancy are entitled to 66 percent of their average earnings for the twelve-week period.

wood, and we hang it like a hammock. If you rock the cradle a little bit, it is very easy for the baby to fall asleep. So I would rock the cradle with one hand, and teach my students with the other hand.

After I had my baby, I changed my life. Even if I didn't have enough money to buy a full meal, even if I could only eat rice soup, I was happy. In the past, I was so scared to speak with people, but after I had my baby I became braver about facing my problems. Before, I would keep silent and stay alone, but after I had my baby I would talk to people. If people asked me about my life, I would speak openly to them about my situation. Even if someone didn't greet me first, I would greet them. I spoke to more people, and I had a kind of social life.

After my son was born, I would talk to him about my life, even before he was able to speak. He's my partner, my family.

My son looks like me. He is a quiet boy and he just plays alone. I could talk to him about anything—he's like my friend. I told him that his father was already dead, but Win Nyut came to my house twice. The first time he came, my son was only a few months old. My son had bad diarrhea at the time, so I took him to the hospital. Win Nyut followed me to the hospital and tried to give money to me and the doctor, but we refused it. Finally he left.

He came to meet my son again when my son was over two and a half years old. He told him that he was his father, and my son asked me, "Mom, he said he is my daddy. Is he?" I said, "No, your daddy is already dead. This man just wants to be with me, that's why he told you that he's your dad. Don't believe what he says." I asked my son if he wanted me to be with that man, and he said no. My son then told Win Nyut that he was not his father, and that his father was dead. I didn't allow him to come into my house again.

I think I will tell my son about who his father is when he is older and when he can understand the difference between right and wrong. Right now, while he's young, it's not the right time to tell him because I think he would be negatively affected. When I was with my first husband, I was always living in fear. I don't want my son to fall into a situation with his father like what I experienced, where he will likely become afraid of the people surrounding him.

I TRY TO FORGET THE PAST

After my divorce, my family still did not accept me. I tried to visit them again, but they still did not believe me. They refused to meet with me, and if I saw some of my relatives or their neighbors in the street, they wouldn't even greet me.

It was five years after I had my baby that they finally accepted me back to the family. It had been quite difficult to support the baby on my own. Since I was a civil servant, I had a low salary. It was just enough to survive—sometimes I couldn't eat.

When I returned to my family, my mom told me that my dad had passed away two years before. She said, "Why didn't you come to your father's funeral?" I said that I didn't know about it. My mom said that she had sent me a registered letter, so I went to the post office to find out why I never received it. They had a record that the letter came in and went out. I found out that the post office gave the letter to the head of the village, but my husband gave that man 3,000 kyats and told him to keep the letter a secret.[7] He knew that if I got the letter, I would go back to my family. My family was in Kyaikto, and I lived in Thanbyuzayat District. The journey takes two days if you take a car and a boat.

When I went back to my family, my mom and my siblings were very negative toward me at first. My mom was just crying and hitting me. They were angry that I didn't come to my father's funeral. But when she looked at my son, she started crying again—she loves him very much. My mom said to me, "You left the family when you were young, so I would like to take care of your son because I could not take care of you." I love my mom and want her to be happy, so I let my son

---

[7] Approximately US$3.

stay with them. I try to forget the past, because I'm happy to be with my family in the present.

I'm happy that my son lives with my family and has so many people that love him, but I'm sad that I cannot stay with him. I am also worried about my mother raising my son because when I was young, she taught me that I could not sit next to boys or bathe downstream from the boys, things like that. I don't want my mom raising my son so strictly.

HE WILL DO THIS AGAIN AND AGAIN

One year after my son went to live with my family, I got bad news from my neighbor. She said my ex-husband had been working as a broker, sending people to Thailand illegally. He was sending mostly girls, not only from our village but from other villages as well. If they wanted to go to Thailand, they would contact my ex-husband. At that time, two ladies had gone with him to Thailand but they were arrested by the police before they arrived. They asked my ex-husband to return their money as he had agreed to do, but they couldn't get any money from him.

Then another woman complained to me about my ex-husband. She said that when my ex-husband was taking her daughter to Thailand, they stayed overnight in Dawei before they got to the border at Kawthaung.[8] In Dawei, there were many girls going to Thailand illegally, so most of them stayed three or four girls to one room. But this girl stayed alone in a room. My ex-husband went into her room and he raped her. They were there three nights, and he raped her every night. He threatened her by saying, "If you talk to other people, I will send you to the police station and say that you tried to go to Thailand illegally."

The girls weren't able to go to Thailand, because when they arrived in Kawthaung they were arrested and sent back to their villages. When the girl returned to the village, she found out she was pregnant.

---

[8] Kawthaung is a city at the southernmost tip of Burma, bordering Thailand; Dawei is another city in the southeast.

She was so sad and afraid, crying every day. Her mom came to talk to me because she was angry and she needed advice. I talked to the girl and asked her, "Where did you stay in Dawei? Which hotel? Do your friends know about what happened?" I said I would help them, since I'd had this experience before. The girl and her mother were afraid but I said, "You have to go to the police station and tell them about what happened with him."

We didn't go to the police station right away. First I went to the police chief's house and met with his wife. There is more understanding between women about this kind of thing. I asked his wife what we should do, and she agreed to help us. She told her husband, and he said, "What would you like me to do to him?" I said, "He is my ex-husband. If we don't do anything, he will keep doing this again and again. I don't want to let him do this again, so I want to handle this the legal way."

The police arrested my ex-husband, and his first wife too. They were working together to send people to Thailand. In court, I testified and explained that my ex-husband had raped me too. My husband was found guilty of both human trafficking and rape. At first, he was sentenced for twenty-five years. But he appealed to the court and paid bribes to a lot of people, and then the sentence was reduced to fifteen years in jail, and his wife was sentenced to five years. My mother was worried. She said, "Why did you do this? When your ex-husband gets out of jail, he will be dangerous."

MONEY IS MORE IMPORTANT THAN THE LAW

When schools exams were over in 2005, I went to stay with my family for the summer season. Three days after I got home, I saw all these well-dressed people coming to my family's house. They looked like they were going to a ceremony. I wondered, *Why are people coming to my house?* I didn't know what was happening. There was a man there who was always visiting our home; I knew him from school, but we hadn't been friendly in school because I was younger than him. All the people gathered in our home, and then my mom said I had to marry this man. She said, "If you don't marry him, your ex-husband will take revenge on you or our family."

So they forced me to get another husband. I was so sad—I didn't want to accept it, but I had to accept whatever my mom wanted. I could not protest. I really wanted to stay with my family, but I could not. I was also afraid to start the life of a husband and wife again. I was so sad to do another wedding like this. The first time I was married, I did not accept it, but I got married. The second time, I didn't accept it either, but I got married again. I was thirty-six years old at the time. Why were they afraid about my ex-husband getting out of jail? He might be dangerous, but I shouldn't be afraid if there are laws and regulations. But in Burma, the law doesn't protect us—money is more important than the law. If you had much more money than I do, then you could get protection from the law.

Corruption exists everywhere in Burma now. The people who have money win the case. Even if you are right, without money you will lose. What we call laws are only on paper—the laws rarely work in reality.

THE ILLEGAL WAY IS STILL BETTER

After one week of being married, my husband decided to go to Thailand illegally to work. I said that I wanted to stay in Burma and continue teaching, but he and my mom both said that I had to go with him. I felt sad to leave my son behind; I have felt sad again and again in my life.

We went to Thailand in April 2005. We had to spend a lot of money at the military checkpoints. Getting a passport in Burma is very difficult, so people say that going the illegal way is still better.

We took a boat from Kawthaung, on the Thailand–Burma border. The man we paid to arrange our journey brought us to a building where we had to wait for three days for the boat; I didn't eat anything the whole time because I had no money to buy food. There were many people from Burma going to Thailand; they were from Mon State, Rangoon, the western part of Burma—so many different places.

The boat ride was terrible; we all had to lie down together on the floor, and they covered us with some plastic. We couldn't get any light or air from under the plastic, so people were getting dizzy and vomiting. But we couldn't move—we couldn't sit, we couldn't stand. We left Burma at 4:30 in the afternoon, and we arrived in Nam Kem around four or five the next morning.[9]

During that time, I felt like my life was meaningless because I had been forced to give up everything. I started to feel like I didn't care anymore about what would happen to me.

WE ARE NOT LIKE HUSBAND AND WIFE

When we arrived in Thailand, my husband and I stayed at his friend's house in Bang Niang.[10] He went around looking for jobs for both of us. We spent around ten days jobless. There are a lot of Burmese migrant workers living around here. It's mostly for economic problems that people leave Burma and go to Thailand.

My first job was working at a construction site, reconstructing buildings that were destroyed by the tsunami.[11] There is still some destruction now. I saw a video about the tsunami and I heard about it from my husband. My husband said that he and his wife were holding each other when the tsunami happened, but they were separated by the wave. He doesn't remember what happened, but when he came to, he was holding a tree and he had no clothes on. He didn't know where his wife was. Then more big waves came, and he saw a foreigner floating in the waves. He caught hold of the man and brought him to the tree, but he was only able to save one person because he had to hold on to the tree. After the waves were gone, he climbed off the tree and saw many dead bodies. His memory was blurred.

---

[9] Baan Nam Kem is a coastal village in the southern province of Phang Nga in Thailand.

[10] Bang Niang is a coastal village in Khao Lak, Phang Nga province, Thailand.

[11] The 2004 Indian Ocean Tsunami killed over 230,000 people in fourteen countries.

He saw many things, like gold jewelry and money, but he didn't think any of it was important—it wasn't precious, because it came from dead bodies.

At the construction site, we had to remove the debris and build new buildings. Sometimes I was breaking old walls, sometimes I was carrying cement, and sometimes I was removing cement blocks. I felt quite sad that I had to do manual labor. I thought, I'm married to a man I did not even want to marry, and because of that I have to work like this.

We had to wear a long-sleeved shirt, a helmet, and tall boots that they provided us, and we had to buy long trousers. They fined us 50 baht[12] if we didn't wear one of these things; that was the rule at the construction site.

I earned 120 baht each day, working from eight in the morning until five in the evening.[13] We had one hour to eat lunch at noon. I usually worked every day, but I didn't go to work if I felt sick. I didn't get my wages on the days that I was sick. There was no insurance for accidents at the work site, so if someone was injured they just had to take time off from working but they didn't get medical attention or medicine. Women get injured more often than men, because they are not as strong and cannot always handle the heavy loads. Also, women work on the ground while men work above on scaffolding, so if something falls from above, it is usually women who get injured.

They provided rooms at the construction site for all the workers to stay in, and we had to give money for electricity and utilities. Each room was about nine square meters; it was very narrow and there was just one door. The roof was made of zinc, so it was very hot. We slept on wood floors. Two people stayed in each room, and we ate and slept in that one narrow room. There were four toilets for about four hundred workers, and the sanitation was very bad.

It was not only Burmese people working at the construction site;

---

[12] Approximately US$2.

[13] Approximately US$4.

Thai people worked there too. There was discrimination between the Burmese and Thai people. Even though we were all working in the same situation and at the same level, the Thai people got higher wages. If it was really hot in one area of the work site, the Thai people avoided that area and stood somewhere watching out for the supervisor. The Burmese people were afraid to do this, so they worked hard. When the supervisor came over, the Thai people would pretend to be working, and the Burmese people didn't want to report them. The supervisor was also Thai, so when Thai workers requested a break, he told them they could rest. But Burmese people could not do this. Even if they could speak Thai, Burmese people had to do a lot of work and they could not take breaks.

When we first came here, we were living only on my wages. My husband was working at a construction site too, but they did not pay his wages regularly. We had to work separately because my husband had a work permit but I did not have any legal status. If the police arrested me, they would arrest my husband too. The boss at my work site paid me regular wages, but the boss at my husband's work site lied to the construction workers and did not give them any wages. It is common for migrant workers in Thailand to receive no wages. Sometimes they will get no wages, and other times they will get regular wages when they start to work in construction, but then later they won't get any more wages.

My husband had some debt at the time, so people came to ask me to pay back the money. My husband had borrowed it, but I had to pay it back. Because of this, I could not send money to my family and support my son. But everything else was fine, because my boss paid me regularly.

The amount of money I got in Burma was not even enough for one person, but with the money I earned in Thailand, I could eventually save a little bit, even though still I had to economize everything like I did in Burma. Before I came to Thailand, I only earned 12,000 kyats per month.[14] No matter how hard you try to economize while earning that

---

[14] Approximately US$12.

amount of money, it is never enough. The Burmese government provided some rice, but the quality was so bad we couldn't eat it. I would exchange it in a shop that sold better quality rice.

THE TRADITIONAL BURMESE WAY

I worked in construction for six months, and then I began working as a teacher at the learning center, here at the GHRED.[15] One of my colleagues informed me that the GHRED needed a teacher, and she told them that I had teaching experience in Burma. I was so happy to work as a teacher again. Most of these children from Burma didn't have a right to education in Thailand, and I would see them playing or working at the construction sites.[16] It seems dangerous for society if they grow up without education, so I loved to teach them. The kids were between five and sixteen years old, but they didn't always say their real ages. If they were fifteen or sixteen, they would say they were twelve or thirteen years old because they really wanted to go to school. The students at the learning center must be between five and fourteen years old. There is also a nursery for children between two and four years old.

When I was working at the learning center, I would leave for school in the early morning and return home in the evening. Like in my past life, I had to do all the housework when I got home. I had to get up early, I had to work, I had to do things for my husband, and I had to do things for myself.

At the time, we had bad neighbors living in our compound. They would tell my husband, "Oh, your wife is just going to the school, she's

---

[15] GHRED is the nonprofit Grassroots Human Rights Education and Development in Khao Lak province, Thailand.

[16] Though Thai policy has traditionally been to keep education open to all children regardless of nationality, in fact, only a small percentage of migrants are actually enrolled in Thai schools, largely due to linguistic, financial, and cultural barriers. NGOs have been working steadily to remedy this situation and its debilitating consequences. As of 2009, for instance, GHRED reports that there are seven learning centers for migrant children in Phang Nga province.

not doing any work," or, "Your wife is a teacher and you're a construction worker—you're not on the same level." They would pressure my husband like this, and also say, "Oh, your wife looks all nice and beautiful when she goes to the school. She's meeting other people and being friendly with them, but she's not friendly with you." They caused arguments between my husband and me. He would go out and drink with the other men, and sometimes when he came home he would yell at me and hit me—it was the same as before. He said that his friends' wives had to stay home and take care of their children and husband—they didn't go outside to work. The men were thinking in the traditional Burmese way, saying that women should stay inside the home.

Every morning I rode in the school bus to pick up the students, because they were so young and traveling could be dangerous for them. My husband's friends said to him, "Your wife goes in the bus with the Thai driver, maybe she'll fall in love with him." So my husband was angry and it caused more problems for us.

I was so serious during this time, because I had to ride with the students in the morning, then I had to work, and after I came home I could not take a rest. I was serious in the sense that I didn't talk to my husband and I was really angry and really unhappy because of the things that my husband and his friends were saying about me and the Thai driver. Also, even though I was working hard for my wages, I couldn't use the money for myself. I couldn't send money back to my family, because I had to give my wages to my husband. I couldn't do this anymore, so I resigned from my job. I thought that if I stopped working, then I wouldn't have wages to give him. I was teaching for more than a year and a half; it was maybe 2007 when I resigned.

I was so happy when I was teaching because I loved being with the children. Even though I resigned, I still go to the learning center sometimes to teach a little bit. When I look back at my whole life, it is only children who give me happiness and make me feel good.

A husband and wife should be able to discuss things openly, give advice to each other, and be friendly. I felt hurt when my husband would hit me, so I said to him, "We should not be wife and husband, because you hit me and you are not open with me. You don't allow me to discuss things with you." Since I said that, we are still living together in the same home but we are not like husband and wife; we don't have sexual relations anymore since this problem.

Now I don't have any permanent work here, but I am attending trainings and going to workshops about women's rights. I am struggling to find a way to survive, and I want to make money for myself, not for him.

Sometimes my husband gives me money to buy food for him, and sometimes I cook for him. We sleep in separate beds now, but we only have one room. He does not support me, but I have an auntie near here who borrowed money from me in Burma, so she is paying me back now once a month. Right now I live on this money, and sometimes I get a little money from some other work.

I LEARNED WHAT WOMEN CAN DO

There are many organizations here, so I attend different trainings and workshops supported by the MAP Foundation.[17] One was a health worker training, so I can help someone if they have a health problem. I also attended a training session on women's rights and leadership. The GHRED and other organizations also had community leader trainings that I attended. After that, I started working as a volunteer at the women's center here.

We never had trainings like this in Burma. When I attended these trainings, I learned what women's rights are, and what women can do. As a woman, I have faced so many problems in my life—I don't want other women and girls to face these problems. Now I can share my knowledge with other women and explain what we should do when we have problems like this. For example, when I was pregnant I had some health problems

---

[17] The MAP Foundation was established in 1996 to aid in protecting and promoting the rights of Burmese migrants in Thailand.

because I didn't have any knowledge about pregnancy. But now I know more because I have attended the health training. I volunteer as the assistant coordinator here because the organizations sometimes hold women's group discussions about community organizing and things like that. I participate in the workshop and share whatever knowledge I have with the women from our community and from the temporary shelter here.

I also help out by sewing uniforms, which they do for income generation here. At first, I didn't even know how to cut or sew the clothes, but now I have learned. In this way, I can help the women's center and I also learn something new. I plan to find a permanent job, and I will continue helping out here at the women's center. I already told my husband that if I get a permanent job, I will not stay with him anymore. I hope I can get a good job, save money, and help other people. I hope that by volunteering with this organization, other women can learn from my experiences.

Sometimes I have contact with my family in Burma. If I can send them money, I contact them; if I cannot send money, I do not contact them. I used to talk to my son on the phone, but my family doesn't allow that anymore because they said he looks unhappy after we talk.

I am able to go back to Burma, but I don't want to go back right now. My relatives took my house and my paddy fields, so now I own nothing there. Also, my family took my savings from the bank to pay for medical treatment when my mother was sick. I'm not sure how they could take money from my account—there is corruption everywhere in Burma. Also, it is difficult to find a job in Burma—it's not like Thailand. I can earn more money working here.

If my son isn't interested in the education in Burma, or if he cannot become well educated there, maybe I will bring him here to have a better life. I feel so hurt to be far away from him; no words can express how I feel.

MA SU MON

32, journalist
ETHNICITY: *Burman*
BIRTHPLACE: *Rangoon, Burma*
INTERVIEWED IN: *Bangkok, Thailand*

Ma Su Mon became involved in Burma's democracy movement in 1996, when the ruling military junta shut down all of the nation's universities for four years. She began studying at the National League for Democracy office, where she met "Auntie"—Daw Aung San Suu Kyi[1]—and was inspired to become a full youth member of the opposition group. As a result of her involvement with the NLD, Ma Su Mon was arrested by military intelligence officers and taken to Insein Prison, where she was subjected to cruel treatment, deprived of adequate food, and held in solitary confinement for eleven months. She was twenty-two years old. Since her release, she has become a journalist and is now living in Thailand, where she is pursuing her master's degree in communications and a career in journalism.

---

[1] Daw Aung San Suu Kyi is the General Secretary of the National League for Democracy (NLD) and winner of the 1991 Nobel Peace Prize. Her party was the decisive winner of the 1990 election. For fifteen of the last twenty-one years she has been held under house arrest. The prefix "Daw" is a Burmese title used as a sign of respect for older women. See appendix pages 455-456 and 464-465 for further detail.

I was born in Rangoon in 1978. My father is a government staff member in the Ministry of Agriculture. I have four brothers and one sister, and I am the oldest daughter. In my childhood I had to wear boys' shirts and shoes because my mom bought us all the same clothes and school uniforms. When my brothers would go out and play like boys, I went out, too, so I could play like them. I acted like a boy—I really liked climbing trees, playing, and running. I could do whatever they did. But my other two older brothers didn't want to take me along to play because I always made a lot of trouble when we were playing games. My brothers had to fix my problems and take responsibility for whatever I had done, so they told me to stay in the house. But I always followed them.

My father is really quiet. He never said much, so if he said one word, it was really big for us. My mom was just talking, talking, talking. We didn't hear her. But if my father said one word, we had to obey.

My mom and dad were really sorry for us. They would always say, "We cannot give any money to you, like other parents. We can give you only education. Concentrate on your education, because it can make your life better. You should do better than your parents." So that's why, even though I liked to play in my childhood, I always focused on my education.

I DIDN'T KNOW ABOUT DEMOCRACY

In 1988, I was ten years old. I was a fifth standard student. My father brought me to see some demonstrations nearby, where a lot of people were gathered, and they were shouting slogans, speaking their minds. I felt happy. But then I could see that my father and my mom felt worried about us; three of my brothers had gone out in the morning, and they were involved in something. We had heard that there was shooting and that the army killed some protestors. I can remember some parts of what happened, but not everything. I think maybe at the time, everyone thought that we could get democracy, but we didn't know what democracy was.

My father said, "We can get democracy right now, because the whole country is demonstrating. We can change our lives." Everyone knew that the government censored the truth about what was really happening in our country, so everyone thought the government had to change.

My father had a very low salary because the economy was bad. He thought that if we could get democracy, if we could get some rights, things could be better. At the time, I thought democracy was just a big thing my father could bring to our home. I didn't know; I just felt happy. We were all shouting, "Okay, now we can get democracy!" When we would play, we would play demonstrations because we saw this kind of thing in front of us.

But after that, a really bad thing happened to our family.

When the new military government started ruling our country after the '88 uprising, they decided to claim some land and force the people living there to move to a remote area.[2] When the government wants to build a government compound, they just claim all the buildings in that place and send the people elsewhere. They had a lot of space and electric fences around their compounds, but I think maybe they were still afraid for their security. After the SLORC took power in 1988, my father said we had to obey them—we didn't have a chance to say no.[3]

They made a new town and sent us there. We had lived for ten years inside Rangoon city, but now, in 1990, we had to move to this new town, North Dagon Myothit. It was two hours away by bus. It had no school, no hospital, no transportation. We had to go to school in another rural area called North Okkalapa on the other side of the river; it was very difficult to go there in the rainy season.

---

[2] In 1988, there was a nationwide popular uprising against Ne Win's one-party rule. In response to the Burma Socialist Programme Party's failed attempts to quell the demonstrations, the State Law and Order Restoration Council (SLORC), a group of generals, took control of the government through a military coup. See appendix VIII for information about the uprising.

[3] Framed as a caretaker government, the SLORC—State Law and Order Restoration Council—has remained in power since the 1988 coup. In 1997 they changed their names to the SPDC—State Peace and Development Council. See appendix pages 465-467 for further detail.

The military government didn't say directly to my family that we had to move. They told the head of our town. We had to give our land to the government without receiving any compensation. This happens in other places too—forced relocation.[4] When we moved to a new place, we had to pay money.

They gave us a deadline to move. Some people didn't want to move, because they were living on the land where their grandparents had lived. The government sent some very big army trucks to send us to the new place with our things. Some people stayed in their compounds, but I heard that if someone didn't move they would use the bulldozer to clear the buildings.

Because Rangoon is a city where people are in the public eye, we were given some time to prepare our things and move, but in other divisions or other states—where other ethnic groups lived—they didn't have any time. They didn't even get a deadline, like one day or two days. They didn't want to move right away, but they had to just do it. The army can do whatever they want in rural areas. If the government says to move, you move. You have no choice.

When we moved to North Dagon Myothit, my father was old at the time, maybe fifty years old. He became really sick with tuberculosis and was forced to retire from his job. When that happened, three of my brothers decided to work for our family. They were about sixteen, eighteen, and twenty years old; my oldest brother was only in tenth standard. They were really young, but they had to find money for us because we had three children who needed to continue their education.

---

[4] Land confiscation and forced relocation by the military junta have been well documented. In 1988, whole areas of Rangoon were cleared and the SPDC's four-cuts policy regularly removes inhabitants in ethnic nationality areas where the military regime has been at war with armed ethnic opposition groups. People are also forcibly relocated in SPDC-backed development projects, like dam-building, throughout the country. For more on the four-cuts policy see appendix pages 461-462.

My brothers sold betel leaf, because everybody chews that in Burma.[5] My brothers were working in a big market, very far from our home. My parents thought they were going out to see friends, but my mom went to the market one day and saw my youngest brother carrying something that was too heavy for him. She cried a lot and said we had to do something to change the situation. My father never forced my brothers to work, he just wanted to see his children become educated people. But my brother said, "This is our responsibility for our family. We're just handling our business." They said they didn't want to keep studying because the education fee was really expensive for the three of them.

I KNEW IT WAS DANGEROUS TO PROTEST

When I passed high school, I was only interested in education. My goal was to be a lecturer at a university. But when I was a first-year university student in 1996, there were student demonstrations at our university. Though I didn't know anything about politics at the time, I followed the older students, my seniors, when they started demonstrating and protesting for democracy. Then the government closed the university without reason.

I knew it was dangerous to protest, but when I started there were a lot of students and many people surrounding us who gave us water and food. I thought it would be fun. I was really happy to continue demonstrating with my seniors and to shout, "We want to study, open the university!" We were demonstrating at the Hledan Junction, a very famous place in front of Rangoon University, near Daw Aung San Suu Kyi's house. At the time, all of the people from different universities were gathering there. When they shouted, we shouted. Then something happened in front of me.

I saw the police come and beat our student leaders. This was really my first experience seeing people beaten in front of me. We had to run. Some

---

[5] Betel leaf is a heart-shaped leaf common throughout Southeast Asia. In Burma, it is chewed with the areca nut (and the combination is casually referred to as "betel nut"), and often combined with tobacco and assorted spices.

of the student leaders pulled me along because I was young and I didn't know where to go. We went to hide, and later we heard on the radio that the police had arrested a lot of student leaders. Some of them had been beaten very badly, almost to death. General Khin Nyunt announced that the military was just protecting the security of our country.[6]

We hadn't done anything—we didn't have any weapons, we just demonstrated in peace—but after the demonstrations they closed the universities for almost four years. My parents were worried about me. "Why did you follow them?" they asked. "You should not do things like that. If you just want to be an educated person, you should concentrate on your education, not get involved in political demonstrations."

During the protest, I didn't know I was involved in politics, I just wanted to do what my seniors did. But then I saw my seniors get beaten and a lot of bad things were happening around me. Some of our seniors said, "You should go back, sister, you are too young and you're a girl." But I didn't like hearing that—I could do whatever I wanted.

I SAW AUNTIE FOR THE FIRST TIME

The government closed the universities from 1996 to 2000. They said they didn't want to open them again because of security concerns, because they were worried that demonstrations would happen again. They arrested all of the students who were active in the political movement. I felt really upset, and I was also worried about my future—I was afraid I'd never be able to study again. None of my college friends knew what to do either, so we started to look for a place where we could get some kind of education. I think I was lucky, because some of my friends who were NLD members invited us to go to the headquarters of the National League for Democracy, where they had a library and also English training

---

[6] General Khin Nyunt was Chief of Intelligence. In October 2004, during an apparent power struggle between him and SPDC Chairman Than Shwe, General Khin Nyunt was removed from power, arrested, and has been held under house arrest ever since.

for youth.[7] We followed them there and we eventually met Daw Aung San Suu Kyi.

When I went to the NLD office for the first time, I was really afraid. I didn't know where it was so my friend took me there, and when we got off at the bus stop, we walked to the office and saw the red sign—it said NATIONAL LEAGUE FOR DEMOCRACY. Their flag has a peacock and a star.[8] I had seen this flag before, because my parents showed it to me when they voted for the NLD. I felt strange and nervous when I entered the building, and I didn't feel safe because we knew about the government's propaganda against the NLD.

A lot of people were at the office, just gathered around and whispering to each other. Before I entered the building, I felt strange because we could not see inside. The office was very old and fading, very dark and narrow, with really old furniture. But when we entered the building, we saw a lot of people who really welcomed us and also some student leaders, like the central youth leader of the NLD. They gave us a place to sit and we saw they had a lot of big pictures of Daw Aung San Suu Kyi and other leaders. We saw a picture of General Aung San, which we had never seen in public before.[9] The pictures were looking down at us.

---

[7] The National League for Democracy is a political party in Burma formed in the aftermath of the 1988 pro-democracy uprising, and is headed by General Secretary Aung San Suu Kyi. In the 1990 general elections, the party garnered 59 percent of the general vote and 80 percent of the parliamentary seats, but the military junta never ceded power to them. In 2010 the military declared the party to be illegal. See appendix pages 465-468 and 473 for further detail.

[8] The image of the peacock has been used on flags as an emblem of Burmese nationality throughout Burma's modern history. The National League for Democracy's flag, which displays the peacock in a fighting stance, was first used by student activists against British colonial rule, in order to connote a sense of power and defiance that the NLD has come to represent.

[9] General Aung San was the architect of Burmese independence. He founded Burma's army (the Tatmadaw) and the Anti-Fascist People's Freedom League. He was assassinated in July 1947, six months before the end of colonial rule. For more on Aung San, see appendix pages 459-460.

I was really amazed when we went to the office. There was so much activity, and some of the members there were important people who might inspire us. Everything was really different from our university classes. We were so happy at the NLD office and we kept returning to study more. I didn't tell my parents about my involvement with the NLD because I knew they would stop me. I had an excuse—I said I wanted to attend computer trainings and go to some places to discuss jobs with my friend. Since the university was closed, my parents said I could go. They said, "You should find some place to learn English and also about computers." So I never lied, but I found an excuse.

At the time we were not full members of the NLD, but we would go whenever they had group discussions about books and poets. Daw Aung San Suu Kyi was also involved in these discussions. They didn't put pressure on us to become full NLD members—they said we could just come and stay with them, because they were really impressed with the students.

Daw Aung San Suu Kyi made a big library in the office. We could find books that had been banned by the government, like history and educational books. There were some books by famous Burmese writers; some of them were in prison or had already died.

I trusted the NLD leaders. The NLD had won the 1990 election with 80 percent of the seats, but then the military government arrested every NLD member who had been elected to parliament. Some of the parliament members have been in prison since 1990. The junta arrested Daw Aung San Suu Kyi, and they put her under house arrest. We call Daw Aung San Suu Kyi "Auntie"—she is the role model of our young generation and all of the party members. We love her.

About a year later, in 1999, I became a full NLD member. When I became a full member of the NLD, it was because I was so impressed by Auntie. I love her work and her actions. The leaders chose some of us from the student movement to accompany Auntie whenever she went somewhere in Rangoon. We also went to Auntie's house to do some political things.

Auntie's house is on University Row. It's really old and big, with a lot of grass in the compound, and it has really simple furniture. The library has a lot of books, and she has a piano too. Even though she is really the leader of our country, she lives like a simple person. Some of the NLD members stayed with her inside her compound to take care of daily things, but other members had to stay outside so they wouldn't create a security risk for her.

From about 1997 until 1999, we would do some activities in her compound, like ceremonies for our national days. Everybody could go and visit the compound then. Sometimes Auntie would put out a lot of sweets on the table and play the piano for us while we had discussions about the books in her library. She'd smile at everybody inside the office. She said our members were like our brothers and sisters—and she called us her sons and daughters, like she was our real mom.

Sometimes we made a lot of trouble and challenged the SPDC, and she worried about our security, but we had to do something more. We challenged the SPDC in many ways. Even though it was against the SPDC's rules, we did political activities in public, like going to the pagoda to pray for the release of political prisoners. It caused conflict, because some of the NLD leaders tried to stop us, but we didn't obey them. But when Auntie told us to stop, we obeyed her.

NOW WE'LL TAKE YOUR DAUGHTER

When I became a full member of the NLD, I was just doing very simple things at first. But things changed after March 13, 2000, when we celebrated Human Rights Day in Burma. March 13 is the day in 1988 that the student Phone Maw died. The '88 uprising happened because of this.[10]

---

[10] Engineering student Ko Phone Maw was murdered by the military on his school's campus while participating in pro-democracy protests. See appendix VIII for more details on the events of 1988.

The NLD had a ceremony for Myanmar Human Rights Day, and we also had a poetry and picture competition. I wrote about my university experience in Burma, about how I was very worried about not being able to continue my education. I wrote that the military government's oppression made me want to fully participate in the political movement; I realized that politics was the new university in my life. My poem won and Daw Aung San Suu Kyi handed me the prize at the ceremony.

We were really busy that month. Daw Aung San Suu Kyi was traveling to our towns to help set up networks of NLD members and to assign student leader positions. Each town had three top youth leaders—first leader, second leader, and third leader. I was chosen to be the third leader in my town.

We knew that we could get arrested, so some of my friends didn't stay at their family's homes. I had been thinking that they would not do arrests during the Burmese New Year, because there is the traditional Burmese water festival. I knew that something would happen to us when our leaders gave us those positions, but I didn't think it would happen so soon. Soon the government started arresting all the members, and then they came to my house.

I was still living with my family in Dagon. It was April 12, which was our New Year in Burma, so I went to the NLD office for some festivities. When I went back home, my brothers picked me up at the bus stop because it was very late. I saw that a really nice car had stopped in front of my house. It was really unusual to see this. It had tinted windows, and we knew that only government officers could use those cars. But we didn't know the car was for me.

I entered my house and went into my room. Maybe ten or fifteen minutes later, someone knocked on the door of my house. I think there were more than twenty people, but some of them stayed outside. Some of them were in uniform, like the local police. There were military intelligence (MI) people—they never wear a uniform. They have walkie-talkies and very short hair. The leader of their group was from MI. I think they also had people from the USDA—they're not soldiers, not police, but they're supporters of the government.[11] The local authority person talked to my mom and said they wanted to check the list of family members. They read my name and said, "Where is Ma Su Mon?"

They just entered my room and started searching everywhere. They found some papers—some official statements and the document from when I won the poetry prize. They took everything. I was really afraid at the time, really nervous. I couldn't stand on my two feet.

I knew that I would be arrested one day if I was involved in political activities, so that's why I knew to ask one question before they searched my room: "Do you have any permission to enter my room?"

"Oh, you're very clever, you're bright. Who taught you this kind of question—did your Auntie teach you that?" They made fun of me like that. But I knew the law—they needed to show a warrant to search my room, but they were just doing whatever they wanted.

When they found the papers in my room, I still felt comfortable because they were official statements, signed by our leader, Daw Aung San Suu Kyi. I believed that it wasn't anything illegal. Then they asked my mom, "Can we bring your daughter in to ask some questions? It will be very short. After that we will give you back your daughter." My mom didn't know that I was involved with the NLD, so she said, "Okay, daughter, you can go. Don't forget the Buddha—pray for him."

IT WOULD BE SHAMEFUL

It took about twenty-five minutes for the military officers to collect all of my papers. They had my mom and the local township authorities sign a paper saying they knew and approved that they were taking me from my home. They blindfolded me, and they were very rough when they put

[11] The Union Solidarity and Development Association is a mass organization formed and led by Burma's military junta. It plays many roles in local governance, including engaging in business, paramilitary activities, and education in subjects ranging from Buddhism to computers.

me in the car. My brothers came very close to the car and said, "What are you doing?" One of the MI officers said, "None of your business. If you want to know, you should ask your sister when she comes back to you." My brothers got into a shouting fight with the MI officers, and then the officers closed the door.

When they took me to the military intelligence compound, there were maybe a hundred people there who had been arrested and brought in for interrogation. I could see the others—some of my friends had been arrested—but we couldn't talk to each other.

The MI officers said, "If you sign this paper, you can go back home right now." The paper said, "I will not be involved in any kind of political movement. I will not participate any more in politics. I will not support this any more."

Some of my friends signed the paper, but I never signed it. It would be shameful for me, because I could not promise that. Some of them signed the paper so they could tell people on the outside what was happening on the inside, but that was a risk for their reputation. Some of the people who signed the paper might continue in politics anyway, but some of them never came back to us. Maybe they were afraid for their family's security, or afraid for their business or something. In our party, if we signed that paper, it was really shameful. It's like you're not thinking about other people, just thinking about yourself.

After I said I would not sign, they divided us all into two groups. They put hoods over our heads, like they do for people getting the death sentence. We couldn't see anything. Then they put our group in a police van, the kind with the bars. There were so many people we couldn't even breathe. We couldn't see each other, we didn't know who was who. Maybe the trip took just a minute, but it felt like an hour until they opened the door of the van. They had sent us to Insein Prison, the biggest prison in our country.[12]

---

[12] Insein Prison was a British colonial prison, now famous for holding Burma's political prisoners.

SOLITARY

The hood smelled so bad. They pushed my head down because the prisoners are not allowed to stand straight when they cross the yard—it's the rule. There was a special door for prisoners to walk through, and it was very hard for us because we had to kneel down when we walked.

After that we had to take off our hoods, and I saw that it was all females in the room with me. I was the youngest. Everybody knew each other from working in politics, and they said, "Don't cry, don't be afraid. We can go back home one day. They can't do anything to us, we will take care of each other." There were some old people, like sixty-five- and eighty-year-old women in our group.

I felt sorry for my father when I was at the prison, because they wrote my family name on a piece of paper that I had to hold when they took my prisoner photo—one photo from the front, and one from the side. I thought, *I am the daughter in prison.* But I hoped maybe my father would still be proud of me.

After that, they put me directly in a cell. It was in a special place, usually for people with a death sentence or for people who break the prison rules—solitary confinement. It was really narrow and very dark. There were three doors—iron, wood, and aluminum.

Everybody is afraid of this kind of cell. We were the first group of people who came to the prison that they put directly into this kind of cell. They put us in there because they didn't want other people to see us, and maybe for other reasons. Other prisoners were in a very big hall together, but we were each alone.

After they put us in the cells, they started interrogations. They interrogated us many, many times and gave us no food for three and a half days. We got one bottle of water in the morning. There was just a little bowl for a toilet, and they gave nothing for us to clean ourselves with. When I saw this, I said, "Why do you give only one bottle, for cleaning my face, for cleaning my toilet, and for drinking? You are not Buddhist. If you are Buddhist, you cannot clean yourself and drink from the same bottle." I really felt angry, so I just left the bottle there.

"You think this is your family home?" they said. "This is prison. You can't complain about this kind of thing."

"Okay, so I will not drink any more. If I cannot get another bottle, I don't want to clean this toilet, and I don't want to drink." Then there was some conflict between the prison wardens, and they talked to the MI. A military intelligence officer came and said, "You want two waters, right? Okay, give them to her." Then I asked about other people, because there were a lot of older women. So they got two bottles for everybody.

For the interrogations, an officer would take me out of the cell and put a hood on me and then lead me. We had to sit on these very high stools so our feet couldn't touch the floor. We sat like that for long hours during the interrogation. They didn't give us any food at that time, but I wasn't hungry. I felt tired, and they just kept talking, talking, talking.

They cover the faces of every political prisoner in Burma. I think maybe they don't want to show our faces to other people in the compound so that we don't know who was arrested and who was released. For example, even if my friend and I were across from each other in our cells, we wouldn't know. We could not talk each other.

During the interrogation, the intelligence officer said to me in Burmese, "You are a very useless person. You all want to destroy the country."

I couldn't listen any more. "Why are we useless people? If we really are useless, why do you spend so much time on us?" And then he slapped me.

When they put me back in the cell, the warden said, "You should not do that any more. They can kill you at any time."

At that time, they were putting pressure on other people to sign the paper. I heard that maybe two or three weeks later, some of them were able to return to their homes. But my parents didn't even know where I was.

THEY REALLY HATED US

When they slapped me, when they interrogated me, I didn't feel anything.

But after those first four days, I saw the food we had to eat and I started to cry. It was rice, but not regular rice—it was the kind we feed to pigs. If it was hot, okay, I could eat it. But it was cold, like raw rice. I said, "How can I eat this kind of food?" and I started crying.

They brought me to another room. There was a very big table with a lot of food. I couldn't stand it—oh my god, it was really delicious food. They said, "You only got involved in politics because of the NLD, right? They were pressuring you, and you made the wrong decision. It's okay, we understand. You can't eat the prison food, right? If you eat this, you can go back and just sign that paper." Then they said, "And then you can tell us some information about who is involved in the democracy movement." I shook my head and said, "Please, I just want to go back to my room. I don't want to eat any more." I saw that this was their strategy, because they thought I couldn't stand this kind of situation. I really wanted to eat the food, because I hadn't eaten for five days. I couldn't stand on my feet, and my hands were shaking. But it was just food.

When I went back to my room, I didn't eat the food in my cell that day. After that, some of my friends said to me, "If you don't eat it, you will die here. Just try to eat a little bit." They were worried about my health, so I thought, *Okay, I will eat it for tomorrow. I want to see my family. I want to go outside. I want to see Auntie.*

They interrogated me for one month. For the first week it was day and night, but after one week, they only questioned me once in a while. They compared the things different political prisoners said and tried to confuse us. "Your friends said you did this, it was you." But we always denied it, whether we had done it or not.

We had to wear the hood every time we were interrogated. It smelled so bad—we could smell blood, it smelled like death. The smell was all around the compound. We had to answer some of their questions. For example, if they asked, "Why were you involved in this political situation?" we would answer, "Because we believe in it." But if they asked about our activities or maybe some secret thing, we would always deny it. If you laughed at them during the interrogation, they would beat or kick you.

I think they do things like that when they cannot control your mind.

I was twenty-two years old when I entered the prison. The man who slapped me was maybe my father's age—maybe I was his daughter's age. They only slapped me, and just once, but they did more horrible things to other people—you can't imagine. We knew that some of the officers at Insein were beating people really horribly. They beat monks and even pregnant women, and after they beat them, the women had miscarriages. We could not understand their minds; I don't think they were human any more. Maybe the prison officers just wanted to do their duty, but I think they really hated us.

They didn't tell me how long I would stay in jail; they just put me in jail with no charges or anything. I was in solitary confinement the whole time. You can't see any light in this kind of cell and it is very cold, made of concrete. You can only walk back and forth. They gave each of us a piece of wood to sleep on in the rainy season, because there are heavy rains from April to July. We didn't have any blankets, and they gave us only two sets of prisoner clothes. Prisoner clothes are all white—a white shirt and a white *longyi*.[13] We didn't wash our clothes in the rainy season, because we were afraid they wouldn't dry. So there was a lot of skin disease, and the smell was bad. Some people got TB; they had problems with their lungs.[14] After six months like this, you feel like you're not even human—no clean clothes, not enough food, dirty hair.

We could leave the cell two times a day. One time was to empty our toilet bowls, take a bath for five minutes, and clean our plates. We were outside the cell for fifteen minutes each, one at a time. After that they closed the door and let us out again at 2 or 3 p.m. to throw away our things and clean one more time.

---

[13] A *longyi* is a cylindrically sewn cloth sheet worn throughout Burma. It generally drapes from the waist to the feet. It is worn by both men and women.

[14] According to the World Health Organization, approximately 1.5 percent of Burma's population becomes infected with tuberculosis every year. High-density prisons compound the spread of communicable diseases like TB, and treatment is particularly scarce in rural areas where the majority of prisoners are held.

When they let us outside, I really loved to breathe the air. I would just look around, and it made me feel really good. I wanted to escape. I would cry, but never in front of them. They were always monitoring us, so if they saw me cry they would come and say something to me like, "You are very brave." It was like they were playing games with us, so we didn't ever show our emotions in front of them. I would cry in the night, when they closed the wooden door. We're human; we missed our families.

When we were outside, we could talk to each other using hand signs. After three months, we would just be saying things like, "Don't give up." But if they saw us talking to each other, they wouldn't let us out for one day. That always happened to me, because I always tried to talk to other people. I would also sing songs in the cell, so they said I was too noisy. They used so many reasons to keep us inside our cells.

We weren't allowed to read or write in prison, but we found many ways to communicate with each other secretly. We would write on plastic bags, using our nails to carve messages, and then roll it up and throw it into someone's cell when we crossed the hall. We wrote messages mostly just about good news we had heard, rumors in the prison. Sometimes it was about a problem, or just taking care of each other. We didn't know anything about the outside world.

WE DON'T KNOW ABOUT THE FUTURE

One morning the prison staff came to us and said, "You should prepare to leave this cell." We thought they were sending us to receive a sentence, or to another prison. But they released all of us who had been arrested on the same day—more than a hundred people. It had been almost one year.

We were really excited when we went outside the prison, because a lot of people had gathered to watch us. There were international journalists waiting to take pictures and ask questions. The officials were smiling for the camera. That's when we knew they were releasing us. I felt confused. They gathered us in front of the prison and one of the highest-ranking military intelligence officers gave us a lecture. He said we should not talk to the foreign press about this issue. He said, "We kept you because of security concerns. But we treated you very well, right?"

After they gave us the first lecture, the military intelligence from our townships put us into cars and brought us to offices in our different towns. Then they gave us another lecture, explaining again that they had arrested us because of a security concern. Then we were brought home by military intelligence and an authorized military person from our town.

The government can do whatever it wants. They arrested us without reason, and they released us without reason. We can't be sure about tomorrow, whether they will arrest us again or not. We don't know about the future.

WHAT DO YOU WANT TO DO?

When I arrived back home, everything felt really strange and new. After almost one year in jail, suddenly I could go outside. I felt really dizzy, and I couldn't walk any more. My legs had become weak and swollen from the prison, because it's very narrow there and we could not walk around very much.

My family was really proud of me. That first night, my parents said to me, "We don't blame you for anything that happened. But you should think about your future now. What do you want to do?"

I went back to the NLD office the next morning to report back about my experience. It was really crowded because so many of us had been released. The leaders welcomed us and asked if we were okay, and told us we should go to the hospital to get blood tests and heart check-ups because we would all be weak from being in jail. They suspected that we might have been drinking unsafe water in jail, and that they might have given us the wrong medicine. I continued going to the NLD office, but not very often.

I felt lonely at home, but my family treated me well. Sometimes I had nightmares and I thought I was still in prison. When I heard a car start near my house, I felt like someone was coming to take me to prison or something like that.

Since the jail food was really horrible, we used to all talk and dream about the kind of food we would eat if we were released. But when I got home and my mother cooked the things I liked for me, I couldn't actually eat it. The smell and the taste were so good, but after one or two spoonfuls, I could not continue. My body wouldn't accept this kind of food for a couple of months. During that time my mom just gave me soup, like chicken soup or rice soup.

My mind wasn't normal. I felt sad, because some of my friends were still in jail. This made me feel sorry, even when I saw the food. Can you imagine this kind of feeling? Every time I drink a nice coffee or eat nice food, I still feel this way.

WE SUSPECT EVERYONE

After I was released from prison, I didn't want to stay around my hometown because our neighbors looked down on me. There were a lot of government officers in my community, so everyone was really scared of me. They talked about it to their children and friends, and they didn't make visits to my home. It made me really sad and uncomfortable; I wanted to run away.

I decided to go to my grandma's village, which was three hours away by boat. My mom said I shouldn't go because of the weather, but I went. When I arrived, someone from the village was using my grandmother's boat and told me she'd died while I was in prison. I didn't cry; I just felt the pain in my mind.

Before, when I had visited my grandma, everybody would be shouting and yelling to welcome me. But this time, it was like I was a different person, and they didn't want me there. I thought maybe my auntie and uncle and cousins would want to talk to me, so I went to their house. But even they were afraid—of me, of the government, or something like that. They knew I hadn't done anything wrong, but they're villagers and they're afraid of everything because they know very well about the SPDC. I stayed about an hour, and then I went back to my parents' house.

We don't trust each other in Burma—we cannot even trust our own family members. In our country, you cannot even sit for one minute before someone sits down next to you; anybody could be MI, and they will watch you. We cannot discuss our political party in public. Some of our leaders say we should not even trust our friends. We suspect everyone.

I DON'T THINK I CAN COME BACK

When I was released from jail, the universities had already opened again. But when I tried to attend my university, they told me I had to sign a paper saying I'd obey the university rules and not be involved in any political movements, or else I couldn't attend class. It was like the paper they wanted us to sign in jail. I said I didn't want to sign the paper, so they suspended me for a year. After a year, I was able to attend without signing the paper.

When I started university again, I was interested in becoming a reporter because I had met some journalists when I was released from jail and they'd suggested it. So in 2001, in my second year at university, I started working with a privately owned journal as a "rookie." I was doing a BSc in chemistry, but I really wanted to be a reporter. I just continued my education to please my parents.

I graduated from university in 2003 and continued working for the journal. There was a lot of censorship by the government; they were always watching these kinds of publications. Inside Burma, we could see everything that was happening around us, but we could not write about it. We could hear what everyone was feeling, but we could not report it. If you report these things, the government will destroy your publication, and the journalists can be arrested.

At the time, we had no official journalism training in our country, but young journalists could take trainings from certain organizations. From these trainings in Burma, people would be chosen to go to Thailand for further training sessions. In 2004, while I was still working at the journal, I did one of these trainings and was then one of the people chosen to go to Thailand. Luckily I got a passport—it's normally very difficult to get a passport in Burma.

I returned to Burma after that training session, and then in April 2005, I got the chance to attend a year-long journalism training in Chiang Mai, Thailand.

In April 2006, I went back to Burma after the training. I wasn't involved in political activities—I was just doing my job as a reporter—but the government still had a problem with me because I had been in prison. They thought I was attending trainings arranged by an opposition group in Thailand. They had gone to my house and asked my parents what I was doing there and who'd arranged it. They tried to link me with the Americans, because they hate the Americans. I didn't know they were still watching me.

The first week I was back, they didn't come to my home; I was usually out every day looking for news stories. But that Sunday, four people from military intelligence came to my house and spoke to my father and me. I was surprised, because they were quite polite. They asked about my trip to Thailand, how I'd arranged it and who had paid for it.

The trainers had said I should report to them if I ever had a problem, so I told them that MI had come to my house to ask questions. My trainers said I should leave Burma. Some of my friends also suggested it. The government says people who go for trainings in Thailand are terrorists being trained to destroy the country—what if they came to my house to take me away? I told my editor I should leave as soon as possible, and he agreed.

I was lucky, because I got help leaving Burma immediately by plane. My father said, "So, you cannot come back to us, right?" I said, "I'm not sure... I don't think I can." My mom didn't say much—she just cried. You can imagine how painful it is for a mother and daughter to say goodbye when they know they will not see each other for a long time, and especially when they know that one of them could even die before it would be possible to reunite. My parents were already old and they had given up so much for me. They allowed me to go because they knew it was better for me. It was really sad.

But I'm lucky, because for other people who've left Burma, their parents don't know where they are. The parents of many student activists don't even know if their kids are dead or not, because some of them have been in the jungle fighting since 1988. I have been gone for almost six years, but some of these activists left their homes in Burma twenty-one years ago. Their family might have moved to another place, but they don't know.

When I call my parents now from Thailand, I cannot talk much about what I'm doing, because I have to think about their security. If it's known they are in contact with someone in exile, they can be arrested. The government can do whatever they want.

I don't think I can go back home again, but I hope that one day it's possible.

THERE IS A LOT OF STATIC

All of the media in Burma, including the two television channels, the radio, and the newspapers, are controlled by the government. Even private journals, books, and music are under the control of government censorship. If they don't like one word they will cancel a whole program. I think this is why even nowadays, Burman people inside Burma don't know about the ethnic minority issues or about international news.

When I was young, I listened to the BBC, Radio Free Asia, and Voice of America with my father. We felt like these radio stations had real news. The government says that stations like that are liars and that they want to destroy the country. People in Burma cannot listen to those radio stations very loudly, and the connection is not clear—there is a lot of static.

After I fled Burma, I went back to Chiang Mai and became a producer and reporter for the Burmese section of the BBC World Service Trust. It was my first experience in radio—I didn't even know how to use an audio recorder, but my editors were always taking care of me and teaching me how to do things. One of the first aired projects I did for them was produced in Mae Sot, where I was reporting about health education and HIV/

AIDS.[15] I had a ten-minute program in which I interviewed people at a medical clinic there. It was really new for me, but after that, I became more familiar with this kind of thing.

When my parents heard my voice on the radio, my father told all his friends. He would tell people at gatherings that his daughter worked for the BBC, and they didn't believe him. It was scary for them. "Well, if you don't believe me you can listen to the BBC," he'd say. He would promote my program, but my mom said he shouldn't tell people about his daughter because she was afraid.

When I did radio shows at the BBC, and now working as a stringer at Radio Free Asia, I don't use my family name. Still, I think that the Burmese embassy in Bangkok knows that I'm a reporter for RFA. That's why government people sometimes go to my parents' house and ask about where I am and what I'm doing. I told my parents they can just say that I'm studying in Thailand, or they can say, "She does whatever her heart is set on doing." And if they start to pressure my parents, they can say that I am no longer their daughter. But so far, they just ask where I am.

It's okay for me to stay in Thailand because I have a student visa from the university where I am studying for a master's degree. When my visa expires, I will have to find another way to stay here. If you hold a Burmese passport in Thailand, it's really difficult to extend your visa or passport. The Burmese embassy has a list of people who work for media and other organizations, so if I went there and showed my passport, they would know my real name and they could take my passport and send me back.

There are a lot of people from the Burmese government in Bangkok, but we don't know who's who. In Mae Sot, it's not safe either. Now even the Thai army goes to the opposition organizations in Mae Sot and Chiang Mai and searches their offices. Sometimes they arrest people. They say they have a reason to search, that maybe the opposition groups hold weapons or

---

[15] Mae Sot is a town in western Thailand, on the border with Burma.

something. We don't know how the government of Thailand is connected to the Burmese government.

Even though I'm now working for exile media outside Burma, it's still very difficult. If I call someone on the phone and say I'm from RFA, sometimes they just stop the conversation. Everybody's afraid. But some people really do want to speak and talk about what's happening inside, so we do not use their real names. We cannot always get both sides, because the government usually refuses to give any information. I don't feel comfortable with this—I want both sides.

Sometimes I can't help having questions in my mind—is this really freedom of press? Are we doing real journalism or not? We have self-censorship—sometimes we hear information about something bad, like a corruption case in a migrant organization or an international organization working on Burma issues, but we don't report all of the information because we have to think about our people and our country's situation. There are a couple of million migrant workers from Burma who are living in Thailand, and most of them are here illegally. They have no documents for security, so sometimes it's better if we don't report certain things that will cause problems for the groups that help migrant workers and refugees.

IT IS NOT ENOUGH

Last year I received an award for my journalist friend, who was arrested and jailed in Burma. It's called the Kenji Nagai Award. Kenji Nagai is the Japanese journalist who was shot and killed in Burma.[16] There was an awards ceremony in Chiang Mai and I accepted the award on my friend's behalf because her family could not come to Thailand to accept the award for her.

---

[16] Kenji Nagai, a well-known Japanese photojournalist, was shot dead while covering pro-democracy protests in September of 2007. His death was initially explained as the result of stray bullets, but Japanese video footage later revealed he was shot at point-blank range by a Burmese soldier who subsequently confiscated his camera.

She was arrested by the government when she was trying to help Cyclone Nargis victims seek assistance. She was so young, and they sent her to jail for a year.

The situation for journalists is really bad in Burma right now. Last month, some young journalists were arrested. The government doesn't like journalists because they are always watching what the government is doing.

I WONDER HOW THEY WILL SURVIVE

When I lived in Burma, I thought the people were really powerless in our country. But now that I'm outside, I see that people from our country face different challenges in Thailand. Migrant and stateless people here have to survive by themselves—nobody takes care of them.[17] I wonder how they will survive.

I sometimes go to a school for migrant workers and children in Mae Sot—they have a big project for the people who live on the garbage dump. I spend time with the migrant children and play games with them. I tell them stories and I donate books and some money. Sometimes I go with my friends from university, and we bring food too. Some of the children are stateless, and they have no opportunity to study. They come with their family when they're three or four years old—they have no hope, no future. If their parents cannot take care of them, they'll become workers, to help their families survive. When I ask them what they want to be, sometimes they answer, "I want to be a Thai police officer." The Thai police are their role models, because they think the Thai police can control everyone. They also sometimes say they want to be a *hua na*—"boss" in Thai—for example at a construction site.

---

[17] In Thailand there are around 150,000 people who fled Burma living in refugee camps and about 1.5 to 2 million Burmese "migrant laborers" working in garment, tourist, sex, domestic labor, and other industries. In Thailand, migrant laborers enjoy few protections. A groundbreaking report by Human Rights Watch titled "From the Tiger to the Crocodile" documents abuses in the workplace and at the hands of the police.

I think what I do is not enough for them, but I don't know what else we should do. I think some organizations and some people do take responsibility for the migrant people, but more should be done for them.

EVERYTHING IS BROKEN

The question of what would happen if Auntie were not here any more is on my mind, because the army has tried to kill her many times. The army tried to kill her one time in 2003 in Depayin, in the middle of Burma. It was before her current house arrest started, and she was traveling all over the country. We heard that there was some conflict between the higher military intelligence and the army officers, and this is why they attacked her. They attacked her while she was traveling and they killed a lot of people. We call it the Depayin Massacre. [18] That is the last time they tried to kill her, but they have tried to kill her many times before.

In one famous speech, Auntie said that she would die for the country if it meant the country could have democracy. She said that if the country would change if she passed away, then she would be ready to die for it, like her father did. At the time that we heard that, we were really sad and very sorry because she has two sons. At her home, she had a big picture of her family in front of her desk, but she never talked about them. Daw Aung San Suu Kyi never gets to see her sons, and she cannot see her granddaughter or her grandson now. When her husband passed away, she could not leave Burma to attend his funeral and she could not see his body again. I am really grateful to Daw Aung San Suu Kyi's family; they may be very hungry to see their mother, but they have given her to us.

If Daw Aung San Suu Kyi passed away, I'm not sure if anything would change. Maybe some student activists like Min Ko Naing would

---

[18] The Depayin Massacre refers to a government-sponsored ambush of a large convoy of National League for Democracy members in May 2003, allegedly aimed at assassinating General Secretary Aung San Suu Kyi.

take responsibility for our country's situation and lead the country. But Min Ko Naing is now serving a sixty-five-year prison term.[19]

After the Depayin case, everybody was silent. In 2007, after they killed the monks in the September revolution, everyone was silent again. There was more fear. It was twenty years between the 1988 and 2007 uprisings. We don't know if a revolution will happen again or not. The people have had enough already, but they are in fear; there is a silence in the land. The people don't smile at all. I never criticize the people living inside Burma because I know their feelings and their pain. This is why Daw Aung San Suu Kyi wrote a book about attaining freedom from fear.[20]

Nowadays I try to think about what we have to do. I mean, we should not just depend on Daw Aung San Suu Kyi. We all put everything on her shoulders, and it's not fair for her; she's an old woman now. I believe in the National League for Democracy, and I believe in their ways, but we have to change something. Our young generation has to take over from the old generation. We have to work to change our country. The youth should prepare for our future.

Right now there are just old people and kids in Burma. In certain regions, there are no youth left. Like me, the youth have all gone to Malaysia, Thailand, and Singapore to try to survive. All people from Burma want to go back, but they have nothing left—no property, no business. We have to start from the very basics. We will need educated people, so we all have to prepare ourselves.

I think there will be a lot of work to do in our country, and that is why I am working on my education. We will need a generation of young, educated people to rebuild our country. There are no educated people left inside Burma. Right now everything is broken—the education system,

---

[19] Min Ko Naing is a well-known political dissident who entered Burma's political arena as a prominent leader of the student protests that took place in the late 1980s. He was formerly chairman of the All Burma Federation of Student Unions (ABFSU), and is currently being held in prison for his role in the 2007 Saffron Revolution.

[20] *Freedom from Fear* is a collection of essays written by Daw Aung San Suu Kyi and published in 1991, one year after her party's victory in the general election.

the health care system, everything. Even as a former NLD member and a former political prisoner, I am no longer involved in any of the political and campaigning activities. Aside from working with AAPP two times, I'm just studying and reporting.[21] I have to make something of myself with the time I have. I'm a journalist and I do the right thing for my people by reporting on Burmese issues.

When I reported on the radio about the government crackdown on the major demonstrations in 2007, I could not control myself. I was crying. My editor from Washington, D.C. said, "You are a journalist, you should not cry like that." I said, "This is my country's situation. I am Buddhist—they have even beaten our monks." I couldn't stand it any more, but I had to report what had happened in Burma.

In 2008, the government had a constitutional referendum, but I wasn't involved and I didn't vote. I don't believe in the 2010 elections— I won't vote in them. The 2010 elections will not be free because the regime is still arresting many people. They're just playing the game. If Burma does change one day, I will go back and report on it.

If I went back to Burma, the first thing I would do is go to the pagoda. I would go to the biggest one, the Shwedagon Pagoda. The Shwedagon Pagoda is the first place I went the morning after I was released from jail. I went there because I believe in my religion and I believe in Buddha. I really want to go back to Burma and pray to Buddha. I also hope my parents are still alive when I go back home. Maybe I will go home tomorrow, or maybe it will be another day. I hope to knock on the door of my home again one day.

---

[21] AAPP(B) is the Assistance Association for Political Prisoners (Burma), a nonprofit started by a group of Burmese political prisoners in March 2000. In 2009, Ma Su Mon participated in their signature-raising campaign called "Free Burma's Political Prisoners Now," which began on Burma's Human Rights Day in 2009 and attempted to collect 888,888 signatures calling on Secretary General Ban-Ki Moon to work toward the release of political prisoners in Burma. A delegation of Burma advocates delivered it to the UN envoy to Burma, Ibrahim Gambari, in June of 2009.

KNOO KNOW

33, human rights/LGBT activist

ETHNICITY: *Kachin*

BIRTHPLACE: *Kachin State, Burma*

INTERVIEWED IN: *Chiang Mai, Thailand*

The first time we met Knoo Know, he was walking around a room full of flip charts and other supplies left over from a long day of conducting human rights training sessions. Knoo Know has worked as a human rights trainer for the past six years. He co-founded a Lesbian Gay Bisexual Transgender (LGBT) rights training program, which uses LGBT rights as a lens and metaphor for larger democracy and peace issues in Burma. Born in the jungle in Kachin State, Burma, Knoo Know was the son of a famous general from the Kachin Independence Army, an ethnic opposition army. Knoo Know described his childhood as an internally displaced person (IDP) and the numerous times that his family and several hundred other Kachin people had to flee their homes because of Burma army (Tatmadaw) offensives into their territory. In 1986, Knoo Know's father sent him to town to begin formal schooling. For security reasons, he was told to change his identity and never speak of his family or his life in the jungle.

I was born in a village in the jungle called Balawng Kawng on September 4, 1977. The only thing my mother told me about my birth was that my father had to deliver me. Since he had previously worked in the KIA medical group, he knew how to do it.[1]

At the time, there was a war going on between the Kachin ethnic group's armed independence organization and the Burmese army, the SLORC.[2] My father was a soldier in the Kachin Independence Army. He was a guerilla and my mother was a schoolteacher. My parents met when she served as a teacher at the KIA 1st Battalion.

Altogether, there were six children in my family. I am the fourth son. I have one younger brother, one younger sister, two elder sisters, and one elder brother—but he already passed away. When I was very young, we stayed for a few years in the area where I was born. It's in Kachin State, close to the China–Burma border. I don't really remember what it looked like.

We were internally displaced people. We had to move from village to village because the SLORC soldiers pursued us and burned our villages down. They were doing this because these villages were supporting the KIA with food, and also because some villagers were related to KIA soldiers. At the time, we didn't call them SPDC; they were SLORC.

When I was four or five years old, the KIA assigned my father to a new post in western Kachin State, with the KIA 2nd Brigade. So we spent several months traveling westward through the jungle to the Hukawng Valley. My memories of that time are not very clear, but I do remember passing burning villages. There were maybe two or three hundred people in our group, but I'm not sure because I was really little.

The SLORC army was always following our people. Sometimes the

---

[1] Kachin Independence Army (KIA) is the armed wing of the ethnically based Kachin Independence Organization (KIO). The organization has been in armed rebellion against the Burmese state since the 1960s, signing a ceasefire agreement with the regime in 1994. For more on Burma's civil wars, see the "Armed Resistance and Counterinsurgency" as well as the "Ceasefire Agreements" sections of the appendix.

[2] Framed as a caretaker government, the State Law and Order Restoration Council (SLORC) has remained in power since the 1988 coup. In 1997, they changed their name to the State Peace and Development Council. See appendix pages 463-465 for further detail.

SLORC sent a plane to watch the jungle in the morning, so all of us had to stop cooking and put out all the fires. The KIA soldiers wouldn't even allow us to dry our clothes because then the SLORC might know where we were hiding. Most of the area where we lived was said to be under KIA control, but since we always had to run away it wasn't really under KIA control. I think it was under the control of both armies.

While we were traveling to the Hukawng Valley, we usually stayed in one place for four or five days, and then we would get news that it wasn't safe, that the SLORC was getting close. Then we would move to another place, and maybe we would stay there for two days, or maybe ten days. Then we would move again.

We usually heard that the SLORC was coming maybe three to five days in advance, but sometimes it was only four or five hours. When we heard they were coming, we didn't take very much from our house. We had a lot of bamboo in our environment, so we didn't need to carry the materials with us to rebuild our house. My family mainly took food, like grains, and if we could carry it, maybe we would kill a chicken that we had. We couldn't carry many clothes. It was just important that we brought a jacket, a shirt, and a small blanket.

And then we ran. While we were running, everyone was shouting and the older people were crying. I helped carry things, but I was very small. Most of the time I was just playing around and very happy because we were going to new places, and I was accustomed to moving around.

Most of the time, we had to keep walking for ten days or two weeks before we found the most secure place to build a new camp. It always depended on whether or not the SLORC was still following us. Sometimes we had to move at midnight because a KIA spy would inform us that the SLORC was getting very close.

If we arrived at the next camp early enough in the evening, we built our huts then. But if we arrived at night, we would just put up a plastic sheet as a cover and stay there. The next morning we would find bamboo and leaves to build our small huts. Everyone helped each other build.

We had to move locations all the time. Sometimes people talk about their hometown, right? They say, "Oh, I miss home." I don't have that kind of feeling. Which place is my hometown? I don't know. Since I was very young, my family was moving around, but at least we were together.

THE FIRST TIME I HEARD GUNSHOTS

After a few months, we arrived in the Hukawng Valley. We stayed in the jungle outside the township, near what the Kachin call the Danai River—on the Burmese map it's called the Chindwin River. My father was put in charge of the KIA army battalion based in Hukawng Valley.

Our group made another village in the jungle, and my family built another house. There were maybe around one hundred households in our village. Everyone lived in huts. I don't remember what the area was like, but my sister told me that there was forest all around when we arrived.

We lived there for almost two years, but we had to run away from our village twice during that time because the SLORC came.

The second time we ran is unforgettable for me. It was around 1985, and I was about eight years old. My father was on the front line fighting with the SLORC in the Pagan area, very far away, and my mom also had to go there. But they couldn't bring us children there because of the fighting. One of our relatives, who was about fourteen or fifteen years old, was taking care of me and my younger brother, who was three or four years old. She was still very young and she didn't know how to take care of us. She was really bad—she beat us every day!

At the time, I was playing with my friend at the river when we heard gunshots. A woman came over to us and said, "The SLORC is coming! You have to take everything. Run!" I was shocked and afraid, so I ran directly to my house because my younger brother was there. The whole village was running and everyone was in shock—we didn't hear that the SLORC was coming in advance. The KIA soldiers had heard the SLORC was coming from the east, so many of the KIA soldiers went east. But the SLORC soldiers were actually coming from the west.

We heard the dogs barking and more people shouting that soldiers were getting close to our village, so we had to do everything as usual—grab everything we could, pack our things, and run into the jungle. But that time we didn't have my mother there, and the girl who was taking care of us had disappeared. My aunt lived near our house, but she had to take care of her sons and her daughter. I was really afraid of the gun sounds. I didn't know what to take. I ran into the kitchen and I put rice and salt in a big bamboo basket—rice is important, and if you have salt, you can cook anything. I tried to catch a chicken but I couldn't. My little brother didn't know what to do. He was in shock, so he just stood there watching me. I took my brother and we ran.

We were both really afraid. Everybody else had their families, so it was really hard for us. I think that was the first time I'd heard gunshots. They were so close, and it felt like everyone was going to die. We ran to the riverside and people were lining up to get on the rafts. There were long lines, and we just followed the older people.

Everyone had to cross the river on a bamboo raft. Some KIA soldiers were near us, giving us reports on the SLORC. "They are getting very close," they would say. After we arrived on the other side of the river, we could still hear the gunshots—*dun dun dun dun dun*—but we were safe. From there, we walked for about three or four hours. I was carrying the big bamboo basket on my head, and it was very hard for me to walk.

When we arrived deeper into the jungle, I realized that I had put barely any food into the basket, only clothes. I took all the things out of my basket. The clothes were useless—torn shirts and cloth. We couldn't wear any of it. Maybe when I was gathering the things, I was in shock and I didn't pay attention to what I was taking.

That night, some older people let us stay in their hut because my brother and I could not build one ourselves. We both cried at night because we missed our mom.

After we'd been there for a day, my father came on his horse. He said he was worried about the two of us. He came to make sure we were fine, but he didn't say much. I was crying, "Ahhh, help me! I don't have anybody. There's nobody to take care of us. Please come stay with us." But he had to take care of all of his troops so he could only stay for a few minutes. He said the SLORC was getting very close so he had to fight them back with his troops.

Two or three weeks later, my father came back again and stayed for just a night or two. He saw that another KIA general was taking care of our group, so he felt okay about that. Then he left again, but I think he was also really sad to leave.

My brother and I couldn't do anything, so we were just crying alone. And then maybe two or three hours after he left, we got used to it because it's been like that since we were very little. My father was not very present in our family—it was like he was a guest. Sometimes my little brother didn't remember him, and he would say, "Oh, this man has come back again? Oh, this man is leaving again."

A BLACK POOL

After one month, the SLORC had left and we returned to our village. But it wasn't like, "Oh, the SLORC is gone now, so let's all go back together." We had a method where four or five expert KIA soldiers had to go to the village first for two or three days to assess the situation. Some of them checked for landmines, and then they marked the areas where it was safe to walk. After the experts checked the whole village, then maybe two or three families would go first. But it was still very dangerous. After the first group of people returned to the village, we always heard something like, "One woman went to the toilet and she stepped on a landmine and was killed."

The whole village had been burnt black; it was like a black pool. You could see dead cows and pigs—they'd even killed the fish in the Danai River. The river was famous for having many species of fish, and it was very easy for us to get fish to eat. Our house was right near the river, and when my mom was cooking dinner, I would go fishing while she was cooking the rice. I could easily get three or four fish; the whole village caught fish like that. But when we returned to the village that time, the first thing we heard was that the SLORC had exploded mines in the river to kill everything.

I never used to think about that time in my life very much, because it was really scary for me. I still don't want to think about it; it's really hard.

WE HAD TO ACT LIKE STRANGERS

My father was a very famous guerilla among the Kachin people. He served as head of KIA military intelligence from about the late '80s until the early '90s. Most Kachin people supported the KIA, although some people were afraid of them. They had very strict policies at the time; some people told me that if you did not support them, they said you were a traitor, that you were on the Burmese side. They did terrible things to you if you were suspected as a traitor.

Because my father was a famous guerilla in the KIA, my grandparents and all of my father's siblings were forced by the SLORC to leave Kachin State and live in Pyin Oo Lwin and Mogok, near Mandalay, where the government could monitor them more closely. When my parents returned after that month in the jungle, I only stayed in our village for about ten days, and then I left to live with my grandparents in Pyin Oo Lwin. My father wanted me to study there, because we didn't have a school in the jungle.

My older brother and my second-oldest sister had left our family first; the next person to go was my oldest sister. Then it was my turn. We had to leave separately like that because it was very dangerous for us that our father was a KIA commander. My mother cried again and again as each child left.

It was 1986 when I went to live in Pyin Oo Lwin; I was eight years old. When I traveled there, it was the first time I had ever seen a train or a car. Two of my sisters and my brother were already living at my grandparents' house, along with our auntie and uncle and many other relatives who had moved there. There were maybe fifteen cousins living there; it was like a dormitory. When I saw my siblings, I had to act like we were strangers. We all had to lie about our names and our pasts for security reasons. My uncle told me that I couldn't even tell my cousins where I was really from. My siblings and I pretended to introduce ourselves to each other, and then we ran to the back of the house and talked. After that we would sometimes secretly meet after midnight, when everyone else was sleeping.

At that time, our grandfather had to go to the police station frequently to explain about my father's actions. Whenever there were some activities in Kachin State relating to my father and his fighting against the SLORC, the SLORC made my grandfather go in and they questioned him about it. Sometimes they even put my grandfather in jail. My grandmother said they were trying to get my grandfather to tell my father to stop his behavior. They threatened that if my father did not stop his actions, there would be big problems for the entire family.

The SLORC secret police were always watching us. Sometimes other Kachin people came to our house pretending to visit, but they were really sent by the SLORC to spy on us.

We always had to remain in Pyin Oo Lwin because the SLORC didn't want my family to travel and try to contact my dad.

It was really difficult to go from living in the jungle to living in the town, and I cried every night in the beginning. I couldn't talk to anyone about my experiences living in the jungle, because my family always reminded me that I would have big problems if I did. I soon realized that nobody would change my situation, so I had to get used to it.

My aunt, my father's eldest sister, also lived with us in the house, and she was very strict. She would beat us terribly, maybe because she was really afraid of our family's situation with the SLORC. I hated her rules and we would fight with each other all of the time

Despite our hardship, most of my family, including my grandfather, supported my father. My grandfather would invite all of his grandchildren into his room and we would secretly talk about Kachin history and the Kachin struggle against the Burmese military. My grandfather told us about how there were groups of Kachin people fighting within the British army during the colonial period, and about how the British favored the Kachin over the Burmese. The KIA formed to fight for an independent Kachin State. The British used to encourage the Kachin people to fight for independence, but now that's changed.

My grandfather was always telling us these kinds of stories about my father and the Kachin struggle for independence. He'd say, "Knoo Know, your father is doing great things." But when I was little, I didn't want to listen to my grandfather's long speeches. I always got sleepy.

Our grandfather died in 1990, when I was about thirteen. It was very sad. He died because someone we didn't know beat him in the street. He didn't die there right away; he passed away four or five weeks later. There was a rumor that the beating was done by someone from the SLORC, but we don't know that for sure. We reported it to the police, but they didn't do anything. When my grandfather died, my father was away on the India–Burma border fighting the SLORC. It was his last battle.

After the KIO started ceasefire negotiations with the SLORC in 1991, we were allowed to leave Pyin Oo Lwin. For the first time in five years, we could talk openly to our brothers and sisters, and I went and saw my entire family in Kachin State. I was so happy to see my parents, but at first it was like they were strangers.

I only stayed one month with my parents, and then I had to go back to school. My siblings and I didn't want to go back because we were really afraid of our aunt there—sometimes she beat us badly. I went to visit my parents every year in the summer for two or three months, after exams finished in February or March.

I THINK HE HAD BEEN OUT OF HIS MIND

I started to fight with my father when I was about sixteen. I would always quarrel with him, complaining about how we had no money for university and how our family was always separated. My brothers and sisters were very quiet and polite, but I was not—I always spoke against him and questioned the things he did. I wanted to study again in the city. I told him it was his responsibility to give me money to study, but he could not.

While I was spending the summer with my parents in Kachin State in 1993, my father started taking me to the military camp with him because he wanted me to join the army. I was sixteen at the time. One day I realized he was planning to take me to the military recruitment center to force me to join the KIA, so I made a plan that night to run away. There was one truck that always carried food rations from the market at the China border, so I escaped by hiding under the sheet that covered the food.

When I got back home, I told my mom about my father's plan and she became really angry. The next day my father said, "I am so crazy, I almost did something really bad to my son." I think he had been out of his mind.

Ever since I was a child, I'd always been really afraid of war and violence. My brothers were always wearing soldier clothes, because they wanted to become soldiers and protect their people. Sometimes the soldiers would take out all the bullets and let the children play with their guns. One time, a soldier accidentally left a bullet in the gun and gave it to our neighbor to play with. The boy gave the gun to his mother and asked her to play with him, so she shot the gun and the boy was killed. I was really afraid of guns after that experience, and I never played with them. Most of the time, I played with girls; maybe that's why I wasn't close to my father.

RUNNING AWAY TO RANGOON

I ran away from home many times because of my sexuality. I was about seventeen years old the first time I ran away to Rangoon. I was so confused about my sexual orientation. I had no information, I didn't know what to do. I hated gay people, and I didn't want to become that kind of person. I really didn't want to become a homosexual, so I had internal conflict. I didn't dare speak to anybody about it. I didn't want to go out with boys, so sometimes I went out with women.

I realized my sexual orientation when I was maybe seven years old. I knew I was attracted to men, but I was conflicted inside. I used to play with girls and sometimes I would put on *tanaka*, but I didn't actually want to go out like that, like a woman.[3] When I was a teenager, it was very difficult for me because I would see a man dressed like a woman and I thought, *Should I wear that? Should I live like a woman?* So I tried it, but I wasn't comfortable like that—I didn't want to be like that.

My feelings were very confused at the time. I wanted to study music, but we don't have music colleges or music subjects in Burma. I also wanted to learn English and study in an international school, but my family had financial problems at the time. I went back and forth between Pyin Oo Lwin and Rangoon; I would run away, and then my sister would come to Rangoon after a month and bring me back to my aunt's house, but then I would run away again a couple of months later.

In Rangoon, I was hanging out and trying to become a professional singer. Since I was very young, I had sung in the church choir and received many prizes. While I was in Rangoon, I sometimes performed solos. Sometimes I would get a gig to sing with my friends, and sometimes I would sing at the karaoke bar. The shop owner would pay me a little money, and sometimes I'd get a few tips.

I sang a lot of English songs. When I was in Pyin Oo Lwin, I became familiar with a lot of English songs because my grandfather didn't like us to play Burmese music in the house. We'd get many pirated CDs and DVDs on the China–Burma border.

I liked to sing easy songs, like oldies, but my favorite music is R&B. I like the divas like Whitney Houston and Mary J. Blige. A lot of songs in English have something for me to think about. Sometimes I listen to them when I'm feeling down, and it gives me courage. Some of Christina Aguilera's songs give courage to LGBT people, so she's one of my favorites. Listening to English songs is also one of the ways that I learned English.

In Rangoon, I tried many times to make it as a professional signer, but I failed. I met with a music producer who promised to make a record

---

[3] *Tanaka* is powder that many women and children in Burma wear on their faces. It is said to be good for the skin and a natural sunscreen.

with me, but after one, two, three months passed, it didn't happen.

While I was in Rangoon, I had a lot of problems. I didn't have any relatives there so sometimes I would stay with someone who I thought was my friend and after a month I'd realize they were a night bird (a student who occasionally does sex work). So I'd move to another friend's place, and maybe they were using drugs. So I also used drugs sometimes. I didn't have anything to eat, I was eating only *mohinga*, a type of Burmese food.[4] I would just have one meal for the whole day. It was really bad.

CEASEFIRE

When the KIO and the SLORC were discussing the ceasefire in 1991, my father was not involved in the talks because he was a fighter and he didn't want the ceasefire. The KIA is the military arm of the KIO, which is the political organization. The new leader of the KIO didn't have as good a relationship with my father. I think he was afraid that my father would seize power because he was very strong inside the KIA.

In 1994, the KIO signed an official ceasefire agreement with the SLORC. After the KIO agreed to the ceasefire, the KIO authorities let my father take a rest because of his health conditions. My father had to go to the hospital because he had shrapnel from a mine stuck in his head from a battle. We asked the KIO many times to help pay for the surgery, but they didn't give us anything at the time.

My father became a drunk, staying at home and drinking twenty-four hours a day. Sometimes he was like a crazy person, maybe because he had trauma from being in battle. It was a bad situation.

When he got drunk he would always say to people, "Are you going to accept the ceasefire? What about my soldiers who died for Kachin State on the front lines? Are you going to pay for that? Your only goal

---

[4] *Mohinga* is a fish broth noodle soup that many consider the national dish of Burma. Though ingredients vary, it often contains rice noodles, fish paste, banana leaf stems, fried onions, and boiled eggs.

is to make this agreement—if we had known that, we wouldn't have fought, wouldn't have died." The former soldiers always thought they would get independence and now they couldn't; maybe that's why he got depressed. There are many soldiers like my father who didn't like the ceasefire.

That was a very difficult time for our family. My father was taking leave for his health, and we had no money. I was still in school, but I eventually had to go back to my home in Kachin State because we had no money to support ourselves.

WHAT MY FATHER ALWAYS TAUGHT ME

I was really confused and angry about my family's situation—my older brother had become addicted to heroin just after the ceasefire and died when he was just twenty-one. My sister couldn't finish college. In September 1997, I had a big yelling fight with my dad. I blamed him for many things, all because we had no money.

"You sacrifice your life for the Kachin people, for your revolution, but what do we have right now? You can't leave the house. We don't have money. Nobody is taking care of us. And now my brother has passed away. The whole family is messed up." He didn't respond to anything.

It was really bad; I shouldn't have said all those things. After our fight, I left for Rangoon again, and that was the last time I saw my father.

My father passed away in November of 1997. I was in Rangoon when I got a phone call from the pastor giving me the news. I really wanted to go home, but I didn't have any money; nobody helped me at first. Two days later, a relative gave me the money. But when I called my sister, she said it wasn't necessary to come back because he was already buried. The ceremony was already finished. My father was buried in Laiza, where he died with one of my brothers by his side.

Because my father was very famous in our area, many, many people went to his funeral. Our family didn't have any money for the funeral, so we borrowed it from other people. Afterwards, we were almost 300,000 kyats in debt and we had to sell my father's rings in order to pay people back.[5]

After my father passed, we were in a really difficult situation. Because my mother had never worked independently while my father was in the KIA, she didn't know how to run a business or how to take care of us. My elder sister hadn't finished college, and the rest of us were still studying, but my mom didn't work. I was sad and worried for the future. And then another feeling came—anger. I was really disappointed with the KIA.

Last year, when my mother got sick, the KIA supported her treatment. My mother has a lot of health problems because she gave birth to five children in the jungle.

After the ceasefire, my father always told me to never become a soldier, but that I should still work for our people.

THEY WERE BLIND

After high school, I went to college for almost three years. I haven't finished yet because I had some issues there. I wanted to study music or English, but there weren't many options. For most Kachin people, the only opportunity to study English or politics or something like that is the theological college. I also thought that I might be cured from being gay if I went to theological college and studied religion. So in the year 2000, I started at Kachin Theological College in Myitkyina.

I went to the theological college for general studies, but I left after two and a half years. The gay and gender equality issues in Christianity were a huge problem for me. Sometimes they didn't allow people to speak about women's issues on the campus, and women weren't allowed to speak about gender equality in church. Sometimes the people there weren't friendly, and they said that a man who acts like a woman could not become a priest or a pastor. Sometimes there would be hate messages in the professors' lectures, so I eventually decided to leave the school. I didn't have any problems with my friends, just the leaders.

---

[5] Approximately US$300.

When I was still in college, my friends from outside college and I started a group that met independently outside the college—we called it our "reading club." We wanted to do something to change the conventions; living there was not good. They were blind and we wanted to open their eyes. I attended my religious classes while going to these meetings secretly.

Our reading club would secretly get books from outside of Burma on subjects like democracy and the rule of law. One of us would secretly keep the book in our house and spend the day alone reading it. Then, that night, we'd pass it to the next person. There were six or seven people in our reading group. Sometimes we met at one of the members' houses, or sometimes we met in the church.

We had this kind of routine for two or three months and then we started to connect with people outside of Burma who were doing human rights and rule-of-law work, including giving trainings about the constitution. We started to meet these people in Laiza; Laiza is an area under KIA control, so we were able to do these things with protection from the KIA.

In 2002, our group met with someone from a human rights organization that is based in Thailand. They were going to do a human rights training program in the China–Burma border area, so we went to participate. That training was the first time we heard about human rights.

It was also the first time we learned that our country had a constitution, and that we have no rule of law in Burma. After that training, we realized many things that we weren't aware of before. I started to realize that even if I could not take action against the authorities, I could start teaching people about their human rights. I had been a Sunday school teacher since I was nineteen, so I knew how to teach people.

We met with the director of another human rights organization after that training, and our group decided to attend some more human rights trainings.

When I first missed school to go to the human rights trainings, my friends wrote a letter to the school administrators saying that I was sick.

NOWHERE TO BE HOME

But starting the second semester, it became a problem because I had missed so many classes. I didn't fail my exams, but two professors had problems with me. There was a policy in the school that none of the students were allowed to be involved in politics.

The academic dean called me into her office to discuss the situation. She didn't accuse me of anything, but she told me that if I continued going to school there, there would be a big black mark in my educational history—I would be recognized as a politically active student. Since it's a theological college, students are supposed to become pastors, not politicians. If you were a politically active student, the SPDC might start watching you.

Another reason I had to drop out of school was because I joined so many human rights trainings in Laiza, and some of the trainings were really long, like five or ten days.

MY LAST CHALLENGE TO GOD

When I was twenty-four, my mom and sisters asked me to marry a certain woman. At that time, I had an inner conflict with my religion and my sexuality. It was a big problem. If my religion had said it was okay, I would have accepted my sexual orientation.

While I was at the theological university, I prayed so many times for my sexual orientation to change. But after the third year, I dropped out. The people there didn't know I was gay, but they thought it, and they said things about how being gay was wrong. I was really depressed then; I tried to commit suicide once, but it didn't work.

One day I went to a prayer mountain in Laiza, and I prayed from morning to night.

"Give me an answer. If you are really God and really love me, please tell me why I've become like this. If Christianity doesn't like gay people, why am I gay?" I prayed like that and said I needed an answer by evening time. This was my last challenge to God. So I prayed, prayed, prayed, and in the evening, the answer was in my head.

154

Okay, I thought, *this is what I am. This is what God wants, for me to be gay.* I felt that if He didn't give me an answer, it meant it was okay to be gay. It was very clear to me suddenly, and I felt amazing. So that's when I decided to come out.

But I realized that before I came out, I had to apologize to my whole family first. I had treated them badly when I was running away from home and staying in other places, and I had dropped out of college. My whole family was really upset when I dropped out. They didn't know what was happening to me—they didn't want me to get hurt.

It's our family tradition that if we do something bad to someone in the family, we wash that person's feet. So I went to buy three towels—two for my sisters and one for my mother—and then I boiled some water. Then I called them into the house and brought them to sit on the bed, with their legs over the edge of the bed. They were all surprised. My mom said, "What's happening? What's wrong?" I just rubbed their feet, washed them, and talked. "I did a lot of bad things, so please forgive me." They asked me, "Why have you been acting like this? You're very strange nowadays. You're a good person, but why have you become like this?" So I told them then that I didn't want to marry that woman. They were just silent, shocked. "Why?" they asked.

"I don't like women."

Then my mom asked, "So what do you like?" And at that moment, my elder sister grabbed me and cried. She knew what I meant. I told them I would never marry a woman in my whole life, that I liked men. Everybody was crying, and they said, "Why didn't you tell us before? It's not a problem with us!" And my sister said, "You are my brother still. My brother." They were all saying it was fine, it was okay. My whole family was really supportive. It wasn't a problem, and they weren't angry. Before that, sometimes I didn't even want to look at my face in the mirror. But everyone loved me. After coming out, I felt like I had escaped from a really bad place. I began to see myself in a more positive way.

RIGHTS AND RESPONSIBILITY

After I left the theological university, I continued working with human right groups underground and attending trainings. Soon after that, in 2002, our youth group received an invitation from a human rights organization to attend an internship program in Mae Sot about democracy and constitutions. I signed up and went to Mae Sot in 2002 to take the human rights training course.

In the course, I had to learn so many things about what has happened in our country. I knew about the Kachin situation, right? But I did not know about the other states. The first time I heard about Karen refugees was when I arrived in Mae Sot, on the Thailand–Burma border. I didn't know that Karen people were also fighting against the SPDC. When I heard the stories of other ethnic groups' struggles, I thought, "Wow, it's the same as us." I had already been in that kind of situation, so it didn't seem very strange to me. But one thing that is different between the Kachin State and Karen State struggles is that the KIA took a ceasefire, but the KNLA has not.[6]

It has been eight years since I first went to Mae Sot, and I am still here in Thailand. Now I am working as a human rights trainer.

THEN IT COMES TO THE DETAILS

I enjoy being a human rights trainer, but I never thought about how difficult it would be to do the trainings. I train many different kinds of people. It's been mainly migrant women whom I train about women's rights. I've also done many trainings with members of different ethnic groups from Burma, and a lot with the refugee community. I have also done

---

[6] The Karen National Liberation Army is the armed wing of the Karen National Union. They fight for autonomy for the Karen people within a federated Burma. Starting in 1949, the war between the KNU and the Burmese army is the longest-running war of the post–World War II era. For more on the KNU, see the "A Brief History of Burma" section of the appendix pages, 460-461.

LGBT rights trainings with non-LGBT people. I discuss topics like basic human rights, gender concepts like, "what is gender," women's rights, and LGBT rights. The topics I discuss depend on the requests I receive.

Generally, when we discuss human rights, everybody accepts the basic concepts. Everybody likes them. But after two or three days, it comes to the details.

Many ethnic people want human rights for their people, not for others. If in the middle of a discussion I say, "Let's talk about our opinions about other people's rights," they will say, "No." They especially don't accept freedom of religion, the idea that you can choose your religion or have no religion at all. It always becomes a big quarrel, because they say that the concept of human rights comes from Western cultures, and that human rights will destroy their cultures. It's very challenging.

I had a big quarrel, a big debate once. We had a workshop where we had to draft a state constitution with several different ethnic groups. They proposed first that the head of state for Kachin State must be a Kachin person, he must speak Kachin, and he had to have stayed in Kachin State for twenty years, something like that. It was a mixed ethnic group, but I was the only one against it. Some of my Kachin friends even got angry, saying, "I will kill you when you arrive in Kachin State." I said, "Let's think about reality. In Kachin State, I will not vote for a Kachin leader who is not going to do good for the Kachin State, who is not educated—even if he is Kachin. But if there is a Shan or Burman who lives in Kachin State and wants to do good for Kachin State, I will accept him whatever his ethnicity is." But the others didn't like this.

This is one thing I started to realize when I attended that first training in Mae Sot. We were discussing human rights, democracy, the constitution—many issues during three months. There were many different ethnic groups there—we had Shan, Mon, Karen, Kachin, and Burman. But I realized that even though everyone was talking about human rights, each ethnic group was only interested in human rights for their own ethnicity. They just want to put their own nationality as the priority. When that happens we have to change our method, use another strategy, maybe another activity, so that they can see other people's rights are also important.

That's just one example. We had other kinds of discussions and debates like that in the training. That's why I was thinking, *We're talking about human rights, but we're not really looking inside these human rights.* I started studying human rights much more deeply because of this.

I also come from a very strong ethnic nationalist background, you know. When I was a child I didn't understand why the government army would follow us. The elder people told us that they would kill us, that they hated our ethnic group. So I really hated Burmese people when I was little. I didn't want to have Burman friends until I was maybe twenty years old. But my father would tell us not to hate Burmese people.

It's bad that many elder people keep telling their children about the old stories—I mean, it's good that they are keeping the history, but not when they are manipulating their children's minds to hate other ethnic groups. That kind of teaching is really the worst. I don't think it's only in the Kachin community, it's in the other ethnic groups too. Everybody knows that the SPDC does bad things, but they have to speak about the state system separately from race or ethnicity. They should speak about them separately, but they don't. They stereotype other ethnic groups. That's why I think education is very important in our area, in our community. Otherwise, people start to automatically believe that all Burman people will do something bad to them. It really becomes their belief.

My father always reminded us not to hate Burmese people. He proved himself by doing what he said. When he arrested Burmese soldiers, he didn't kill them. Sometimes, he brought them to our house, fed them, healed them, and released them again. I think that's why my whole family doesn't have a problem with the Burmese ethnicity; many Kachin people in our community didn't like us because of this.

When I talk about human rights, I always, always talk about responsibility too. Some other educators and facilitators will only talk about human rights, but it's very important to me that I always discuss rights and responsibility in my trainings. I tell them, "If you have this right, then that other person also has this right. So you have to take responsibility for that other person's rights as well."

Two years ago, I worked for the gender and women's rights program as the assistant coordinator, and then as the program coordinator the following year. As a man, it was a challenge with the Burmese community. The women's groups were always joking about a man doing women's rights work, and they would laugh in front of many people and say, "Oh my god, how are you going to do that? Is that going to work?"

One of the reasons I started working on women's rights and gender issues was because of my mother's experience. My mother's life was very hard. She sacrificed a lot for her family and she gained very little. When my father was away, my mother had to do everything. Everything. And she really wanted to stay with her children, but we had to live apart.

THE FIRST BARRIER

The first barrier I encountered whenever I was doing any activity was being gay. People would discriminate, and they didn't want me there. Even if I was talking about ethnic issues, the people in the group weren't comfortable.

One time, the facilitator raised the issue of gay people from Burma. Everyone said, "No, no, no—we will kill them. We don't accept gay people." So I just kept silent and didn't talk about that issue. I didn't say anything during that training. This was a group of people all doing human rights training, and they all said "No way" about accepting gay people.

That's why I started to do the Lesbian Gay Bisexual Transgender human rights program. It is a big challenge because many Kachin people are very conservative Christians. Kachin guys tell me, "You could be very useful working for all the Kachin people, but you are doing LGBT rights, such a useless issue. We're talking about and fighting for human rights while you're talking about this useless LGBT rights issue."

Many of my friends know about my father and they say, "Your father was very brave and he sacrificed for the people. Now you're doing this useless gay issue." I answer them by asking my own questions. "Do you know how hard it is being a gay man? Or dealing with the way men treat gay people?" They don't have any idea. I told them that I'm committed to working for all the people of Burma, not only for the LGBT people.

I usually discuss basic human rights concepts before LGBT rights in my trainings, because then they will learn about concepts of equality and that all human beings are born free. After two or three days talking about human rights, we begin to discuss gay rights; then they can understand that gay people are included in these concepts. But it's very challenging.

I don't know much, firsthand, about the experience of LGBT people in Burma, because I came out publicly after I arrived in Thailand. When I was inside Burma, I was homophobic, tense and suspicious—I didn't like gay people because I wasn't secure with myself.

The most visible gay group in the Burmese community is the transgender people. Most people in Burma believe that being gay means you are a crossdresser—a man who wants to become a woman, or a woman who wants to become a man. So they don't believe that I'm gay because I'm not wearing women's clothes.

It's very easy to find transgender people in the Burmese communities in Rangoon and Mandalay. Most of them are marginalized in the community, often poor and uneducated, but there are also some very famous and rich transgender people. I think most of the celebrity hairdressers and makeup artists are transgender, and some of them are very popular, rich, smart, and talented. But they're not interested in politics, in rights, in LGBT issues. Right now, I'm trying to get in touch with them.

General discrimination in Burma is the same toward all transgender people. Everyone will shout at a transgender person walking down that street—shaming them or calling them different names. This is normal. I wasn't thinking about my sexual orientation when I was about twenty-one, but by the time I was twenty-four I understood that I didn't want to be transgender. When I wore a skirt or a dress, it was very uncomfortable for me. Sometimes I put on lipstick, and it was okay at first, but I didn't like it after an hour or two. Many young gay men in Burma have the stereotype that if you love a man you must act like a woman—this is the wrong concept. That's why I have to do a lot of education in the community.

At one of my trainings, I met a transgender person who took hormone pills and now has big breasts. After I finished the training, he said, "I'm so disappointed with my body." I said, "What's wrong?" and he said, "I didn't know gay men could live like you—I thought that to love a man, I had to be a woman. That's why I tried to become like a woman, but now I don't want this body."

It's been getting better over the past ten years for the community of gay men in Burma. We have a lot of social networks, for example.

I've never heard about other programs like ours, but inside Burma they have sexual health and HIV/AIDS education for gay men. Just this year we set up one Burmese LGBT networking group for LGBT rights, and we have eight networkers inside Burma.

We have four or five people working in our LGBT program, and two of my assistants are also gay. Our friends support us—they distribute our publications to LGBT people inside Burma, and if I'm doing a training session in Burma, they will organize for the community to attend.

Maybe one day we can remove Section 377, the sodomy law that we inherited from British colonial times. It still exists in Burma, and it makes "unnatural sex" an offense; if you commit that crime, you can be sentenced to prison for ten years. The SPDC said they haven't practiced this law for a long time, but since the law still exists, they could use it if they wanted to. It's a problem because many police officers know the law still exists, so they can harass the transgender community a lot by arresting them or interrogating them at their houses.

Just last week, my best friend called me on the phone and said he understands my feelings now. He said he met with a young boy who was sixteen years old, and he asked if he knew Knoo Know. "Oh, the faggot from Burma," the boy said. Then my friend got really angry. Now he really understands why I am working on this issue.

BOTH GOOD AND BAD

One thing I want to say is that because I have experienced a lot of human rights abuses in my life, the experiences are like a fuel for my future work. I think my childhood had a big impact on what I chose to do. Sometimes I blame my father, but in the end, I see that it's the whole system, this government, that impacted my life. So basically, I think this is what I can do for that right now. That's why I chose to do this kind of work. I come from a situation of conflict and human rights abuses, so these themes are not new for me.

My organization is also trying to educate people about the meaning of elections in preparation for the 2010 elections inside Burma.

I don't accept the constitution and the election. I don't agree with them. But this is another window, a door. I hope the election will provide some opportunities. I think they are giving some space for political groups who want to do something, but the space is very tight.

It's very difficult to say what I think of the KIA–SPDC ceasefire; it's hard to express articulately. My opinion is that the ceasefire is both good and bad. It is good because we are not at war and civilians aren't being killed anymore. People can now travel safely. But on the other hand, the KIA didn't have a good strategy when they took the ceasefire, so some of the areas like those that my father controlled have now fallen into the hands of the SPDC. Corruption among the KIA officers is huge—it's not surprising, since they spent almost their entire lives in the jungle with no money and no good facilities, and then the SPDC gave them the chance to do different kinds of business after the ceasefire. Now they have a lot of nice cars and they stay in nice buildings. They are not thinking about the past and about how many soldiers have been sacrificed.

I will not stop, no matter what. I want to see all people equal in our community and also in our Burma in the future. That's what I live by.

SAW MOE

49, bookshop owner, former SPDC 2nd lieutenant,
and current KNLA trainer
ETHNICITY: *Karen*
BIRTHPLACE: *Rangoon, Burma*
INTERVIEWED IN: *Thailand*

Saw Moe met us for interviews in the evenings, after closing up his bookshop in Thailand. He methodically described his time in Burma's army, giving matter-of-fact descriptions of battle after battle, and eventually the event that forced him into exile. Saw Moe works part-time as a trainer for the Karen National Liberation Army, one of the armed opposition groups he spent much of his career fighting.

My parents are Karen, but I cannot speak the language because I grew up in a community of mostly Burman people in Rangoon, which is far away from Karen State. When I enrolled in school I had to say I was Burman—if I said I was Karen, people would discriminate against me. There were around sixty students in my class, and more than fifty of those students were Burman, so there were very few ethnic students. I couldn't use "Saw" at the beginning of my name because that is what Karen people use, so I used a Burman name instead. But the students knew I was Karen anyway, so I was called "rodent Karen" and "smelly Karen." That's what they called all the Karen students.

When I joined the military, I still could not say I was Karen because I felt like I would not be promoted if they knew I was Karen. The Burmese military is dominated by the Burman ethnic group, and other ethnicities usually cannot advance in the military.

I joined the military voluntarily when I was seventeen. I joined because I liked fighting. As a young man, I wanted to be in battle, going from place to place. I planned to be a brigadier general or a colonel. It was 1979 or '80 when I joined. My family didn't like that I was in the army because they were afraid I would die in battle.

When I joined the army, the training course was six months long. In our course, there were about two hundred and fifty trainees. We had to train to have strong bodies first, so we could defend ourselves. For example, we had to run many miles each day. We had to learn how to shoot guns—we had to learn the "one enemy one bullet" system. When we practiced shooting targets, we had to search on the ground for every bullet that had missed the target. If you were missing even one bullet, you were not allowed to have lunch. If we made mistakes, the trainers beat us. We had to learn to follow all commands in order to avoid the beatings.

As soldiers, we were automatically members of the Burma Socialist Programme Party—the party of the former military regime—so we had to learn about party policies.[1] During that time, the enemies we had to fight were the Karen National Liberation Army (KNLA), the Shan State Army (SSA), the Communist Party of Burma (CPB)'s army, and the

---

[1] The Burma Socialist Programme Party was the only legal political party in Burma during the years 1962–1988. In 1971, the BSPP changed from a small cadre to a mass party with around 1 million members. The party congress met periodically and repeatedly "elected" Ne Win as its chairman. For more on the Burma Socialist Programme Party, see appendix, pages 462-463.

Kachin Independence Army (KIA).[2] The CPB was our main enemy.

We had to learn about our enemies' backgrounds and histories, how they started, what their aims were, and what type of fighting force they were—their artillery, their mines, and defense strategies.

We were also trained in psychological warfare—propaganda. We had regular training until six o'clock, and then we had the psychological warfare training. There were two main things that they trained us to do: one was to believe in the propaganda, in the policies of the socialist party, and the other was to follow orders. You could not ask any questions, you could only listen. They trained us very well. The military trains soldiers how to do psychological warfare campaigns—how to persuade someone who dislikes you to like you, and how to make things unclear. For example, if we did bad things in a certain area, we would make the people believe that we didn't do those things—that was part of the army's strategy in areas where we were active. It was important for us to understand how to make other people or groups look bad too. We had a very rational way of lying to the people for our benefit. We would be very friendly with some people and show them a lot of things they could believe, while we had a hidden purpose.

We had to train and study very hard, but we had enough food and we were all learning together.

All the trainees had the same spirit and we were all very happy, because we had chosen to join the army. Now it's different—now the army has to force young people to join. Leading up to 1988, fewer and fewer soldiers were joining the army. Then after the '88 uprising, we started forcing young people to join the Burmese army because they didn't wish

---

[2] The Karen National Liberation Army (KNLA), the Shan State Army (SSA), the former Communist Party of Burma (CPB), and the Kachin Independence Army (KIA) are among Burma's most active and well-organized militias. They controlled considerable amounts of territory in the 1970s and 1980s. In the 1990s and 2000s, internal conflict and increased regime advances greatly diminished their capacities. See the appendix for further information about non-state armies and their protracted conflict with Burma's central government.

to join anymore—they hated the army.[3]

WE HAD NO FEAR

After training, I was sent to Moulmein, which is the capital of Mon State. At the time, there were a lot of battles happening. First we had to go from Moulmein to Mong Hpayak in Shan State.

Mong Hpayak is the region where the United Wa State Army—formed after the Communist Party of Burma collapsed—is now based.[4] It was a very long trip; it took us one week to get to Mong Hpayak. There were no villages nearby, only the forest and some army bases. I had wanted to go there, but then I became scared when we started fighting.

I was so afraid when I first heard the gunfire and the artillery. But after a month, I learned the sounds of the bullets so I could recognize whether or not they were dangerously close. I also realized that it's human nature—all human beings are scared to die, even our enemies.

Whenever we started to shoot, we would first find a place to hide ourselves and then we'd start shooting. Then, when we started fighting, our blood would get hot and we didn't care if we lived or died. After gaining experience with many battles, our minds became stronger—we had no fear.

When we were fighting the Communist Party of Burma, our strategy was to first fire artillery to clear them out of their fighting positions, and then we would play music. It was propaganda, to soften their hearts and change their minds. I don't remember the name of the singer, but it was a classic song by a very famous singer in Burma. While we played the

---

[3] In 1988, there was a nationwide popular uprising against Ne Win's one-party rule. For more on this student and worker uprising, see the 8-8-88 section of the "A Brief History of Burma" in the appendix, pages 463-465.

[4] The United Wa State Army formed after the collapse of the Communist Party of Burma in 1989. Along with many other ethnic armed opposition groups in the early 1990s, the United Wa State Army signed a ceasefire agreement with the military junta.

song, both sides would listen, but some of our troops would secretly be sneaking up on the CBP soldiers. It was part of our strategy, and we'd fight again after the music ended. We were very happy in these battles.

Our operations in Mong Hpayak lasted six months at a time. During the operations, we would have about eighty to a hundred soldiers, but sometimes only thirty soldiers would survive the operation. Many, many soldiers died because of landmines.[5] A lot of people on both sides died when we seized control of a Communist Party base, so we held a lot of funerals.

If someone is injured by a landmine on the battlefield, then we have to take a knife and cut his leg above or below the knee. Then we have to sew up the wound right there on the battlefield; otherwise, if the wound is left exposed, this person can die from infection. The powder in the landmines was poisonous, so it could kill a soldier easily. When I've had to cut a soldier's leg like this, I felt very uncomfortable. Whenever I saw a fellow soldier dying, I felt sad, of course, and I would wonder when it would be my time to go.

One time a bullet grazed my head during a battle. While I was fighting, I thought it was just sweat on my head—I didn't realize it was blood. But there was a lot of blood, and my friends noticed. After the battle, they sewed up the wound with thirteen stitches. If the bullet had hit one millimeter deeper, it would have entered my brain and killed me. I was lucky to survive.

I think dying is also about karma. For example, I would step on a mine and it didn't explode, but then it exploded when another person stepped on it. One time, we were shot at while we were eating, and a bullet hit my plate but it missed me. Karma is interesting; I had good luck.

---

[5] Both the Burmese military and many non-state armed groups have used landmines as part of their strategy in the long-running civil war. According to the Global Health Access Program, "Eastern Burma is the most heavily mined area in the world, with approximately 1500 landmine casualties annually, accounting for 5 percent of deaths."

After the fighting, we didn't feel afraid, only hungry. I would fight and then I would eat—just like that. We would bury the dead bodies and say that it was just their turn to die. I'd think about how my turn would come sometime too, but how I could not be sure of when. I was only eighteen at that time, and fighting was the only thing I knew.

After we completed a six-month operation, we would take a one-month rest, and then return to the battlefield. During the rests, I would get permission from the army to go to Rangoon and visit my family. I went back and forth like that for three years.

NO FEAR, NO WORRIES

After three years in Mong Hpayak, I was sent to another part of Shan State that is west of the Salween River. There, we were fighting the Shan United Revolutionary Army (SURA)—which no longer exists—and the Shan State Army (SSA).

The battles felt different there. There were villages in the area, so sometimes battles happened in the village. Both sides had army bases, and we had to use mobile tactics and ambushes—this included using machines to listen to the enemies' communication. Sometimes we found out that the enemies had gone to the village, so we would go there to fight them. By the time battles started, the villagers had already run away. If we thought that a particular village was supporting our enemy, we would fight them with mortars and artillery and then burn down the whole village.

During that time, I didn't believe the enemy was bad. They were doing their own thing, and we were doing ours. I just wanted to be a soldier; I wanted to be in the army and go to new places. So I felt very happy. The unhappiness would come later.

All the battles in this part of Shan State were very, very intense. Sometimes we lost, sometimes we won—it was always different. If many of our fellow soldiers died and we lost, then we felt very sad. If many enemy soldiers died and we won, we were happy. If we had to run away—for example, if the enemies had more soldiers than we did—then we felt very disappointed. But by that time I had no fear, no worries. Nothing. We spent three years in that area.

WE WERE TRAINED TO DISTRUST THE U.S.

In 1986, I went to Mogaung in Kachin State. We were fighting against the KIA—the Kachin Independence Army—which is part of the Kachin Independence Organization.[6] For these battles, we were also moving around. There were a few villages in that area, but it was mostly forest.

The people in Kachin State were satisfied with their lives, even though they weren't rich. They had enough food and they had their traditions. I cannot speak Kachin, but sometimes I could speak with people there who understood Burmese. They were afraid of us. We associated with them, but we weren't so friendly, because we were Buddhists and they were Christians. In the army, there were few Muslims or Christians, and we stayed in Buddhist villages.

It was difficult to associate with the people there, because we were suspicious that they had contact with Western countries. Colonel Seagrave from the U.S. Army had been a missionary in Kachin State, and he had trained the Kachin people.[7] In the army, we only trusted in socialism, which is why we were worried about the West. We were trained to automatically distrust the West, and we were worried about U.S. attacks on Burma. That's how the Burmese generals controlled their soldiers, by persuading us that we had to be prepared for a U.S. attack. They turned our feelings against Western countries. They used

---

[6] KIA (Kachin Independence Army) is the armed wing of the Kachin Independence Organization, which rose to power in the 1960s. The KIO signed a ceasefire agreement with the State Law and Order Restoration Council in 1994. For more on Burma's ongoing civil war, see the "A Brief History of Burma" section in the appendix.

[7] During World War II, the Allies armed and trained some ethnic militias to fight against the Japanese occupation. Colonel Seagrave was a famous doctor who worked in Kachin State during the war.

an enemy that was far away from Burma, because maybe if you can't see the enemy, you will be more afraid. America had been in Vietnam, and they had a joint training program—Cobra Gold—with Thailand, so we thought it was possible for the U.S. army to attack us.[8]

Like everyone else in Burma, we got our news from the military government's state-run media, so as soldiers we had very poor knowledge. We didn't get information from outside the country, which is still a problem. Only later, when I went to Thailand and learned about international law, I realized a U.S. attack wasn't really likely.

WE WOULDN'T BURN THE WHOLE VILLAGE

In 1986 I was made sergeant. I was head of a platoon, which usually had about twenty-five soldiers. I was still young, and at the time I just wanted to fight.

When we launched military offensives, we needed villagers to carry our ammunition—if only the soldiers carried it, we couldn't carry enough and we'd run out very quickly. We couldn't use helicopters like the U.S. army, so we had to use people. We would ask the village head for a certain number of men and a certain number of women. We had the men carry weapons and ammunition, and the women carried rice for us. When we asked the villagers to carry ammunition for us—to be porters[9]—they were supposed to get wages equivalent to 10 baht per day, but the high-level officials would keep their wages.[10] However, the porters did get to eat the same rations that we ate.

---

[8] Cobra Gold is a U.S.-Thai military exercise held annually in April and May. The United States funds Thai civilian and military professional development. In return, Thailand hosts U.S. Navy ships that often port in Phuket and Pattaya.

[9] Portering is a form of forced labor in which the military forces citizens to carry supplies, weapons, food rations and equipment for soldiers traveling from one area to another in Burma.

[10] Approximately US$0.30.

If the villagers ran away and the village head couldn't provide the number of people we asked for, we chased the villagers. The Burmese military didn't persuade the villagers to be on their side—they just made the villagers afraid.

The situation for porters has changed a lot over the past twenty years. Now, instead of going to the head of the village to recruit people for work, the Burmese army abducts villagers and forces them to be porters. In the past, there were many soldiers who joined the army voluntarily; they were educated and had good minds, so they didn't treat the villagers so rudely. But people hated the army after the '88 uprising, so we had to start forcing young people to join.

When I first joined the army, most of the soldiers joined voluntarily and supported it. We went to many places and learned many things in these new areas—everywhere in Burma is very beautiful, so we were very happy. When we visited places, I would learn some of the local language and try to tease the many beautiful ethnic girls there. But now, the soldiers in the army aren't educated and they don't have good minds—they don't know how to treat the villagers, and so the situation is worse.

When we were in Kachin State fighting the KIA, our superiors told us that the KIA were separatists—they wanted to separate from our union. We believed that if we eliminated the KIA, then Kachin State would be peaceful.

Most of the fighting happened in the jungle, but the KIA would go to the village when they needed rations. Twice we got news that they were going to the village, and we sent around fifty or sixty of our soldiers to fight them close to the village. But the KIA soldiers had to retreat because there were only a few of them, and they also didn't want the village to be destroyed. Both times, the villagers knew that the two groups were coming, so they had run away.

We had to walk all day when we were in Kachin State, searching for the KIA soldiers. We were climbing up and down mountains from 6 a.m. to 6 p.m., looking for them according to the intelligence we received from local villagers or from high-level army officials. The KIA soldiers would usually stay in the jungle, maybe near a natural pool of water somewhere deep in the valleys, so we tried to guess their locations. It wasn't easy to find them—I was only successful maybe one out of every ten tries.

Usually we slept under the trees, on top of plastic bags and with blankets to cover our bodies. We carried seven days of rations at a time—rice, yellow beans, and oil. We cooked in the forest. Sometimes we would cut down banana trees, take out the core, and then cook it with the beans to make a curry. The food was always very delicious to us because we were very hungry and tired. Sometimes we ate more than our rations because of our hunger, so our rations would run out after only five days. In order to survive for the next two days, we had to ask for rations from the villagers—we demanded the rations through the village heads. The villagers could not refuse us because we knew they gave rations to the KIA.

We didn't have much meat in the jungle; we usually only found vegetables. When we found animals, like snakes or geckos, we would kill them and eat them. There were tigers in the area, so sometimes we would chase after a baby, a female, or an older tiger. One time, we caught a small tiger and sent it to the Rangoon Zoo, but I'm not sure if it's still there.

THEY JUST BURN EVERYTHING

When we were near villages for military operations, we would sleep in there. If the villagers didn't like us, they would run away when we arrived—in this case, they would be shot dead, because the army officials would think they were insurgents.

Some officials would burn down a whole village if they saw the villagers run away, because they'd say it was a rebel village. But I tried to understand the villagers. If the villagers ran away, I would ask the head of the village why. I understood that the villagers were caught in between the Burmese military and the rebels, but it was our order to burn the village if the villagers ran away. We knew not to argue with an order or to ask for the official written order, because in the Burmese army you cannot go against any order you get from someone higher than you. However, officials are able to carry out orders in different ways.

In my platoon, for example, we would burn only three or four houses and then report that we had burned the whole village. But some groups from the military would burn whole villages, even the rice fields and the livestock—everything. Some officers aren't patient; they don't have good hearts. If they get the order to burn, they just burn everything.

Some of my fellow soldiers weren't very educated, so they were very brutal. They would drink too much alcohol, so we had to control them and tell them not to do that. Some of them also really liked to chase girls, so we had to tell them not to do that either.

THEY DIDN'T TELL US THE
PEOPLE WANTED DEMOCRACY

In '87, I came back to my battalion in Moulmein in Mon State, and then I was sent to southern Shan State again. We had to fight against many groups: the Shan State Army (SSA), the Shan United Revolutionary Army (SURA), the Pa'O National Organization (PNO) army, and then the Mong Tai Army (MTA).

On August 16, 1988, we had to return to our base in Moulmein, because there were major demonstrations throughout Burma, and rumors of a coup. We drove for three days straight—day and night on the truck—to return to Moulmein. Throughout August and in September, the demonstrations got very big. They spread to many cities and towns. There were different types of people demonstrating, including rich people, poor people, monks, and students. We were told by our superiors that the people were rising up against the system because they didn't like the Burmese Way to Socialism.[11] They told us that the people were

---

[11] The Burmese Way to Socialism was Ne Win's plan to build the Burmese nation post-independence. For more on the Burmese Way to Socialism, see pages 461-462 of the "A Brief History of Burma" in the appendix.

rioting and we had to control them—they didn't tell us that the people were actually asking for democracy.

We only had one battalion in Moulmein, and we were responsible for controlling the demonstrations, but we didn't get any specific orders about what to do to the demonstrators.[12]

There were five groups of soldiers in our battalion, and our officers sent us to the areas where we had relatives or where we knew people. If we were friendly with the locals, we could talk to them and ask them to be calm. When the people didn't listen to us, we demonstrated how powerful our weapons were—we didn't shoot, but we showed them how big they were and told them how many people would be killed if we fired them.

We told the demonstrators that if they wanted democracy, they couldn't cause riots. They had to negotiate with the new government, which would come, because at that point the military coup had taken place.[13] We told them that the soldiers couldn't give them democracy. We said it was their choice, but that if we had to use our weapons to control them, they would die—we had to follow our orders. Then the people listened to us. Since I was in Moulmein, I didn't know what was going on in Rangoon.[14] But in Moulmein, only two or three people died during the demonstrations.

At the time, the soldiers didn't actually know why the military had executed the coup. We were very young, and we just knew what the military leaders told us—that the military had to be responsible for the country, to lead the country. They told us the demonstrations were not

---

[12] A battalion is a unit of soldiers. In Burma's armed forces, the Tatmadaw, there are approximately 200 to 500 soldiers in a battalion.

[13] On September 18, 1988, a small groups of generals overthrew the Burma Socialist Programme Party and sent the army to crack down on the demonstrators.

[14] It is typically estimated that 3,000 people were killed during the crackdown. However, some estimates run as high as 10,000. For more on the uprising and crackdown, see the "A Brief History of Burma" in the appendix.

good. We didn't want an unstable situation, and we had to listen to our orders. Our leaders told us that the military would hold elections, and would no longer be in control after the elections. We didn't actually think about anything critically—we just knew that we had to follow orders. It was not really socialism; it was more like a dictatorship using the cover of a socialist system.

I NEVER THOUGHT ABOUT THE FACT THAT I WAS KAREN

On January 10, 1989, after the demonstrations had died down and the coup had taken place, our battalion was sent to Karen State. We started an operation against the insurgent groups there—the KNLA, the New Mon State Party, the Karenni Army, the SSA, and the SURA. We realized they were very active in illegal trading along the border, so we wanted to eliminate their sources of income. After every six months of doing an operation, we got one month to rest, and then we were sent to a different area.

Then we were sent to attack the KNLA base at Maw Poe Kay. We called the KNLA soldiers "insurgents" because we wanted to make them look worse, like they were even lower than rebels. We considered thieves to be the lowest level, then robbers, then insurgents, then rebels, and then revolutionaries.

Our brigade had five battalions. We attacked the Maw Poe Kay KNLA army base on March 25 at 5 p.m. We didn't finish fighting until the 27th, at 5 p.m. So many soldiers died on both sides. We were shelling them and there was also fighting on the ground. Some of the Karen soldiers were in trenches, and the vibrations of the shelling exploded their eardrums. I saw so many casualties, and I kept wondering when I would get shot, when I would get injured or killed. But I just continued fighting.

The Karen used a lot of landmines, and they shot with a type of bullet that can tear your body apart. There were a lot of casualties, a lot of soldiers who lost their legs. Also, there was no cover at the KNLA base because they had cleared out the trees. The Karen had very good defense.

We had about 3,000 soldiers and they probably had around 500. I think we lost about 450 soldiers, but we didn't have time to bury them.

Some of our soldiers were so hungry that they were crying. We joked that we didn't want to be Burmese soldiers in our next lives, because we were so tired and hungry, and we had to fight so heavily. Our joke was that we prayed to become U.S. soldiers—they can use helicopters for fighting, and after they fight, they can eat really good food. Soldiers in poor countries like Burma have to carry all their artillery and food rations, but soldiers in developed countries can use vehicles or helicopters. We had seen a movie with U.S. soldiers, and we saw that they were given food after fighting. We had to cook our own food, and sometimes we couldn't cook anything because the enemy would see our smoke.

After the battle, we took ten days rest, and then we continued to fight. Our next battle was at the Mae La KNLA army base. At the time, the Karen villagers had already fled to the Thai side of the border, so there were no villagers there. The villages were already destroyed, so I didn't see any houses when we arrived, only rotting posts. The civil war had been going on for about forty years already, so all the villages in that area had relocated.

At the Mae La KNLA base, we were fighting the KNLA, the ABSDF, and the "Three P's"—the People's Patriotic Party—at the same time.[15] The PPP was in Karen State because U Nu had fled to that area. There were so many groups working together, because our military was very big. They needed help from each other.

The battle took twenty days, and then we took over the Mae La army base.

While we were fighting against the Karen, I never thought about the fact that I was Karen too. I didn't think about anything—I just wanted

---

[15] The All Burma Student Democratic Front (ABSDF) was a guerilla army formed by students who fled the 1988 military crackdown and fought alongside many of the ethnic groups against the dictatorship military junta. The People's Patriotic Party (PPP), originally the PDP, was a political party/armed group founded by former President U Nu, which fought alongside the ethnic militias against the Ne Win–led government.

to be a soldier. We were taught that the KNLA were rebels, and we were the good people, so we had to fight against them.

WE HAD TO KNOW OUR ENEMIES

Saw Moe attended Officer Training School (OTS), where he studied military strategy, including psychological warfare, counterinsurgency tactics, and the strategies and weaponry of foreign nations, including the U.S., Germany, and England. He graduated in June 1993 and became a second lieutenant, sharing responsibility for a company with two other officers. In September 1993, Saw Moe's platoon fought the KNLA for three intense months before taking over the Kway Ee Toung KNLA base. In 1994, he was responsible for overseeing soldiers involved in construction projects in Pyay, Taunggyi, and Irrawaddy Division.

In 1995, we were asked to go to Pathein, in the Irrawaddy Division, to practice fighting alongside the air force and the navy. The army, the navy, and the air force were all training together and showing each other their tactics. We wanted the enemy to think we were all just practicing, so then we could surprise them by all going to fight. After training, three divisions went to Karen State to take over Manerplaw.[16] This was known as a "liberated area" because many opposition groups had their headquarters there, like the KNLA and the ABSDF.[17]

At the time, the Democratic Karen Buddhist Army (DKBA) had recently split from the KNLA, so we were cooperating with them.[18] The

---

[16] Manerplaw is the former headquarters of the Karen National Liberation Army (KNLA) and the All Burma Students Democratic Front (ABSDF). For more on Burma's civil war, see pages 460-461 of the appendix.

[17] Burmese dissidents use the term "liberated area" to describe those places along the borders where the opposition groups continue their activities.

[18] The DKBA broke with the Karen National Union and signed a ceasefire agreement with the government in 1994. The leaders of the group complained that as Buddhists they did not have enough of a voice in the Christian-dominated Karen National Union. For more on Burma's civil war, see appendix pages 460-461.

DKBA knew the geography of the area, so they showed us how to get to Manerplaw while avoiding landmines. The DKBA also showed us how to enter Manerplaw through a back route, so that if the KNLA soldiers ran away they would run into Burmese soldiers again. The KNLA retreated when they realized we were blocking both ways, so it was easy for the Burmese army to take over Manerplaw. Because of the DKBA's assistance, the fighting was easier for us and there were fewer casualties.

After Manerplaw, the opposition groups no longer have big liberated areas.

I BELIEVED EVERYTHING I TAUGHT

After Manerplaw, my battalion moved to eastern Shan State, to a place called Mai Ton. We spent six months there training new soldiers, including child soldiers.[19] I didn't have any feeling about the child soldiers; I just saw that they were recruited. Many of the young soldiers were very homesick and they always asked to go back home. But the older soldiers like me never felt homesick, because we'd been in the army for a long time already.

In January 1997, I went to Mai Sat, where I had even more responsibility because I had become a captain at that point. I was in a very difficult position, because the upper-level officials would give me orders—to burn certain villages, for example—which I had passed on to other officials. Sometimes the officials who had good hearts would tell me they couldn't do it; they were friendly with me, so they would tell me if they didn't want to carry out the orders. But then the upper-level officers told me I had to follow orders and that complaints were not allowed, so I was stuck in the middle. I realized I could not have compassion in this position—

---

[19] Burma is frequently cited as being one of the countries with the most child soldiers in the world. The Optional Protocol to the Convention on the Rights of the Child sets eighteen as the minimum age for direct participation in hostilities, for recruitment into armed groups, and for compulsory recruitment by governments.

I had to just give orders and the other officers had to follow those orders.

If something went wrong, I was also in a difficult position. For example, if I was told to give the order to burn a village and there was some kind of problem afterward, we would say, "You ordered us to burn that village." But the officials would say, "Where is the official order?" The orders were not written down, so there was never any official proof that the directive came from above.

They also trained the upper-level officials to understand how soldiers behave, to control them and make them accept certain things. The Burmese army has a strict system of control—they use it to maintain their one-order system, to change people's minds and make people follow their orders. It's how they mold the soldiers so that they don't think critically about anything—they just follow orders. Usually their strategy is very successful in getting people to do what they want them to do.

The system in the Burmese army is to just follow orders—we didn't think or feel, we just followed orders. We had been soldiers since we were young, so it became normal for us to see death and injuries. I experienced a lot of difficult things while in the army, so now that I am in Thailand, I have heartache.

HUMAN BEINGS MAKE MISTAKES

Once, I was patrolling a rebel area with my soldiers. I was sleeping on the ground in the valley, and my soldiers were staying in the mountains. I woke up in the middle of the night because I heard a noise, but I thought it was a car wheel bursting or something like that. We had never had a battle there, so we weren't expecting any rebels to come. But when I woke up in the morning, the villagers came to inform me that some of my soldiers had died—they had been ambushed. Several soldiers died, and a few were injured. We tried to search for the rebels, but we couldn't find them. They could have been hiding in the village in plainclothes.

I think it was my fault. I'd deployed the soldiers too far from each other. The area was normally quiet and peaceful with no rebels, so I'd gotten careless.

During my twenty-five years in the army, I'd never had any problems with the higher-ups; that incident was the first time. But I knew many officers who had gone to prison because of similar incidents; sometimes officers went to prison if they lost a battle. If a case is brought to the military courtroom, it's certain that the person will go to prison. All of the judges are military officers.

The military officials launched an investigation into the incident, and then my friend, another officer, called me and said the division commander had signed a sentence saying I had to go to prison for more than five years. When I heard the verdict, I felt really upset. At that time, other people didn't know yet. My friend told me, "Well, you can flee or you can go to prison." I told him I wouldn't go to prison—I would run away.

I think normal human beings make mistakes, and it's normal that you win some battles and you lose some. You can't say what will happen. But even though I had been in the military for a long time, they couldn't forgive my mistake.

I got on a motorbike and decided to escape to Thailand.

I THOUGHT I COULD CONTRIBUTE SOMETHING FOR MY PEOPLE

I didn't have any plans when I arrived in Thailand, so I stayed with a friend and worked in a shop. When I got to Thailand, I had the chance to read books about human rights and democracy, and I started to see that the Burmese military does many bad things. I realized that things needed to change in Burma; people must be allowed to complain. The more I read these books and spoke to people here about democracy, the more I could analyze the situation.

Since I am Karen, another Karen person here contacted the KNU/ KNLA, and they asked me to teach and write the curriculum at their training school. It may seem strange that I'm working for the KNLA after twenty-five years in the Burmese military, but I don't think about the past—that's just my nature. I didn't think about any of that, I just made the decision to help people. I thought that by working with the KNU, I could contribute something for my people.

When I train the KNLA soldiers, I talk about the different battles I was involved in. I analyze the battles for my students so they can understand why the KNLA lost, and learn how to win in the future.

When I was young, I couldn't say I was Karen at school or in the military because I would be discriminated against. But here in Thailand, you can say who you are. It's open. It wasn't that I didn't have a Karen spirit in Burma, but I couldn't express my feelings until I got here. I have a strong Karen spirit, but I don't discriminate, so I will help other ethnic groups if they ask—I feel like we should help each other. I think a federal union would be best for Burma, because then the ethnic groups would have their own states, their own autonomy. But if the ethnic groups separated from the union, it wouldn't be good for Burma. It'd be like if New Mexico and Hawaii separated from the United States and started their own governments.

I don't think it's fair for people to hate all SPDC soldiers. Even if we hate a group of people, we have to learn about them and try to understand them, so we can negotiate with them. It's normal for an ethnic group or any group of people to make mistakes. If you want to be educated, you should learn about other people; you should learn about your enemies and make peace with them. I don't want people to be racist. Teachers play a very important role, because they can show students different ways to see things. They can show them the right attitude.

I believe that most of Burma's ethnic armed groups are racist—they only want to fight for their own group. The Karen only want to fight for the Karen, the Mons fight only for the Mons. But now the ethnic groups want to cooperate more, which the Burmese military doesn't like. A lot of groups here say bad things about the SPDC, but they will never find solutions until they understand what the SPDC is doing and how they think. The ethnic groups have to be very united. Right now, even the different Karen groups are not united.

I am staying with a friend now. Even though I'm not very worried about my security here, I still have to be very careful when I travel here in Thailand. I don't have official documents to be here, so I could be deported and then arrested when I'm brought back to Burma.

For the first six months that I was in Thailand, I was worried that the Burmese army would find me and abduct me. The Burmese army will only come for people here if they think that person's important—for example, Pa Doh Mahn Shar was shot dead on the border.[20] So if they think I'm important, I will have to die. But if I'm not important to them, they won't think about me.

I recently met another Burmese soldier here in Thailand who had also fled the army, and I had to tell him not to be afraid of me. Because of how the army system is in Burma, even soldiers who have both fled the army and live in another country still fear each other.

IF AMNESTY IS OFFERED

From the outside, people are very surprised with the big changes I've made in how I live my life. They ask how I could do all those things with the SPDC in Burma and then come here and work for a group opposing the SPDC.

I'm surprised by the changes too, but I don't think about it, so I don't care so much. I talk to someone, and then it's finished, I don't think about it anymore. If I see them again, we start new. It's just my nature.

---

[20] Pa Doh Mahn Shar, then General Secretary of the Karen National Union (KNU), was shot in his home in Mae Sot, Thailand in February 2008. Many speculate that his assassination was the result of his refusal to comply with the Burmese government in the run-up to a constitutional referendum.

I feel much better here in Thailand, because I don't have orders from above and I don't have to order anyone else around. Before, I was a soldier, and now here in Thailand, I've opened a bookstore because I like reading a lot. Now I have many books in the shop so I can work there and read. I'm trying to learn new things, so I read a lot. I only have my own schedule that I make; I feel free. Most of the books I sell are in Burmese, so it's Burmese people who come and buy.

About three-quarters of my customers are girls. I don't think boys read many books.

In an hour, I will go buy books and bring them to my shop. I sell so many types of books: philosophy, English-learning, dictionaries, journals, and other kinds. I want to have a bigger bookshop, so I can put more kinds of books in it and people can go there to read and drink coffee. It would be okay if they didn't buy a book—they could come and read, and maybe another day they would come and buy.

I'm happy to live here in Thailand. I don't miss Burma very much, because I am settled here and I want to stay. If change happens in Burma, I would go back, at least to visit. But I am worried that even if change happens, and even if amnesty is offered, as a former SPDC soldier I may not be okay.

If democracy comes to Burma, I don't think the soldiers in general should be held accountable for human rights abuses. Some specific officers should be accountable if, for example, they carried out an order too strongly and attacked people. I think the person who is the most accountable is the Commander-in-Chief of the Burmese Army, Than Shwe, because it is a one-order system—all orders come through the ranks from him.

Maybe when I get very old, I may go back. When I die, I want to be in Burma.

KHINE SU

38, migrant worker

ETHNICITY: *Burman*

BIRTHPLACE: *Eastern Pegu Division, Burma*

INTERVIEWED IN: *Mae Sot, Thailand*

We met Khine Su in her home on the busy dump site where she lives and works with her husband, collecting plastic to be recycled. We were introduced by a group of exiled activist monks who run community projects for the dump's residents. Only three miles from Thailand's border with Burma, the dump is home to eighty families from Burma who find it a place of both opportunity and daily challenge. Khine Su told us about her life in Burma, where her village was caught in the middle of fighting between the state army and Karen National Liberation Army.

The rice fields in my village are beautiful. If you saw them, I don't think you would want to go back to your country again. I miss working in the rice fields as a child. I miss home, especially when the rainy season starts, because my friends and I would work and share stories and sing all day together in the rain. I miss our singing together the most.

I had a happy life until I was ten years old. But after I turned ten, I didn't have a peaceful life anymore. The problem started when the rebels came to the village and started asking for rations, food taxes. They asked for whatever they wanted. The rebels are the KNU.[1] They are fighting against the Burmese regime because they dislike the SPDC and they don't want to see the Burmese in their area.

The rebels ask for food, and the government also demands the same thing. We can't deny either side what they ask. If you don't give them what they want, you will be asked to work for them. Most of the time, they forced those who couldn't give taxes to porter. Both sides did this. This was the villagers' fine if they couldn't pay taxes to the government.

We gave the rebels the taxes, but when the regime's soldiers found out, they made trouble for the villagers. The government soldiers also started coming and asking for rations, food, taxes, and money. Then the rebels found out that we were giving rations and taxes to the government and they started making more trouble. This is how the problem started.

Because we lived in a black zone—Eastern Pegu Division—we faced problems from both sides, from the government and from the rebels.[2] The black zone is a terrible area to live in because the rebels are active there. The regime calls these areas black zones because they are where some villagers have supported or joined the rebels. A white zone is an area without fighting.

The government soldiers would not ask for the same amount of money every time. Sometimes, if they needed a lot, we had to give them

---

[1] The KNU is the Karen National Union. It is a political organization with an armed wing—the Karen National Liberation Army (KNLA). The KNU fights for the autonomy of the Karen people and is dominated by Karen Christians. It has been in armed rebellion against the central government since 1949. For more on the KNU see the "A Brief History of Burma" in the appendix, pages 460-461.

[2] Black zones are free-fire zones set up by the junta to rout out insurgents. They are part of the junta's four-cuts policy, which divides the country into black, brown, and white zones. The brown zones are controlled partly by the government and partly by insurgents. White zones are fully government controlled. For more information, see the "Armed Resistance and Counterinsurgency" section in the "A Brief History of Burma" provided in the appendix.

a lot. If they needed a little, then we only had to give them a little. If you didn't have money to give to the government soldiers, then they would tell you to go with them and work. The higher authorities from the city gave orders to build roads with forced labor, then the local officials would tell us what to do.[3]

There were about a hundred people doing forced labor at the same time. The people were not only from my village but from other villages as well. We had to come together and work. In one day, six or seven people were responsible for digging one hole or trench. Then we had to carry the dirt and small stones from one place to another. They used the dirt and stones that we dug up to make roads.

We had to do different kinds of jobs for the Burma army. For example, sometimes we had to dig bamboo out of the ground so that we could make fields and do farming for the army. We also had to help build the army camp. We worked from around eight o'clock in the morning to about twelve, and then we could take a one-hour rest. At 1 p.m., we had to start working again. The army never gave us payment.

When they called us for forced labor, we had to stay for two, three, four days—whatever they decided. We had to bring our own food and sleep at the work site. It was a little bit far from our home, similar to the distance between the Mae Sot rubbish dump and Myawaddy.[4] Usually we had to work once every two months, but during the summer we had to work one to three weeks every month. We had to work more in the summer because this is when they built and repaired the roads.

When I did forced labor, I was very angry because I was so tired. If we could not carry heavy loads for the government army, they were really rude to us. It was difficult to earn an income when we had to go do forced

---

[3] Human Rights Watch and the International Labor Organization have documented the widespread use of portering and forced labor by the Burma army.

[4] Mywaddy and Mae Sot are two towns lying on opposite sides of the Moei River, which forms the border between Burma and Thailand. The Mae Sot rubbish dump is approximately 5 km from Thailand's border with Burma.

labor, but we couldn't do anything about this situation. Anytime they wanted, we had to go and work for them.

OUR VILLAGE WAS A PEACEFUL PLACE

When I was young, my family was poor, but we had a good house. Our house had three rooms: one was for cooking, one was for sleeping, and one was like a living room. All together there are five children in our family. I am the oldest. My brothers, sister, and parents are still in Burma.

Growing up, I was very close to my mother and father. My parents are Buddhists and were very, very religious. They would go the monastery to say their prayers and to pay their respects to the monks. My parents would go around the village and collect money for the monastery, and then they donated their labor to help build the pagoda. There were also some churches in our village because there were Christian Karen people living there.

The day of the full moon was very important, and everyone would come together. On the day of the full moon, people go to the monastery for ritual worship. I loved celebrating the full moon very much. People made a variety of snacks and exchanged the snacks with each other. People from the towns had machines to make dried cakes, and it was easy for them. In our village, we would use rice and sticky rice to make traditional homemade cakes by hand, which was a bit tiring, but I liked it a lot. I might say the quality of the snacks made in the village is better because they're fresh. We would send the cakes to the monastery, and then the villagers would sit together and eat the remaining cakes. It was a very happy occasion.

We had a government school when I was young, but the school only went up to grade one. Children whose parents could afford an education had the chance to go to school in another town, but those who couldn't dropped out from school after grade one and studied in the monastery. Because we were poor, our parents could not send us to school, so I studied at the monastery every other day.

The abbot always requested that my parents allow me to study in the monastery, which is why I had the chance to learn there. I was very happy there. I studied with four friends, and the abbot taught us things like the five precepts in Buddhism.[5] I especially loved seeing the animals—the abbot fed monkeys and deer. The monkeys could understand human language and were trained to do chores at the monastery, like washing the clothes. Whenever I saw them I was very happy.

On the days that we did not go to the monastery, we had to go to the rice fields to work with our parents. To cultivate rice paddies, you must first cultivate the young seeds. Once the young seeds are ready, you replant them in another field. The work is not difficult. We would get up at 6 a.m. and cook food, and then we would go to the field and work there until 5 or 6 p.m., and then we'd go back home. There was a break once a day for half an hour. The one thing that was very painful is that we had to bend over the whole day and we would get pains in our backs and sides.

While working in the fields, some people sing and some people talk. There were some famous songs that we sang. At the time, the singer May Sweet was famous. At special ceremonies, like novice monk ordinations and weddings, we would listen to her songs as they played on the loudspeakers and we would memorize them. This was our only chance to listen to the songs because we didn't have any cassette players. We'd remember the songs by heart and then we'd repeat them in the field. Every day we sang songs. Someone was always singing very loudly and beautifully.

Our village was a peaceful place. We worked in the fields and we lived a simple life. But when we became older, because of the conflict that happened there, our village became an unhappy place.

---

[5] The five Buddhist precepts direct that laypeople should abstain from killing, stealing, sexual misconduct, lying, and intoxication.

LIFE WAS NO LONGER NORMAL

The parents in the village knew very well how to deal with both sides, with the rebels and the government soldiers. It was important to give both sides what they wanted. Sometimes the rebels and the government soldiers would enter the village and start to fight. They shot at each other, and some villagers were wounded and died. Life in the village was no longer normal and everyone started to have problems in their lives.

When I was ten years old, I made a pilgrimage with my family for the summer water festival.[6] For the pilgrimage, we visited a pagoda in a village that was a day away. When we got back to our village that night, we realized there was a problem. The rebels were drunk, and then the government soldiers came and they started to fight each other. My friend was in front of me and I told her we needed to hide. At the very moment that I pushed her forward into a trench, a bullet came and hit my friend in the upper arm. I was very, very sad that she was wounded—I recognized that she had been like a shield for me. Fortunately, she didn't die. There were many people who were wounded that night, and some people died.

My parents were very flexible with me, and they gave me lots of freedom. Our parents had to give us a lot of love, because if they scolded us or restrained us too much, we could be convinced to join the rebels. The rebels show children things like cell phones, swords, and guns to try to encourage them to join them. I also saw the rebels, but I would always run away from them. I heard that five children went to join the rebels at their camp, and only two of them came back to the village—the other three had died in the forest. I felt very sad for the young people there who could be recruited to fight.

One time, two girls and three boys from our village were taken to Thailand to work because they were orphans. They were told they could

---

[6] Thingyan is the Burmese New Year water festival that usually falls around mid-April. During the five-day festival, people throw water on each other to wash off the previous year's sins and start the new year off fresh.

get work in Thailand, and then they were taken to work as housemaids, to wash clothes, or to work in restaurants. The children were about seventeen or eighteen years old at the time. The person who took the children never came back again, and we never heard more about what happened to them.

Sometimes I imagine that maybe the children have gone on to pursue a good education and reach a higher position in life. Sometimes I imagine their lives like this. But I don't know exactly what has happened to them and I feel sad. They were my friends when we were young, so I wish I could see them again. It is very difficult to imagine the lives of my old friends.

WE HAD TO TAKE APART THE HOUSES

One night, when I was about nineteen years old, some young government soldiers were staying in our village. They were eating chicken, singing, and using a kind of dried leaf that is like a drug. Unfortunately, the rebels attacked that night and twelve government soldiers were shot dead. One village member also got shot and died on the spot. Only one soldier escaped because he was with his girlfriend at the time. We were very worried when the soldiers died, because we thought something might happen to our village. We were also worried that some unexploded bombs would later injure our villagers.

One month later there was a special funeral for the government soldiers with all of the villagers. A government battalion came to the village to provide security. They came by foot from another place; I don't know where they were stationed. When they did a security check in the village, they said they found one area that had more than twenty unexploded bombs left by the rebels. The bombs could have nearly destroyed the whole village.

After they discovered the bombs, the government decided that they wanted to move our village closer to the city because it was very remote and difficult to monitor. There were fights very often between the rebels and government soldiers, and I don't think they wanted to see any more fighting.

The government ordered that the villagers relocate to another place, and that all houses be destroyed.[7] We had to abandon our village and lose our property. Everyone started to take apart their houses, remove the roofs, and destroy the roofs. We didn't want to wait for the government army to come and burn down the village, so we took apart the houses ourselves. We did this to show that we were following orders, and to prevent the army from completely destroying our village. Everyone was really sad and crying—we were really attached to our village and no one wanted to leave.

The place where the government soldiers told us to move was not close to other villages and towns. Only a few families decided to relocate to the new site. Some villagers abandoned their houses and went to stay in nearby villages where they had relatives, and the rest of the people stayed in hiding in our village. Our family also decided not to go the new site because we would have had nothing to do there—there were no fields to grow rice, so we didn't want to go. But we no longer had a house in our village, so we had to hide in the trenches, in my family's *bon gin*, a trench where people hide underground to be protected from fighting.

LIVING UNDERGROUND

Each family in the village had its own *bon gin*. You can survive an attack, as long as it's not a really big one. You enter a *bon gin* through a hole in the earth, and then you cover it with some stones so that it remains hidden. The cover on the trench is about one and a half feet thick, and the *bon gin* has wood on the bottom so that you can sleep in it. The walls are covered with bamboo mats with soil over them. The space in our *bon gin* was high

---

[7] Land confiscation and forced relocation by the military junta have been well documented. In 1988, whole areas of Rangoon were cleared, and the SPDC's four-cuts policy regularly removes inhabitants in ethnic nationality areas where the military regime has been at war with armed ethnic opposition groups. People are also forcibly relocated in SPDC-backed development projects, such as dam-building, throughout the country. For more on the four-cuts policy, see appendix pages 461-462.

enough for people to sit up, but not very wide—just big enough for our family. There was a system for circulating the air in and out. We kept our clothes, food, and dishes in there. Sometimes when there had been fighting in the past, we would go there for a day to hide, but this time it was a lot longer.

Fighting sometimes broke out while we were hiding, but sometimes there was no fighting. It was mostly skirmishes. The fighting was in different places around our village and in nearby villages. I heard the gunshots. We heard fighting about once every five days, but sometimes fifteen days could pass with no fighting.

All seven of my family members went together to hide. It was very tight and uncomfortable living underground. After a long time, we became very bored because the place was so narrow. When it was peaceful outside, we would go outside and cook rice and then dry it so that we would have something to eat while the fighting was happening. We couldn't cook anything while we were hiding in the *bon gin* because then the government army would know where we were—we would be shelled to death. We stored our water and food in big bottles. Whenever it was time to eat in the *bon gin*, my whole family would cry because we were so unsatisfied with our food. We only had the dried rice and nothing else.

My younger brothers hiding in the *bon gin* with me were about eight and nine years old, so we were okay because we could tell them how to behave, but it was really difficult for people with babies. Sometimes we would check the security situation, and if it was possible, we would go to visit our friends in another *bon gin*. The head of the village was always checking on the security situation to see when we could leave. He would go aboveground, and whenever it was possible, the villagers would work on our houses and check on our fields. But during the fighting we would spend almost all day, every day, underground, talking about when or how we would be able to come out again.

After a month had passed, the families slowly started coming out from underground. We would check aboveground to see how many people had come out. While this was happening, some government soldiers came to know that we had to dig the *bon gins* to survive, and that the villagers had been hiding underground. They started feeling really sad about the situation, and they regretted what they had done in the village. So at that time the government started giving us supplies, like mosquito nets and blankets. The rebels also started to feel bad, and they left us a letter describing a place where they had left some meat for us. They couldn't bring it into the village, so we had to go and retrieve it.

Both sides started to realize their fighting had caused such a bad situation for us and they regretted it, but it was *nowanda*—regret when it's too late. We had already suffered enough.

I was so happy when my family and I came out from being underground. Although it had only been one month, it felt like an entire year had already passed.

NO CHANCE TO SAY NO

When we came out from being underground, different villagers were choosing different pieces of land and rebuilding their homes. Whoever claimed the land first got to have it. If you built on it, it was yours. This is how it works in a conflict area.

The villagers all agreed that we did not want to move, and we decided to formally protest the order we had received to relocate the village. We said to each other, "Even if we die, we will never leave our village."

The order to move had come from the local level. Since the higher authorities in Burma can override the decision of the lower authorities, the villagers made a petition and sent it to the higher authorities, above the township level. We sent our signatures to the higher authorities and they finally said we could stay.

Only one week after the villagers started to rebuild, the people who had gone to the government's relocation site came back because they found that there was no opportunity for them to work there. But after the decision was made not to move the village, the government told some of the nearby villages to resettle in our village in order to make it bigger.

The other villages were in a similar situation to ours, so they combined our villages. The others didn't want to relocate, but they were forced to. The government uses this relocation strategy to control people, and the government soldiers forced the movement of villagers. The government allocated land to the new villagers—they took our entire acre and a half and gave us nothing back.

After we petitioned the higher authorities against relocating, the lower authorities said nothing, but then they made us do a lot of forced labor from then on because we had gone against them. We had done forced labor before, but for years after that incident, they made us do harder work.

I had to carry weapons, especially bullets, on the mountain. I remember very well one time I fell down on the mountain, while camping. The mountain was so difficult to climb up, and the soldier shouted at me from behind. I shouted back that I fell because it was difficult to climb up the mountain. The soldier was afraid that the bullets would drop down behind us and roll far away down the mountain, so he'd shout at us.

I had to carry fifteen or twenty kilograms while climbing up a mountain. How could I carry that? I would fall down, for sure. I was very angry that he was yelling at me. But you had to carry it. No discussion, no chance to say no. If something was very heavy, five people had to carry it. If there was a kind soldier, sometimes he'd help me carry the load; otherwise we had to carry it ourselves the whole trip.

There were porters of all ethnicities in my area, including Burmese, Karen, and Indian. The ethnic minorities had to porter very hard, but there was no separation, we all had to carry together. I felt very upset at seeing this situation and also very, very sad that ethnic minorities like the Shan and the Karen were also suffering. They suffered like me and I was sympathetic.

I COULD NOT OPPOSE THE ELDERS

A group of government soldiers was moved to our area for military operations, and they stayed in a nearby village. They would stay there for six months of each year and then go to other areas. I came to know one of the soldiers because I visited that village often and he also visited my village. I was around twenty-seven or twenty-eight years old when we met, and he was older than me. He became friendly with me, and then one day he approached my parents, brothers, and sisters to tell them that he loved me.

Since I hated soldiers, I didn't want to marry one, but the elders suggested he would be an appropriate husband for me. My first worry was that I would become a widow after marrying him, because he had to go to the front line during military operations. He had to go around to many different areas. I could not oppose the elders because they were respected, but I already had someone in mind whom I intended to love. He was my childhood friend from the monastery where we studied. We hadn't said we loved each other yet, but we had an understanding between each other. But my parents agreed that I should marry the government soldier.

His relationship with the village was very good because the situation at the time was quite calm and quiet. Since he was a soldier, he only stayed in our village for a short time. He had no relatives in my area, so only his soldier friends came to the wedding. He went to my parents and asked for me in front of the elders, and then we offered food to monks and listened to a religious sermon. To make the marriage official, we offered tea to the elders and the people at the wedding. There were quite a lot of people enjoying the wedding, but I was both happy and unhappy during the wedding ceremony. I was unhappy because I thought about how I could become a widow if he passed away in the battlefield, but I was happy that he was respectful and had requested permission from the elders and my parents to marry me.

After the wedding, he stayed with me for six months. Then for the next six months, he had to go to another area for a military operation. After that he came back to his battalion and to me. I stayed with him in this way for three years.

One day when he went out for an operation, he stepped on a land-mine. I only found out about it a month after he got injured because he was far away. I got the message that he was hospitalized in the Mingaladon Military Hospital in Rangoon, but I didn't receive any news about how serious my husband's injury was—I only knew that he had been injured by a landmine.

I was crying when I heard he'd gotten injured, and I didn't know what to do. Other people usually bring snacks and things to eat for sick people, but I didn't know what to buy. I couldn't buy anything anyway because I didn't have any money. I didn't know what to say; I felt worried and nervous because I had never experienced this before.

When I arrived at the hospital, I could talk to him but he looked very weak. His lips had turned blue and his skin was pale. I cried a lot when I saw him, and he also cried. He requested that I go and stay with his brother. He told me not to go back to his village because it was far away and it wouldn't be easy to visit often.

As soon as I looked at him, I knew my husband couldn't survive—his leg was cut off above the knee. As far as I know, it had taken him one month to get to the hospital. Although the landmine had only wounded his ankle, he bled too much and his leg started to rot and the bone marrow became poisoned from the landmine. I saw that he was in very much pain.

He died during the night. I had been in the hospital for about fifteen days when he passed away. I heard the news from a nurse. Men and women had to stay in separate rooms, so I was not with my husband when he died.

His brother was in charge of the funeral and organized everything. No relatives from my family came because it was a long way from my village to the hospital. I cried during the religious sermon and when they took his body for cremation. I was thinking about memories of him. I couldn't eat for two days. I thought about his desire for me to stay with his brother's family so I could live happily and without any troubles. But I was also thinking about my parents and my siblings. I am the eldest of my siblings, and I felt worried about my younger siblings staying at home because they were still young. I was most worried about how

I would survive and whether my family would be happy for me to stay with them after my husband died. I was very grief-stricken while thinking about these things.

In the end I went to Irrawaddy Division to stay with the family of my husband's brother. That's what my husband and his brother wanted, and his brother felt sympathy for me. My husband and his brother had been the only two people left in their family after their parents passed away.

It was summer when I went to Irrawaddy Division. People there live along the riverbank, and most people work as fishermen. The houses are small and built of bamboo, unlike the houses in our village, where we could find plenty of wood in the jungle. When I was living in his brother's house, I spent most of my time doing housework. The family didn't want me to do work except for housework, such as cleaning. They were government personnel, selling clothes in a shop owned by the government.

I was depressed after my husband passed away. Most of the time I was thinking about how to survive and work. I was really worried about how to face the future. I was also worried about the stigma usually attached to widows. People gossiped, saying, "How can widows survive without their husbands? When their husbands were alive, they survived on their husbands' work and they couldn't work for a living. So how can they work now?"

I stayed there for about two years and then I went back to my village. I was unhappy staying in Irrawaddy Division without my husband, and I had been living away from my parents for a long time. My brother-in-law's family wanted me to stay with them, and they cried when I returned to my village. I was very sad to see them crying, but I was very eager to get back after such a long time away from my family.

MY SECOND HUSBAND

I met my second husband when he came to my village to work—we were working together and that's how it started. Now it's seven years already that we've been married.

It was a small wedding ceremony. We invited relatives from both sides to come. It's normal to invite the whole village to the ceremony in Burma, but I was so sad—we couldn't invite the whole village because we couldn't feed them. On that day I was again both happy and sad. I was happy because both of our families understood each other, and they didn't want us to end up with a heavy debt for the cost of the wedding; they were satisfied if we just showed respect and paid homage to them. But I was sad because we could not invite all of our relatives and friends. I wore just a simple dress; it was short and lacy.

During the ceremony, I kept focusing on my husband being drunk. He had a lot of friends who pushed him to drink. He started to drink, and then the men were shouting at each other. It was not good; I did not feel full of happiness. I was angry with him for being drunk that day, and I did not want him to be my husband. My memory of that day has become an upsetting thing.

Normally he is good, but if he drinks he makes me feel very troubled. He goes out and sings karaoke, but he never makes trouble for others, only me.

IT IS BETTER IN THAILAND

I left Burma three years ago. We lost our house and our land because of the fighting, and I wanted to earn money to buy them back. We were living together in Burma when we decided to leave for Thailand.

My husband and I were doing nothing special before we left; we were only in the field working, planting. In Burma we worked so hard and we were so tired, but we got very little money. We were talking about how to find work. In Burma there is work, but you cannot earn good money. In Thailand, if you work hard you can earn about 100 baht a day.[8] It is much better in Thailand, and that's why we decided to come over here.

---

[8] Approximately US$3.

We had to take two buses to reach Thailand. We took the bus from Pegu to Myawaddy, and then we came directly to Mae Sot because my cousins were already living here. We left with just a small bag.

To make our living here in Thailand, we collect plastic from the rubbish dump. There is a car that buys the plastic and pays us. I collect plastic bags, bottles, and old carpet. I work every day and get 40 to 50 baht per day.[9] One kilo of plastic bags is worth 2.5 baht, and one kilo of plastic bottles is 4.5 baht. But the buyers only choose the good plastic when they buy it.

I start working very early in the morning and work until 12 p.m. I take a rest of one to two hours for lunch, and then I start working again until 5 or 6 p.m. The amount of money we earn is okay for one day, but we don't have any extra. Sometimes I end up 100 or 200 baht in debt.[10]

There are good and bad things about being here. When I first arrived here at the rubbish damp, I couldn't collect plastic bags because it was so smelly that I vomited everything that I had eaten. As I watched the other people collecting, I vomited. But later on I became used to the smell and the place.

There are many houses here on the dumpsite and there are also people who live nearby off the dumpsite. The people who live at the rubbish dump live together happily most of the time, but sometimes there is conflict. We sometimes have conflict when trucks do not come to dump a lot of rubbish, so the people have to grab the rubbish in a hurry, and people are angry at each other and accuse each other of collecting rubbish in their area. Also, sometimes foreigners come to the rubbish dump to donate things for the people collecting rubbish. People who have a good relationship with the donors take more donations than others, so conflicts start.

The only thing I like about being here is that I can work; otherwise

---

[9] 40 to 50 baht is approximately less than US$2.

[10] Approximately US$6.

I don't want to stay here for long. Nobody wants to live here for a long time.

BOTH SIDES ARE RESPONSIBLE

If I get enough money, I want to go back to my village and buy back my old house and my old land. That is our plan.

There are people coming here from my village, so we're able to get some news. They say that the situation is getting better in the village, so we have hope. There are some peaceful areas, called white zones, where there are good leaders. Some village leaders tell both sides, the rebels and the SPDC soldiers, not to bring any guns into their village, otherwise their armies cannot come into the village. Sometimes the rebels and the SPDC soldiers will eat and drink together. The SPDC and the rebels both have the responsibility to live together peacefully, because if they do, then we can all eat well, we can all live well.

The people who have committed crimes in Burma, such as the military and the rebels, have to suffer on their own because they made their mistakes on their own. The punishment will come to them through their karma. Some SPDC soldiers are bad, but some are good; some rebel soldiers are bad, and some are good. As to why I have experienced so many difficulties, it is difficult to complain to someone. And I don't want to complain about only one side—both sides have a responsibility to take care of the people.

If I could do anything right now, I would plant trees and vegetables. What keeps me going is my desire to survive. My main aim is to live a normal life; I want to have a better standard of living. If I achieve this aim, I want to be able to make donations and share with others. This motivates me to keep working.

NAW MOE WAI

28, mother

ETHNICITY: *Burman*

BIRTHPLACE: *Pyinmana, Burma*

INTERVIEWED IN: *Mae Sot, Thailand*

Naw Moe Wai spoke to us on a bench outside the Mae Tao Clinic in the bustling border town of Mae Sot, Thailand. Her three-year-old daughter, Phyu Phyu, ran around laughing and shrieking gleefully as we chatted. The two had traveled over 450 kilometers from their home near Burma's new capital, Naypyidaw, to seek medical care. Medical assistance is inaccessible to many living in Burma due to the high costs of treatment and lack of options for the poor. According to the World Health Organization, in 2000, Burma's healthcare system ranked 190th out of 191. The Mae Tao Clinic serves Thailand's population of Burmese migrant laborers and refugees as well as many who live inside Burma.

I gave birth to my second daughter Phyu Phyu in 2007. Two days after I gave birth to her at home, I realized that she couldn't defecate. I had noticed that she had the shape of an anus but there was a small round ball attached to it, so I thought the doctors at the hospital would be able to remove that successfully in a short amount of time.

Many village people in my area believe that a mother must not leave the house during the first five to seven days after delivery. Since I could not go out, my elder sister took my newborn daughter to a few clinics. She had to pay 3,000 kyats to each clinic for the doctor's examination,[1] but none of them could solve my daughter's problem—they said she was born without an anus.[2]

My sister and her husband took Phyu Phyu to the Naypyidaw Hospital that same day.[3] I didn't have money to cure her, so some people lent money to me so that she could be treated.

My sister's husband came back at four in the morning and said my sister had to stay at the hospital with Phyu Phyu. The doctors had to do a colostomy on the side of Phyu Phyu's stomach instead of on her buttocks, so now she passes stool through a hole in her abdomen.[4] This was because the baby had the shape of an anus, but not the canal that joins it with the lower intestine. The surgery cost 100,000 kyats.[5]

My father told me I should cut off my attachment to my baby, because my husband and I didn't have money to cure her. My mother went to the hospital, but she didn't take me along because she was worried that my attachment to my baby would grow when I saw her again. They tried to give her up for adoption to someone who had money, but no one adopted her.

I feel very sorry for my daughter because she was born like this and no one loves her; the relatives from my husband's side don't love her. But ever since I delivered her, I'd become attached to her and felt responsible

---

[1] Approximately US$3.

[2] Imperforate anus is a birth defect where the rectum is malformed. It occurs in about 1 out of 5,000 infants.

[3] Naypyidaw is 200 miles north of Rangoon, and has been Burma's new capital since March 2006, when the government built it specifically to serve as the capital.

[4] A colostomy is a surgical operation in which a piece of the colon or large intestine is diverted to an artificial opening in the abdominal wall in order to bypass a damaged part of the colon.

[5] Approximately US$100.

for taking care of her—I couldn't abandon her.

When I arrived at the hospital in Naypyidaw, I felt so sorry for my baby I didn't know what to say. I asked the nurse why the doctors could not make the anus on the buttocks, and she replied that they'd tried their best to do this, but the baby's intestine was too short to reach her buttocks. The doctors needed to do an X-ray to figure out how to treat my daughter further, but the hospital was not big enough to have an X-ray machine.

Cleaning my baby's surgical wound was very complicated, but after three days, the nurses wanted me to do this without their help. I had to buy the materials to dress the wound, and I had to pay for the baby's medicine at a pharmacy. Every morning the nurses came and collected fees for cleaning and for use of the bathroom.

I experienced discrimination at Naypyidaw Hospital. I wanted the nurses to take care of my baby and explain things to me, but they would not answer my questions. They weren't friendly. They only answered my questions if I bought them apples or tea leaf salad as a bribe.[6] They don't treat the patients equally. If a patient has money, for example a military official, they care for the patient very well, but they don't do that for poor families. I just wanted my baby's wound to heal quickly, and I wanted to leave the hospital as soon as possible because I didn't have enough money to stay there for a long time.

After five days, a doctor came around to check the patients and she told me that the baby was well. She said that if I could take responsibility to clean the baby's wound, then we could be discharged from the hospital. I didn't get any further explanation.

In order to open up my baby's anus and reverse the colostomy done in Naypyidaw, we had to seek advanced medical treatment in either Rangoon or Mandalay. I don't know why the hospital in Burma's capital

---

[6] Tea leaf salad, or *laphet thote*, is an integral part of Burmese culture. It serves a multitude of purposes, including as a palate cleanser and to welcome guests. Its flavor is colored by the use of fermented tea leaves, shrimp, peanuts and an assortment of sauces and spices.

city is so poorly developed. I tried to find out the cost, but I knew I wouldn't be able to afford it. I even had to borrow money to pay for my trip to Naypyidaw—how could I afford the surgery? Then people told me it would cost 2 million kyats.[7] I thought, *Please don't say that! I'll never have that amount.* We tried to ask for donations from other people, but it was too much; we couldn't get it.

I ended up coming back home with my baby. I just regarded her condition as misfortune.

I STILL WANTED HER TO HAVE TREATMENT

I fought with my husband. I wanted my baby to have medical treatment, but I only made 1,400 kyats for a whole day's work selling rice and corn.[8] It wasn't enough, because I had to spend 700 kyats for basic daily needs. Also, daily work was sometimes not available. So my husband and I agreed to play the two- and three-digit lottery, but then we became addicted—it was a big problem.

The most I ever spent on lottery tickets was 200 kyats, but my husband would spend thousands of kyats.[9] This was one reason we started to have problems between us. I was hoping that if we won, I would be able to buy cotton and the other materials for my baby's wound. I ended up in some debt, but not very much.

One day, a woman who had gone to work in Mae Sot, Thailand told me she could take my daughter to get medical treatment there. My husband told me not to go all the way to Mae Sot, but I was already planning to go. He asked for my ID card and all of the child's medical records, but I didn't give them to him because he would have burned them to stop me from going. I told him and my parents that if I didn't go to Thailand, the

---

[7] Approximately US$2,000.

[8] Approximately US$1.40.

[9] Approximately US$0.20.

child would never become a normal human being. It's hard for me to talk about how my husband acted.

I was really happy thinking that my daughter would get medical treatment. I had always wanted to find someone to help her—if a person could help, I would do whatever that person asked. I would do it for my daughter.

I got all of my daughter's medical records and my ID card, and I followed the woman to Mae Sot. I had never heard about the clinic and the organizations there, so I thought at first that the woman was paying to cure my daughter—I thought maybe she was very rich. I didn't know that the clinic and the organizations were helping people by giving free treatment.

When I arrived in Thailand, my daughter was two years and four months old.

I WANTED TO HELP THEM, BECAUSE THEY ARE CURING MY CHILD

At the Mae Tao Clinic, there were lots of patients whose illnesses were more serious than my daughter's. I found there was no discrimination in how people treated each other there. From the Mae Tao Clinic, my daughter was sent to the Mae Sot Hospital. They examined her, but they didn't tell me anything. While we were there, a translator asked me, "Why did you come to get medical treatment here? Naypyidaw is very developed and Than Shwe is very rich—he celebrated his daughter's wedding so splendidly, with diamonds.[10] Won't he be able to cure your baby?"

The Mae Tao Clinic connected us with the BCMF—Burma Children

---

[10] General Than Shwe serves as Commander-in-Chief of the Myanmar Armed Forces and chairman of the State Peace and Development Council (SPDC). He also heads the Union Solidarity and Development Association (USDA)—a mass organization that coordinates government at the local level. The amalgamation of positions means that Than Shwe is the effective leader of Burma's ruling military junta.

Medical Fund—who sent us to Chiang Mai with an interpreter.[11] When we first arrived in Chiang Mai, I thought my daughter would immediately get surgery and recover very soon—but then I found out it could take years. But the BCMF actually provided us with accommodation and food, and they gave my daughter and me some clothes as well. Everybody was so friendly. At the hospital in Chiang Mai, I became friendly with the nurses. Here in Thailand, if a nurse or medic asks you to do something, they say "thanks" to you after you help them; it is very surprising to be treated with respect. I stayed in Chiang Mai for a month and a half. I was very happy because I could help cook, clean, and wash clothes for other patients. I wanted to help them, because they are curing my child.

Right now we have to stay at the Mae Tao Clinic in Mae Sot until Phyu Phyu can have the surgery, and then we will have to go to Chiang Mai again.

Here in Thailand babies undergo the anus operation by the time they are seven months old and they recover completely by the time they are a year and a half. But my child is now three years old and she hasn't had the medical treatment. If I had known earlier, I would have come here.

I DON'T WANT TO GO BACK

I miss my village, because it is where I grew up. But the standard of living is high here in Thailand—people here use electricity switches and they cook with automatic rice cookers. We can also get free medical treatment here through the Mae Tao Clinic, and it doesn't feel like people

---

[11] Mae Tao Clinic does not send patients to Chiang Mai. This is done through the Burma Children Medical Fund (BCMF) or Burma Adults Medical Fund (BAMF). When patients get sent to Mae Sot hospital and get a referral letter to Chiang Mai for treatment, they go back to the Mae Tao Clinic and then get referred to the Burma Children Medical Fund program, which is independent of the Clinic. It funds the accommodation, transport, surgery and other costs involved.

discriminate against each other.[12] I never saw that when I lived in my village, so I want to tell my parents about it.

Even though I miss my family in the village, it's better for me to stay here to improve my daughter's condition. I miss my parents and my elder daughter, who is nine years old. I left her in Burma with my mother and father. My husband went back to his village, so he is living there.

When we lived in Burma, the other children wouldn't play with my daughter and she didn't talk much, but now she is very confident—she plays and talks a lot.

I don't want to go back to Burma. I found out from other people that children can study English, Thai, and Karen languages here, and they don't have to pay a tuition fee at schools for migrant children. I will look for a job, and then I will send money to my parents so they can send my older daughter here—I want her to get an education. In Burma, I could only send my child through grade four because the primary school in our village only goes that high. After that, parents have to send their children to town to continue school, but I would not be able to afford that, and my daughter would end up doing work like the people in the village. I want my daughters to become educated people, because if they have an education they can choose what to do and they can help those in need.

---

[12] Burmese migrants receive free medical treatment at the Mae Tao Clinic, which is located on the Thailand side of the Thailand–Burma border. However, migrants are not treated for free in Thai hospitals.

MALAYSIA

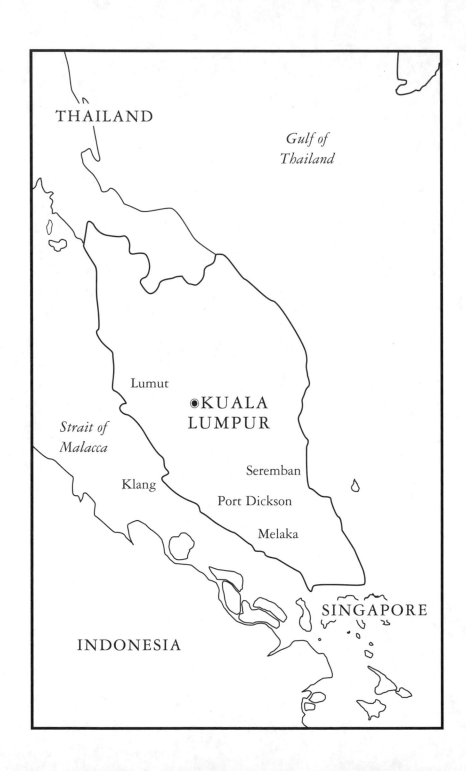

AYE MAUNG

34, former prisoner and SPDC army porter
ETHNICITY: *Chin*
BIRTHPLACE: *Chin State, Burma*
INTERVIEWED IN: *Kuala Lumpur, Malaysia*

Aye Maung was studying to become a pastor in Burma before he was abruptly imprisoned and then forced to porter for the Burmese military. We met Aye Maung in Malaysia, where he and his family lived in a precarious situation, hoping to be granted resettlement to a third country. Aye Maung sat with us in the Chin Refugee Center, a community center founded and managed by Chin refugees. The refugee center sits in the shadow of Kuala Lumpur's gleaming Petronas Towers. The unmarked entrance to the center leads to a narrow, winding staircase; the office itself is full of activity, with many recently arrived refugees from Chin State seeking advice and assistance.

One night the prison guards yelled for me to get out of my cell. They made me line up with the other prisoners, and they chained us all together, one by one. They put us in a military car, and they didn't tell us anything. But as soon as they called us that night, we knew we would be made porters. We were afraid, because we had heard that most porters die. Only the prisoners who have money can pay to not become porters.

The government doesn't have much money, but they have prisoners. So for them, it makes sense to use us for army porters—if we die, they lose nothing. But if they use horses or helicopters to carry their loads, the government loses money if the horse dies or the helicopter breaks. It's easy to take a prisoner and make him a porter. That's how the SPDC thinks about it.

That night, they brought us to Palaw,[1] southeastern Burma, which is in the area of the Karen National Union (KNU).[2] There were about 185 porters and 250 soldiers. Most of the soldiers were Burman, but maybe about thirty of them were ethnic minority people. The porters were mostly ethnic minorities—Rohingya, Karen, Rakhine, and a couple of Chin, like me.

We left Palaw on January 28, 2006, and began walking to an army camp that was a two days' walk from the border. We started our journey around 3 p.m. and slept that night in a village along the way. The next morning, we continued walking. We followed the stream, but it was hard because there was no trail. Sometimes a few porters would walk ahead to clear a trail, and we would follow. We were carrying so much—machine guns, ammunition, and rations for all the soldiers and for ourselves.

Some machine guns were so big that eight people had to carry them. We hadn't gone through training, and we weren't allowed to rest, so some porters couldn't handle it. If one of us couldn't walk any farther, the soldiers would just kill him. They didn't want to leave behind any prisoners who were alive.

If someone tried to take a rest without permission, the soldiers would beat him with their guns. They would beat him so much that he couldn't

---

[1] Palaw is a town in the Tenasserim Division, which is the southern most part of Burma, bordering the Andaman Sea.

[2] The Karen National Union fights for autonomy for the Karen people within a federated Burma. Starting in 1949 and continuing until today, the war between the KNU and Burmese army is the longest-running war of the post–World War II era. For more on the KNU, see the "A Brief History of Burma" section of the appendix, pages 460-461.

walk anymore, and they'd leave him there to die. People kept dying. My friends kept dying.

WE USED TO GO FISHING IN THE SMALL STREAM

I grew up in Chin State. Everybody in my town was Christian, and the majority of the people were Baptist.

I lived with my mother, father, three sisters, and brother. My father was a government clerk, and his salary was 1,000 kyats each month.[3] At the time, one ration bag cost 1,000 kyats, and each month our family needed two ration bags. And then we had school fees and other needs. We had our own farm, and we used it to feed our family—that's how we survived. Many families in our town had farms; some people grew corn, or cotton, or rice paddies. We had a rice paddy.[4] I was ten years old when I started helping my family farm. It was very hard, but our farm was very beautiful. There was a little stream, mountains, and a small valley. We used to go fishing in the small stream.

It was a small town, and we had a very good community. When I'm falling asleep, sometimes my hometown and our family farm appear in my mind. Even now when I'm telling you about it, it's appearing in my mind again.

WHATEVER THE MILITARY TOLD US TO DO

There's a military camp in the same region as my hometown. The government tries to have Buddhist monks wherever there is a military camp in Chin State, to try to get Chin people to convert to Buddhism. So it's like they have a mission, because we lived in a Christian town.

Whenever the military needed work done in the camp, they would

---

[3] Approximately US$1.

[4] A paddy field is a flooded piece of land used for growing rice.

come to our town and make people work for them. You didn't get paid, and the military never provided food. The military would say, "Oh, today we need thirty people to work at our camp." So the head of the village would appoint people to go to work for the military camp, and no one could say no. If you said no, you'd get arrested.[5]

I started getting called to do forced work for the military when I was seventeen years old. Sometimes I had to work at the military camp, and sometimes on road construction. Sometimes we had to spend a week at a time at the work site for the road construction. But for working at the military camp, we would just go one day at a time and then go back home to sleep. Sometimes we had to porter in Chin State for two or three days. So whatever the military told us to do, we had to do, and without getting paid. That was the problem.

We had to worry about food and school fees at the same time as working for the military with no pay. We were very angry, but we couldn't deny them. If we did, we would have to flee from our town. And even though we were very angry, we had to smile.

I heard that if someone from the Burma army married a Chin woman, he would get a promotion. The reason he'd get a promotion is because when he married a Chin woman, he would convert her to Buddhism. The Burma government wants one religious system and one language system, but we are Christian. There is no government college or government university in Chin State—I think this is because we are Christian.

I went to Rangoon for university to study theology. My parents were very happy, because they wanted me to study. I traveled to Rangoon with my friend, and we were so happy and thankful to go there. When we arrived, we saw how big it was and thought, *Wow!* We were just villagers, so we had never seen a city like that before—it was marvelous for us. The buildings were so big, and there were roads with cars. For us, Rangoon felt like the biggest city.

---

[5] The routine taking of villagers for forced labor in Burma is well documented by the International Labor Organization.

WHEN WE ARE YOUNG,
WE FEEL LIKE IT'S IMPOSSIBLE

After my father retired from his government job as a clerk, he became involved with the NLD.[6] But even though my father was involved in politics, I wasn't involved. In Burma, when we are young, we feel like it's impossible for anything to change. What Aung San Suu Kyi said was always very good, but to a young man like me, it seemed impossible. We see the government with guns and military power, but the other party has no guns, no power. How can they win against the military government? This would be very, very difficult. So to regular people like me, it seems impossible for the NLD to win. Maybe we don't understand Burma politics, but where I lived, that's what we thought.

I did my bachelor's degree in theology, and after that, I was taking my master's in divinity. And then in the summer of my first year, they arrested me, even though I wasn't involved in politics. I shouldn't have been harmed for this, but that's how the military government acts in our country. It's frightening what happens to people. My father was energetically participating in the NLD, and he had to go each month to the township executive office to sign a paper because he was involved in politics. I don't know exactly what the paper said, but he told me that he had to go sign it every month. But he wasn't harmed, and I was.

The summer of 2003, I had gone back to the village for vacation. There was an NLD event planned in Chin State. At the time, we didn't think there would be any problems.

But the military intelligence came to the event, and they took photos—they had my photo. That very night the police came to my house and arrested me. But the next morning they released me. They made me sign a paper saying, "I will not participate again in the NLD party."

---

[6] The National League for Democracy is a political party in Burma formed in the aftermath of the 1988 pro-democracy uprising, and headed by General Secretary Aung San Suu Kyi. The party was the decisive winner of the 1990 elections. See appendix pages 465-468 and 473 for further detail.

I wasn't in the NLD party, so I just signed it.

Later, I returned to Rangoon for my studies. I was only there a few days before they arrested me again. At around 3:30 a.m., about ten people entered the house. Some of them were in the Burmese police uniforms, some were in military uniforms, and some had no uniforms. I didn't know at the time, but later I found out that the ones without uniform were from military intelligence. They showed me the photo taken of me back in Chin State.

"Have you see this?" they asked.

"Yes, I've seen it."

"Do you recognize this?"

"Yes."

So they tried to handcuff me, and I said, "Why? What's wrong? I'm not in the NLD party. I just went to an event. I am a normal man. I am a good man." But they didn't listen.

They held me for ten days, and they gave us food only once a day—just enough to survive. I was so hungry, so I ate whatever they gave us.

They asked me, "Are you in the NLD?"

"No, I am not."

They asked me many, many questions. And when I answered, if they didn't get what they wanted from me, they would just beat me. They would strike me, kick me, torture me. After ten days, I was sent to Insein Prison. At the gate to Insein Prison, they made me sign a paper and they told me that my sentence was three and a half years. There was no trial.

Everything stood still. I had plans for my life—I didn't know I'd be put in prison. It was very, very severe. For the first three months in prison, I couldn't think about anything.

PRISON

There were many people at Insein—Karen, Kachin, Chin, and Burman people. We slept on the floor. There were eighty people in each prison room, and each room had one monitor. The monitor is a prisoner who teaches other prisoners how to live in the prison. For example, the monitor showed us that when we talked to guards or prison police, we had to stand with our arms out. To punish us, they would make us stand with our knees bent, in a half-squatting position. We would have to stand like that for half a day. I never got punished like that, because I tried to follow the rules as much as I could. If we followed whatever orders the guards gave us, nothing happened to us.

I was put in the political prisoners section. Many political prisoners are sent to Insein. Since it's very big, they make a separate area for political prisoners, and then there is a section for the important political prisoners—the very great men. But they kept the regular men together. I was with five men. We all lived the same way, just normal life. They didn't really talk about politics all the time, but when there was news— like when Aung San Suu Kyi was sentenced to house arrest for another six months—then they talked about their politics. I wasn't so interested in this—as I said before, I think it's very difficult to implement these politics in Myanmar because the government is very strong. So I agreed with what the prisoners said, but I didn't think it would happen.

I stayed there for five months, and then they moved me to Moulmein Prison.[7] At Moulmein, I was not put with political prisoners. They watch the prisoners, so after five months at Insein, they saw that I wasn't political. I don't know why they didn't just release me; they gave me no reasons.

To me, Moulmein was better than Insein. It's smaller, and we had a better understanding with the guards. The longer I was there, the more I shared an understanding with the guards, so that gave me a bit of freedom for where I could go and all that. I stayed in Moulmein Prison until the day I became a porter.

---

[7] Moulmein is the third largest city of Burma and the capital of Mon State. It is 300 km southeast of Rangoon, at the mouth of the Salween River.

WE SHARED THE SAME LACK OF FREEDOM

When we walked through combat areas, the SPDC soldiers would make the porters walk in front. In the forest, it's easy for KNLA soldiers to shoot the SPDC soldiers, but if the porters walk in front of the army, the KNLA soldiers don't dare shoot—they don't want to shoot porters.

Sometimes there were landmines. One time I saw a porter step on one and lose both of his feet. But another time it happened to a captain. As always, we were walking with the porters in front of the army but the porter didn't set off the landmine, the captain behind him did. Two soldiers lost their legs.

Most of the time, I didn't think about the landmines. I just walked. The load was so heavy, and we were always very tired. No time to think about the landmines, only about how we could carry on and get to rest. After the first village we stayed in, other villages we passed were empty. We saw no one—the SPDC had cleared the villages.[8]

On that trip to the army camp in southeastern Burma, my leg became swollen. I thought I could not carry my load any longer. But I knew that if I didn't carry anymore, I would die. I told the soldiers that my leg was swollen and asked them to give me less weight. He shouted, "What do you say now, porter?" He shoved me and beat me. "No, I cannot carry this!" I told him again. He beat me again. But when they only hit us with their hands, we were not so afraid because we could recover again. If they beat you with their guns, you wouldn't recover.

It took us five days to walk to the government army camp. By the time we arrived, only 147 porters remained. Thirty-eight people had died on the journey to the camp. When we made it to the camp, we could finally take a rest. We were very, very tired. But after a week, another bad thing happened. Four porters who were sick tried to flee, and the

---

[8] For more on the SPDC's four-cuts strategy, which includes the clearing of villages, see the "Armed Resistance and Counterinsurgency" and "Ceasefire Agreements" sections of the "A Brief History of Burma" located in the appendix pages 461-462 and 465-466.

army caught them that very same day. The soldiers killed those four people very brutally. They broke their arms and cut their tongues. Then they hanged them from a tree, and they made the rest of us watch. They wanted us to be afraid, so no more porters would try to run away again. After that, we were so afraid.

The government sends around ten battalions and 500 porters to this army camp every year.[9] But out of those 500 porters, only 70 to 100 return. So many porters die every year. The year I was there, it was also like this. See, this army camp was a Karen village before, but now there are no more Karen people there—only an SPDC army camp. All the Karen villagers in the area had to move to Thailand, because the SPDC cleared them out. The army would go into the area and kill everyone they saw, even if they were civilians.

During the day, we would stay by the river. The soldiers made us stay in the sun all day, and it was so hot. If we moved, one of the captains beat us. We had to stay in the same position until evening, with no water. They wouldn't even allow us to bathe for seven days. We were very dirty, and we smelled so bad. On the seventh day, they finally let us bathe, and they fed us well. But after a month, many of the prisoners were sick, since we didn't get to bathe often. Some of the weaker porters began dying, one by one, often from malaria. I kept wondering, "Is this how I will die?"

At the camp, malaria was a big problem. When I got sick with malaria, I was shaking for three days. All of my Karen friends told me that I shouldn't just sit there, that I should drink hot water and run. If you do this, you can survive. So I tried this—I drank hot water and ran around. I actually did recover, but ten days later I was sick again.

When twenty prisoners had died at the camp, the captain became afraid that we would all die. So the soldiers gave us good medicine and good food for five days. I finally recovered, but by then there were only about 115 or 120 porters remaining. We all grieved so deeply at the time,

---

[9] A battalion is a unit of soldiers. In Burma's armed forces, the Tatmadaw, there are approximately 200 to 500 soldiers in a battalion.

watching our friends die. We loved each other and took care of each other, because we shared the same lack of freedom.

Soon after I recovered from malaria, we started to work again as porters, travelling back and forth with rations from the camp to another army camp on the Thai border. During the rainy season, which begins in June, it takes one month to go back and forth to the border camp by climbing through the mountains. At that time, you can't follow the river to the border, because it rises high and becomes too wide to cross. So we climbed the mountains instead. It was like this: go up a mountain, go down, go up another mountain, go down again.

The rain was so heavy when we were climbing through the mountains. Heavy rain, morning to night. We got up at five in the morning and started walking around 6 a.m. each day. We would walk all day, through the rain, with our 25 kg bags of rations for the border camp.[10] In the mountains we used plastic to collect rainwater. We used the water to cook rice, because if we didn't eat, how could we survive? How could we carry? At five in the evening, we would take a rest and find a place to sleep. First we had to make sure the rations did not get wet, so we made a tent to store them. Second, we made a tent for the soldiers. Since we were in a KNU area, we had to be on guard. But for the porters, there was no tent. We could fit only our heads and chests under the tent and had to leave our legs outside. Our bodies got so wet through the night. We woke up in the morning with our *longyis* so wet, and then we'd start carrying again.[11]

The first time we climbed that mountain I actually wanted to die because I knew this was the first time, and that I'd have to go many more times. *I know I will die*, I thought, *so let me die now, easily. Let me not suffer in the future again.* But then I remembered my father and mother, and how sad they would be if I died there. The only reason I could survive is that I'm from Chin State, and as a child I was always climbing in the

---

[10] 25 kilograms is approximately 55 pounds.

[11] A *longyi* is a cylindrically sewn cloth sheet worn throughout Burma. It drapes from the waist to the feet, and is worn by both men and women.

mountains. Only because of that could I survive this mountain journey. Every time we took the trip, two people would die. The whole time, we were walking through a KNU area, but we saw no Karen people. Only destroyed villages.

One time, the captain told us that we had lost the way. It was the rainy season, so the path was very slippery. We made our way to a cliff near the river, and we set up camp there for the night. It was already dark, but since we were in the forest and it was a KNU area, the army didn't dare make a fire. So we stayed in the dark, in the cold.

When we finally arrived at the border camp after losing the way, we were so hungry. We were very thin. Our hands were so sore. But when we arrived at the camp, we saw that one porter had been left behind. We hadn't noticed before, because we could barely even take care of ourselves. It was so dark and rainy on that journey, so the army didn't keep track of us either. We only knew that we couldn't fall behind, or we would surely die. So when we saw that we had left one porter behind, we went back to find him the next day. But he was already dead. He had died from the cold, and because he was too weak to go any farther.

We were always weak because we never had enough food on these journeys. They only fed us twice a day—at 11 a.m. and 7 p.m. They gave us rice, and we would take banana shoots and crush them into it. We could only go on if there was at least something in our bellies.

If we tried to steal from the rations, the soldiers would beat us. The army checked what we had when we left the first camp and when we arrived at the camp, so we dared not steal. If we lost any of the rations, we were punished. Because the food they gave us was barely enough to survive, in one month five of our friends died from the hardship. If porters died while we were climbing through the mountains, we had to leave them there. We couldn't bury them, because we had no tools for digging. But when porters died at the army camp, we buried them as much as we could.

One time when we were climbing the mountain, one of our friends, a Mon man, was severely beaten by the soldiers. But he kept climbing. When we reached the top of the mountain, we left him to rest there while we continued on to take the rations to the border camp. We stayed two nights at the border camp, and then we went back to find him. We found our friend sleeping there, with maggots crawling from his anus. But he was still alive, so all the porters said to the army, "Please, we will carry him. We will carry this man to our camp, and we'll take care of him." But the army didn't allow it. "No," they said. "How can you carry him?"

We begged the soldiers. We had already left the rations at the border camp, so we had no more to carry. We were about fifty porters, so we could carry him back to the camp and take care of him. We begged them, but the soldiers said no. And then the soldiers made us throw our friend off the cliff. They made us throw him off the cliff while he was still alive. We were so sorry for our friend, but as prisoners, we could do nothing. We had to throw him. We felt so much sorrow, all the prisoners. That day, I told myself to run away from this life.

ESCAPING DEATH

For the first three months, the soldiers treated us badly like this, as if we were enemies. The regional colonel was very angry when those sick prisoners ran away, so all the soldiers saw us as enemies. They watched us carefully, and we didn't dare talk to them—we just carried the loads. But after three months, there was some mutual understanding with the soldiers, and they started to trust us more. At the same time, we prisoners would always try to please them. We tried to do whatever they wanted, because if we pleased them, they might give us some food.

I believe one reason that soldiers treat the porters so badly is that most of the soldiers did not willingly become soldiers. Some people who are in prison know that if they join the army they will be released. So that's how some people get out from prison. Some of the soldiers are very young, maybe fifteen or sixteen. At the time, I was about thirty years old. Some of them don't have a mother or father. The army tells them, "Ah, come. You join, and we will take care of you." So they join the army. And if soldiers run away from the army, they are imprisoned.

The officer life is very different from the normal army life. The officer's salary is about one lakh,[12] but a normal soldier's salary is only about 30,000 kyats.[13] You can't survive on this in Burma. The regular soldiers' salaries are not high enough and should be increased. Also, the officers rule over the normal soldiers very cruelly. They can do whatever they want, and they have opportunities. But the normal soldiers are stuck. If they run away, they will be imprisoned.

When we were carrying the rations, the soldiers were also very tired. If a porter could not continue, the soldiers had to take care of it—so they would just kill him. I think it's the officers that made them do this. The officers told them, "Don't look at the porters as your friends. They're prisoners. Thieves, murderers. Don't give them any chances."

In actuality, many prisoners are arrested not because they are murderers, but just because they did things like sell lottery numbers. The lottery is illegal in Burma. Just for selling a lottery ticket, someone can get one and a half or two years in prison, and be sent to porter.

My strategy to survive was to appease the soldiers and to make friends with them. But porters can die at any time. For example, if a soldier got angry and just shot me with his gun, nothing would happen to him. I would just die, like a chicken or a rat. To Tenasserim Division, they send about 500 porters every year. Of the 500, fewer than 100 porters make it back to the prison. If you survive, you survive.

A HOLE IN THE GROUND, COVERED WITH BAMBOO

Staying at the army camp was always so hard. The soldiers fed us very little, and we wore only the clothing we had when we first arrived at the camp. Our loads had been so heavy while walking to the camp that we had thrown away our extra clothing. We spent six months in the same clothes.

---

[12] Approximately US$100.

[13] Approximately US$30.

There was an officer who went crazy at the camp after about five months there. One night, around 2 a.m., he went outside and they couldn't find him. They finally found him under a tree, just sitting there and thinking. The porters never knew exactly what happened, but we saw them take him away and put him in a prison. The prison was just a hole in the ground, covered with bamboo, and they kept him inside.

One day things started to change for me. I was assigned to cook for the prisoners at the time. That day we were not given the full ration of food for the prisoners. The prisoners reported this to a major, and he came to check. He called me and asked, "Did you cook all the rice I gave you for the prisoners?" I explained that there was only a little left.

"Who left only this?" he asked.

"It was the sergeant," I said.

"Where is the rest of it?"

I had to tell the truth. I admitted that the sergeant had taken the rice away. The major was angry about this, so he punished the sergeant severely. Then the sergeant got angry with me. "Oh, so you reported me?" he said.

"No, I didn't." He slapped me and told me I had no right to reply.

"If we travel together to carry the rations," the sergeant said, "I will kill you."

I was so afraid. In the camp area, it was very easy for the soldiers to kill porters. There were only ninety-seven porters left at that time. My friends tried to encourage me to run away. They said that if we went to carry rations, they would accompany me and help me run away from the camp. I felt it was my chance to leave. I could not escape death if I stayed, so I had no choice but to try to escape. I thought, If I die, I will die. If I live, I will live.

GOOD, STRONG MUSCLES

By the end of July, we'd already been at the camp for six months. Somehow, the soldiers trusted that we would not run away. We usually had breakfast at 11 a.m., so everyone was there taking food. The guards were having breakfast too. During this time, I ran away and made it to the stream. Since I'd stayed in that area for almost six months, I knew the way to town. I didn't dare walk on the path, but I stayed near it. I walked for the next three days. During the night I slept on the ground, just like we always did as porters. And for food, I ate banana shoots. This kept me alive.

During those three days of walking, I thought about how simple the life of a porter is, and also how easy it is for us to die. I thought about my friends who died. Some of them had good, strong muscles, but they died anyway. Maybe they died because they didn't have a strong mind, or a strong heart. As I thought about what I'd faced in my life as a porter, I realized again that I had only survived because of my love for my mother and father. If I didn't love them, if I didn't have them to love and take care of me, I would have died as well. But I was still alive. I had survived.

FOR REFUGEES, THERE'S JUST NO LAW

When I arrived in town, a schoolteacher helped me and let me stay at his house. He took care of me and helped me get to Kawthaung, the southernmost town in Burma. I decided to go to Malaysia because there are so many Chin people here, including my elder sister and my younger brothers—they had been living there since before I was arrested.

In Kawthaung, there was an agent who sent people to Malaysia. The payment was nine lakh, but I didn't have it.[14] So the agent paid for me, and agreed that my older sister could pay him in Malaysia. From Kawthaung, I first fled to Ranong, Thailand. It was August 2006 when I left Burma. I came by boat to Ranong, which is near the Malay border. The boat ride was five or six hours long, and there were about twenty of us on the boat. There were Mon and Karen people, who were also going to Malaysia with the agent. When I was in Kawthaung, I was still afraid.

---

[14] Nine lakh, or 900,000 kyats, is approximately US$900.

But when I arrived in Thailand, something lifted in my mind. I felt like what I feared had just flown away from me.

To pass through the Thailand–Malaysia border and into Malaysia, they put me in a car. They put two of us in back, on the floor behind the seats. And that's how we entered Malaysia.

Living in Malaysia is like another life for me. I think I have had two lifetimes—it's really great, and I'm fortunate. Before, I felt like I was mostly dead, but here I am, alive. And even though I struggle in Malaysia, Malaysia is my only hope. We face many, many problems here, but maybe this is my great test—my opportunity to have a life again.

I first heard about Malaysia in 1989, because there were Chin people here. So I heard about it, and we also saw Malaysia in videos. In the videos, the houses looked very good, the police seemed so nice, and the roads looked very good. So I thought it must be very good to live in Malaysia, right? But when I really came here, I saw that there are so many problems. It's different from what we saw. It's very hard to live here. If we go out at night, there are robbers who take our things away. And we have to worry about the police. Malaysia is one way for the Malay people, but for refugees, there's just no law. Whatever they want to do to us, they can—it's unsafe for us.

One day, I went to the cemetery and looked around at the gravestones. I saw some Chin people who had died in Malaysia, and I saw their ages— nineteen, twenty, and twenty-eight years old. Some Chin people commit suicide because they cannot face their life anymore but they don't dare return to Burma. Of all the Chin people who die here, I think 98 percent must be under the age of thirty. Not all of them are suicides, just some. In Myanmar they are afraid for their life, so they come here. Then here, they suffer more. They work, but maybe after two or three months, the boss still won't pay them and they have to pay for food and a place to stay. So those are the problems they face, and some of them commit suicide.

I've had some problems with work. Sometimes the boss didn't pay us, even after a month or two of work, so we had to try another job. Fortunately, my brother and sister living abroad help support me. If they weren't living abroad, I couldn't afford to survive here. Thirty people will stay in one flat—one couple here, one couple living over there, children over here—everyone in one big room. It happens in many places here. All the refugees live like me.

We have a coalition for the different ethnic groups from Burma—COBEM.[15] We work with people from the other ethnic groups, and we meet together at COBEM after work. The Chin is the biggest group of the COBEM members, so we are like leaders.

But it's hard to have friendships here, because of our living situation. I don't have any Malay friends. It can be very difficult to be friends with Malay people, because of how they see us. We only speak with Malay people when we are working.

I am helping here at the Chin Refugee Center—the CRC. I've been working here for two months, but before I was working in construction. I would come here to visit sometimes, or to help interpret for people. There are some free clinics for Chin refugees here, so sometimes I would go and interpret there. I enjoy working here now, because we help with the many problems that arise. For example, some Chin women have been raped while out working at restaurants in the city. The women come to us first, and we help them go see UNHCR and the police. When we can help people like this, it makes me very happy.

We don't really have any security here at the CRC office. We just take a gamble. The police don't come here, so we have maybe an unofficial agreement. If they arrest a refugee who has a CRC card, the police will call us. We beg them to release the refugee, and then they usually do. We also have NGOs helping us when refugees get arrested.

In general, I think Chin people have a very strong community. Maybe it's different in some parts. But here in Malaysia, Chin people have a very, very difficult life. They are refugees, and they live and eat like refugees. But when a Chin person dies here, the Chin community makes a condo-

---

[15] The Coalition of Burma Ethnics, Malaysia (COBEM) represents the Chin, Kachin, Rakhine, Shan, Karen, Mon and Karenni ethnic communities in Malaysia.

lence service. It costs about 10,000 ringgits, which is a very big amount of money for us.[16] But if we face death with the whole community, we can afford it. The reason is that we're used to sharing with each other—it's what our forefathers did in Chin State.

SOMETIMES I THINK I AM NORMAL NOW

My whole family has applied for refugee resettlement. I married my wife in Burma just before I was arrested. She came here in 2007, a month and a half after me. Now we have two children, a boy and a girl. One is three weeks old, and the other is a year and one month.

I want us to have a normal life again. When I was in prison, I was eager to have a family, the children staying peacefully at home, and the father coming home from work to his children. That's what I imagined.

After facing the deepest difficulties as a porter, I try to forget them. I arrived in Malaysia and there were many Chin people here—even my villagers and my relatives. When they asked me to tell them what happened, I said, "Let me take a rest first." I felt that what I had seen was very normal, but I think it will take time for me to recover—to feel like everything is really normal.

Sometimes I think I am normal now, and I try to do things for my Chin people. I do whatever I can do. Then sometimes I see a police officer, and I'm afraid. But what I feel isn't just normal fear—it touches me really deeply. I need to build up my psyche, my mind. I need to try to be normal again, so I can do whatever I can for my people.

I hope that I will be able to resettle someday, and live my normal life again. I want to resettle in the U.S. I've had my DHS interview already, so now I am waiting for the decision.[17]

I'm very disappointed with the Burmese government, because ever

---

[16] Approximately US$2,940.

[17] The U.S. Department of Homeland Security is responsible for the ultimate decision on refugee resettlement status.

since they imprisoned me, I've lived in fear every day. They sent me to work as a porter just to kill me; they let porters die. When my friend was dying in front of me as a porter, I knew I could die like that too. At that time, I didn't know how I should pray. I thought, *If I actually survive and leave the life of a porter, I will give my time to those who suffer like me.* That's what I decided. But now all I can do is live in fear of the Malaysian police. There are just so many things I cannot think about yet. What will happen in the future? We really, really don't know. Even tomorrow is a question—we don't know. But this is what I'm trying for—if I can do something for whoever has suffered like me, I will—here in Malaysia, and maybe somehow in my resettlement country.

I don't know what job I will have in the future. I have worked in construction here, so maybe I'll do that. But I'm taking classes now, and then I want to do theological study. Preaching is the job I like; I'm a pastor, but I can't do it here in Malaysia. I have no congregation, so I have to do work like construction. My life is totally different right now.

My father and mother are still alive. My elder sister and youngest brother live abroad. My other sisters live in Burma. Her husband is a pastor. And then there's me. So, this is our family. I told everybody that now I'm a normal person.

Because I've already died, my hope is that the life I have now is not for me, but to work for the people who suffer here. So here at CRC, I'm working for this. I work for my family and my community.

THAT'S HOW THIS CROOKED COUNTRY IS

The NLD will never win the government. The regime in Myanmar will never change. Also, the ethnic armies like KNU and KIO will never be able to overthrow this government. They're wasting life by fighting like this. Meaningless dying. How many people have already died? How many ethnicities are suffering in our country now? The Karen, the Chin, the Kachin, the Shan, the Rakhine, the NLD political party—they all suffer. Why?

We need international action against the Burma government. We can only change the government with the help of the international community. The 2010 election is coming now. The government is trying to create a friendship with North Korea. What do they want? I know, everybody knows—they want nuclear weapons. So that's how this crooked country is. If the international community takes action, people in Burma will be very happy. In my view, they can't do it on their own.

Now we're just searching, just trying to live our lives in a safer place. Someday, some of us will go to another country and study, and help work for the needs of our country and our Chin people. Today things are very hard for us. I'm a refugee, I had to flee the country, so of course whatever I say will have a bias against the Burma government. I think refugees always have an injured psyche, so it's hard to find the very good things in life. But after time, I think it gets better.

I appreciate this book, because people will read about what the government does in Burma. I hope many people in China, India, and Thailand read it, so they understand what is happening nearby in Burma.

I think that if you publish stories about what's really happening, the Burmese government might have to improve. Sometimes the Burmese government does good things when they can be seen. But when they're behind a screen, they do whatever they want. So if we make it known to people what is happening behind the screen, then the government will become afraid. This book will do so many good things for the people of Burma. This is what I hope.

Since our interview, Aye Maung and his family were resettled to the U.S., where Aye Maung currently attends a theological seminary.

KHINE KYAW

18, refugee

ETHNICITY: *Rakhine*

BIRTHPLACE: *Northern Arakan State, Burma*

INTERVIEWED IN: *Kuala Lumpur, Malaysia*

Khine Kyaw is a Rakhine teenager who fled Burma to avoid forced conscription in the Burmese military.[1] Within a week, he went from being a normal sixteen-year-old—hanging out with his friends and working on his family's farm—to living and working illegally in Thailand, cut off from almost everything he knew. We met Khine Kyaw in a community refugee center in Malaysia, where he lived and studied. Although he had to spend most of his time within the center for his own security, he still managed to sport a styled hairdo and self-customized, funky jeans. Khine Kyaw gently and thoughtfully recalled the unexpected path his life has taken. Several months after our first interview, Khine Kyaw found a job at a cookie factory in Penang, Malaysia. He is awaiting further information about his possible resettlement to a third country.

---

[1] Rakhine is the original word for the majority Buddhist ethnic group that lives in Arakan State. Arakan is the name given by the British to describe both the state and the people. In this book, we use the term Arakanese for anyone from Arakan State and Rakhine to demarcate the ethnic group.

*   *   *

I was sixteen when I had to flee Burma. Several days earlier, three government soldiers had kidnapped me and forced me to join the government army. I just wanted to stay in Arakan State, to live with my family on our farm, and one day become a singer. I felt so much pain leaving my home, and I kept thinking about how I would never go back there again.

It happened in late 2007. I had the day off from school, and I was walking around when I came across three government soldiers who were drunk. They were in their thirties, and they spoke to me in Burmese. In Burma there are many languages, but all the soldiers speak Burmese. They said, "Come with us." They said they wanted me to go with them to their camp to help with their work. When I refused, two of them grabbed my arms and pulled me away. I was very scared and I was shouting for help, but there was no one around. I had no idea what I should do. I only felt fear.

I'd heard that this happened often in Arakan State. Government soldiers would go out to look for recruits and just collect boys from the village streets.[2] The kids are usually alone, happily going around the village when they are arrested by a soldier. I think the Tatmadaw takes young boys because they don't have enough men joining the army.[3] The boys don't agree but they are forced to join. The soldiers would also come to our village and harass the women and children. Sometimes they would eat at a restaurant and refuse to pay the bill. Sometimes they even raped women. In Burma, the Tatmadaw has all the power and they can do anything they like.

It took about half an hour to get to the camp. On the way, I asked the soldiers to take me home, but they replied that they were taking me

---

[2] Burma is frequently cited as being one of the countries with the most child soldiers in the world. The Optional Protocol to the Convention on the Rights of the Child sets eighteen as the minimum age for direct participation in hostilities, for recruitment into armed groups, and for compulsory recruitment by governments.

[3] The Tatmadaw is Burma's armed forces, founded by General Aung San to fight the British. Since 1962 Burma has been ruled by its military. See the Brief History of Burma section of the appendix for further details on the Tatmadaw.

to the camp and that they would only respond to my request after we had arrived there. I thought that they would release me after I'd helped them with some work.

They brought me to Battalion 376, a small government army camp. I asked them again to let me go home. They refused, and then they ordered me to sign a paper agreeing to enter the military. When I refused to sign the paper, one of the soldiers punched me in the forehead four times. I couldn't see very clearly at the time, but I think he had a ring on his finger. After that, he was punching and slapping me. It hurt very badly, and as long as I wouldn't sign the paper, the soldier kept hitting me. It felt like it lasted for hours—it was like hell. I was so scared that eventually I signed the paper. They didn't give me anything to treat the injury on my head, so I have a scar now.

After they beat me, the soldiers took me to a hut and told me to stay there, on the floor. There were five or six soldiers around. Some of them stayed in the hut and some were sitting outside. I was afraid to stay there and I didn't want to be a soldier. Things are very bad living in the army. They force the young soldiers to do very hard work and they pay them a low salary, not even enough to pay for their food and clothing. Although they are soldiers, their superiors order them to carry very heavy things like stones for building roads, and they force them to plant and harvest rice. I didn't want that future for myself. I was so young, and I was supposed to be in school.

I decided to escape. The door to the hut was not locked, so I escaped while the soldiers were sleeping, between midnight and one in the morning. At first I just started running without knowing where to go, but later I remembered the way to my house. It took me over thirty minutes to get to my mother's house, and I was afraid the whole time.

When I got home, my parents were very happy to see me. They had been searching for me all over and asking the people in the village if they'd seen me. When I explained what had happened, they became very worried. My mother told me I had to run away because the government army would come and search for me. She was worried that they would come and arrest me. The army searches for and arrests people who flee from them, and then they force them to join the army again. My mother told me that I could no longer stay in my home. I didn't know at all what would happen next—I just knew that my signature was on that paper, agreeing to join the army.

Three or four days after I got back, my mother contacted my uncle about sending me to Thailand. My uncle told me to be strong, and he said, "Don't worry. I am in touch with my friend who lives in Thailand—I will send you to him." Then my mother introduced me to a guy from the village who was working as a broker on the Thailand–Burma border.[4]

Words cannot express how sorry my mother felt to say goodbye to me. I said goodbye only to my family. I think all my friends must worry about me when they think of me now. I was very young at the time, and I was always hanging out with them and visiting them when there was no school. I wish it were possible to see them again, but it's only a dream for me to go back to my country. I feel very sad when I think about it because I will never get the chance.

I DIDN'T KNOW WHAT TO DO

I escaped in a boat that went from Arakan State to Kawthaung, which is on the border of Burma and Thailand.[5] The boat carried over 100 bags of rice, and there were another four or five people traveling in it. They were Chin and Rakhine. We each had to pay the broker 6,000 baht for the boat ride—it was expensive.[6] During the nine days we spent on the boat, they talked to me and tried to make me feel better. We had enough food and drinking water on the boat, and we would go into the sea to bathe.

I felt safe on the boat because we went directly to Kawthaung with-

---

[4] A broker is someone who is paid for assistance in illegally crossing a border.

[5] Kawthaung is a city on the southernmost point of Burma, about 800 km from the capital, Rangoon. It is a common border crossing between Burma and Thailand.

[6] Approximately US$200.

out stopping on the way. When we reached Kawthaung, we crossed into Thailand in a small boat. On the way there, my mind wasn't clear. I didn't know what I would have to do when I arrived in Thailand. I had heard that it was nice, but I had also heard that it wasn't safe. I thought that if I made smart choices while living in Thailand, it would be better than living in Burma. I thought that, compared to the situation in Burma, people in Thailand earned enough money each month for their food, clothing, and shelter, and that the country had electricity all day and night for their citizens. But in Burma, everything is the opposite. Burmese people don't have enough food to eat, even though they work the entire day. It was my thought that Thailand would be better—a small child's thought. I didn't know how hard it would be.

THE PRAWN FARM

I had to stay two days at the broker's apartment in a village in Thailand. There were some other people there, mostly Rakhine, who had come to Thailand for all different reasons—persecution, economic problems. I was the only young person there without family, so most of them called me *Nyee Che*, which means "younger brother" in Rakhine language. They asked me why I was coming to Thailand so young, and they gave me information about living there. I felt like they would take care of me.

While I was at the broker's apartment, he contacted a man about finding work for me. The man looked at me and felt nervous about giving me a job because I was so young. In the end he decided to give me a job at a prawn farm, frightening away the birds so they wouldn't go into the prawn pond.

The prawn farm was far from any town or village. I liked that job because I could act like a child, running around and scaring the birds. First I would try throwing firecrackers at them, but if that didn't work I had to run after them. The birds came twice a day, in the morning and evening. They didn't usually come in the afternoon, so I had free time to relax.

They gave me a small tent to sit in during the day, near the grid of prawn ponds. I tried to control my thoughts when I was sitting in the tent; even though I wanted to go back to Burma, I pretended to be happy.

I slept in a separate room that my boss gave me, and they gave me a pot and some rice so I could cook. Since I was just a kid, they only paid me 1,500 baht each month—the other men got over 4,000 baht per month.[7] My salary was not enough. I had to pay back some money to a man who fed me when I arrived in Thailand, and I had to buy some clothes.

When I first arrived there, I didn't dared leave the prawn farm because I didn't have any documents—I could be arrested by the Thai police if I went out. After a while, I went out and encountered the Thai police. They interrogated me and I had to pay them money for my release. In Thailand, when Burmese people are caught without documents, some of us are sent to jail and some are sent back to Burma. I was a stranger there and the worst thing was that I could not speak Thai.

I didn't really know what I should do at that time. I couldn't live in Thailand forever, but I couldn't go back to Burma. I didn't know if I should stay in Thailand or go to a new country. I was very young and I didn't have any friends there. I was very lonely, and I missed my friends and family in Burma. Sometimes I felt that I wanted to go back to Burma because Thailand was not my country. There were no other young people working at the prawn farm, so I didn't talk to anyone about this.

I really liked working on the prawn farm, but I wanted to leave that job because my salary was very low. After working there for two months, I got in contact with my friend who lived near the Thai–Malay border. He was one of my new friends that I'd met when I first arrived in Thailand. He said I could get 4,000 baht a month by working with him on a fishing boat. He got me a job on the fishing boat, and I left the prawn farm without any problems from my boss.

---

[7] 1,500 baht is approximately US$50; 4,000 baht is approximately US$130.

WE ALWAYS FEARED FOR OUR LIVES

Another person working at the prawn farm decided to leave with me. We took a bus to the port town and stayed there one night. The next morning, we prepared to go to sea on the fishing boat. We prepared food, drinks, and also ice for keeping the fish we caught fresh. My first day on the boat, I got seasick and was vomiting because I had never worked at sea before. I couldn't stand on my feet, I could only lie down. The next day I felt a little bit stronger and only a little dizzy. On the third day I felt even better, and then by the fourth day I was used to it.

There were about eight of us living on the boat, including the captain, and we worked each day from start to finish. I tried hard to do what they wanted me to. During our breaks, the other workers and I talked to each other like friends; I could talk about my feelings with them. Because I was young, the boss called me *Dtua Lek*, which means "little boy" in Thai.

Sometimes we prepared hooks to catch fish whenever we had a short break. We could sell those fish on our own to make a little extra money, apart from our monthly salary.

When it started to get dark, we had to shine a light under the boat so that fish would gather around the light, and then we would catch them in a net. We couldn't see the land—we could only see fishing boats around us, and the lights from other boats at night.

My salary was 4,000 baht per month, and I could get another 1,000 baht per month by selling fish I caught on my own.[8] We spent fifteen days at a time on the boat, so we went to land twice a month. We sometimes visited the shops where my co-worker's friends worked— they were also illegal workers—but I didn't go to many places because I feared being arrested.

The Burmese people there had small shops selling betel nut and ciga-

---

[8] 4,000 baht is approximately US$130; 1,000 baht is approximately US$30.

rettes.[9] These people had good relationships with their landlords, who allowed them to open their shops, but they had to pay the police bribes in order to keep the shops open. The Burmese people were informed of raids by their landlords ahead of time, so they could avoid arrest and move their shop to another port.

I really didn't like working on the fishing boat, but I tried to be happy. My co-workers and I always feared for our lives, because when we came to land after fifteen days at sea, gangsters would be waiting. The gangsters were Thai people, including Thai Muslims. There are many Thai Muslims in southern Thailand, and they are fighting for their own state. The gangsters are not afraid of the police. They knew we would have money when we got to land, so they would come and put a gun to a fisherman's head and ask for money. If you didn't give them money, they would shoot and kill you. They never pointed a gun at me, but they did hold me up with a big knife two times.

My co-workers and I didn't want to sleep on the boat when we were at shore, because we were afraid to be killed by the gangsters. If you died, your body would lie at the bottom of the sea without anybody knowing. I felt very frightened living in Thailand.

The first man I saw killed was a fisherman. He was an ethnic Pa-O from Burma, and he was in Thailand illegally.[10] One day when he was on land, he slept on the deck of the boat while his friend slept inside. Some gangsters came on the boat and asked him for money, and the fisherman cursed at them because he was drunk. They started beating him very badly with their fists and with sticks. His friend inside the boat saw him being beaten, but he didn't dare help his friend—he would have been beaten too, and they would have died together. The next morning I saw the man's body in the boat, and I thought about when my turn would

[9] Betel leaf is a heart-shaped leaf common throughout Southeast Asia. In Burma it is chewed with the areca nut (and the combination is casually referred to as "betel nut"), and often combined with tobacco and assorted spices.

[10] Pa-O is an ethnic nationality group that lives mostly in Burma's Shan State.

come. In Thailand, it's easy to take away a life—it's like killing a chicken. There were no laws to protect us because we are illegal migrants, so we had to be careful every single day. For example, we never went out alone when we had to go out to buy things.

Another man who was killed was drunk one night and singing karaoke at a place not too far from our boat. I think the man was Cambodian. His body was found beside the karaoke shop. My friends and I saw the police checking the corpse the next morning. It was covered in so much blood. His throat had been cut. We didn't get too close.

There is so much violence in Thailand, especially on the coast. One killing after another. Living there was like hell—I was very, very eager to leave.

Sometimes I saw people from other countries relaxing, swimming and playing on small islands. I felt sorry about my life when I saw them, because I wanted to be happy like that. They could go to any country they wanted to, and they could relax and not worry about food or clothing, or about penalties for being illegal. We wanted to escape our suffering, but I had nothing, not even a chance. I couldn't control my sadness when I saw them.

I HAD NEVER WALKED FOR SUCH A LONG TIME

After about three months of working on that fishing boat, one of my co-workers told me he was going to Malaysia. I was afraid to go with him at first, so he said I could contact him after he arrived. He gave me a phone number and left. He was like a brother to me, always showing me what to do and what not to do. I felt like I could trust him, because he helped me distinguish between good people and bad people. He was twenty-two or twenty-three years old, also Rakhine. After he left, I continued working on the fishing boat for another month. When he was settled in Malaysia, he got in touch and said, "Why don't you come meet me?" I said I wanted to go, so he paid a broker to take me there.

I didn't tell my boss that I was going to Malaysia. The next time we were on land, at the end of the month, I hid for three days in my friends' grocery shop near the beach. I never went back to the boat.

The broker picked me up in a car and took me to his place, which was in a town on the border between Thailand and Malaysia. I had to stay there for three days because we were waiting for another person he was taking to Malaysia. The brokers never take only one person—they wait until they have at least three to five people so they can make more money for each trip. The broker took care of me because my friend in Malaysia had sent him a lot of money—1,500 Malaysian ringgits.[11] I traveled by bus with three other people to the border. We were all from Burma—Rakhine, Chin, Karen, and Karenni. When we arrived at the Thai–Malay border, we could see a highway and a rubber tree forest. We couldn't go on the highway, so we had to wait until around seven or eight o'clock that evening to cross the rubber forest.

I thought it could be dangerous to cross the rubber forest because there were many police on the border. We heard that if they saw people crossing the border, they would shoot them with their guns. They also had dogs to chase the people who were crossing.

We looked around to make sure we didn't see police, and then we all started crossing the rubber forest with the broker. We walked all night. Some parts of the rubber forest were very dense and hard to cross, but other parts were clear and easy to walk through. While we were crossing the rubber forest, we got very dirty from the mud—we were the color of the earth, so the police could not see us.

After three hours of walking, my thighs were red and had abrasions and my muscles were tired. I had never walked for such a long time. Sometimes I couldn't keep walking and I felt like I would fall down.

When we arrived at the Malaysian border, there was a small hill. We drank from a small pool of water in the ground, the way an ox would drink. At the border, we had to take off our clothes to jump over two electric fences—we didn't want them to get caught, so we threw them

---

[11] Approximately US$475.

over the fences. It felt like we were soldiers in training. It was really difficult to go over the fences, and I was very afraid because there were Thai police with dogs searching for illegal immigrants.

After we had jumped the fences, we put our clothes back on. We saw many police standing with their dogs, but they couldn't see us because we were hiding in the rubber forest. Everyone was afraid because the dogs could smell people, and if the police saw us, they would shoot and kill us on the spot. I think I was more afraid than the other people because I was a kid and I had no experience crossing the border. The broker said not to look around, to just stay silent and look straight ahead while we crossed the field. He told us to walk under the trees.

I think it was July 6, 2008 when I crossed into Malaysia.

I AM ALWAYS AFRAID BECAUSE I AM ILLEGAL

I thought it would be nice to get directly to my friend's house without having any obstacles on the way. Before going to Kuala Lumpur, the capital of Malaysia, we all rested at a construction site which was near the forest in a small town. It was far from Kuala Lumpur. We slept there for one night, in huts inside the contruction site. I was scared because I heard that there were one or two raids in that area every year. In the morning, they sent us one by one to stay with our friends or family. We went to Kuala Lumpur by bus, accompanied by the broker.

When we arrived in Kuala Lumpur, we hadn't been able to bathe for three days and we had been wearing the same clothes for a long time, so we all smelled very bad. We didn't want to sit near other people, because we were afraid they would smell us.

I am always afraid because I am illegal. Right now I feel afraid too.

THE UN IS LIKE A MOTHER AND FATHER TO ME

After arriving at my friend's house, I got the chance to work in a cookie factory in Kuala Lumpur. After I'd been working there for one month,

I noticed someone who was observing the workers in the factory. I just thought he was a customer coming to buy cookies. After a while he left, and then about fourteen police and immigration officers surrounded our factory and came inside and asked the workers to sit down. We were all making cookies, but we were forced to sit. Then they asked for passports from us, which we didn't have. About fifteen of us got arrested—there were two Rakhine people including me, and the rest were other ethnic people from Burma.

The Malaysian authorities arrest many illegal migrants from Burma and other countries. If people from Indonesia or maybe countries in Africa are arrested, they have a chance of getting help from their government. But I never saw the Burmese government come to help the Burmese people.

I didn't have any legal documents but I showed them my Rakhine refugee card, which is issued here by the ARRC—the Arakan Refugee Relief Committee. But the police didn't accept it and they handcuffed every one of us and took us to the police station. The police took me to jail, and I stayed there for fifteen days. They fed us a small plastic bowl of rice twice a day, but it wasn't enough to eat.

We had to sleep on the cement floor in only our underwear, with no blanket. The place where we ate was practically the same place as the toilet. There was no drinking water, so we had to drink the same water that was used to flush the toilet.

All ages stayed together and there were between seven and ten people in each cell, depending on the size of the cell. I think I was unlucky because I was in a cell with two Indian men and two Chinese men who were all bigger than me. They had been arrested for an opium case. As soon as I entered the cell they slapped my face and were using crude language, asking me where I was from. Then they said things to me like, "I will fuck your ass." I was very afraid. The new people in jail have to do what they're told by the others. Because I was young, they told me to clean the toilets and give massages to the older people. If I didn't listen to them they would beat me. They did that for about one week.

I was finally able to contact the ARRC. It makes me feel strong that my community has an office like this. I was so happy when I found out about it, because I never dreamed there would be something like this for my community. The ARRC is helping Rakhine refugees in Malaysia, negotiating with the government, NGOs, and the UNHCR.[12] It's especially good for health problems; if we get sick, our office helps us go to the clinic and pay the cheapest price. The Rakhine people in Malaysia must have an ARRC ID card to live in their community center because there are often police arrests.

When a Rakhine person is arrested by the police, the ARRC can help them get released. But once the Arakanese person is taken to court or to jail, the ARRC can't help anymore. One of the ARRC leaders came to try to free me, but he couldn't do anything, so he contacted the UNHCR for me.

Some UNHCR officers came and interviewed me in jail. As soon as they saw me and my co-workers, they greeted us warmly and gave us encouragement. They told us not to be afraid, that we would be freed.

"We'll try as much as we can," they said. After they gave a report to the UNHCR about my arrest, a UNHCR officer came to the jail and gave me a paper saying I was registered as a "person of concern." Then I was freed. I was very, very happy.

The fifteen days I spent there were like hell for me, because I had never been in jail before. Once the UNHCR came, it was the happiest day of my life. Since I don't have many relatives here in Malaysia who can help me, it's like the UN is a mother and father to me. They're the only ones I can depend on.

Before I got registered for my UNHCR card, the UNHCR interviewed me again and again. I have done at least three interviews with the UNHCR, I think. Aside from those interviews, I had never told my

---

[12] The Office of the UN High Commissioner for Refugees is a United Nations organization with headquarters in Geneva, Switzerland. The primary mandate of UNHCR is the protection of refugees and finding solutions for refugees, including assisting in the voluntary repatriation of refugees to their home country, integration into the country of asylum, or resettling refugees to a third country.

life story—this is the first time I've explained my history. After I passed the interviews, I got my UNHCR registration card. In September 2009, I have to apply for resettlement to a third country—it's called RSD.[13] I can't go back to Burma; I would have to return to the military because I signed that paper.

IT'S LIKE WE ARE UNDER HOUSE ARREST

After I was released from jail, I joined the ARRC and started attending their school and living there. I've been at the ARRC for six months. They have an office where they provide English-speaking classes and computer classes—I take both classes. Even though I am lucky to live here, I still feel very unhappy. I was happier when I lived in Arakan State, because I could go outside. I was a citizen, so I felt very free. In Malaysia, we can live with our Rakhine community but we have no opportunity to go outside. It's like we are living under house arrest. Police are everywhere, and they always ask for money from refugees if they see them. The police don't even accept refugees' UNHCR cards.[14]

I don't feel like I can relax here because even though we're from the same community, I still feel like a stranger. I just came and asked for permission to live here. Sometimes I don't know what I should do—should I be doing something? Should I sweep the floor? I want the community leader to like me, but I don't know what the best thing to do is. Some of the other students here have parents, and even though they have hard jobs, they can support their children with some money. But I have no one, so it makes me upset.

---

[13] Refugee Status Determination is the process by which a government or UNHCR determines whether someone qualifies as a refugee. Refugee status is granted based on a strict set of criteria, and once granted, confers the right against forced return, as well as a host of other rights, including the right to obtain travel documents or the right to UNHCR's international protection.

[14] For more information about the refugee situation in Malaysia, please refer to pages 484-485 of appendix.

I've been able to talk to my mom twice since coming to Malaysia. First I had to send a message to a small town near my village. I told them my name, what village I come from, and then I asked them to send a message to my family to arrange a phone call. The message takes only one day to get to my family. The first time I spoke to my mother on the phone, I said, "Mother, do not worry for me. I live in the Arakan Refugee Relief Committee center, so I'm not alone. There are many refugees here. We are living together and studying together here at the refugee center." I felt both happy and sad to speak to her. Sometimes my words could not come out. I found it difficult to talk to her because I was feeling really choked up. I almost cried, but the tears did not come. The sadness came like waves in the sea.

THEY HAD NO POWER TO HELP US

I was arrested at a celebration for Aung San Suu Kyi's birthday, on June 19, 2009.[15]

The party was organized by the local branch of the National League for Democracy (NLD). I didn't know very much about Aung San Suu Kyi. I just knew that many people in Burma like her and support what she is doing. My friends called me to go with them, so I followed them because I had never been to a party like that and I wanted to have a new experience.

We had barely started the ceremony when a police car arrived. The police surrounded us and they had clubs—we were very surprised. They asked me to show my identity card, passport, or Malaysian citizenship documents. I showed them my UNHCR card and they said, "Okay, come to the police station. We'll talk about it later." So we got into the car and went to the police station.

---

[15] Daw Aung San Suu Kyi is the General Secretary of the National League for Democracy (NLD) and winner of the 1991 Nobel Peace Prize. Her party was the decisive winner of the 1990 election. For fifteen of the last twenty years she was held under house arrest. The pre-fix "Daw" is a Burmese title used as a sign of respect for older women. See appendix pages 455-456 for further detail.

At the station, the immigration officer was checking if our UNHCR cards were real or not. The officer took my card and wrote down my name and card number. They were also asking other people for passports and testing those. They made a record of our documents and then left without saying anything. We were left with the police officers, and they released some of the people who had passports. All of us who had UNHCR cards, as well as the refugees who had no cards, had to go to an interrogation camp in Petaling Jayar. They kept me at the camp for one week.

Later I understood that, according to Malaysian law, we didn't have permission to hold the celebration. We were supposed to apply for a permit first. We had relied on Anwar, the opposition party leader in Malaysia, to help us, but I think there were also problems between his party and the Malaysian government. The government arrested us to show that the opposition party had no power to help us.

After interrogation, we were sent to jail. Many journalists and cameramen came to the jail to take photos and interview us about our birthday celebration for Daw Aung San Suu Kyi. There were Rakhine, Karen, and Burman people in the jail, with five or six people in each cell. The journalists wanted to see what was happening in the jail and they took many photos—it was like we were actors. The thing I was most worried about was that the Burmese military would see my photos and see that I was involved in Aung San Suu Kyi's birthday celebration. I worried that the Malaysian government would send me back to Burma. If they did, the military would end my life in Burma.

After more than two weeks, the UNHCR came to release us from the jail.

IT'S BEEN MY DREAM

If Burma got democracy, or new leaders in the government, I would go back and live there happily because Arakan State is one of the most beautiful states in Burma. It has rivers, the sea, mountains, and a lot of greenery. Since I was young, around seven or eight years old, I used to go along with my father to the farm, where we grew rice paddies. Farming was very hard work, but I felt so happy there. I had no intention of leaving.

I don't think we can get democracy in Burma easily. Right now we have Than Shwe, the head of the military regime—he is getting old and will die soon. He will choose the next person, someone with the same opinions as him, to control the country after his death. I don't think we can get democracy in Burma by being peaceful and asking, like Aung San Suu Kyi does. She has been asking for it for so many years throughout her life. I believe the only way we can get democracy is if all the ethnic groups from Burma work together to fight the military regime with guns. I don't really know about the armies fighting the SPDC, but I've seen pictures of some of the ethnic armies fighting the SPDC on the border between Burma and India.

Most kids haven't experienced as many bad things as I have. I'd like to read stories about people who've had experiences like mine, so that I know about the people who've suffered the same way I have. I want to believe they've all become more experienced in life.

I don't want to take things quite so seriously now. Because I have experienced serious problems, I don't care about small problems and regular daily hardship. I want to study, because I'm at the age where I should be studying—it's the right time. There was a high school in my town in Burma, but I only attended up to sixth standard. Now that I have my UNHCR registration card, I might get the chance to go to a third country.[16] If I get that chance, I will try to study again there. I would like to learn a language like English, and some computer skills for my future.

I really like pop music, so I'd like to be a pop singer—it's been my dream since I was young. Whether that will come true or not, I don't know. But I believe that after I attend college, or get some higher

---

[16] Third-country resettlement refers to when a refugee is resettled in a country other then the one that they fled to or the one they are fleeing.

education, I will have more experience than now and I'll be able to make a decision about what I should be. But right now I want to be a singer, and I want to get an education so I can change my life.

PA TLUANG

30, former missionary

ETHNICITY: *Chin*

BIRTHPLACE: *Thantlang Township, Chin State, Burma*

INTERVIEWED IN: *Kuala Lumpur, Malaysia*

As a young man in Chin State, Pa Tluang always wanted to be a preacher. Over 90 percent of the Chin—an ethnic nationality group from western Burma near the Indian border—are Christian. Pa Tluang's family was against the idea of him becoming a missionary, as they feared the consequences in a country ruled by a repressive Buddhist regime. Despite the well-known hardships for missionaries and the threat of religious persecution of non-Buddhists in Burma, Pa Tluang followed his dreams and trained to be a missionary. He was sent on a mission to the neighboring Arakan State, where his plans were quickly and violently unraveled.[1]

During school, whenever our teacher asked about our ambitions, I would

---

[1] According to the UNHCR, there are 82,200 refugees from Burma living in Malaysia, of which approximately 38,700 are Chins. According to community refugee organizations in Malaysia, the actual numbers are higher than the UNHCR estimates; they estimate there are approximately 50,000 Chin refugees in Malaysia.

NOWHERE TO BE HOME

say I was interested in being a missionary and a preacher. It had been my ambition since childhood.

I was born on August 25, 1979, into a Christian family from the Lai tribe of Chin State.[2] Lai is one of the Chin tribes. I am from Thantlang Township, in the middle of Chin State, and my village is near the border of India and Burma. It is on the peak of a mountain and so the roads are difficult. The local people of my village are all Chin, and they are Christian—there is no other religion. The villagers belong to two separate churches: the Church of Jesus Christ—CJC—and the Baptist Church. We have some differences in doctrine—for example, the CJC members do not believe in original sin, while the Baptists do. I love Christianity because I believe all creatures have been created by God, as it says in the Bible, and I firmly believe in Him and all He has done.

When I was in the eighth standard in 1994, I was only about sixteen years old. I asked my mother to allow me to join a mission to convert non-believers called the CCOC—Chin for Christ in One Century.[3] The CCOC was formed as a follow-up program for American missionaries in Burma, to continue the work of the missionaries. I wanted to serve as a preacher because Jesus left a message to his disciples to go and preach around the world, but my mother disapproved of this and so I didn't join. None of my relatives agreed with the idea either, because so many people had already died during their time as missionaries.

Most of the members of the government are Buddhist, and I believe they hate Christians. They insist that the country should be one race, one religion. Christian believers are persecuted, tortured, and forced to leave their homes and family. People fear that they will be arrested and tortured when the soldiers come to their village and see preachers. That's why many villages, especially Buddhist ones, do not allow preachers to

---

[2] Lai is a subgroup of the Chin. The Chin are comprised of six major subgroups: Asho, Cho, Khuami (M'ro), Lai (Laimi), Mizo (Lushai), and Zomi.

[3] The CCOC was formed in the late 1970s with the goal of converting the entire Chin population to Christianity.

stay in their town. I heard that during the time of the CCOC, fourteen missionaries passed away—they were all killed by local people.

The next year, during my ninth standard, I told my mother that I would like to join a theological school instead of having a normal, formal education. When I told her this, she was so sad—she wanted me to finish high school instead. So I stayed in school, but by 1998, I was having too many financial problems to continue my studies. I started working as a ward servant in a hospital while still studying for my matriculation examination—I'd already failed three times. The matriculation exam is very important for all high school students in Burma, because it decides whether or not they can go to university or college. Since I could not pass my exam, I quit my job in 1999 and finally made the decision to work as a missionary for my career.

I couldn't tell my mother face to face that I was leaving to become a missionary, because I was worried that she might not agree to it again. So instead I left her a letter:

Mum, do not feel sad. I am going to join the mission. I believe you'll forgive me for disobeying you since you know it has been my ambition since childhood to be a missionary.

I WROTE MY THESIS ON CHIN CULTURE

In April of 1999, I went to Kachin State to start training and working as a missionary. I don't know the connection exactly, but the missionary project I worked with was supported by an organization in Washington, D.C. I stayed in Kachin State until the end of the year.

The following year, I went through southern Chin State and was a missionary in four different townships. During that time, I converted one villager. Most of my experiences at that time were difficult, and I encountered many problems. Some villages warmly welcomed me, but in other villages, they didn't allow any Christians to enter the village. The villagers would trick us and give us the wrong directions to another village. Sometimes we'd have to sleep in the forest because of that.

I thought I was poor at preaching, and so I decided to study deeper and pursue a bachelor's course in theology. I first studied for a LTh— License of Theology—for four years. When I finished the LTh course, I studied for another year at a seminary in Rangoon Division. There, I wrote my thesis on Chin culture. After a total of five years, I finally received my bachelor's degree in February 2006.

I HAD ALREADY PREPARED FOR THE WORST

When I had first decided to pursue missionary work full-time in 1999, that was also the last year of the CCOC. That year, the CCOC was changed into the CMC—the Centenary Mission for Christ.[4] As soon as I had heard this new program would be finished in 2013, I decided that I would join the CMC before it ended. So in 2006, when I was finally ready to mission again, I joined the CMC. The CMC told me that I would be sent to mission in Arakan State. While I was preparing to travel, I heard that a church deacon in Taungup Township in Arakan State had been beaten to death by the police, the village head, and a monk. But my heart was burning to join the mission, and I didn't care whether I died or not.

I talked about it with my mother. She didn't think that I should go, but I wanted to because within the state there are many K'Cho-Chin, a sub-ethnic group of Chin.[5] They are looked down on by the Rakhine, and I wanted to help them and lead them.[6] And besides, I had no choice—the CMC program did not allow me to choose the place, so I had to go to Arakan State.

---

[4] Centenary Mission for Christ (CMC), which ran from 2000 to 2003, focused on missionary work outside of Chin State and helped to further the goals of the former Chin for Christ in One Century (CCOC).

[5] K'Cho-Chin live predominantly in southern Chin State and in northern Arakan State. The women are traditionally distinguished by their tattooed faces.

[6] Rakhine is the original word for the majority Buddhist ethnic group that lives in Arakan State. Arakan is the name given by the British to describe both the state and the people. In this book, we use the term Arakanese for anyone from Arakan state and Rakhine to demarcate the ethnic group.

I had never met a Rakhine person before I went to Arakan State, but I'd heard about them through my friends—how they are rude and how they are bad. But I insisted on going to Arakan State. Before I left my village, I told my mother that if I died in Arakan State to please donate my thesis to the youth in my village. I thought that it would be nice to leave something to help them understand Christianity.

I left Rangoon on May 30, 2006, with some higher-ranking preachers who accompanied me to Taungup in Arakan State.[7] We arrived that night, and left again early the next morning for the village, arriving on June 1. The preachers told me nothing about what to expect for my mission, but I was already well prepared for the worst.

When we arrived in the village, one of the preachers who accompanied me introduced me to the villagers, who were K'Cho-Chin. I was warmly welcomed by the K'Cho-Chin elders and the village leaders. Most of the K'Cho-Chin villagers were Buddhists, and some were Christians who had been converted by missionaries. After they'd become Christian, they built up a community and shared the Bible with each other to improve their spiritual movement. They also sometimes managed a temporary space for all the missionaries.

Although I had been warmly welcomed, that first night the village youngsters tried to shoot me with slingshots, with dried clay as bullets. Then again on the second night, and the night after—they continued this for two months. They never hit me, but they tried. The other Christians watched out for me and they were always around me, so the youngsters couldn't hit me and they got angry. Then after two months, all the youngsters of the village surrounded my house and pelted it with stones. I was sleeping inside the house and was very scared by the noise. Fortunately it was not life-threatening. Because I had already prepared for the worst since I'd left, I never thought about turning back home.

---

[7] Taungup Township is a municipality in southern Arakan State.

At the start, I dared not introduce Christianity, and so I would ask the locals about their lifestyle and their culture, and we talked about that. There were Rakhine people residing twenty minutes away from the K'Cho-Chin village, and I always went there to buy vegetables, rice, and groceries. I helped them on their farms and also with building their houses from bamboo.

The Rakhine were wiser than I expected. They had favorable living standards, and in their morality, they were fine. Most of them, especially those studying in the school, were kind and communicated with me very well. Only the leaders of the villages disliked me and didn't communicate with me much, as they didn't accept missionaries in the region. The Rakhine have been influenced by Buddhism for many years, so they don't want to convert to Christianity.

Those first few months, I was so sad when I found out that they disliked Christianity. They strongly believed in Buddhist reincarnation, and they also thought of Christianity as a path to poverty, because those who are Christians are also very poor.

Before I arrived at the village, there was no one who had been baptized. Then on Christmas Eve 2007, I converted and baptized three K'Cho-Chin villagers. We were having a worship service, and then we went to a nearby stream for the baptism. Some Buddhist K'Cho-Chin villagers watched us in amazement because they had never seen this before. At around noon, Burmese soldiers and the VCC—Village Council Chairman—came to our village.[8] They knew that new converts were being baptized and they didn't like that. The SPDC soldiers would usually come to the village, but there was a problem that day specifically because of the baptism. The village is only one mile from the other Rakhine villages, and so the villagers were in the area and they had seen us. I expected that something might happen, so I had already told the new converts that if the soldiers asked them why they were being baptized

---

[8] Village Council Chairman is the head of the local Village Peace and Development Council (VPDC), which is in charge of local government under the Burmese state.

to reply that it was not because of me, but that it was their own choice to be baptized. The three new converts agreed.

I saw them coming. They were a big crowd, and they came and surrounded us. The Buddhist people were shouting that they would kill all the Christians. They beat me up in the church, and then the police, monks, and the chiefs of nearby Rakhine villages took me to the nearby VCC's house. I told them, "I will follow you as you wish," so they didn't need to tie me up or carry me there. Some leaders of the church followed me to the VCC's house, and some ran away. Both a police officer and a soldier interrogated me there.

They didn't do this with the other preachers because I was the only outsider. I was also the one who was responsible for that church. In the interrogation, they asked me why I'd come there. They asked me if I had any recommendation or permission letters from the government. I claimed that I used my own freedom to do this, but they replied that all the words they spoke were the law. They said they didn't like their children to be taught in Sunday school; they told me that there was no right to teach children who can't choose, who are under ten or eleven years old, because they don't know what is good and what is bad. Afterward they confiscated my identity card and told me not to have the worship service anymore. I was forced to sign a paper saying that I would also not teach Sunday school. I usually taught them *sol-fa*, staff notation and music, and they also stopped that program.[9] I was forbidden to have Christian worship service, and to celebrate Christmas.

On that same day, the Rakhine youth, other Rakhine people, soldiers, and the police cut down the houses of the Christians with saws. My own house was burned down. I saw who burned my house—the village chief was involved in that, and so were a monk, two Burman soldiers, and many police. The rest were about 150 local people who had followed them.

---

[9] *Sol-fa* is a reference to the *solfège* method of sight-singing by learning a particular syllable for each note of a musical scale (do-re-mi-fa-so-la-ti).

MY WIFE IS COURAGEOUS

When I first arrived in the K'Cho-Chin village, the year before the baptism incident, a Chin woman involved with the youth group came and greeted me. She often came to the church for choir rehearsal. Since we lived in the same village, she also took care of me when I got sick and that's how we got to know each other. Eventually we fell in love and we were engaged to get married by the pastor.

My wife and I married in a church in February 2007, in the K'Cho-Chin village. Both of our families and the leaders from the Lai Baptist Church in Rangoon approved, and the leaders arranged our marriage in the village. We celebrated, and served our guests tea and rice. It was a very pleasant time, especially because all the arrangements were made by our religious elders and by my wife's relatives. We played cassette tapes, and there was a choir. It went smoothly.

My wife is courageous and patient, and she is also very devoted to Christianity. Because of her efforts, her parents and her grandmother were also converted. In October 2008, we had our first child. Her name is Grace. I was not at home at the time my wife delivered because I was traveling and preaching, but I arrived home five days later. I was very happy because our baby was God's blessing.

Before I arrived, the K'Cho-Chin village had a primary school, but after some people converted to Christianity, the primary school was closed. The school was accused of allowing Christian children to study, and so the government ordered to shut it down. Afterward, the chief of the Rakhine village, who was also in charge of the K'Cho-Chin village, forbade the building of any school in the K'Cho-Chin village after they heard that some villagers had converted their faith. So my wife started informally teaching writing to some of the children in the village. One night, when she was teaching at our house, a monk and some Burmese soldiers came to the house along with the Rakhine village chief, and they started hitting her. Around that region, it is said that if someone is a Chin, he or she doesn't have the right to study past the fourth standard.

The non-Christian villagers and the Rakhine feared that the K'Cho-Chins would get ahead through education.

Chin people in Burma also face discrimination when it comes to traveling inside Burma and in the ability to have an ID card. Almost every town has a checkpoint on the outskirts of town, where people could be arrested or fined by Burmese military soldiers for not having an identity card while traveling out of town. So many people do not dare to travel.

I believe the Chin people in Arakan State living in the region have even more problems, because of both their religion and their ethnicity. The Chin people in this region get treated very unfairly. For example, one VCC can rule many villages, but only the Rakhine can serve as VCC and the Chin people pay more taxes and even need to get the VCC's permission to kill their own livestock. Furthermore, the Chin people who wanted to kill their livestock had to pay 6,000 kyats for permission from the chief.[10] If the livestock owner slaughters without paying, the chief would fine that person more than 6,000 kyats for breaching the rules. This policy was enacted only for the Chin people who had migrated to Arakan State. In this region, the Chin people had to pay whatever the government demanded from them, whenever it was demanded.

I WAS LEFT UNDOCUMENTED

There was a second incident. On Christmas Eve 2008, twenty new converts were baptized. Around fifty people, including people from surrounding villages, came for the Christmas and baptism celebrations. The next day, I was conducting a sermon at the church; the sermon was about when the prophets announced that Jesus would soon be born into the world. Suddenly another big crowd came. I could see them coming as I was preaching and I became afraid. I knew something was wrong. They

---

[10] Approximately US$6.

started shouting that they would kill every Christian and that they would destroy Christianity. They claimed only the Buddha as God.

Some church members started running right away. Then they started beating everybody. I was punched in my eye—even now my eye is still not good. Among the crowd, there were soldiers, police, village leaders and a monk. Apparently the local people had reported us. But even if there were people in the village who wanted to stop the crowd from attacking the Christians, no one dared to get involved in that incident. The soldiers give the orders and they are the law.

On that day, seventeen out of the twenty new Christian converts converted back to Buddhism. Only three were left. They had been called to the military camp in the village and interrogated about their baptism. A police officer and a few monks asked the new converts if they had been forced or persuaded by someone, and seventeen of them replied that they had been persuaded. They feared being tortured and having atrocities committed upon them by the Burmese military, so they abandoned their new beliefs. But the three that were left, their belief was unchanged, and they claimed that they themselves chose to be baptized. No one had pushed them. Luckily, they were not beaten up or punished, but the police officer said the three new converts would no longer be considered part of their tribe, and they would be removed from the list of registered villagers. Among them, one woman was forced by her family to leave her house.

My whole body hurt because I had been beaten so many times. I was arrested and taken to another village where I was beaten and tortured by them again. I prayed as my eye bled. I was taken to a lockup in the nearby Rakhine village, an unofficial detainment center for all perpetrators. Whenever the soldiers and policemen came they would beat my shins with a stick. They accused me of violating the law, because I had been told not to conduct any more gatherings, teach the children, or baptize any more converts. I was accused of violating all the "promises" that I'd given them during the first raid the year before.

My identity card had already been confiscated during the first raid, and in the second raid, they prepared to kill me because they accused me of being a supporter of the CNA—the Chin National Army.[11] They wanted to kill those in the CNA because it was formed by people who don't like the current military government. They accused me of having no identity card and said I must be from a rebel group. In reality, I don't think they really suspected that I had any connections to the CNA at all. They just accused me of this because they wanted a reason to detain me. These kinds of incidents, they never appear in court and they never make trial. The Burmese military does whatever it wishes. Even if we appeared in court, we would lose because we have no right to defend ourselves. Like I said, they are the law.

I was held in the jail for one week. I was so frightened. I prayed all the time. I was in fear because that group of Buddhist Rakhine people, soldiers, and police had killed one of the deacons after my arrival there. During my imprisonment, some fellow Christians came and told me that they'd received information that I would be killed because of my suspected connections with the CNA. When they confirmed that I was to be killed, I decided to break out of the jail.

It was early morning. No light. I was locked inside the room and I didn't know whether there was a guard outside or not. But I wanted to escape because I wanted to live for my God, to serve him longer. The lockup was not a normal lockup. It was in a village, near the river, and it was built from bamboo. I broke through the wooden window frame on the back side of the lockup and escaped. That night, I had to sleep in the jungle.

I was headed for my home village, and traveled from place to place with the help of my fellow Christians. I was lucky to have Christians in every village help take care of me. They arranged all my travels and sometimes they even accompanied me between villages. There was a nurse who treated my injuries at the request of my Christian friends. I recovered, thanks to her, but my eyesight is still blurry to this day. In order to avoid the army and police, I chose footpaths. If we heard that

[11] The Chin National Army (CNA) is the military wing of the Chin National Front (CNF). The CNA opposes Burma's military regime.

military troops had arrived in certain villages, I would wait and hide in another village until they'd left.

The journey took me three weeks. To be honest, I was scared to go back because of how the villagers might receive me. When I got home, I knew that my parents had already deleted my name from their family registration card, because it was near the time of the referendum. The constitutional referendum was held on May 10, 2008 by the military government of Myanmar in order to know whether the people of Burma approved of the new constitutional draft.[12] Those who were absent at the time of registration were all deleted. My mother said the representatives of the immigration department had come and told them to delete the names of family members who were not staying in the village at that time. Also those who were living in Malaysia and other foreign countries, their names are erased from their family registry. The government only held the referendum because they wanted to deceive the world into thinking that the people in Burma approved their constitution.

So when I got home, I was left undocumented. I could be arrested at any time and charged by the Burmese soldiers with whatever they wished. I felt unsafe in my home village and so I dared not stay. At that time, my wife and daughter were still in the K'Cho-Chin village, and so I needed to go back to them.

I went through the whole journey by foot again. It was faster than before but it still took more than two weeks to reach my wife. At the start of the journey, I was very scared about traveling alone and what would happen to me once I arrived and the K'Cho-Chin villagers saw me. But as I neared the village where I had missioned for three years, met my wife, and started to raise my child, I could not wait to get back. I stopped being afraid. I entered my wife's family farm at night to avoid the villagers and the army. My wife was crying, and she was amazed and overjoyed to see me—she thought I had died.

---

[12] For more on the 2008 constitution and referendum, see pages 469-470 of the appendix.

During my absence, the Burmese military threatened to arrest my wife if she couldn't bring me back to them. And so when I returned to the village, it was impossible for us to live there any longer. It was also impossible to go back to my home village. I stayed on our farm for three nights, and then in May we managed to flee to Malaysia.

STANDING ON THE EDGE OF DEATH

I first heard about Malaysia during my bachelor's studies in theology. I'd heard that there were many arrests and raids on Burmese people, so I knew going there that there would be many difficulties. But I decided to go because there are lots of Chins in Malaysia, and I hoped that they could help me and I could rely on them. In Thailand there are only a few Chins, but in Malaysia there were people I was familiar with—many of them were from my native village in Chin State.

My wife's relatives helped us with the initial expenses for leaving Burma. From our village in Arakan State, we walked on foot to a sea port, and from the port we went by boat to Thailand. From Thailand, we contacted a broker who was willing to help us get to Malaysia.[13]

The whole journey took around two weeks. It was very difficult. We were never sure whether we would live or die. We had no choice but to ride in any vehicles and boats arranged by the broker—there were eight people traveling in our group with the agent. In order to avoid being arrested by authorities, we would sometimes walk by foot across the deep jungles at night. We crossed forests, villages, and fields. We often slept in cars as there were no other places to sleep. We were with our newborn baby the whole time, but she is a very good child—even on our way to Malaysia, she never cried.

Although I was with my family, my trip to Malaysia was the hardest journey I'd ever faced, because I was leaving my home country. I'd never

---

[13] A broker is someone who is paid for assistance in illegally crossing a border.

imagined leaving Burma. Along the way, I would sometimes secretly cry by myself. We were in such despair, but we encouraged each other by reminding ourselves that God would bring us safely to Malaysia and grant us a better life there.

When we finally arrived in Malaysia, there were many more hardships than I'd imagined.

Making a livelihood has been especially hard here. After a week, I found work laying wires. But it was very difficult for me because my eyesight is now so poor, and my boss complained about this. I went to the hospital and I was told that I needed treatment for my eye, but it would be expensive, about 5,000 ringgits.[14] My employers often cheat me on my salary, and so I haven't been able to get treatment.

There is no organization that helps us, but many relatives and friends give us a hand. Still, we cannot even afford to pay our rent—sometimes we just have no money. If we feel sick we have no money to go to the hospital. During the day we eat rice, eggs, and vegetables. But sometimes I worry that we are starving. I feel like we're standing on the edge of death.

THEIR OWN GOD

Life in Malaysia isn't for me. I am always thinking about our survival, and how to earn money. I am always worried about our lives here. We cannot contact our parents because we don't have enough money. But I have nothing to talk to them about anyway, except the poverty and the difficulties we face here.

I don't want to stay in Malaysia. I don't like it here because there are so many raids. If I could get a UNHCR card, then it would be easier for me to find jobs and maybe to get asylum in another country. I don't know much about the UNHCR, but I do know that it helps those who fled their countries, and those who are helpless.

---

[14] Approximately US$1,500.

I do wish to become a preacher again. Even though I don't think Burma will gain democracy—since the generals want to keep their thrones—I would want to go back to Burma if there were any possible way, because we are facing a lot of difficulties here. I am absolutely in despair.

Right now I can't have any dreams or hopes for my future. I can only pray to God. I think God will punish those who attacked me. Even though they are not Christian, they have their own god, and their god may not be happy with them. I think God is teaching me through these difficulties and hardships, because the more difficulties and problems I have, the more I trust in God.

KO MG MG

30, fisherman
ETHNICITY: *Burman*
BIRTHPLACE: *Pegu Division, Burma*
INTERVIEWED IN: *Puchong, Malaysia*

Ko Mg Mg left Burma ten years ago in an effort to relieve his family's crippling economic situation, which was exacerbated by forced labor imposed by the Burmese military. When we met Ko Mg Mg in a small, refugee-initiated Burmese community office, his pneumonia had left him physically frail. He had spent the day of the interview writing down his story in a notebook, because he knew his pneumonia would limit his speaking ability. Ko Mg Mg was warm and candid while recounting his personal history of being caught in a cycle of trafficking and slave labor in the Southeast Asian fishing industry. He maintained a gentle smile during the many hours we spent together.

When I was nearly twenty years old, I decided I had to flee from Burma. The first reason I had to leave was because I was afraid to be taken for forced labor. The second reason I left is that I wanted to get a good job to support my parents.

    I don't remember exactly, but it has been over ten years since I've had contact with my family because of the many difficulties I've encountered. I don't know where my parents are now, or if they are alive or not. It makes me feel so sorry. My family does not know, but I am now an HIV patient.

In Thailand I did many jobs, but even though I tried so much, I didn't earn any money. At first I thought that after I got money I would send it to my parents, that I would contact them. But slowly, slowly, there was no contact because I didn't earn any money, and now it has been a very long time. HIV is a very serious disease, so now I cannot work and I cannot send money.

I feel very sad when I think about my mother and father, and when I remember their personalities. If I talk about them I will probably start crying, so—I'm so sorry. Every time I remember them, I miss them.

NO ONE CAN ESCAPE FROM THEM

I was born in the lower part of Burma, in an area called Pegu Division. I lived in a village. There are five members in my family—my father, my mother, my two younger brothers, and me. We rented our home—it was on the ground floor, and it was very small, with only one room. My father was a mechanic, and my mother was a housewife.

Where I come from there are many Burmese military camps, so the ethnic rebel groups are also there, always fighting with the government. This means that our village and nearby villages are battlefields for the ethnic groups and the Burmese soldiers. During battle times, we have to go with the military to carry their rations and their arms. This is called forced labor in our country. Some people also call it portering. The military comes to your village and says that you have to go to porter. If you don't go, they will arrest you. We faced this reality all the time; they never let us be free. They even took women, children and elders, so I was even afraid for my grandparents.

One of the ways that the military called us to do forced labor for them was to go to the village head's house, and then call the whole village with a loudspeaker. They would say, "Okay, the whole village must come to us for a meeting. We have something important to say to you." So the whole village would come, sit on the ground, and the soldiers would point their guns and say who had to go with them.

There are many types of forced labor. Sometimes the military came inside the village and called a few people to go with them to clean the whole military camp. You would stay morning to evening and they would release you within one day. That was okay. There was also short-term forced labor like cleaning the road.

If you couldn't go for short-term forced labor—maybe because you were very busy working or maybe because of sickness—you had to hire people to do the forced labor in your place. You had to pay 1,000 kyats to one person for one day.[1] At first I was paying people to go for me like that. After that, the military told us directly, "Okay, if you can't do the forced labor today, you have to give us 2,000 or 3,000 kyats." The military even made the head of the village do forced labor. No one can escape from them.

There was also longer-term forced labor. I never did this, but other people in the village did. The army would take people and make them walk in front of the soldiers on the way to the battlefield, so that the laborers would be the first to step on the landmines. If you're taken for this kind of forced labor, you have to run away.

When there were no battles, the government soldiers would come into our village and ask for food. We had to give them food at least once a month. They would take all the rice, some chickens and pigs, and sometimes even our cows.

MAYBE I WOULD FIND SOME GOOD JOBS

I went to school through sixth standard. At the start of seventh standard, I struggled. I dropped out when I was around twelve years old. First, I was not a good student, as I was playing with my friends. Second, I had

---

[1] Approximately US$1.

to think about my family's economic problems, and I had to help them.

After I dropped out of school, I stayed in my village for about eight years doing forced labor and many different kinds of jobs. I worked with my uncle, who's a truck driver—he carries goods from one city to another. I was staying at my mother's house, but sometimes my uncle and I would go for two or three days or longer. My uncle gave me a small salary, and with this money I helped my father and mother.

Because of the economic slow-down, and with only my father earning a real income, we sometimes didn't have enough to eat. I thought that if I left, maybe I would find some good jobs and escape from forced labor. I was really worried that I would soon be taken for long-term forced labor.

THAILAND

I decided to leave for Thailand with two friends from the village. I am sorry to say that most of my friends were in a similar economic situation. One of the people who left with me was my best friend Aung Soe. We went down to Dawei, in the lower part of Burma, and from there we went down to the southernmost city in Burma, called Kawthaung. We had to be careful, because the Burmese military doesn't allow people from one state to easily travel to another state or city.[2]

In Kawthaung we found brokers who agreed to send us to Thailand, but to cover the agent and travel fees we had to agree to work for them once we'd arrived. They took us in a small boat and sent us to a coastal city in southern Thailand. They gave us jobs on an illegal fishing boat, and we had to work for six months to pay back our broker fees.

In Thailand I had to spend most of my time out at sea. We always spent at least one month out. The longest time I was at sea at any one time was maybe three or four months.

---

[2] Travel restrictions are enforced by checkpoints throughout Burma, especially in areas where non-state armed groups are active.

There are many fishing boats, and the captains are usually from Thailand. Before going out to sea, the captain calls to the different workers, "Okay, how much money do you want?" And the advance may be a limited amount. You can ask for 500, 1,000, or 2,000 baht, and this would be your advance.[3]

When the bell started ringing in the morning, we had to wake up and get ready to work. On a typical day, when the first bell rang, we would put the nets in the water. After we got the fish out of the nets, we would put them in a box with ice, put the boxes inside the storeroom on the boat, and then we could rest a little. When the bell rang the next time, we had to go and put the net back in the water. We had to take the net out three, sometimes six times a day. If there were many fish in that area, we would have to do it again and again, two or three hours apart. By that time we would be very tired, and if we didn't do the job as they said, the captain would beat us. Sometimes we got body and eye injuries, and we could not carry on.

If someone gets sick, the way they're treated depends on the captain. If the captain is good, he'll give you some medication. But some captains killed workers—they dropped them into the sea if they were too sick to work. So many people have been thrown into the sea. One time, I saw a captain ask a Thai worker, "Do you know how to do this work?" The worker answered, "Oh no, at home I never did this kind of job." So the captain just threw him into the sea, and then the fishing boat went home. I think he must have died.

After three or four months, we got to go back to land again, but most of the time the employer didn't give us a full salary. After you come back from working on the fishing boat, almost all captains put a gun on one side and the money on another side—"Which one do you want?" That's how they threaten you.

If we choose money, they will give us so little that it's almost as if

---

[3] 500 baht is approximately US$15; 1,000 baht is approximately US$30; 2,000 baht is approximately US$60.

we didn't get any money at all. Some captains say, "Well, we didn't get so many fish, so we have no profit—so you cannot get a salary." If we asked them seriously for our money, we would get shot. I was paid, but never even half as much as they said they would. If they told me they would give me 5,000 baht, I might get less than 2,500 baht, something like that.[4]

If the captain was good, I was happy to work. But never mind how good a captain is, he'll never want to give the right salary and payment for hard work. Even though this made me unhappy, I was happy when we could go to land with even a little money.

WE NEVER BELIEVED THEY WOULD TRICK US

After a year, one of my friends said he wanted to go to Ranong, a city in Thailand that is very close to Burma—it's the city nearest to Kawthaung. My friend asked me to go with him, so I accompanied him along with Aung Soe and one other friend. The three of us went with my friend, but when we reached Ranong, we realized we were part of a trade. My friend had sold us to an illegal fishing boat.

On that fishing boat, my friends and I met with a lot of difficulties while working. We didn't get paid anything, and the employer beat us. After a very long time—maybe after over one year of working on the boats—we got a chance to flee. We rushed to the bus station and got tickets to a city called Pattani. We didn't know the place. When we got there, we met a Burmese couple who said they would help us find jobs. In Thailand there are many Burmese people facing difficulties like me; when we meet Burmese people like that, who've lived in Thailand for a long time and speak Thai fluently, we rely on them for help. The Burmese couple allowed us to sleep at their house for free for seven days. Then they told us that they didn't have any jobs available for three months, and that we had to pay them to stay with them during those three months.

---

[4] 5,000 baht is approximately US$160; 2,500 baht is approximately US$80.

After three months, a fishing boat came in and the Burmese couple handed us over to the captain. Because the boat was still on land, the captain said, "You three have to stay on the boat because on land there are many police." So he left us on that boat and they all disappeared. After the captain came back an hour later, we realized we'd been sold a second time.

We never believed that the Burmese couple would trick us, or bring us difficulty and trouble. They talked with the captain in Thai so we couldn't understand, and then they just left us there.

I couldn't do anything. I could only feel angry and disappointed. I didn't know anything about Thailand and I didn't know how to get help.

INDONESIA

After the Burmese people sold us to the fishing boat, we stayed on that boat for much longer than we'd ever experienced. The boat went to Indonesia—I never thought I would reach a country so far away.

It took us nearly two months to get there. All along the way we stopped and fished. Eventually we arrived at a small island in a very rural area, where there were no motorbikes and no cars.

We would go out to sea and come back to the island to sell the fish. We had to unload all the fish boxes from the ship and take them to the harbor, but the boxes were so heavy that we couldn't do it well. We were beaten so much because we couldn't do what they said.

One day, we heard that our captain had bought a gun, and we thought this meant he would shoot us the next time there was a problem. My friend Aung Soe and I discussed what we should do. Aung Soe and I had gone to Thailand from Burma together, and he was always by my side. He's my best friend because he has a good mind, and I can share everything with him. After discussing our situation, Aung Soe and I finally decided to run away together. While the boat was docked, the captain would sometimes be staying below deck on the fishing boat, or drinking, or having fun at the harbor, so that was the only chance for us to run away.

We jumped in the water and swam to a nearby island. I was so frightened that I was taking care to not make any sounds while swimming. After we swam to land, we slept there for one night. The next morning we walked through the island and reached a very small village. We were saved.

THEY BUY PEOPLE TO WORK FOR THEM

When we entered the village, the locals came to know that we were foreigners. They tried to ask me where we were from, but we didn't understand each other at first. Eventually we got a place to live there, in the household of a large family.

The family was very good to us. They fed us, gave us a place to sleep, and they gave us a job cutting fruit with them. I didn't want to stay very long there because it was so boring—every day was the same.

After three months, someone told Aung Soe and me that a fishing boat captain was coming to capture us. Aung Soe said that if a captain found a worker who'd run away, he would kill him. We were so afraid that we decided to flee from that village and try to get back to Thailand.

Aung Soe and I ran away together and found the Indonesian police. I explained our story—our problems with the captain, and how we wanted to go to Thailand. I trusted them, and thought that they would save us. They said they would help us to go to Thailand—but they were just pretending. They arrested us. Then two different captains came— one of them took me, and the other one took Aung Soe.

When I was staying on that island, I didn't realize that the illegal fishing boat would try to find me. But now I know that there are many illegal Thai fishing boats between the Indonesian islands that never give salaries—they only buy people to work for them. The captains contact the Indonesian police when many workers have fled from their boats because of the tiring work and the beatings. Then, when the police arrest a worker, they send him back to the Thai boat. Maybe they get money or they get something paid back to them.

After the police handed me over, the captain took me to his fishing boat, and some Thai people tied me by the hands with a rope. I had on handcuffs and I was hanging. The captain beat me with the back of a scalpel and left a scar on my head. I was so afraid that they would kill me, so I said, "I will do a good job for you." I was tied up all night, until the next morning.

The fishing boat went around the islands catching fish. There were Mon people working on the boat, and I became friends with one of them. The Mon are one of the ethnic groups from the southern part of Burma. When our boat eventually reached a village, my friend and I jumped from the boat and escaped. From there, I had to go from village to village for nearly two years, trying to survive.

Finally, after I had been traveling for a long time, I reached a village where there were many Thai fishing boats that had some Burmese workers. I went to one of the boats and I asked for a job at the port. I told them that I wanted a salary of maybe 100,000 Indonesian rupiah,[5] which is very little money for them. I worked at the port and they gave me the money I asked for, as well as eight or nine tins of oil.

I STARTED TO THINK THIS WAS FATE

At that time, my only wish was to go back to Thailand because I had no acquaintances in Indonesia. In Thailand I had some friends, some different kinds of jobs available. I'd get little things to survive on even if I didn't get a full salary or full payment. I worked at the port and every time a fishing boat came in, I told the boat workers my story, that I wanted to go back to Thailand. They pitied me, but they said I couldn't go with them because of many different inconveniences.

One day, after waiting for six months, a Thai fishing boat came in. As usual, I told my story to them. The captain told me that one of his friends had five Burmese workers, but that they didn't know how to work on a

---

[5] Approximately US$11.00

fishing boat. He asked me if I wanted to work there, so I said yes and he sent me to that boat. After a few months in that fishing boat, we reached Pattani, Thailand, and I went to the house of the Burmese couple who had sold me. I asked them to give me back my money, but they said they didn't have any.

At first I was angry at the people who'd sold me, betrayed me, lied to me. But after some time, I started to think that this was fate. In Buddhism, it's like karma, the consequences of the past life. Burmese people believe that if you are in trouble or face difficulties, it's because you did not do good things in your past life. I am relieved by this thought every time.

HE DIDN'T KNOW THAT I'D SEEN HIM

Once I was back in Thailand, I started to live in Pattani city again. I made some friends after a while, and one day one of them told me that he wanted me to do a job on a fishing boat with him. At that time, I was between jobs and had nothing to choose from, so I had to take another job on a fishing boat.

I joined him and we went to one of the boats, where there were four other Burmese workers. The captain was Thai and his name was Amon. One day, before going out to sea, my friends had a drink on the fishing boat. When Burmese drink beer, they talk too much, and then they fight, and then afterwards everyone is friends again. From the outside, people would think we were fighting, but we weren't really—Burmese people are just like that. So that day, we were being loud—we were talking and shouting a lot. I went to the back of the boat to get something to drink and Amon was nearby, drinking on a boat next to us. Because we were very loud and it sounded like we were fighting, Amon got very angry. He went over to my friends and he shot all four of them dead. He didn't know that I'd seen him.

I fled immediately from that fishing boat for Malaysia.

WE HAD A NONSTOP CONVERSATION

In 2007, I reached Malaysia. I traveled to Klang Valley and stayed with a friend. One day I went to a place on the coast with many fishing boats—I had to look for a job there because I only knew how to do that kind of work. There were many other Burmese people there, maybe from Arakan State.

I told them about my difficult situation, and they fed me—they cooked for me and we had a conversation. I told them I had a best friend called Aung Soe whom I had originally gone to Thailand with, and that we had been working together in the same fishing boat. Just as I was telling them my best friend's name, I saw that Aung Soe was walking down to the fishing boat—it was amazing! When we first saw each other, we told each other about what had happened since we separated. We had a nonstop conversation for nearly four hours!

A short time after I'd found Aung Soe again and started working on the boats, I started to feel seriously ill. I decided to go to the ACTS clinic just outside of Kuala Lampur.[6] When I went there, they said that they needed to check my blood; I didn't know at that time what they were looking for. But after they checked my blood, they said there was HIV in it.

IT IS A SORRY SITUATION

When I found out that I had HIV, I was very frightened and disappointed. I knew the disease was very serious and couldn't be cured—it could only lead to death. I got seriously sick; I became thin and so tired. I went back to the ACTS clinic and was then hospitalized.

In Malaysia, they don't recognize refugees and asylum seekers. They see us as illegal migrants. For Malaysian citizens, it's very cheap to get medication and health care. If you're a foreign citizen and you have a permit, it is possible to get care, but for refugees and asylum seekers, we

---

[6] ACTS is a faith-based organization that serves refugees and asylum seekers in Malyasia. The organization has two locations as well as mobile health units.

can't get any medication at state clinics and hospitals if we don't have UNHCR documents.

HIV and tuberculosis medicines are very expensive in this city—only hospitals and medical centers have them, and you can't get them freely. The hospital asks if you have a UNHCR document, and if you have it, then you can be hospitalized. If we can show it, we pay the same medical costs as local people. But it does not benefit us much, because we still do not have enough money to pay.

At the clinic, they tried to get the UNHCR to help me. In 2008, I went to the UNHCR to try to get refugee status and a UNHCR document. After I had tried so hard, they gave me a document saying that I was under consideration to be registered as a refugee—not a real refugee card. So it is not a UNHCR card, but with this document we can go to the hospital.

I got that document in June, and the day they gave it to me they referred me to a community home for people with HIV. The UNHCR called them, and they brought me to their center. The center is very small. They provide HIV patients with some antiretroviral drugs, so I stay there. The community home provides many rooms for HIV patients to stay in and rehabilitate, while the community center offers some classes and activities. Because we don't have any money to pay, they allow us to stay for free.

I would like to say something, but it is very difficult to say. The center is not very good for those of us who are not Malaysian citizens because they mostly focus on Malaysian people—those with HIV and drug addictions. They help people from Burma because of the cooperation of the UNHCR and many ethnic organizations, but they make us do things like cleaning—if a patient can walk or stand, then he has to clean. At times it's no problem, but once I was so seriously sick that I couldn't even eat, I couldn't walk. I was so disappointed because they still made me clean. For meals, they provide us with leftover food that is past the expiration date and then maybe some bread. It is a sorry situation for the refugees.

I know that one of the refugee organizations provides the community home with an amount of money for each HIV patient. Many churches and many organizations also donate to them. We see every day that they provide the clothes, food, and materials, but none of it goes to the patients—not to Malaysians, Chinese, or Burmese.

Later on, after many interviews about my RSD—refugee status determination— the UNHCR officer said that I was not eligible for refugee status.[7] I didn't receive refugee status because I answered a question wrong at the last interview. The UNHCR officer had asked me, "Can you go back to Burma or not?" At that time, because of the interpreter, I misunderstood that as "Do you *want* to go to Burma or not?" So I explained to him that I did want to go back. But what I didn't say was that I couldn't go back because of the forced labor, and that the military would look for me.

The UNHCR was not able to provide me with a Burman interpreter. Sometimes ethnic minorities don't understand Burmese language very well, so they don't understand what we say and they could interpret it in a certain way that means Burman people might be refused asylum or refugee status.

The officer thought I said I could go back to Burma. He said that if you could go back to Burma, you weren't eligible for refugee status. They gave me a rejection document, but the interpreter said to me, "You can write an appeal letter within one month." So I found an organization to write the appeal letter for me, but when I sent the letter to the UNHCR, they told me my letter was too late. It was over.

Because I am staying with other refugees, I know many stories like mine. Burman people are facing difficulties with interpreters. A lot of people say that Burman people are not refugees. They think that because most of the military is Burman and because Burmans are Buddhist, that

---

[7] Refugee Status Determination refers to a title given by government or UNHCR officials to individuals seeking asylum or international refugee status. The status is granted based on a strict set of criteria, and once granted, confers the right against forced return, as well as a host of other rights like the right to obtain travel documents or the right to UNHCR's international protection, relocation, or assistance as a refugee. See appendix pages 482-483 for further detail.

NOWHERE TO BE HOME

the military government never persecutes us—it is not true. For example, Buddhist Burman monks suffered in the 2007 uprising.

The military has only one philosophy: to maintain their power. They kill without discrimination. If you are Burman, they can still kill you, just like that.

I WANT FREEDOM

I can't do any job now because of pneumonia—if I speak too much or walk for a short distance, I feel so tired. I have had pneumonia in the lower airway many times. It's very closely related to asthma. I take two tablets a day of the HIV drug—that's sixty tablets a month.

I didn't tell any of my acquaintances or my friends that I have the disease. One or two of my friends called me to visit their homes, but I told them I couldn't go—I gave some excuse. I feel so much shame and I don't want them to worry for me. Since I got HIV, I have had no contact with Aung Soe, my best friend. He doesn't know that I have HIV. We haven't been in contact since last year, I think.

I don't want to go back to Burma, because if I went back I would have to tell my parents that I have the disease. I feel so much shame— I don't want them to see that I have HIV.

I now regret and grieve so much. Before, when I had a bit of money, I used to find happiness with beer, girls, that kind of thing. Maybe that's how I got the disease. I really have so much regret.

Because I've had so many bad experiences in my life, I am not sure how to decide if a person can be trusted or not. A friend is someone who, even if they've got only one thing, they will give it to their friend. A friend never takes. So I don't know who to trust anymore.

I want to feed and support my family before they die. I want to find them. I'm always thinking about how to support them; it's in my mind every day. Now, my biggest desire is to be cured, so I can support my parents. I want freedom from the disease.

TAN HTAY

23, refugee, detainee

ETHNICITY: *Karenni*

BIRTHPLACE: *Karenni State, Burma*

INTERVIEWED IN: *Kuala Lumpur, Malaysia*

We met Tan Htay the day after he was released from a detention center in Malaysia. Tan Htay fled Burma after SPDC soldiers confiscated his family's land, shot and killed his uncle, and took Tan Htay to do forced labor at their military camp. Although he was able to run away from the SPDC camp and escape over the border to Thailand, he was accused of being a Karenni Army rebel and found himself unable to return to his country. Tan Htay decided to migrate to Malaysia, where he knew some friends from his village were living; he soon became one of more than 83,000 (according to the UNHCR-Malaysia) officially registered Burmese refugees in Malaysia. The Malaysian government actively employs three branches of its enforcement agencies to arrest and detain illegal immigrants. There are also no refugee camps allowed in Malaysia. According to the UNCHR, there are some 10,000 additional Burmese refugees in Malaysia still unregistered, but others put the number much higher. These men and women survive on the margins as illegal migrant workers, without any protection.

I was arrested in April 2009.

At the time of my arrest, I was working in a restaurant in Kuala Lumpur, washing dishes. There were about thirty Burmese people working there. When the police and immigration officers came, they asked us to sit down in a line and show our passports—all of the customers could see what was happening. They checked our passports with a machine. Out of thirty of us, only three, including me, held a UNCHR card.

I had been registered by the UNCHR in August 2008. When I arrived in Malaysia, a friend who worked with a Karenni community organization asked me whether I had any documents to stay in Malaysia. Since I didn't, he promised to help me get a UNCHR card. I gave him all my personal details, and he helped me start the process of applying for refugee status with the UNHCR. After my friend submitted my information, I was called by the UNHCR to undergo an interview. When I finally got my UNHCR refugee card after undergoing several interviews about why I left Burma, they told me to contact their office whenever I was sick or if I got arrested by the police and immigration.

When the police raided the restaurant, the other two UNCHR document holders and I were separated from the other Burmese people under arrest. They took the UNCHR cards and put them in a small bag. The immigration officials told us that UNCHR cardholders are not allowed to work. We replied, "If we don't work, how can we get food to eat?" Then we were all handcuffed, and everyone was told to get in the vans. The immigration officials told us that they were taking us to the detention camp.

That night, I was taken to the Putrajaya Immigration Office. They checked my name and address and I was put in a cell for transfer to the KL camp.[1] We arrived at the KL detention camp at 5:30 a.m.

There were only about 100 people held in each cell block. Some of

---

[1] KL Camp is the Kuala Lumpur International Airport Immigration Detention Center. The KLIA Immigration Detention Center has a capacity of 600 detainees but usually holds an average of 1,200 prisoners at one time, with many refugees detained for months at a time.

the Burmese in that camp had UNHCR cards or Burmese passports, but some had nothing.

It was like prison there. We were not allowed to leave our building. There were four toilets there, but they didn't have any walls or doors. The toilets were very disgusting because of a lack of water. Drinking water and bathing water were the same—as a result, many detainees suffered from diseases.

Three or four days after we were arrested, some officers came and took us to be interrogated. If we couldn't answer their questions due to language difficulties, they hit our faces with books.

Two weeks after the interrogation, we had to go to our court trial, where the immigration officials submitted our paperwork to the judge. Eventually, after four weeks in the KL camp, they sent the verdict. We had to sign our verdicts, but I didn't understand it when I signed it. I only learned what it said later, from other people who lived there. It said that if you were a UNCHR card holder, you had to stay in the camp until the UNCHR came to get you. If you held a Burmese passport or fake passport, you would be deported.

After I signed my verdict, I was given a green piece of paper that said I had already undergone a trial. Document holders and illegal migrants were separated, and I was sent to Semenyih camp. I was lucky I got to move to Semenyih camp because I had a UNHCR card; otherwise, I would have gone to prison.

THEIR MINDS ARE AFFECTED

The Semenyih camp is located in Kajang, a township in Selangor State. In the camp, there are five cell blocks that hold about 1,500 people in total. Each block holds 300 people and one of the five blocks was for women. Semenyih camp was bigger than KL camp, and it accommodated more detainees. Also, the people detained there come from different countries, including India, Indonesia, Bangladesh, and Vietnam. In my block there were about 160 Burmese people.

Every morning while I was at Semenyih camp, I was told to clean the floor. We were not fed well—for example, on Tuesdays and Fridays we were given chicken curry as breakfast, but the chicken had already been left in the fridge for a long time and was rotten and smelly. The women and children were also not fed sufficiently.

In each block there were fewer than ten toilets, without walls or doors. There were two tanks with a little bit of water. The water was like in the KL camp—used both for drinking and bathing—and was located by the toilets.

The opportunities to see a doctor were very limited; I think there was an NGO that diagnosed the detainees and provided medicine. Only ten people from one block were allowed to visit the clinic at a time, though there were always more than ten people who were suffering from sickness. People were exposed to diseases, especially skin disease, because the place was not hygienic. Quite a lot of people suffered.

One time, twelve people from our cell block wanted to go to the clinic, but the number allowed was only ten. Two of the sick people were taken to a room and punched by the guards instead of being sent to the clinic. Their eyes were bruised and their legs were burned with lit cigarettes. The rest of us were not happy that they tortured the detainees like this, so we refused to squat with our bottom up in the air like we usually had to do five times a day.

We had to stay in a squatting position five times a day while they checked the cell blocks. Each time took at least an hour and half because they counted all of the detainees. If we asked questions while they were interrogating us, they kicked us. We frequently faced torture in the camp—sometimes we were beaten by the officials. They reminded me of the soldiers in Burma.

Police and immigration interrogators wearing yellow helmets searched for cell phones and cigarettes in our cells two or three times a week. Everyone had to stand outside in the heat. If the police found any phones, or if they found we'd made contact with people from outside, they beat us seriously. If they found anything forbidden, the owner was taken upstairs and beaten at least ten times with a pipe on the soles of his feet. One time, a friend of mine who was about twenty-one years old was ordered by the interrogators to look for phones in a rubbish bin where people also frequently spat. He refused, so he was seriously beaten right in front of us. His mouth and arms were wounded and bleeding.

If the police found any cigarettes or cheroots, they would call the owners over and beat them.[2] Then they would force the individuals who'd been caught to stay with the insane people who were all kept together in one cell. There were six people who had gone mad during their time in detention. They got no medical treatment.

One day the interrogators found out that my friend and I smoked. They took us upstairs and then beat and kicked my friend until his feet were bleeding. They even forced me to hit my friend's face. Then they beat the soles of my feet ten times with pipes. I was also forced to sleep with the insane people for one night.

I was in the Semenyih camp for two and half months. The UNHCR tried to take all the Burmese people—there were nearly 650—out from the detention camp, but it is more difficult for them to help those who don't have their UNHCR card. In our group there were only about thirty Burmese people registered by the UNCHR. Yesterday I was finally released.

There are more Burmese people than any other nationality at the Semenyih Camp. In general, there are more Burmese in the camps now because of the continuous arrest of Burmese people in Malaysia and the fact that the Malaysian authorities are no longer deporting Burmese to Thailand, as they did before.[3] The Burmese have been staying at the camps for months, and the number of detainees continues to rise.[4]

---

[2] A cheroot is a cheap form of cigar made popular by the British during colonization.

[3] In part as a reaction to a U.S. State Department report on trafficking in Malaysia, the Malaysian government has reduced the number of deportations; in turn, the detention centers have become more crowded as people are detained for longer periods of time.

[4] See appendix pages 484-485 for more information about the refugee and detention situation in Malaysia.

Those Burmese people in my block who had no UNHCR registration were sent to another detention camp. The Burmese government said that it would not help the Burmese people in the camp unless they held Burmese passports. People of other nationalities got help from their embassies. Some people did get help from the Burmese embassy because they found ways to pay them, and some other people paid the Malaysian immigration officers and got released.

A BETTER FUTURE

Now I am released, so I feel a little happy. I am going take a rest for a week and look for a job again.

I am married, and I don't want to be illegal here in this country anymore. It is not safe to stay here, so I want to resettle to another country where I can study. Now I don't have any children, but I want to have two—a boy and a girl—and I want to see my them become educated people, like doctors. I want them to have a better future.

BANGLADESH

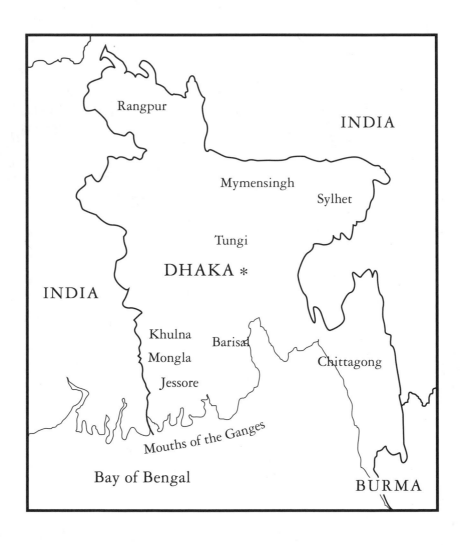

FATIMA

30, refugee

ETHNICITY: *Rohingya*

BIRTHPLACE: *Maungdaw Township, Arakan State, Burma*

INTERVIEWED IN: *Kutupalong makeshift camp, Bangladesh*

We met Fatima one afternoon in the dense and sprawling Kutupalong makeshift refugee camp, near Cox's Bazar, Bangladesh, where she and over 20,000 other stateless Rohingya refugees have made a settlement next door to an official refugee camp. We sat with her inside her mud home, speaking intensely for hours. She kneeled during the five hours of our interview, smiling sweetly and, at times, gently crying while recounting the many trials she experienced in Burma and since her exile in Bangladesh. A dozen or more of Fatima's neighbors passed by, listening and nodding as Fatima described the fear and daily harassment she encountered as a Muslim woman in Burma.[1] Fatima now lives in Bangladesh with her husband. Unregistered as a refugee by the UNHCR, she, along with many of the camp's

---

[1] According to a 2009 report from Human Rights Watch titled "Perilous Plight: Burma's Rohingya Take to the Sea": "The Rohingya are descended from a mix of Arakanese Buddhists, Chittagonian Bengalis, and Arabic sea traders... Centuries of coexistence with Arakanese Buddhists was bifurcated by British colonialism, when the boundaries of India and Burma were demarcated. As a result, the Rohingya became a people caught between states, with the majority situated in newly independent Burma in 1948."

inhabitants, are denied official protection and left without sufficient food or other basic resources.[2] Limited employment options, coupled with the risk of arrest and deportation, leave Fatima and her husband with an uncertain future.

I was born in central Maungdaw District, in Arakan State. In my village there were about 200 Muslims—once upon a time there were a lot more, but so many have fled. There was a NaSaKa base only a ten-minute walk away, with three or four hundred people. I saw the NaSaKa every day.[3]

The NaSaKa has Buddhist Rakhine people and all the ethnicities except Muslims. They occupied my village and made a camp that was bigger than the village itself. Their families stayed there as well, with people of all ages—old, young, everything.

As Rohingya Muslims, we had to inform the NaSaKa about everything, because they say to us, "You are not local people in this country. You are a guest, so you have to do everything that we say." The NaSaKa says that because Burma is not a country of Muslims—it's a country of Buddhists.[4]

We had to pay the NaSaKa. When our family grew in size, we needed to build another house, and we had to pay the NaSaKa for this. If I made a chicken farm, I needed to pay money to the NaSaKa. If our family had four or five chickens, we had to give one to them. If anybody died, we also had to give money. If a woman got pregnant, she would have to inform the NaSaKa, and then she would have to pay after she'd given birth, to register the newborn.

Some of my women neighbors were attacked by the NaSaKa—they

---

[2] Kutupalong's makeshift camp population was over 30,000 in early 2010, but according to the Arakan Project it is now reduced to under 30,000.

[3] The NaSaKa, an acronym for "Nay-Sat Kut-kwey Ye," is a border task force established in 1992 under the direct command of the SPDC. They are frequently cited for human rights violations against the Rohingya.

[4] For more on the Rohingya's official status in Burma, see the section "Rohingya: A Stateless People," pages 478-481 of the appendix.

were arrested and then raped in detention. When the families came to know of this, they had to go to the NaSaKa base and give some money for the woman to be released. If a family was not able to give enough money, the NaSaKa would keep the woman, and the family had to beg the people in the village for help. Once they raised the money, they could return to the NaSaKa and pay for the woman to be released.

Many women who come to Bangladesh from Burma have been raped. I think that many of the Muslim women in this camp, for example, have been raped. If people come to know that a woman was raped, nobody is interested in marrying her; it will be difficult for her.

Women are victims of torture. For this reason, we look for another Muslim country; that is why we are here in Bangladesh today. I was also a victim.

HE NEEDED NOTHING BUT PRAYER

My five siblings and I never went to school when we were young. I had three sisters and two brothers; I was the third born. I would have liked to go to school, but my family didn't have enough money for the school fees, even though it cost very little—1,500 kyats for one student.[5]

My father was a day laborer, cultivating rice. He was religious—he needed nothing but prayer. My father would gather the people and tell them to go to the mosque for prayer time. One time, while my father was reciting the Koran, the army came and took him and some other people for forced labor—they forced the people to build embankments on a shrimp farm north of our village. The army kept my father for three days—during that time my family thought about him a lot, and we cried.

I only remember that one time, but I think they took him other times too. The army would come to our family and demand a person for

---

[5] Approximately US$1.50.

forced work, so my father would try to find someone to go in his place. If my father wasn't able to find someone, then my father went himself.

THEY ARE DRUNK AND CRAZY

I was around twelve when my father passed away. He died of diarrhea in 1990 or 1991. At the time, my mother was pregnant with my little sister. When my father was sick, we went to the village doctor—he was our neighbor, so it only took five or six minutes to get him. When the doctor came to our house, he just took my father's temperature and gave injections. For just one day my father was passing stool, and then at midnight he passed away. He was buried the next day.

To honor our father in the Islamic tradition, our neighbors made a *janazah*, and they kept the dead body in front of them.[6] We started crying, and finally the people buried him. We spent one day praying.

Because my father was gone, I was obliged to work. The standard duty of men was to earn something for our family, but because my father was no more, my mother sold cakes to earn money. Since the very beginning, my mother has done a lot of things for us, and since my father died, she's always supported me. My mother is very affectionate toward me, but she isn't educated—she just knows how to read the Koran.

My mother made the cakes at home. We made two kinds of cake because there are two types of rice. She used flour and some sugar and coconut in the first kind. The other kind she would make is called winter cake. She collected green rice and threw it in to make the cakes—it was tasty. One cake cost 50 kyats, which was expensive at the time. The other one cost 25 kyats. In one day we would make 500 kyats.[7] My mother gave cakes to me and my two brothers, and then we would go

---

[6] The *salat-l-janazah* is the Muslim funeral prayer. The community gatherers and the *imam* (prayer leader) is present.

[7] 50 kyats is approximately US$0.05; 25 kyats is approximately US$0.025. 500 kyats is approximately US$0.50.

to the market to sell them. We didn't have any entertainment. We lived a miserable life.

When walking down the street, I always felt stressed about the Na-SaKa, like they could come and attack me. They are drunk and crazy—I was always thinking like this. More than once, the NaSaKa took everything that I had—all of my money and all of the cakes I was selling. I didn't say anything to them. They took my things like that eight or ten other times. Whenever they took my things, I had to start begging from people to survive. I didn't get money, but I would get a little bit of rice from other Muslims.

WE NEVER GOT MY LITTLE SISTER BACK

My little sister's disappearance happened in my village. She was carrying rice to the market alone when the NaTaLa villagers came in a group and snatched her.[8] I was twenty-two, and my sister was eleven or twelve years old. There were a lot of people around when the NaTaLa villagers took her, but they just sat there.

The NaTaLa villagers were sent by the Burmese government from other areas of Burma to live in our village. Some of them dress like the NaSaKa, and people are very scared of them. The government sent them to torture the Rohingya people.

My family members and I rushed to the NaTaLa village to demand our sister after some villagers told us what happened, but the NaTaLa villagers beat us. They just said, "Go away from here."

There is no way to get justice. My mother brought the matter to the local VPDC chairman, but in vain.[9] If you go to the NaSaKa, they say,

---

[8] NaTaLa is the acronym for the Ministry for Development of Border Areas and National Races. Model villages created by the SPDC in Arakan State are built through the confiscation of Rohingya lands and with Rohingya forced labor, with the intention of further displacing Rohingya communities.

[9] The Village Peace and Development Council (VPDC) is in charge of local government under the Burmese state.

"The NaTaLa villagers are sent here by the government, so we can't do anything against them." We never got my little sister back and I miss her. We have lost her. We think she might have been killed.

IT WAS A GOOD TIME IN MY LIFE

When I was around twenty-three years old, I got married. My husband's name is Rashid. He lived near our village, and I knew him before we married because he is my cousin. So his family and my family, they talked about our marriage and they agreed with each other.

I was excited to get married, but I was scared about the NaSaKa.

The government doesn't allow an Islamic wedding ceremony unless you pay them a lot of money and obtain official permission first.[10] If a Rohingya wishes to get married, they have to submit a request to the government and they have to pay money, and then the NaSaKa gives permission papers for marriage. After girls turn eighteen, they have to go to the NaSaKa and say they want to be married. Then the NaSaKa demands bribes with the marriage application. If you have some family members living abroad they will send you some money and then you give the money to the NaSaKa, and the NaSaKa will give the papers. Whoever can pay the money will be able to marry.

We have some people in our own community who are informers. They know things in our village and they collect information for the NaSaKa. In the evenings, they enter the NaSaKa camp and they tell everything that they saw inside the village. For example, if one lady is married but she was not allowed to be married, the informer will go and tell the NaSaKa. Then NaSaKa will go to your home and beat you and arrest you. If the NaSaKa enters someone's home, the neighbors don't say

---

[10] A local decree in northern Arakan State mandates that Muslims must obtain official permission to marry. Rohingyas must go though what the Inter Press Service refers to as a "veritable obstacle course" to obtain a government marriage certificate. For more on this, see the "The Rohingya: Stateless People" section of the appendix, pages 478-481.

anything—they just sit. They're clearly scared. If you can't pay the bribe for your release, you can go to jail.

When my family and Rashid's family had agreed about our marriage, my mother and my uncles went to talk to the VPDC chairman. He assured them that he would arrange everything with the NaSaKa officer in charge to obtain the marriage authorization. Later, the VPDC chairman demanded money from my mother to bribe the NaSaKa officer. The VPDC chairman also took my photograph to submit with the application. The chairman prepared the rest of the necessary documents to be deposited at the NaSaKa camp. The chairman did not take all the money at one time; my mother paid him in installments, as the chairman kept asking for more money.

I don't know how much money my mother paid for the application, but it was a lot. She initially sold one bullock and paid the money from the sale to the VPDC chairman; then she sold our second bullock and again paid the money to the chairman. One day the chairman delivered a paper and told us it was the marriage permission. Then my mother sold her last bullock and used part of the profit to pay the chairman; she gave the rest to my uncle so that he could buy the dowry items for the marriage: a mat, a pair of pillows, a trunk to keep my clothes in, and also some new clothes for me and for Rashid. My mother also bought three or four kilograms of beef from the market so that she could offer food to the guests at the wedding. I was scared about the NaSaKa, but I felt very excited about the ceremony.

Finally, we got married to each other. I was about twenty-three years old; my husband was about twenty-two. I don't remember the exact year. Both families invited their relatives and provided food for the ceremony, which lasted one day. About twenty people came to each set of in-laws' homes. Our relatives and neighbors came to our homes and brought ornaments, earrings, nose rings, and necklaces. They made me wear them and I was totally dressed up. I was obliged to wear the veil as well. We then called the *maulvi*, who leads the mosque, to perform the religious marriage ritual. He recited some verses of the Koran, and then finally we were married.[11] After the wedding, my husband's family came to take me. I was in a good, happy mood. It was a good time in my life.

MY LIFE WAS ALWAYS AT HOME

After I was married, I went to my husband's house and started leading my life over there. I lived with his extended family, ten or twelve people. I got up very early in the morning to say my prayers and then start cooking. My main work was only cooking, nothing else. I would cook fish and rice, and then sometimes I would go out to fetch water. My life was always at home—because I was married, I had to stay at home according to Muslim law. My husband and his father would go out to chop wood, and we survived on their very small salary.

For me to be a good Muslim, I need to sit five times a day in prayer. I need to recite the Koran and read from the Kalimah, which is from the Koran.[12] Muslim women are not allowed to go to the mosque, so they say their prayers at home.

From the time when we are twelve, thirteen, or fourteen, we are obliged to wear the veil. When I wore the veil for the first time, I just stumbled. That was at first, but later I got used to it. In Burma, we must take the veil and an umbrella when we leave the house.[13] It is a big training. It took me about two years to get used to it.

People say that if you don't wear the veil, you are not a good Muslim woman. If you want to keep with your religion, it is very important that you wear it.

---

[11] *Maulvi* is an honorific title given to Sunni Muslim scholars.

[12] Kalimah literally translates as "the word." Affirmation of the Kalimah is the first of the five pillars of Islam. One commits through reciting the phrase, "There is no god but Allah, and Mohammad is his prophet."

[13] It is common in Burma for men and women to use an umbrella to shield themselves from the sun.

IF YOU WANT CHILDREN,
WE'D BETTER LEAVE THE COUNTRY

About six months after Rashid and I were married, I became pregnant. Just at the time when I found out I was pregnant, some neighbors who were also married compared my marriage permission paper with theirs. We realized that mine was not genuine—my family had been cheated. My mother went many times to visit the VPDC chairman, but he simply said the NaSaKa officer had been transferred, so we had to reapply for permission. My mother had already sold everything, so she had no money left to apply for permission again.

I heard that many people got punished by the NaSaKa because of unofficial marriage, and that the NaSaKa summoned women to their camp when they suspected they were illegally married—the proof was usually pregnancy or the birth of a child. I had no other option except an abortion. I was already four months pregnant when my neighbor helped me and brought a root from a local midwife.[14] I paid the midwife for her help.

I was scared—some women had died trying to have abortions. But the root worked within one night and my pregnancy was aborted. I was unable to walk and unable to eat. I felt guilty, and then I started experiencing problems. Everything, even breathing, made my whole body very weak and vulnerable. It was terrible, really horrible.

In my culture it's a big expectation for women to have children. This was supposed to be my first child, but in Burma I just couldn't afford to have any children. It was horrible for me. I did it because I was scared about the NaSaKa. If the NaSaKa comes to know that you're pregnant, they will come and demand money, because then they know that you are married without their official permission—then my

---

[14] According to the Arakan Project, abortions are usually performed by local midwives using a stick or a concoction of herbs. The tablets commonly used by Rohingya women for their abortions are smuggled from Bangladesh to Burma.

NOWHERE TO BE HOME

husband could be sent to jail. They will torture you. So I was obliged to abort the child.

According to my religion, it is not right to abort children—it's a big sin. I think that according to the Buddhists, it's also not good. The NaSaKa knows about the abortions, so why do they behave as they do? I don't know exactly; I don't know what is in their hearts. The NaSaKa are Burmese people, but I think perhaps they don't want the Muslim population to increase—perhaps they only want the Buddhist population to increase.[15]

I became pregnant two more times in Burma. I aborted the second pregnancy within three months and the third pregnancy within less than two months. I got tablets from the doctor those two times because using the roots was painful. They are Muslim doctors, so they do not tell the NaSaKa. If I went to the Rakhine doctors, they surely would have informed on me. The tablets took more than one day to work.

At that time, we didn't know about condoms because we had no education about that. Now we know about them, so we are using them.

I would like to mention one thing—sometimes my husband would get very angry and hit me. "Why don't you give me a child?" he'd say. The beating was not so serious; my husband would slap me on the cheeks and say, "I cannot give you everything because I don't have much more money. I cannot pay for you any more." I would ask him why he beat me. I told him that he knows about the NaSaKa, that he is scared of the NaSaKa too and this is why I needed to abort the preganancies. He was furious, because he had to pay money each time I aborted a child. I would also be sick for several months after each abortion. For this reason, my husband felt annoyed. He was stressed because of me.

I didn't say anything when he did that, but at that time, I felt like leaving him. But I didn't leave, because that is not allowed according to our custom. I was with my husband and I didn't go anywhere.

---

[15] The Rohingya have been subjected to myriad policies that isolate them from the rest of the Burmese population. For more on these policies see the "The Rohingya: Stateless People" section of the appendix pages 478-481.

Finally I told him, "If you want children, it would be better if we left the country."

THERE IS A BOAT TO BANGLADESH

The NaSaKa can torture people and demand bribes for any reason they want. I got married according to my Islamic law, but the NaSaKa came and took my husband away because we did not have a genuine marriage permission document.[16]

Just after my third pregnancy, a local informer had gone to the NaSaKa to denounce our marriage. It was midnight when the NaSaKa came to my in-laws' house with the *sein gaung*.[17] My husband and I were sleeping when they ordered us to open the door, and I immediately went to hide in another room.

We didn't answer, so they broke down the door. They had guns and weapons. They found my husband alone in the room. The NaSaKa and the *sein gaung* looked for me but did not find me. Then they took my husband away with allegations of illegal marriage. His mother ran after the authorities, begging them not to take him away. My parents-in-law tried to take him back from the NaSaKa but failed.

Rashid was detained in the NaSaKa camp for two days, and he was beaten and interrogated. Then he was sent to the Maungdaw detention center while the authorities investigated whether or not he was illegally married.[18] While he was in detention, he was forced to work a lot and he got many injuries.

After my husband was released from jail, we decided to flee to

---

[16] According to the Arakan Project, the male in the couple is generally prosecuted under Penal Code Section 493 "for marrying a woman by deceit" which prescribes a sentence of up to ten years imprisonment, but average prosecution is four to five years.

[17] The *sein gaung* is a local leader of ten houses, reporting to the VPDC chairman.

[18] According to the Arakan Project, he would have been held in a detention center for pre-trial detention. Bribes are demanded to avoid prosecution and secure release.

Bangladesh. He said if we stayed in Burma, it would have to be without ever having children. There is a boat that takes people to Bangladesh; we only had a little money, so my husband went first. Since we didn't know how we would survive in Bangladesh, he said he would call for me once he had settled down and found work. It was also safer for us to go separately, because the NaSaKa would arrest us and send us to jail if they suspected we were traveling.[19] We had to be very careful because there were informers for the NaSaKa around the village.

I HAD NO EXPECTATIONS AT ALL
THAT THEY WOULD BE FAIR

After Rashid left, I left my in-laws' home and returned to my mother's house to start living with her again. A month or so passed and I received a message from a person in my village who had secretly visited Bangladesh. He said that he'd spoken with Rashid and learned that he was trying to settle in Teknaf.[20]

Then one night, another NaSaKa officer came to my mother's home and started knocking. I took some time to open the door because I had been sleeping. One of the NaSaKa soldiers broke down the door and he said, "You took too long to open the door," and then he kicked me on my thigh. I fell down and they started beating me. There were about eight to ten men altogether. The officer said, "You don't have the marriage document," and he tried to get more money from us, but we didn't have any. If they feel like torturing any family, they will do it with any cause, whether it's fair or not.

They searched our house and our yard and asked about Rashid. They also opened my trunk to see if there were any of Rashid's clothes or belongings. The NaSaKa men grabbed me and my mother begged them

---

[19] For more on restrictions to Rohingyas' movement in Arakan state, see appendix pages 479-480.

[20] Teknaf is a town in southeastern Bangladesh, which borders Burma.

not to take me away. She asked them why they were taking me, and they replied, "The other officer took her husband, so now I will take his wife." My mother tried to run after us and stop them, but they just beat her. She is over sixty years old.

During the arrest, I just stayed silent and let them do what they wanted; I knew there was no point in begging. I let it be. I had no expectations at all that they would be fair.

That night they took me to the NaSaKa camp. On the way to the camp, they started touching my body. When we arrived at the camp, three or four drunk NaSaKa guys attacked me. They brought me to a little room with tin walls and locked me inside. I was thinking that the NaSaKa was going to send me to jail, or torture me or rape me.

They didn't say anything to me at the NaSaKa camp, but I don't understand their language anyway because I speak Bangla.[21] I just sat like a ghost. They beat me, they tortured me, and then they raped me— I didn't do anything. I just kept silent.

The morning after my arrest, my mother was going mad, and she immediately went to see the VPDC chairman. He told her not to worry because the NaSaKa wouldn't find evidence of my illegal marriage since I did not have a baby and Rashid was not there. But he said the NaSaKa arrested me because an informer had denounced me, and so they would surely demand some money for my release. The chairman went to the NaSaKa office, and then he told my mother they demanded 200,000 kyats.[22] My mother sent me food and water, but I didn't take the food, only the water. I had been tortured again and again, so I'd completely lost my appetite.

There were more than fifteen soldiers involved in assaulting me— each night, different people came. They raped me again and again in the night, and even in the daytime. I said to the Almighty, "Why, Almighty,

---

[21] Rohingya people speak a dialect of Chittagonian, a language of southern Bangladesh. Educated Rohingya people also speak Burmese.

[22] Approximately US$200.

did you send me here?" I couldn't stop crying. I didn't understand what
had happened to my life.

My mother informed the local Muslim villagers about the danger her
daughter was in, and my in-laws, my uncles, and some villagers at the
central mosque gave my mother some money to help. I didn't know what
would happen to me. If my mother was able to get the money, I knew
I could leave. I sat crying, only crying and crying. I was raped constantly
every day. When the NaSaKa men raped me, I felt as if vultures were biting
me all over my body and that they would bite me until I died.

It took three days for my mother to collect the money, and then she
went to the NaSaKa and paid. When they let me leave, they just said
"Okay, go." But I was unable to walk. My family members—my brothers
and my mother—had to carry me. Seeing them, I felt like I'd been given
a new life. My mother asked me what had happened to me. I explained,
and they cried. Then my mother said, "You can't live here; you must leave
this place."

What happened to me is common. So many Muslim woman have
been tortured by them. If you have money, you can get tortured less. If
you don't have money, you get tortured. I don't know why they do this—
only the Almighty knows.

I was so tired and exhausted, and I had not eaten during the three
days in detention. I stayed at home for a long time and tried to regain my
mental strength; I had been tortured so much that I had fallen sick. It was
fifteen days until I could walk again and take a little food. After a month,
I decided to join my husband in Bangladesh. My mother managed to collect some money and she gave this to me. I walked to the river to take a
small ferry boat to the Bangladesh side of the river. From there I had to
take a bus to Teknaf, where I thought I would find Rashid.

I DIDN'T WANT TO DIE IN BURMA

I didn't feel sad leaving Burma; I was thinking about how it would be
in Bangladesh. I wondered how I would find my husband. While travel-

ing, I was thinking that Bangladesh is a Muslim country and that we are Muslims—I thought, Muslims like other Muslims. I thought that if you go to Bangladesh, you get a better life, better than in Burma. This was my thinking.

I gave 2,000 kyats to the fishermen in Min Ga Lah Gyi.[23] They had a boat and carried me and some other passengers from the Burma side to the Bangladesh side. I took my clothes, but I could not take luggage because if I did, then the Burmese government would have arrested me—they would have known I was traveling from Burma to Bangladesh.

I was scared coming here, because I didn't have any relatives in Bangladesh—I just knew that my husband was here. I also thought about how the NaSaKa could torture me, so I prayed to the Almighty to let me die in Bangladesh, not in Burma.

When I arrived in Teknaf, I didn't look for my husband straightaway. First, a woman gave me shelter in her room and arranged a job for me grinding spices in a restaurant. Then I tried to find Rashid but he was not there. A month later, a group of Rohingya women left to go to Nazirartek in Cox's Bazar.[24] They advised me to accompany them because the wages were far better in Cox's Bazar, where a woman can earn up to 100 taka a day.[25] I went with them and I rented a room with other women in Nazirartek. I found a job sorting fish, but the employer only paid 60 taka per day.[26] I asked the people there, "Do you know Rashid? He has come to Bangladesh and he is my husband. I am looking for him." One person I knew from Burma said, "Yeah, Rashid lives here. He is at sea with a fishing boat."

I waited fifteen days, and finally the boat came in with my husband. Finally, I had found him! I was excited to see him. My husband felt very surprised when he saw me. He said, "I thought you were in jail!"

---

[23] Approximately US$2.

[24] Nazirartek is a sea town in the Cox's Bazar district of Bangladesh.

[25] Approximately US$1.40.

[26] Approximately US$0.85.

NOWHERE TO BE HOME

After we found each other, we stayed in Nazirartek for six months. My husband didn't allow me to work, so I just stayed home and cooked food while he worked. It was a happy life for me. But when there was an increase in our rent, my husband couldn't afford to pay it, so we moved back to Teknaf. But the rent was a burden for us there as well, so when we heard that a makeshift camp had started in Kutupalong, we decided to go there.[27]

WE ARE LIVING IN HELL HERE

We moved to the Kutupalong makeshift camp two or three years ago. We knew how to come to this camp because there were a lot of people gathered here. On the way here, I was crying because we didn't have shelter.

Initially I raised a shanty on the hill, but the Bangladeshi officials demolished my hut and others' huts as well.[28] Then I rebuilt again a bit further away, but when they officials found out, they came once again and destroyed the house. The Bangladeshi officials destroyed our hut three times, and each time we just waited. When they went away, we started building again nearby, in a different section of the camp.

The Bangladesh Forestry Department says this is their property, and since this is their property they can destroy our house. When they come, we don't say anything. We say we don't have any property, we just have dishes and jars, so we just take these and we go away. The three times that my house was destroyed, I thought, *I will go. Because today I make*

---

[27] Kutupalong makeshift camp started growing in early 2008. According to the Arakan Project, as the camp's population increased, the Bangladesh authorities began to destroy sections of the makeshift camp on three occasions during June and July 2009.

[28] According to MSF (Doctors Without Borders), "The Rohingya population at the Kutupalong camp have been told that they cannot live next to the official refugee camp, supported by the Bangladesh Government and the United Nations High Commissioner for Refugees (UNHCR). Nor can they legally live on adjacent Forestry Department land." Houses were destroyed to create a corridor between the official camp and the makeshift camp.

it and tonight they break it. It was really horrible. We couldn't endure it. Sometimes we felt like committing suicide, thinking, *What can we do? Where will we go?*

After the third eviction I met a registered refugee who said, "If you want somewhere to stay, there is a place where we plant vegetables and you can stay over there. But you have to pay 200 taka."[29] Because we live on this land now, the registered refugees cannot plant vegetables here anymore—and if they don't plant, they can't earn money. So if we want to stay here, we have to pay them 200 taka.

We paid the money to the registered refugees; we don't know if they are leaders or not. That's why I'm here today, and why we made this house here, near the latrine. To make my house, I just collected wood from the forest. I bought the plastic material leftover from rice bags at the market, and then I used it to make the house. Each piece of plastic was 6 taka.[30] We don't have much money to make our house, and I'm not able to build two shacks. When the rain comes, rain will fall into the house and we have to let the soil dry. We just make a ditch and drain the water out, and then we rebuild our hut again when the sun comes.[31]

The registered refugees look down on us and make some problems for us. They have latrines, but they tell us that we are not allowed to go there. We live near the registered camp, but in order to use the toilets, we need to pay ¼ kilogram of rice each month.[32] The registered refugees can come to the unregistered camp if they wish, but we cannot use the facilities in the registered camp unless we give them rice. If our little children go to the registered camp and cause any trouble, then the registered adult refugees come to the unregistered camp and beat the adults. If they come here and start to beat us, we don't tell anyone;

---

[29] Approximately US$2.85.

[30] Approximately US$0.10.

[31] For more on conditions in the camps, see page 476 of the appendix.

[32] Payment is to offset the costs of cleaning.

we just stay silent because we know we don't have any protection or identification.

If we go outside of Kutupalong, then other people can catch us and we'll have nothing. We can't do anything. We are scared of the Bangladeshi authorities. Even the registered refugees have told the police to break our homes. We are living in hell here—our homes are always broken, we are always starving. But it is still better than living in Burma.

HARDLY ENOUGH FOR THE FAMILY

I live with my husband and two nieces in Bangladesh. The girls are fifteen and eleven. My older sister and her husband died, and so my nieces came here just a year ago and found me. I need another shack for my nieces; we do not have enough space. My younger niece is now in another house doing household work. My older niece will soon be married off to another camp resident. I feel good about them living with me; they're very good to me.

It is difficult for us to work in Bangladesh because people know we are Rohingya—they think the Rohingya are occupying their land and causing problems and crime. They think we are going to steal their work and destroy their forests.

Rashid has always been sick, even before our marriage. Now he hardly works three or four days a week. If he worked seven days a week, he would become sick. He always suffers from fever. In Bangladesh, while collecting firewood in the hills, he once put something inside his ear because his ear was itching, and that object got stuck in his ear. Since then, he often feels severe pain and he has become totally deaf. I took him to an MSF clinic, but they only gave him some painkillers.[33] Now I have to look after everything and support my family. I often go to the hills to collect firewood with my niece, and that is my main livelihood. What Rashid earns is not enough for the family.

---

[33] Médecins Sans Frontières (Doctors Without Borders) is an international medical and humanitarian aid organization.

I felt comfortable when we first came here because we had a way to earn money through cutting wood. But now, when more people started coming—other people from Bangladesh or Burma—the Bangladeshi officials came to know about it and they sometimes come and arrest unregistered refugees.

For this reason, I am unable to provide more support to my niece. That's why I must have her do other work.

I have a lot of problems living my life here, so it would be better if I could get UNHCR registration.[34] If foreigners can help to make Burma pacified, peaceful, it's okay—the registration is not important. But because my country isn't peaceful, it is very important to be registered. If Burma becomes a country like Bangladesh, for example, and I get the opportunity to go back, then I can go to your home and you can come to mine. But in Burma right now, we can't do this.

If we get human rights, then we will go back to Burma. Or we can go to another country and it will be better. Otherwise, we'll die here.

DO NOT SEND ME BACK

Last year, I went to the MSF clinic and found out I was three months pregnant. All the medicine I'd taken for the abortions had caused a lot of health problems for me, but then I took some different medicine and I felt like I could become a mother. Before, there were a lot of problems that caused quarrels between my husband and me, but now it's okay.

While I was pregnant, the Bangladeshi authorities arrested my husband when he was in Ukhia, on his way to work. My husband and thirty-one other residents of the makeshift camp were arrested by the Ukhia police during the crackdown. They were all sent to Cox's Bazar. They

---

[34] According to the Arakan Project, in Bangladesh, the 28,000 Rohingyas still remaining in two camps are recognized as refugees and benefit from limited protection and assistance by UNHCR. However, it is estimated that up to 200,000 more live outside the camps. See appendix page 476 for more details.

put him in jail for three months. It was very difficult for me to survive during that time. Even though I was pregnant, I went outside to work in local cultivation. I was paid 25 taka per day, and I worked right up until I gave birth.[35] It was so difficult, and it wasn't safe for me, but if both of us couldn't work then our baby would have really suffered.

I was so sad when Rashid was arrested, because I thought he would be repatriated—everyone said prisoners were being transferred back to Burma. I informed Rashid's mother about his arrest. Rashid's parents had fled to Bangladesh too, and his father had died at the Dumdumia Tal; his mother then got a room at the relocated site in Leda.[36] She had 1,000 taka and she borrowed 2,000 taka by pawning her registration card and book provided by an NGO. She gave the 3,000 taka to a lawyer, who managed to release Rashid on bail.[37] I really did not expect that he would be released early, but luckily my mother in-law was able to help him.[38]

Now my baby girl is twenty-five days old. I really hope Allah will let us live in this country forever instead of in Burma. I know Burma is our country, but we can never go back unless we are treated like citizens. We don't even dream of living peacefully in another country; now we just dream of being registered refugees.

If an NGO or the UN could help me, I need food and I need materials for my house.[39] I need a blanket. If my baby gets wet from the rain then

---

[35] Approximately US$0.35.

[36] Like Kutupalong makeshift refugee camps, Dumdumia and Leda are both unofficial refugee camp in the Cox's Bazaar District of Bangladesh.

[37] 1,000 taka is approximately US$15; 2,000 taka is approximately US$30; 3,000 taka is approximately US$45.

[38] If convicted for illegal entry in Bangladesh, Rashid would have faced indefinite detention, as Burma usually does not readmit Rohingya. Some prisoners in Cox's Bazar jail have been there for nearly twenty years.

[39] The two NGOs that work to serve the needs of the Rohingya refugees living in Fatima's area are Islamic Relief, an international NGO that works to empower local communities to overcome poverty and Muslim Aid, founded by Yusuf Islam (formerly Cat Stevens) to do similar work.

I do not know what will happen, she is so young and I am very scared what will happen to her. If my husband goes out for work and earns money, then we can have food. But if my husband can't work, then we don't have food and we have to starve. Today we haven't had any food since the morning.[40]

When we were in Burma, it was a difficult time for us. When I think about what's happening in my country, I feel like crying. In our country, we have no safety, we have no security. The rulers of Burma are good to other groups, but not to Muslims. It's no problem if people call us Rohingya, because we are Rohingya—but we are Burmese people too. We are Burmese Muslims.

Now that we are here living in Bangladesh, it's like an open sky. We feel much better here than in Burma. Even though it is just a hut that we have, it feels like our house. I think we'll get peace here. My request is to not be sent to Burma; I do not believe there will be any change there. Even my brothers have fled to Bangladesh now, though I have not found them yet. Only my mother remains in Burma. But my future is up to God Almighty. And what the Almighty will give away, I will take.

---

[40] In 2009, MSF (Doctors Without Borders) found that 90 percent of those living in the makeshift camp were severely food insecure. See appendix page 478 for more on the Rohingya living in exile in Bangladesh.

HLA MIN

18, former child soldier

ETHNICITY: *Burman*

BIRTHPLACE: *Hlaingthaya Township, Burma*

INTERVIEWED IN: *Cox's Bazar, Bangladesh*

Taken off the streets at nine years old and forced to become a child soldier, Hla Min was fighting on the front line in Karen State by age fourteen. He traveled for an entire day to meet us in Cox's Bazar, a coastal city home to many Burmese refugees in Bangladesh—the country to which he fled in 2007 after the Saffron Revolution.[1] He told us his story until 1 a.m. that night, knowing it would be our only opportunity to meet before he returned to work on a tobacco farm the next day. Hla Min is one former child soldier in a country frequently cited for having the most child soldiers in the world.[2] Analysts have pointed out that the Tatmadaw's ongo-

---

[1] In 2007, Burma's ruling junta drastically reduced government fuel subsidies, which led to a hike in transportation and commodity prices. Thousands of monks subsequently launched the Saffron Revolution, a nationwide monk-led uprising that grabbed the attention of global media and was brutally suppressed by the SPDC. For more on the Saffron Revolution, see page 468 of the appendix.

[2] The Optional Protocol to the Convention on the Rights of the Child sets eighteen as the minimum age for direct participation in hostilities, for recruitment into armed groups, and for compulsory recruitment by governments.

NOWHERE TO BE HOME

ing forced conscription of minors is one of the crucial factors allowing the military to increase its size and therefore its strength.

I'd like to tell you the story of how I joined the army as a child.

I was nine years old, and I was living in the Hlaingthaya Township in Rangoon Division. It was a school holiday on the full moon day in November, and we were making a picnic. Traditionally, during school holidays, students in Burma have to hold a ceremony to honor their teachers, and then we make a picnic with our friends. At around 8 p.m., one of my friends and I went out to buy some chicken. At that moment, an army truck came and took us.

When they pulled us into the back of the truck, I found there were six or seven soldiers inside. My friend and I thought they were killers and I was worried. They made us lie down on the floor—there were no seats—and when I tried to shout, they covered my mouth with their hands. They said, "You keep quiet, you have to come with us."

My friend and I were afraid but we didn't say anything to each other. I had heard from my parents that soldiers beat and arrested people in my village. I'd also heard that soldiers shot people in the street, so I was afraid that they might kill me. The drive felt very long and I had no chance to run away.

When the truck stopped, we got out and I saw the army base. My friend and I had been brought to a Burmese army battalion in Rangoon Division.

I FOUND CHILDREN THERE

When we arrived at the army base, my friend and I were brought to separate cells. They were like prison cells, and they chained the doors shut. I had no chance to talk to my friend.

The battalion compound was big and had dormitories, garages, a big banyan tree, and plants inside. There were many soldiers living there, but I don't know how many. After two or three days, I was asked to carry water. They didn't give me a military uniform; I just had on my own pants and shirt. On a normal day, I had to get up before 6 a.m. and work during the day. I worked with my friend every day. We had to fetch water, water the plants and garden, and also help do chores and cook in the kitchen. I did everything as asked by the cooks and sergeants. All of the work was very tiring and hard because I hadn't had any experience working before.

I was given only two meals a day, at 10 a.m. and 5 p.m. Most of the time I had the meals alone, but sometimes I got to eat with the cooks, or with my friend in the kitchen. Sometimes I couldn't eat because the rice and the curry were not good. They provided only rice, bean curry, morning glory, roselle, and gourd—only the cooks ate meat and fish.[3] If they had leftovers they'd give them to us, but sometimes after eating I wasn't full and I'd be left hungry.

At night, I was confined to a cell where I slept alone. There was no chance of escape, and I didn't think I would be able to succeed if I tried because the gates were guarded by so many soldiers.

My friend and I were very lonely while living at the army base. When we first arrived, we were not allowed to talk to each other. We were confined to separate rooms and we weren't allowed to play together. After working all day, finishing dinner, and washing the dishes, we were locked up in the rooms again. Sometimes they scolded and beat me when I dropped a bucket of water, or a plate or bowl.

During those times, I missed my home very much. I cried for my mother and for my family. I was the youngest of five, and I would play with my brothers and sisters and go to school with them. My parents really loved me and they always made me happy. Sometimes when I cried, I was beaten by the cooks and by the sergeants. Sometimes they slapped me and sometimes they beat me with a stick. While they were beating me they would say, "Why are you crying? Stop your crying!"

---

[3] Roselle is a hibiscus plant often used in beverages in Southeast Asia.

I lived like this for about two months inside the Rangoon army base. I didn't know what was going to happen to me next.

WHEN I WAS GROWN UP

After about two months at the army base, I was sent to a recruitment center. I think it was called the Mingaladon Recruitment Center. When I first arrived, I found almost seventy children there who were around my age. There were some children who had also been picked up from the street.

We had to get up at six o'clock in the morning, and then everyone had to make their bed and wash themselves. After that, we went to the dining hall and had fried rice with a fried egg and a cup of tea for breakfast. The food at the recruitment center was much better than at the previous army base. After breakfast we started working out, doing exercises like push-ups, pull-ups, and running. We ate our lunch at ten-thirty a.m. and then everyone took a nap. After napping, we were allowed to play football or wrestle.

Sometimes the soldiers let me play with the other children, and sometimes they asked me to fight with other children. The leaders would come to us and tell us to wrestle, so we had to fight with each other until one of us fell down—the person left standing won. Sometimes I won, but sometimes I lost. I tried to beat the others and when I won, I was happy because I was given snacks. If someone won, they'd give a snack to them or buy them clothes. Sometimes the army soldiers and officers told me, "When you grow up, you will have to hold a gun like me." When soldiers told us that, we felt really pleased.

After football or wrestling, we took a shower at 4 p.m., and then we had dinner. After dinner, we'd go back to the dorms and watch military fighting movies. We watched movies about fighting between soldiers and rebels almost every day. We were asked to go to bed at 8 p.m., and everyone slept in their own bed on the floor. The dorm where I stayed had a wooden floor, brick walls, and a zinc roof. The door to the dorm was made of iron, and it was locked and guarded by soldiers outside while we slept.

At the recruitment center I got to stay with many other children and I had time to play. The adults there indulged us and never made us study or read books. We were free to move around the recruitment center however we wanted, but we were not allowed to leave. The compound was guarded by lots of adult soldiers. I spent two years like this at the recruitment center.

When I was grown up—around thirteen or fourteen years old—I was sent to a training center for four and a half months in Pathein, in Irrawaddy Division. The recruitment center sent me there in one of its trucks. The training center was very far, and it took almost an entire day to get there. I was very tired when I arrived.

At the training center, we had to train in the heat under the bright sun, and even in the rain. There were more than 250 trainees there, and the training was very hard; sometimes I couldn't stand it. They asked me to run with a gun, and I was punished if I failed—my trainer would come and kick me with his shoe and then make me stare directly into the sun for an hour.

We were fed some rice with bean curry and dried fish and a little bit of fruit. The food was not good. After dinner we had to do night duty, guarding the gates of the training base. Sometimes I felt homesick during my training and I would cry; I wanted to see my mother and my father.

Every morning we had to declare our loyalty to the army. By the time I'd completed training, I started to believe in the army. I was granted a uniform, a gun, and my private rank ID number—I was a soldier. After they gave me these things, I started to feel a little excited and confident that I could handle this kind of work. I believed I would be able do things like go to battle, like the soldiers who had trained us.

My friend and I were separated after we completed training; I don't know where he was sent. I was sent to Light Infantry Battalion number 564 in Arakan State, which is very far from Rangoon. When I was there, I was sometimes asked to cut wood and clear the bushes in the forest. But most of the time, I just did tasks at the battalion headquarters as directed. Then, a few years later, I was sent from Arakan State to the front line in Karen State.

THE FRONT LINE

I was around fourteen years old when I was ordered to go to the front line. My officer told me, "You have to go and fight the guerillas in Karen State." During my training, and then at our battalion meetings, the leaders always preached about how cruel the rebels were, so at the time I believed the guerillas were trying to take my country and kill my people.

We were asked to search for the guerillas and fight them. I was sent to the front line with soldiers who were older than me, and also some who were around my age. I had to dress in uniform and bring a rucksack with my rations. My rations included rice, a thin blanket, a mosquito net for sleeping, and a tarp for the rainy season. I also had to carry my gun, four cartridges of bullets for it, and two grenades, as well as two big cases of bullets for the unit's machine guns, which were a type of light machine gun made in Burma.

I was beaten and slapped three times by my captain because I was too slow folding up my tarp. I had to roll it, fold it, and put it in my bag, but my captain said I didn't do it right and then he beat me. As punishment, I had to carry the unit's cooking pot.

We had to move around a lot while we were in the jungles and mountains. It took us over four months to go around and search for guerillas. Sometimes we starved because food rations had not been sent to us by our battalion, so we ate anything we could find.

We slept in a different place every night. When the sun set, we had to camp at the nearest possible spot. When it rained, we had no place to take cover. Sometimes we didn't have a chance to sleep because we had to sit and do guard duty at night. Everyone had to do it.

One day, while I was carrying the pot, I heard a blast behind me and I fell down, unconscious. When I woke up, I thought I had lost my legs, but it wasn't a landmine, it was a remote-controlled bomb that had detonated. It had hit my backside and my head—the shrapnel had injured my right ear and cheek, my back, chest, and arms, but the pot had helped to protect me.

More than 100 soldiers had been walking together when the blast happened. The guerillas were behind us and they had set off remote-controlled bombs as we passed through. Four other soldiers and I were injured. The injured were taken by the Signal Corps to an emergency medical clinic set up by the army, and we received emergency medical treatment there.[4] The clinic was small and could only accommodate ten patients, but they provided emergency medical treatment to the injured soldiers, especially those who had lost their arms and legs. The people in the clinic were very sympathetic to me. From there, I was sent to Taung Hospital to recover.[5]

WE COULD NOT REFUSE THEIR ORDERS

It took me about a month to recover. After I was better, I was sent back to my army battalion and then on to the front line again.

While we were on the front line, our officers ordered us to completely destroy the local people. They told us that even the children had to be killed if we saw them. I saw soldiers abducting young girls, dragging them from their houses and raping them. At the time, I felt that those girls were like my sisters.

Sometimes the officers would find one of their soldiers who they didn't like, or who was very frightened, and the officer would order the soldier to do that kind of thing, like rape the local women. If the soldiers did not follow the orders, they were shot or beaten. We could not refuse their orders; we had to follow them.

I once saw the guerillas at their camp in Three Pagodas Pass in Karen State. I didn't know anything else about them at the time other than they looked like us—they had black skin and they wore uniforms. I felt sympathetic for them because we had a base to go and rest at, but they had to stay in the jungle all the time.

---

[4] Signal Corps is the branch of an army responsible for military communications.

[5] Taung Goat is a township in Arakan State, the southwestern-most state in Burma.

MY FIRST TIME IN BATTLE

There were some battles on the front line in Karen State. One time, four soldiers were on the top of the mountain keeping guard, while twelve other soldiers went down to get some water from the stream at the bottom of the mountain. I was halfway up the mountain, doing security patrol with three other soldiers. Two additional soldiers were deployed below us.

It usually took about fifteen minutes to get water. Before the soldiers went down to get water that day, the guerillas had already laid down some remote-controlled bombs that were all connected by wires. When the soldiers went close to the stream, the bombs exploded. All of the soldiers at the bottom of the mountain died.

Then the guerillas turned toward us to fight, because our soldiers on the top of the mountain were shooting at them. Those on the top of the mountain gave us orders. I crouched near a rock for cover. It was my first time in battle, and I was both very excited and very frightened, but I just fired back. The battle went on for more than half an hour. One of the soldiers who had gone to get water was still alive, but the guerillas approached and shot him dead. Two of the four soldiers who were doing guard duty died, and the two soldiers deployed below us also died. The guerillas fought against us for half an hour and then retreated. When the battle had finished, there were fifteen or sixteen of our soldiers killed, and some of the guerillas had died as well.

When the battle finished, we still had not eaten and we had no water. We were so exhausted, but we were ordered to march after the guerillas. Some soldiers could not walk, and they were beaten. The captain said to us, "If you cannot continue this battle, I will kill you." One of my friends asked permission from the captain to use the toilet. When he went, he took his gun with him and committed suicide. He couldn't go on. Another one of the soldiers, one of my friends, was hungry and he cut a banana from a tree. When he did that, a landmine got him. I saw him lose both of his legs.

I cannot say why I survived the battle; it depends on your luck. Some people were hit by mines and some were killed, but I was saved.

After the battle, I accompanied the injured soldiers to an area away from the front line. From there, I was sent back to my battalion in Arakan State. I was very sorry because I had to leave without any of my friends. I was also very sad when I saw the survivors of the battle who had lost their arms and legs.

I wanted to desert from the army whenever I thought about my family, but it was not possible for me. If I deserted, I would be jailed.

I WOULD RATHER BE KILLED

I was in Buthidaung when the Saffron Revolution started.[6] There was no uprising where I was. It had started in Sittwe and then it spread to Rangoon. My commanding officer said everyone must be ready. We were told that if the monk or student protests grew, and if they were fighting against the authorities, then we needed to fight back. If the students and monks used sticks, we had to use sticks. If the students and monks used slingshots, we had to use slingshots. If they used guns, we had to use guns.

Then I was sent to Sittwe to attack the monks. At this time, I started to feel really bad about the army.

We took four powered schooners to Sittwe. It took about three hours. We were about seventy soldiers. When we arrived, our leaders told us to make slingshots with mud pellets and use them to attack the monks. I had to make 500 pellets. We were equipped with sticks, slingshots, and guns. Our leaders told us that it didn't matter if it was monks or students—they were marching together, and we had to shoot at them both.

I was in the streets in Sittwe for three days monitoring the protestors, but we didn't do anything to the monks and students because they were

---

[6] Buthidaung is a town in Arakan State, the southwestern-most state in Burma.

protesting peacefully. At first, I thought that the monks and students were just rioting, but later, I learned that they were protesting because of the people's hardship and suffering. They were demanding that the government do something to solve this problem the people were facing. I realized it was similar to the situation in our battalion, because soldiers are poor and get only a small salary. The people who were demonstrating had many difficulties similar to those of soldiers' families. I felt very empathetic and I realized that what the leaders told us was not true.

Since that moment, I stopped believing in the army. I really respect monks and I could not do this to them, so I decided to flee. I felt confident about my decision. I decided I would rather be killed than stay and attack the monks.

One friend and I discussed how we were gaining nothing by working as soldiers, and we decided to run away from our battalion together. We tried to escape many times, but failed.

One day that October, my friend and I packed up all of our things to try escaping again. We were back at our battalion in Buthidaung. At five in the evening we left the dormitory and came across one of our battalion's commanders. He was suspicious of us and ordered us to follow him. When we got to the door of his dormitory, he asked, "Are you trying to run away?" We denied his accusation. He opened up our bags, asked us questions. He beat us, but we didn't tell him anything. He told us we would be sent for at 7 p.m., and we would be kept in a cell. Then, while he was speaking, he turned to go inside his dormitory—at that moment we left our bags and ran away.

The Buthidaung stream was next to the battalion headquarters. We swam across it and then we took the jungle road by the coast from Buthidaung to Maungthaw. While we were running, we didn't talk about anything except our route. We just said, "Turn right here," and, "Left there." We slept for a night at a monastery. We saw people on the way, but I didn't talk to them because we were in Arakan State and I am Burman—if I spoke in Burmese, they would automatically know I was a soldier. My friend is Rakhine, so he spoke their language; he asked people for help in finding our way. We had no food as we went on, and we could not sleep because we had to avoid the NaSaKa forces, who were searching for us after we'd escaped.[7] We had to be careful because there were NaSaKa forces located right on the border.

From the jungle route, we arrived at the border on the bank of the Naf River. It took us five days altogether to reach the border to Bangladesh. I didn't know much about Bangladesh. We just ran to escape, but Maungthaw was the only way to run, and if you proceed from Maungthaw, you go to Bangladesh. That's why we decided to go there. If we had stayed in Maungthaw, we would have been found and arrested.

When we reached the Naf River, the boat operators told us that the other side of the river was Bangladesh. We asked them to take us over, but they refused because we had no money. Out of fear of the NaSaKa forces there, we decided to swim across.

The Naf River is wide and deep, and we crossed during a time of flooding; the current was very fast and strong. We started swimming at around nine-thirty or ten in the morning. I saw only one tree in the middle, and I made it my target. Sometimes we swam normally, and sometimes we floated along the current lying on our backs because we were tired. There was one buoy in the middle of the river where we stopped for a while. It took nearly one hour to get across the river.

When we arrived at the Bangladesh riverbank, there was a Rakhine village. There were also some BDR—the Bangladesh border guard force.[8] I don't think that they saw us; if they had seen us swimming across the river, we would have been apprehended. When we arrived in the village, my friend spoke with the people. He told the villagers that we were soldiers, and because we had to swim across the river, they sympathized with us.

---

[7] The NaSaKa, an acronym for "Nay-Sat Kut-kwey Ye," is a border task force established in 1992 under the direct command of the SPDC. They are frequently cited for human rights violations against the Rohingya and other people living in Arakan State..

[8] The BDR is the border guard of Bangladesh. The acronym derives from its former name, the Bangladesh Rifles. Since 2009, it has been known as the Border Guards Bangladesh.

We stayed in the village monastery that day, but soon we heard that the Bangladeshi police or the BDR might come, so we had to move into the jungle and hide. Some men from the village told a Rakhine friend of theirs in Cox's Bazar that two soldiers had arrived from Burma. He came to get us and brought us back to his home. He took care of us. His name is Aung Tun.

NOW I'M NOT THE SAME

Life is very difficult in Bangladesh. When I first arrived, Aung Tun and his family looked after me. But they are also poor and I felt bad that they were giving me so much, so I try to survive by myself now. Now I am staying apart from them and working on a tobacco farm to survive. Sometimes I feel ill there because I don't get to have meals regularly.

Aung Tun helped me because I am a young boy and because we come from the same land. I told him my story and he told me about how he also left his homeland after 1988. When he told me that the military government killed monks and students in 1988, I was very surprised.[9]

Aung Tun is a politician, and he always talks with me about the political situation in Burma. Now I know that the guerillas are fighting for their freedom, for their rights, and that they don't like the ruling military regime. When I was in the army, I thought the guerillas were trying to break my country, to destroy my country—this is how I used to think. Not now, now I'm not the same.

I think the insurgents will fight until they get their freedom. I understand why they fight; I agree that you should fight for your rights. Right now I don't want to say anything about the soldiers in the Burmese military, but I see the ruling general as a king of hell or a demon.

---

[9] In 1988, deteriorating economic conditions sparked nationwide protests against the ruling government. Though an accurate count is hard to determine, it is typically estimated that 3,000 were killed during the crackdown, however, estimates run as high as 10,000. See appendix 463-465 for information about the uprising.

I don't know why people join the military. As for myself, I was forced to be a soldier. If I had stayed with my family, I would not have been a soldier.

IF THEY RECRUIT SOMEONE, THEN
THEY CAN QUIT THE ARMY

I have had no contact with my family since the army took me. I don't remember a lot from when I was young. I may not even be able to recognize my family. I do remember that we were a poor family, and that the village I was born in had some farmland and some trees.

I remember that when I went to school for the first time, my family was really happy.

I liked going to school because I like to learn. I never got to study in the army. I was only taught about guns.

My family may think that I have died, or that I am lost. I would like to see my family but I don't know how to look for them. When Nargis devastated Burma, I heard on the radio that there were casualties and destruction, such as trees falling down and villages destroyed in the Irrawaddy and Rangoon Divisions.[10] I don't know what happened to my family when Nargis came; I'm not sure if they are alive or dead.

I don't blame my parents for what happened; I don't blame myself either. It is not my fault. I can't blame anyone except the SPDC government. I think the army takes children because they need to strengthen their forces, increase the number of soldiers. I think there is a reward for each soldier who catches a child. Any time a soldier recruits someone to join the force, they get a lot of money. Older soldiers told me that if they recruit someone, then they can quit the army.

---

[10] Cyclone Nargis was the name of a storm that ripped through Burma's Irrawaddy Delta in 2008. Marked by 132 mph winds and a storm surge of twelve feet, the cyclone was the most destructive in Burma's recorded history. It killed an estimated 140,000 people and razed 700,000 homes to the ground.

I think the soldiers who forced children to join the army should be killed because they didn't think of the children as their own sons or daughters. I also think that the soldiers who have raped women should be killed, because they didn't think of the women as their own sisters.

I BELIEVE I WILL GO BACK ONE DAY

I'm registered with the UNHCR in Bangladesh. I applied for refugee status with the help of some Burmese people living in Bangladesh— they told me that it was very useful and important for me since I am living here now, so I applied. The UNHCR accepted my application and then I had two interviews; the first one was ten days after I first turned my application in. After one year, the UN recognized me as a refugee and issued me an ID card.

One time when I was working on the tobacco farm, police came to catch people from Burma and I had to run away. I went back to my room and I searched for my card but I realized I had lost it. I have already informed the UNHCR about what happened, but the UNHCR hasn't given me a new card. I don't know the reason. I believe that if I have the ID card I will be protected.

I have so many difficulties trying to survive. I don't know the local spoken or written languages in Bangladesh. In order to have a good future, I need help from others. I need an education or vocational training to help me survive. I grew up in the army so I don't have an education. I am illiterate. Right now, in order to survive, I have to work on a tobacco plantation and live day to day. But I want to have a career. I like driving vehicles and, if possible, I'd like to improve my life by having a career as a mechanic. I want to have a place to stay and food to eat.

I have met some Rohingya people in Bangladesh.[11] In Burma, soldiers used to beat the Rohingya people, so some Rohingya are really angry

---

[11] There are tens of thousands of Rohingya refugees who have fled persecution in Burma and who are now living in Bangladesh.

at soldiers. Some Rohingya people here are kind to me, and some hate me. I understand why people don't like Burmans—I also believe that they are bad. I don't mean the people are bad, but I believe the authorities like the SPDC and the NaSaKa are bad.

I WAS LIKE AN ANIMAL

I was like an animal while growing up in the military. I did everything that I was told, and in turn, I received the food they provided. In life outside of the military, you can have hobbies and find other things you're interested in. In the military, you will never find those things.

I started to learn about Aung San Suu Kyi when I arrived in Bangladesh. Here, I have the freedom to learn. In 2009, I participated in a protest to demand freedom for Aung San Suu Kyi and to gain democracy in the 2010 elections. I decided to join the protest because I want people in Bangladesh to know about Aung San Suu Kyi, and because I'd like to motivate people inside Burma. I felt happy to participate. We walked for thirty days from Dhaka to Cox's Bazar. Six men and seven women did the protest together. As we were walking, Bangladeshi people encouraged us along the way.

I hope that Aung San Suu Kyi will be free. She must be free first for there to be democracy. If a lot of people inside Burma and also the UN support Aung San Suu Kyi, then we will get democracy and human rights. Only then will I be able to go back to Burma and have the chance to see my family again.

U KHAMA INDA

30, monk

ETHNICITY: *Rakhine*

BIRTHPLACE: *Arakan State, Burma*

INTERVIEWED IN: *Cox's Bazar, Bangladesh*

At twenty-seven years old, U Khama Inda was one of thousands of Buddhist monks who marched in the 2007 Saffron Revolution, Burma's monk-led uprising that grabbed the attention of global media and was brutally suppressed by the SPDC. Today, U Khama Inda lives in a makeshift monastery in Bangladesh with a handful of other exiled Burmese monks. U Khama Inda fears that if he returns to Burma, he will be arrested and tortured.

I am a monk, and since 2003 I have opposed military rule, after a student was brutally beaten in public for protesting a soldier's actions.

In 2003, I was twenty-three years old. At that time, I had been in the monkhood for six years—three years as a novice monk and another three years as a fully ordained monk. I was living in Ponnagyun, Arakan State. In the monastery that day, we had heard about a protest happening in town, but the abbot prevented us from going outside. He said everyone had to stay in. As a monk, my daily activities included meditation, gathering alms from the people, and teaching people about the tenets of Buddhism. I was reading and doing my lessons in the monastery, when five student leaders came to ask for the monks' help. They said that soldiers were unfairly beating the students at the protest, and asked that the monks help deal with the situation.

They explained why they had started the protest. They were students at a high school near Ponnagyun Pond, on the same street as a military compound. It was examination time and one student couldn't do his exam well, so he went outside and sat in front of a restaurant to try to relax. There was a crazy boy sitting in front of the restaurant too. People usually gave snacks and money to the boy and asked him to dance. The student gave some money to him and asked the boy to dance, but a drunk SPDC soldier came and started beating the boy. The student tried to stop the soldier but the soldier got angry and started beating the student with a brick and broke some of his ribs. The crazy boy was okay, but the student had to be hospitalized.

It was around 2 p.m. when that happened, and many students were leaving the school building. When they saw that the student had been brutally beaten, they were immediately united in their anger at the soldier. They decided to protest the soldier's brutal actions at the army battalion base later that afternoon. They wanted to demand that the military take action against the soldier and pay the medical costs for the injured student. Before this incident, the relationship between students and soldiers had been calm.

About 300 students started to gather in front of the army base at around 5 p.m. There were a number of soldiers in the compound, but only about fifteen soldiers equipped with guns were guarding the entrance. The students were about to enter the compound with the intention of asking the military leaders to resolve the problem, but the soldiers shot their guns in the air to frighten them. This made the students even angrier. They started to throw pieces of brick at the soldiers, who responded with slingshots and abusive language, ordering the students not to come any closer. The soldiers used small stones and marbles to shoot the students. Some of the students were hit in the head, face, and other parts of their body. Many of them were injured, and some had to be hospitalized.

I always obeyed the abbot in my monastery, but when the students came and asked for our help, I felt very strongly that I could not stay in the monastery while this situation was happening in town. I was very shocked by the SPDC's behavior, but I had also witnessed the government and military's oppression of the people since I was a little boy. The abbot was worried that the monks could get injured, but we were young and active—when we heard about such an atrocity, rather than being afraid, our dissatisfaction grew. That's why more than 100 monks decided to follow the students back to the army base to participate in the protest. We went there for justice. It was the first time we had opposed the authorities.

When we approached the base, the soldiers tried to attack the protestors by using slingshots and shooting guns into the air. Police officers came to try and settle the problem, but they retreated after they were beaten by the soldiers. People realized then that the police didn't have as much authority as the military.

We pulled back and tried to re-organize the protesters. As this was happening, a soldier approached us and threatened, "If someone is courageous, they can come forward."

After breaking up the protest, the senior SPDC commander came to negotiate with the monks and try to settle the problem. "We are all Buddhists here, so we will settle the problem very peacefully," he told us. The monks responded strongly. We said, "Okay, if you'd like to settle the problem, what will you do with the injured students who are in the hospital now? You have to take care of everything. You have to pay for all of their medical expenses."

The senior commander promised to settle the problems peacefully and take care of the students. The military promised to cover the medical costs for the student who had been initially wounded, as well as those injured in the protest. They provided all the medical costs, but some students had to treat their wounds at home after being discharged from the hospital before they had completely recovered.

But after one month, the soldiers tried to arrest both the townspeople and the students who had been involved in the protest, especially those who had taken leading roles. More than forty people were arrested, and I learned that some of them had been sentenced to twenty years with hard labor. In prison, they were forced to break stones and cut wood for the army. Some students were able to flee from the labor camp and they told me what happened when I met them again. But some of them are still in prison.

In my opinion, the government sentenced the students like that to show that the regime can do anything it wants. They really can do anything; there is no justice. It was shocking to see the oppression happening before my own eyes. The night of the arrests, I thought about all the people who suffered and who were injured that day, and I felt very sad about how it had all happened. I thought about how we have no justice, no rights. We, normal citizens, had nothing, not even the right to speak out. It made me feel like I wasn't human. Whatever the military wants, we have to do.

After the protests in 2003, I made the decision to do something for my people and to work against the SPDC's oppression. That was my first time participating in a protest, and since then, I have been committed to working for the people. This is how I changed my thinking and became involved in the democracy movement.

CHILDHOOD WAS LIKE A BAD DREAM

As a child, I thought soldiers were bullies. I saw soldiers and police come to our village to call people for portering and forced labor. When I heard they were coming, I used to hide in my home, or in the forest behind my house.

The economic situation was getting worse and worse at the time. Villagers were unable to trade freely. Taxes were higher. Farmers were forced to sell rice to the military, and land confiscation happened more and more frequently. Three acres of my family's farmland was confiscated by the government in November 1992. The military confiscated the land to establish a rice-buying center. The government bought paddies from the villagers to store in a barn, and decided that they wanted to make their barn on our land.[1]

Boys as young as fourteen or fifteen years were forced to join the army. Some of my friends were taken by the army, and others joined because they were young men who didn't have jobs.

When I recall my childhood, I think that what happened to the people in my village was very inhumane. People, even children such as myself, had to run away from our own homes. It was very frightening. Sometimes I feel it is following me like a bad dream.

IT'S ALL I'VE EVER WANTED TO BE

I started my monastic education when I was five years old. I went there because the government school didn't offer a good education; the teachers didn't come to school regularly, and the schools had days off most of the time. It's still like this in Arakan State today.

When I was seventeen, I started to live in the monastery and I became a novice monk. I was initiated as a novice monk along with my brothers and my cousins in a big, traditional ceremony held by our two families at the monastery. It is our Rakhine tradition to invite all the villagers and monks to the big pavilion beside the monastery for the initiation ceremony. Before the novice initiation, the novices-to-be must make a procession through the village with Rakhine drums in the front of the group, and then the parents offer all different things such as food, robes, furniture, and medicine to monks in the village monastery and nearby villages. People around the village make donations to the monks as the procession goes through the village, and they also provide food to guests

---

[1] The term "paddy" has a variety of uses; most commonly it refers to cultivated rice with intact husks, or to a lowland rice field.

who come from nearby villages. The people also come to see the monks at the monastery, where the monks deliver Buddhist scripture to the people. My initiation ceremony lasted two days.

I felt happy during my novice ceremony because my parents made a big donation to the monks. Even though I had to live away from my family in order to be a novice monk, my parents agreed to it because a monk's life is peaceful. I missed my family, but I would say prayers for them in the monastery.

In 1999, when I was about nineteen years old, the abbots sent me to Ponnagyun to pursue my higher monastic education.

So far in my life, I've decided to be a Buddhist monk and it is all I have wanted to be. I choose this life because I find Buddhism and life as a Buddhist monk to be very peaceful. As for the future, I am not sure—I cannot tell you if maybe I'll change or something. Before 2003, I never thought I would be an activist in an underground movement. I never thought of myself as someone who was actively against the SPDC. But as I've been getting older, and as I've witnessed brutal oppression and thought very deeply about it, my mind has become more and more determined every day to oppose the military government.

OUR LIVES ARE CONNECTED

After the incident in 2003, I became involved in educating the public and organizing the monks. I became involved in a secret movement of people within the country who oppose the SPDC. I joined the movement because of the people's social difficulties. I wanted to save them from having to fear the government.

Several monks and I started by organizing locally first. We began by showing other monks how the people were being brutally oppressed and experiencing extreme poverty. We raised awareness about how the people's suffering was having an impact on monks' lives. The lives of monks and laypeople are closely related. Monks depend on donations and alms from the public to survive.

Other monks agreed with my ideas, and some of them also became involved in working to educate and help the people in their local areas. Monks started to organize and help the people in their local communities the best that they could. Some monks in other places weren't receiving any donations, and they had no place to stay. We created links with different groups of monks in other towns and cities, and sometimes we would work together to educate people.

After the 2003 protest, we also started to monitor the military's activities and the SPDC's oppressive actions. Sometimes I would try to counter the actions of the SPDC officials. For example, in 2004, some SPDC officials came to make ID cards for the local people, but they asked the locals for money. The authorities are supposed to issue ID cards free of charge, and it is unfair that they force people to pay a lot of money for them. If you don't have an ID card, you're not able to travel anywhere. The people didn't dare say anything to them, but I said, "Why are you asking for money from the people?" I tried to directly oppose the SPDC's extortion. The officials didn't listen to what I said; they just told me to stand aside.

When we started organizing, we had to do it very secretly. We had some difficulties because of the security situation, and we had to be very careful about who we talked to and who we invited to be part of the process. We were sure that if we organized openly, we would be arrested or something bad would happen. If the authorities knew we were organizing, they would crush our organization. So, we would use letters to secretly inform each other about meetings and then come together and discuss the situation in our town. In our discussions, we would secretly decide what actions we should take. We had some older monks who were more experienced in activism and organizing, and they guided us in what to do. Later, some activist laypeople also became involved in our organization and helped show us what to do. We secretly planned demonstrations targeting the military government. However, we decided that we had to wait for the right time to make our plans happen.

WE DO IT FOR PEOPLE, NOT FOR POWER

In 2006, I moved to Sittwe, in Arakan State, to continue my monastic education. The Saffron Revolution first began in Sittwe, and I actively participated. The Saffron Revolution got its name because the movement was led by monks who wear saffron-colored robes. In mid-August, 2007, a number of monks in Sittwe started to protest against the soaring price of petrol. After the fuel prices were hiked, the prices of different commodities also rose. The price of rice doubled. Before the petrol price hike, rice cost only 300 kyats per kilogram, but after the price hike, the price became 600 or 700 kyats.[2] It became very difficult for people to survive daily.

This also impacted the monks very seriously because monks depend on people's donations of food. When monks went out to collect their alms, the people could not donate anything, so the monks didn't have any food to eat. The people would come out crying, "Reverend, sorry, we have nothing to donate to you today." When we heard of these kinds of woes from the people, the monks felt upset. We decided we should do something for the people.

About a week later, the monks arranged a meeting to encourage people to join a protest. There were more than 200 monks, university students, and community members together. The reason for the meeting was to speed up people's involvement.

During the meeting, we decided to protest the high fuel prices and the people's poverty. We wanted the government to reduce the price of commodities in Arakan State. We decided to organize the protest not only for the local people, but for the nation—we knew that if we started, the nation would follow.[3]

---

[2] 300 kyats is approximately US$0.30; 600 and 700 kyats are approximately US$0.60 and US$0.70, respectively.

[3] Sittwe was the first city that monks gathered in to demonstrate during the Saffron Revolution. Protestors from the 88 Student Generation group staged a protest in Rangoon on August 19, 2007.

We thought that with many people demonstrating, the government would be forced to become aware of the people's suffering. We knew that protesting was very dangerous in Burma, but we thought that the peoples' suffering was more dangerous because they didn't have enough food. We worked to gather the people and start a demonstration.

In the last week of August, we started protesting with more than eighty monks and two or three hundred laypeople. We decided to start the protest by reciting the *Metta Sutra*. The *Metta Sutra* is a special prayer and verse in the Buddhist scripture for the well-being of the people. We recite it for peace and happiness, and freedom from suffering for all beings. Wherever monks go, or whatever they do, such as participate in a ceremony, they must first show compassion for the people and all beings—so we used the *Metta Sutra* prayer to show compassion for the people in the 2007 protests. When you show compassion, others can understand you more easily. This was not the first time we had used the *Metta Sutra* prayer during protest. There were monks involved in the 1988 protests who had also used the *Metta Sutra* to show compassion for all beings.

We started to recite the prayer when we first started marching in the street. We chanted this: "May all living things live in peace and be free from danger, anger, and poverty." We chanted this, aimed at all creatures in different directions of the universe by addressing "south, north, east, and west." People encouraged the monks, first paying homage to us, and then joining us in the protest.

On that first day, the authorities didn't give us any serious problems. They just warned the monks not to protest in the streets and to go back to their monasteries. But on the second day, the senior SDPC government officials sent the order to disperse the protests by beating us.

By the second day, there were maybe one or two thousand people marching on the streets of Sittwe. Students and ordinary people joined the protest and demanded democracy and human rights. As more people joined, we became more enthusiastic. It was surprising to see lots of people showing their support. We felt very courageous because we had the opportunity to say out loud what we had silently been keeping inside.

Then the military and police started breaking up groups of demonstrators by firing tear gas and beating them with canes. There were equal numbers of soldiers and police, and they arrested and beat the monks who were demonstrating. I was beaten. The soldiers and the police had no targets when they were beating people; they'd wave their stick and whatever they hit, it didn't matter to them. They also threw stones and shot people with catapults. The protesters were dispersing with bleeding wounds on their heads and bodies. When the police started to get even more violent, I was forced to run away with the other monks. When we were running, I was fortunate that a cane didn't hit me, but I fell down, and some other people stepped on me while they were running.

From what I saw, not all of the police came forward to beat the people. But some of the junior police had come forward because of pressure from the higher authorities. If they didn't come forward to beat us, they would also be beaten or even arrested.

The authorities started trying to arrest the monks, especially those who were taking leading roles in the demonstration. The intelligence units and soldiers also came to raid monasteries very late at night. Some monks were arrested and no one heard anything about what happened to them. Later we heard that they were taken to remote prisons and interrogated, seriously beaten, and killed.

The authorities came looking for me because I was one of the leaders of the protest and I also reported information to exile media. But when the police came to raid my monastery, I was not there. I knew it wasn't secure enough for me to stay inside, so starting from the first day of the protests I had decided to change locations and stay in a different place in the city. When I heard that they had come to find me, I decided that I had to flee completely from Sittwe. If they arrested me, they would force me to leave the monkhood, and they would beat and interrogate me. In Arakan State, monks were forcibly de-robed and imprisoned. Many had disappeared after arrest. I had no idea what to do to for my security other than escape from the SPDC's hands as fast as possible. I fled to Bangladesh that day.

In Bangladesh, I heard on an overseas radio program that after the police had used violence against the demonstrators in Sittwe, more people became involved in the protests every day. The protests were spreading to Pakokku and Rangoon. I heard that police had arrested and beaten more monks involved in the demonstrations, and had used tear-gas bombs and guns on the crowd.

When monks throughout Burma heard the news about the beatings and killings, they demanded that the government apologize. The monks said that if the government didn't apologize, they would launch a nation-wide strike. This meant boycotting the offering of alms from the main authorities and military families. Burmese monks officially launched the strike on September 18, 2007, refusing to accept alms from military families and turning their alms bowls upside down. Monks in exile also actively demonstrated—including here in Bangladesh.

Nowadays, there are many monks who don't accept offerings by the military authorities. Without an apology, we will never open our bowls to the government's donations. Hundreds of monks were killed, and some of the monks' leaders, such as U Gambira and U Ithariya, were sentenced to jail. They are still there now.

A REAL BUDDHIST COUNTRY

Burma is not a real Buddhist country. In Buddhist culture, men and women pay respect to monks and consider them sacred, because it is monks who have maintained and preached the Buddha's teachings since he passed away. Although the ruling generals consider themselves as Buddhists, they are not following the non-violence teachings of the Buddha. They commit atrocities to maintain their power.

As a Buddhist monk, it is my responsibility to continue using nonviolent means to fight for democracy. With compassion for all beings, we can overcome our difficulties and suffering. People might criticize our nonviolent movement, but as I am a Buddhist monk, I cannot use violence. When we started the Saffron Revolution, we felt compassion for the people's suffering and felt we should do something to help free them from suffering. Like this, we started a movement. Now we also want to continue building this kind of movement for the future, because there will be no democracy in Burma without this.

There are many difficulties for me to survive in Bangladesh. There are very few Buddhists and monasteries here. The monasteries cannot accommodate even one more monk because they are in a difficult situation themselves. I have been registered with the UNHCR, but it has not provided any help. Although I am free from the military government, I am living with worry and a lack of security in everything. I want to go back to Burma. After I arrived here, I couldn't have any contact with my family. I miss them. But if I go back, it is sure that I will get arrested. What will happen to me in the future is uncertain.

I wish I could study here in Bangladesh, but I can't; I'm just trying to survive. I'm living with the help of the organization I work with, which is known as the IBMO—the International Burmese Monks Organization. We formed the IBMO in November 2007, after the Saffron Revolution, because so many monks had to leave Burma and were scattered everywhere, but we needed to be organized. The other name for our organization is Sasana Moli.[4] The name relates to our mission, which is to safeguard and defend Buddhism in Burma. The Burmese military government has been beating and killing monks, and even now monks are continually monitored at monasteries, and when they travel. But despite the government's restrictions, some monks are still trying to do what they can for the people.

We want to support the monks' democracy movement in Burma, and also be able to launch the movement internationally, to protect the monks in exile—some monks are here in Bangladesh, others are in India and so on. Through the IBMO, we are able to connect with other monks to share critical information and organize. Even though I fled from Burma and am living in Bangladesh, I still oppose the Burmese government and

---

[4] Also known as the International Burmese Monks Organization, "Sasana Moli" translates as "the crown jewel of the monastic community."

I'm still involved in the movement against them. Sometimes we go to the Burmese embassy in Dhaka and demonstrate in front of it—we demand that the Burmese government stop oppressing its people.

The Saffron Revolution taught me that despite whatever violence is perpetuated by the SPDC, we should continue to fight and stand for our beliefs. We should protest peacefully and not withdraw. We should stand firm and go on. We need people from all walks of life to participate. Everyone should fight so that we can have democracy.

If all the people in Burma work together, then I think it is certain that we will have human rights and democracy. With the public's participation in the movement, we can overthrow the military government. The democracy movement is not only for the Buddhist people in my country, it's for every person—Muslims, Christians, everyone. We work for everyone.

I hope that international governments do something for the people of Burma, to help solve the problems we have. Right now we are suffering severely in all respects, while the government is trying to hold the 2010 election to prolong their rule. We need help—the people cannot overthrow the government alone.

BURMA

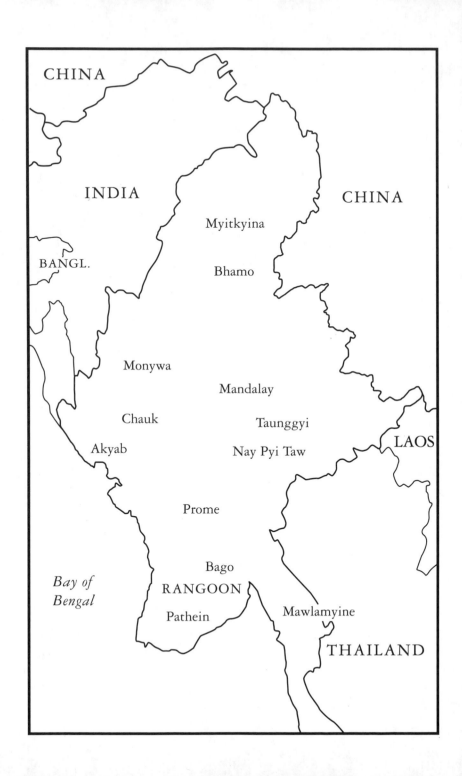

AUNTIE HLA

50, *Cyclone Nargis survivor*

ETHNICITY: *Burman*

BIRTHPLACE: *Irrawaddy Division, Burma*

INTERVIEWED IN: *Rangoon, Burma*

During the interview Auntie Hla sat upright in her chair, her legs crossed with both hands clasped over her right knee. Her brightly colored longyi *and button-down blouse were both neatly ironed. She spoke to us about surviving Cyclone Nargis, a storm that ripped through Burma's Irrawaddy Delta in 2008. Marked by 132 mph winds and a storm surge of twelve feet, the cyclone was the most destructive in Burma's recorded history. It killed an estimated 140,000 people and razed 700,000 homes to the ground. Though Auntie Hla smiled and laughed when we first met, recalling her experiences with the cyclone brought tears to her eyes.*

I didn't know about the storm before it came.

It happened just after the Thingyan water festival. Before the storm, I earned money by going to sell coconuts in Rangoon each week, and my son worked on a passenger ship that went through the waterways between

Rangoon and the Irrawaddy Delta.[1] We were living with my stepsister in a village in the delta. I was in debt after my husband passed away, so I'd sold my house and farm. I had borrowed money from others as an investment in my business selling coconuts. Sometimes I lost money because I had a bad day of selling.

I celebrated Thingyan in the village with my son, because he didn't need to work during the festival. When I saw my son, he suggested that we could build a new house and live there together. My son was thirty at the time. He had been married, but he divorced his wife because her parents were against their marriage.

After the water festival, I went to Rangoon and my son took the ship he worked on to a workshop for repairs. On April 29, I came back from Rangoon. I arrived in the town where I usually transferred boats. It was raining heavily and it was windy. The sky was very cloudy and a little more gray than during the ordinary rainy season. The workshop where my son's ship was being repaired is on the way to my village, so when I was on the boat to my village, I wanted to stop off there to see him. But because of the heavy rains, my boat couldn't stop. As we passed the ship, I saw some people cooking on it, but I could not separate my son from the other people. I went directly back to my village, and had the idea to try and visit my son again. But I couldn't go then because it rained constantly every day for two or three days.

I didn't know the cyclone was coming. My village is very close to the sea, so we always have storms and it's always windy. Some people said there was an announcement on the radio that a storm was coming, but I didn't have a radio so I didn't know.[2] Some houses owned a radio, but they

---

[1] The Irrawaddy Delta region is a vast, densely populated area that is both Burma's largest rice producer and vital to its fish harvest due to its rich soil, streams and rivers.

[2] Indian government weather forecasters say that they gave their Burmese counterparts ample warning of the cyclone's severity as early as April 26, but did not receive a response. On May 2, the Burmese government sent out warnings to residents in the danger zones, but many residents remained unaware of the severity of the coming cyclone. For more about Cyclone Nargis and the SPDC's reaction see, appendix VIII.

did not listen to the weather report.[3] Even those who'd heard the news didn't think the storm would be as heavy as it was, because they had never faced a storm like Nargis in their whole lives. They didn't think it could be that strong. But this was not an ordinary storm.

I HAD NEVER SEEN WIND LIKE THIS

On the evening of May 2, I ate dinner with my stepsister, my brother-in-law, and their sons. We were having some after-dinner conversation when it started raining. It was a little windy, a little dark. Then it grew darker and darker. The winds became stronger and stronger, and the rain became heavier and heavier. The trees in front of my house shook. At eight o'clock, the wind was very, very strong—I had never seen wind like this. Our neighbor's house was made of bamboo and we watched it shake. Then we saw the couple who lived there run to their parents' house.

My stepsister's house was mostly made of wood, so it was stronger and more resistant. At the time, I thought the wind would just last for five or ten minutes and then be finished.

We didn't move, we didn't leave our house. One of the walls of our house, the one where we kept our altar and statue of Buddha, was made of bamboo. Soon that whole wall fell. We pulled it up again and tied it with a rope. The roof of our house was made from leaves; it hadn't flown off, but it was shaking very much.

Then the tide from the sea came in. In our village, the houses were not so far from the river, so it wasn't unusual. But that day, the tide came not only up to the river but past it and then well onto the land. It came quickly—we could see the water on the street in front of my house. If you put anything into the water, it would be taken away with the waves. My brother-in-law was a fisherman, and I said he should get his boat, which

---

[3] Typically shared by community members, radios are critical to receiving accurate news throughout Burma that would otherwise be censored by the military junta's information blackout.

was at a nearby river, and bring it back to the house. We thought that no matter what happened with the storm, we could stay in the boat.

It took my brother-in-law an hour to bring the boat back. By that time, the water was starting to rise over the front steps of the house. My brother-in-law tied a rope to the boat and pulled it right up to the house. My stepsister was very afraid; she didn't know what to do. But I was not afraid, so I reassured her and told her to get in the boat.

I carried some things from the house to the boat—shoes, some clothes, some pagoda statues. The water was now up to my knees. The wind was growing stronger and the house was starting to fall, so I told my stepsister, "Hold on to the boat and don't worry about the shoes." I tied the boat to the house and to a heavy wooden trunk so it would not be carried away.

The neighbors were running and shouting, "Go to the monastery! Go to land!" Everything was getting destroyed and the water was everywhere. When I stood in my house, the water had gone up to my thighs, but when I stood on the street, the water was up to my chest.

Then the tide came again and again. The people who had boats were okay—they climbed into them. The people without boats were running and shouting with their children and babies, and some were falling down in the water. Coconut trees were falling everywhere. People went running down the streets toward high land, and my brother-in-law started pushing the boat toward higher land as well.

Once we reached higher land, near the house of my brother-in-law's parents, we used many ropes to tie the boat around big trees to anchor ourselves. My brother-in-law's parents also got into the boat. It rained all night, and we had to constantly bail out the water from inside the boat so that it did not sink.

At first, during the cyclone, the winds were from the southeast. But after about 3 a.m., the winds came from the west. It was continuous—there was never a quiet time between the wind switching directions. We heard houses falling around us. My stepsister's house was strong, but it also fell.

I didn't know what time it was exactly, but around five or six o'clock in the morning, the tide started going down, but it was still windy. The sky was so red that it looked almost like fire.

During the night, I could only see the people I was in the boat with: my stepsister, her husband and sons, and my brother-in-law's parents. But when the sun rose, we saw all of the houses that had partially or completely collapsed. Some of the houses had disappeared and floated away with the water. Some boxes and other materials had arrived in the water from other villages. At that point, I put my stepsister and her sons in a small house nearby that was still standing. I don't know whose house it was, but I wanted to protect them from the rain.

Two or three other boats with families in them also arrived near the house. We were afraid of getting hit by a zinc roof, because a lot of roofs were flying through the sky.

It was still windy for another hour or so. After the tide went down, the boat was back on land.

ONLY ENOUGH WATER TO WET THE MOUTH

There are two main parts of my village, a southern part and northern part. No one died in the northern part where we lived—the houses were just destroyed and the police station totally fell. In the southern part of the village people died because that part is a little lower and there are a lot of fields. I don't know how many people died there exactly. About seventy people died in the western part. In that area, near the cemetery, five people died in the same house. Only one woman died in the eastern part of the village, where a tree fell on her. We had to dig to get her body out from under it.

The morning after Nargis, people counted who was lost in each family and they searched around the village and found some of the bodies of the people who had died. They found villagers' bodies in the corners of houses or in fields or in the rivers, and then they took them and buried them. Some people's bodies were found because they started to smell. If we found a person's body and knew the family it belonged to, we called the family members to bury the person. If we didn't know which family the body belonged to, we would bury it ourselves.

After the water went down, we had run down to see our house. It was partly destroyed, and it had fallen halfway to the ground. There were two monasteries in my village, but one of them had been destroyed during the night so there was only one monastery left to stay at. I didn't want to stay there because it was full of people.

My stepsister and her sons stayed in the house near the boat, and I stayed on the boat with my brother-in-law and his parents for three or four days. We made a roof with bamboo and leaves to protect us from the rain. Everywhere people wanted to die. There was no food to eat, no water to drink. Every house used a big pot to store drinking water in, but the sea water had entered the pots, so there was no drinking water. Fortunately, there was one water tank left in the monastery. The monks gave one bottle for every family. When we took a drink, it was only enough to wet the mouth.

We were hungry, but there was no rice to cook. Some rice shops gave people free rice, but it wasn't good because it had gotten wet. The first day they contributed sixteen cans of rice per family, but we could only use it the first day because it went bad after a day. The next day they contributed one rice can per person, so if you had four family members, they gave you four cans.

We tried to get a fire going to cook the rice, but all of the wood was wet. There was a rich man who had a house situated on the higher part of the land built with brick. I went to the house and asked to have some dry wood to cook and he gave me some.

People from the village were saying, "What should we do? We have no food to eat. We're hungry." We ate coconuts and drank coconut juice because so many coconut trees had fallen. Some people didn't get food for two or three days. The monks at the monastery also contributed food. At first they contributed rice and curry, but after one day they did not have enough rice to give to the villagers, so they boiled the wet rice in water and gave us the soup.

THANKFUL JUST FOR A DROP

During those first three days, nobody came to our village to help. We didn't have any contact with the city and we couldn't use the telephone. There were no ships or boats coming or leaving. There was no food to sell in the restaurants or food shops.

I believed someone would arrive in my village to save us. I hoped some government authorities would come—I wasn't sure who would, but I thought some authorities would arrive. But I imagined that since we didn't have any contact with another village or another town, other people didn't know what had happened in my village.

After five days, some officials arrived with a helicopter. They brought rice, food, and a fresh-water machine. Altogether, there were six helicopters in one day. The officials said it had been a big storm and the strongest part had gone right through the southeastern part of our country.

I wasn't angry that it took five days for the government to arrive. Some families were dead. Other some families had no food to eat. I don't know if they were angry or not. But I was very thankful just for a drop of water.

The government constructed camps near the southern part of the village for the people who wanted to go there. But in my village, not many people wanted to go to the camp because it was far.

A helicopter bringing food and water arrived every day. They also brought a doctor. The local authorities contributed firewood and one can of rice per person.

About two weeks later, we got tents and mosquito nets from the ICRC—International Committee of the Red Cross. Donations from many organizations came to my village. An Italian organization gave a bag of things to each household. The bag included: a pot to cook rice, a small pot to cook curry, five plates and five bowls, one steel cup, five spoons and one big spoon, a knife to cut meat and vegetables, one kilo of beans, some soap, one towel, two longyis for men, a blanket, two T-shirts, a nail clipper, five toothbrushes and toothpaste; and a plastic box where we could keep drinking water or oil if we faced a difficult storm or flood in the future. I was so happy, I almost cried. It was enough for our family's survival—for cooking and drinking. We thanked the donors by sending them blessings in our prayers.

I didn't see any international donors come to the village because the local authorities distributed everything. I only saw Burmese people who provided the materials locally. So I am not sure where all of the donations came from. I asked a volunteer once and he said some of them came from Japan and from the Burmese Traders Association.

IN MY MIND, MY SON WAS STILL ALIVE

After Nargis, I didn't know if my son was still alive or not.

I was hoping this storm had only happened in my village. Two or three days after Nargis, we still didn't have any contact with the town where my son's ship was being worked on. Four or five days later, the shopkeepers from my village had to go to that town to buy some food and other supplies. When they came back to my village, they told me that my son's ship and another ship had both disappeared. The people who worked on those ships were also missing.

When I heard that, I didn't think he was dead because he could swim very well. He was very young and active. I thought he could have floated along the water and landed somewhere else where some people saved him.

We rebuilt my stepsister's house with the help of many other villagers, and I stayed there, waiting for news about my son. During this time, I sometimes volunteered for the military and the local authorities on construction projects. The soldiers were working too, and they treated me well.

There were five people missing from my son's boat—the manager, two of his family members, my son, and another young man. I went so many times to the ship manager's house to inquire about my son. The manger's wife said she had taken a boat along the river to try and find them, but she had no success. If I had the money, I would have searched for them with a boat like she did.

There were lots of rumors saying that the men had amnesia after the storm and were now living in a different township. The manager's wife went to investigate the rumors and try to find them, but she still didn't find my son or the others.

People in the village said that the five people, including my son, had tried to save the ship because they were very faithful to their boss, and that if they had abandoned the ship they could have survived.

A few months after the storm, the ship owner got news about where the ship had sunk. It was totally damaged—if they lifted it with a crane or something, the ship would be destroyed. One month later, the owner tried to get the ship out again, and this time they tried to just get some parts of the ship, but it was still stuck.

Finally, the manager's wife told me that if my son and the other men were still alive, they would have come back home sometime during that six-month period. Eventually we made donations to the monks to hold a funeral ceremony for the men at the place where the ship had been tied before it disappeared. In Burmese culture, we usually donate to the monks seven days after somebody passes away, but I didn't think my son was dead, so I didn't donate for six months. In my mind, my son was still alive and had arrived somewhere else. I thought he would turn up.

As soon as I donated for my son's funeral, I left. I didn't want to stay anymore. I had to assume that my son had passed away. I was unhappy, and I couldn't control my mind—maybe I was going mad. I knew that if I didn't leave this village, I would only think about my son's death.

IF WE CAN PREPARE

After my son died, I didn't want to stay in the delta anymore. I decided to go to Rangoon to stay with my relatives and look for a job.

I found a job through my relatives, working as a live-in housemaid for a family in Rangoon. When I first met my boss, I told her, "I'm honest and I can do anything you want me to."

I'm currently living in the house where I work. Every day I get up early in the morning, cook rice and curry, and then go to the market. I also wash and press clothes. I feel like I'm in my own house while working for this family. They treat me like a sister and share their food with me. They also buy me clothes and give me 15,000 kyats per month.[4]

When I'm sixty to sixty-five years old and no longer working, I'll have to go to a home for the elderly because I have no son. I'm saving money in preparation for this. I only buy the things I need, and I don't buy any beauty products because I am already middle-aged.

After the cyclone, some construction companies built houses to donate in my village. But only some people got the houses, like the president of the village and some other rich people. I didn't know how to get a house and I didn't want to ask about it because the village leader already knew about me and my situation.

I hope we never again have to face a disaster like this in my country, but if we can prepare and a storm actually comes, maybe there will be less damage.

I lost only one person. Some lost many people—whole families were lost. If I compare my situation with theirs, mine was not as bad.

---

[4] Approximately US$15.

KHIN LWE

29, former political prisoner, journalist
ETHNICITY: *Burman-Chin*
BIRTHPLACE: *Rangoon, Burma*
INTERVIEWED IN: *Rangoon, Burma*

Khin Lwe was soft-spoken yet forthright as she recounted her experiences as a journalist and relief volunteer during Cyclone Nargis. In 2008, Nargis devastated Burma's Irrawaddy Delta, leaving an estimated 140,000 dead and destroying 700,000 homes. In the immediate aftermath of the cyclone, the authorities arrested some journalists reporting on the disaster, as well as some people who took the initiative to do relief work. The regime targeted former political prisoners and others who they suspected might organize people politically.

I was arrested during my first job as a journalist. It was in June 2008, soon after Cyclone Nargis. I was a political prisoner for over one year, and I was released just three months ago.

My parents and relatives didn't want me to be a journalist. They thought it would be too tough of a job in Burma. They wanted me to be a lawyer because they thought that was a more appropriate profession for me. But they couldn't stop me from being a journalist—it was my ambition.

I WOULD GIVE MYSELF FEVERS

I was born in Rangoon in 1981. When I was young, my parents worked as government servants. For their jobs, my parents traveled frequently and separately to other divisions and states. Because of my parents' frequent travel, I lived in Sagaing Division with my grandparents. I am the oldest in my family, ten years older than my sister. My grandfather was a police officer in Sagaing Division and my grandmother was a schoolteacher. At exam time, my grandmother would go to school with me and stand outside the window while I took the exam. After each question I would hold up my exam for her and ask, "Is this right?"

While I was living with my grandparents, I missed my father so much that I would give myself fevers. My grandparents would call for him to come back and visit, and after he arrived I would recover. That happened again and again.

As a child, I liked reading very much. I read lots of books, all kinds. My mother also liked reading. She didn't like us to play outside, so she would give us books to read. I liked translated books, like the classics, biographies, and contemporary novels from other countries. Then I became interested in political books toward the end of middle school. One of my favorite books is about Burma's independence movement before the Second World War—the student movement and student strikes. I didn't read books about the current political situation in Burma, because most of the political books in the library were just biographies of politicians.

I learned about the 1988 uprising from my parents, not from books.[1] The only thing I remember about the uprising was the government broadcast of the events. Protesters beheaded some people, and someone captured it on video. The government got the footage, and after the

---

[1] In 1988, deteriorating economic conditions sparked nationwide protests against the ruling government. See appendix VIII for information about the uprising.

uprising, they broadcast the beheadings.[2] My parents didn't allow me to watch, but I saw it anyway. That is the one thing I remember. I was afraid. I didn't know which side was right or which one was wrong. The only thing I knew was that it was an awful image.

YOU COULD SENSE THAT WE WERE OPPRESSED

After graduating high school in 2000, I had to wait two years before I could begin studying law at Dagon University in Rangoon. There was a backlog of students from when the government closed the universities from 1996 to 2000 because of the 1996 student strikes.[3]

My aunt and uncle had both gone to university, but compared to their experiences of student life, mine were not entirely good. When they were in college, the buildings were famous, historic buildings. But when I was at Dagon University, the buildings were completely new. There were no trees, and in the rainy season it flooded. The environment was bad, and the teachers were young and unqualified.

Furthermore, when my aunt and uncle were students, there were arts organizations and associations at every university. Music, literature, and dance groups were legally and freely allowed to form. But after the '88 uprising, university organizations were banned by the government—not even arts and literature organizations were allowed. I think the government banned them because they were scared of student movements.

I felt deeply sad that we weren't allowed to form associations and clubs, but it couldn't be helped. That's why my friends and I decided to create our own unofficial organization. We were frustrated—we felt like we had fewer rights than students in other countries, and even students of the last generation. We wanted to write and share our feelings, so we

---

[2] For more on protester's backlash against police after the demonstration, see "The 8-8-88 Uprising" section of the "A Brief History of Burma" in the appendix.

[3] For more on the 1996 student strikes, and subsequent university closings, see the "A Brief History of Burma" section of the appendix.

published our poems and essays as small books. There was a tea shop where we liked to hang out; it was our place. There, we shared what we'd been reading, writing, and learning. I remember when a famous Burmese translator translated *The Class*, a novel about student life at Harvard University.[4] Many university students borrowed or bought this book; we liked it very much. You can imagine how we felt, seeing the differences between their experiences and ours.

One day, a student posted a notice on campus for a Burmese literature group, and he was arrested and received a seven-year sentence. After this happened, we were scared but we decided to continue publishing.

My friends and I didn't write poems or essays that were political, but when you read them, you could sense that we were oppressed. But since our publication wasn't official, we didn't have to submit it to the scrutiny board.[5] We printed our books on a Gestetner copier. After the third or fourth book, we heard a rumor that the university administration had started to watch us closely. When we heard that rumor, we stopped producing books. At that same time, at another university, some students had been arrested for publishing a similar kind of small book of poems.

ALL BURMESE CITIZENS BECAME JOURNALISTS

All through university I wanted to be a reporter because I wanted to earn money while keeping up my interest in literature and writing. I applied to work at a weekly publication, but I couldn't take the job because my parents didn't want me to work while I was in school. They just wanted me to be a lawyer.

---

[4] *The Class* was written by Erich Segal. It details the lives of five 1958 Harvard students through the perspective of their twenty-five-year reunion.

[5] The Printers' and Publishers' Registration Act requires all publishers to register and submit copies of their publications for approval to the Press Scrutiny and Registration Division, formerly called the Press Scrutiny Board.

After I graduated in 2005, I had to do an internship at the chamber of law for a year and a half to get my license to become a lawyer. But after the internship ended, I still decided to become a reporter instead of a lawyer. My parents couldn't stop me.

The 2007 Saffron Revolution was another one of my main motivations for becoming a journalist. While it was happening, many young people, including me, were searching the internet for information. We would find out where the monks were gathering and send group emails to our friends so we could all go there. Then we would take photos and document our experiences in order to share information with our friends and groups. During that time, all Burmese citizens became journalists. I knew then that it was what I wanted to do professionally. Journalists can speak for the rights of the people.

The Saffron Revolution was not only about politics. It was also about social, economic, and religious rights. The monks stood in front of the crowd to represent what the people were feeling. They wanted to show that all the people living in Burma were having economic and social problems—they didn't even have enough money to donate to the monks anymore. When the Saffron Revolution was first rising up, I felt happy and satisfied. Then the crackdown made me so sad and frustrated, because someone I was close to got arrested. I was very, very worried about what would happen after. I didn't want it to continue anymore.

I can't analyze the impact of the Saffron Revolution politically, but I think the coming November 2010 election and political progress is the result of the Saffron Revolution. At least one important message got out: how we had been oppressed for many years. People were defiant, people revolted again. After the '88 uprising, there were nearly twenty years of silence, and then in 2007, we spoke out against our oppression.

After the Saffron Revolution, people became more aware of politics, especially the younger generation. Even though young people weren't involved in politics, they became interested after 2007. Also, some middle-aged and elderly people changed their views on the government because of the crackdown on the Buddhist monks. In Burmese villages, we are very Buddhist; we don't even step on a monk's shadow. So when the Burmese military beat the monks in the Saffron Revolution, it was the worst thing they could have done.

THE STORM

In 2008, I began my career as a journalist. One of my friends introduced me to the editor at a weekly publication. I didn't know anything about journalism, and the editor had to teach me how to chase news tips and how to interview.

The day of Cyclone Nargis, I was in Rangoon at work, using the internet. I had only been a journalist for three months when the storm hit. Before the cyclone, there were weather announcements in the newspaper and on TV, but people didn't think much of the announcements. Even as a journalist, I felt the cyclone warnings were normal, because Burmese people are used to the rainy season. There were often cyclone and storm warnings for fishermen and ships, so we just expected torrential rain and strong winds. We didn't expect the serious damage that occurred.

My brother and sister were on the internet, and they got the information that the cyclone might be very disruptive. I don't know where they found that information, but I got an email from them around 2:30 p.m. that day that said, "There is a very strong cyclone heading towards Lower Burma." At about 3 p.m., I got information from one of our weekly publications that Hine Gyi Island, in the western part of the Irrawaddy Delta, had been totally destroyed.[6]

My brother told me to go home early, but I was too busy because that day was the paper's weekly deadline. By the time I left, it was 7 p.m. I left for my aunt's apartment—I sometimes slept at her apartment one or two nights a week. On the way, there was rain, but it wasn't heavy and the wind was not so strong yet. When I got to my aunt's, I was tired and went

---

[6] Hine Gyi Island (or Haigyi Island) refers to an island on the southwest corner of the Irrawaddy Delta, where the Burmese Navy was based and where Cyclone Nargis first hit.

to sleep. At around midnight, the sounds of strong winds and breaking glass woke me and my aunt. We were on the second floor of a four-story building, and a window on the floor above us had broken. My aunt was worried the glass had fallen on her car, so I took out my camera and opened the window. A tree had nearly fallen outside, and glass was still falling from the window above ours. I couldn't get any pictures, because the wind was so strong. My aunt finally closed the window. I was scared. It was the first time I'd experienced a storm like that.

I went back to sleep, and when I woke up again it was 7 a.m. and the cyclone was still going, the winds were still strong. I thought about how I wouldn't be able to go to my office that day, and I fell back asleep.

Between ten-thirty and eleven in the morning, the wind stopped. The storm was over.

At 11:15 a.m., my aunt and I left the apartment for lunch. I was so surprised when I first saw that most of the trees were down—it was like a jungle! Then we discovered the food shortage. People had to queue in the small grocery store to buy eggs or rice. In the bakery, people were waiting to buy doughnuts and bread for their lunch. Hardly any vehicles were passing, only a few people in private cars.

I went back to my aunt's house and got my camera. Then I went back out and began walking around the city taking pictures. Many people were out on the street looking at the damage. Trees had fallen across every road, and every road was blocked. Some people were cutting the trees to clear the road. Then I saw a ferry on the riverbank of the Rangoon River—the water had carried it all the way onto the bank.

When I was taking photos near a temple, a man told me, "Take a lot of photos and send them to the news. Send them to the local media." Sometimes people encourage us to take photos and cover these kinds of events.

I felt I had to report this event. My aunt had let me go out to buy food, but I forgot the food because I was taking photos. I walked two or three miles in about three hours, and I had to report what I saw. I didn't feel hungry, I could only focus on being a reporter. At that time, I didn't know much about the ethics of journalism and I wasn't very skilled. The only thing I knew was that I had to report what I saw there.

I wanted to take photos, but I didn't want to ask people about their experiences at first. Everyone looked so depressed because of the shortage of food and water and electricity. I was depressed too. Everything was totally shut off.

I WALKED AROUND THE CITY, MOSTLY TAKING PHOTOS

That first day after Nargis, I took photos around Rangoon and then I went to report to my office. But when I got there, I couldn't work because the office was still closed. The publication was suspended for two weeks because of the electricity shortage.

Two or three days after the storm passed, I heard more news about the damage in the Irrawaddy Delta. I called my uncle and heard about the situation, about how many people had been killed in the cyclone.[7] I knew some of those who had died. In the delta area, the death toll was very high. My uncle was in Pathein, a port city in the Irrawaddy Division. He told me some of the cyclone victims were arriving there with no clothes, and that the people of Pathein were donating clothes to them.

After the storm, I stayed with my parents on the outskirts of Rangoon. For the first two weeks I walked around the city, mostly taking photos, but I also listened to people and gathered information about their experiences.

In the first week, all of Rangoon had trouble getting access to food and water, but in the following weeks the situation on the outskirts of Rangoon worsened. The area of Rangoon is huge and very densely populated. The people there are mostly day workers, and every day they have to work in order to buy their daily food. When Cyclone Nargis struck,

---

[7] The vast majority of the approximately 140,000 casualties of Cyclone Nargis occurred in the Irrawaddy Delta, where waves reached over twelve feet.

most of the businesses shut down, so the people didn't have work, which meant they didn't have any income to buy food.

A small hut is not much work to fix. It's only about ten feet around, but people couldn't fix their homes because every day they had to spend all their money on food. To buy one small hut, they had to save money for two or three months, a little bit at a time. After Nargis, when all the huts collapsed and were destroyed, they stayed in other people's houses, and sometimes moved into abandoned houses. I went to a temple in the Rangoon area where about three hundred cyclone victims were taking refuge. They'd lost their homes and all their belongings.

The local media and government radio issued cyclone warnings three days before it happened, but they didn't tell us how to evacuate or how to protect ourselves. They only issued the warning that there would be a cyclone. If people had known exactly what was going to happen three or five days in advance, they could have protected their homes—instead they had to leave their belongings and evacuate.

The authorities had to repair their own compounds, so they didn't help the victims right away. Their offices were also damaged, and they had to help themselves. During that first week, people were cutting up the trees in the street with knives and small handsaws to try and make some repairs. Then the government started to help us.

For us, it is normal that the government didn't help sooner. They don't have a system in place for emergencies. Later, the government declared that there were no cyclone victims in Rangoon, only in the delta.

REPORTING WASN'T ENOUGH

Two weeks after the storm, my office opened back up and I was able to give some photos and information to my editor. When our office got the internet connection back, I was able to see news about the cyclone. A group from my office collected all our photos and put them on a CD to get them to the outside media. We tried to find someone who could deliver the information.

Although my colleagues and I wanted to share the story of Nargis with the outside world, at that time we were more interested in helping people than in reporting. My colleagues and other reporters were helping with donation efforts to support people in the delta, and we traveled to the delta area together.

The first trip to the delta that I took was with my friends and colleagues. It's not far from Rangoon, but it took two or three hours to get there because transportation was so poor and the routes were damaged.

The second and third times my colleagues made trips to the delta, I didn't go along with them. I helped them prepare for their trip by buying things with the donated money to send to the delta. I also collected information to send back to the donors. My colleagues told me about the situation they saw on their second and third trips. They reported that the government had begun closely watching the local donors. The police, plainclothes government informants, and local authorities watched where the donations were being made and when the donation carts came into town.

One time when my colleagues were in the Irrawaddy Division distributing donations, the police questioned them seven times. Each time the police asked where they came from, their names, what they were donating. My colleagues had to give the names and addresses of the donors. After that happened to them, they didn't go back to the delta.

At that time, I was busy taking care of victims in the Rangoon area. I thought reporting alone wasn't enough. Many people were gathering rice and clothing to donate to the victims, but they couldn't provide all that the victims needed. Our government had given donations and support to the Irrawaddy Delta. In Rangoon, we received government aid one week after the cyclone, but in other areas they waited more than a week. It is still hard for me to understand the government's response and what they were thinking. Why didn't they respond instantly? It is my opinion that they didn't have a disaster response system, and they didn't know enough to create one. Also, we are a poor country, so the technology, the transportation—everything—was slow to respond.

For those few weeks, I helped with donations in the mornings. Then we prepared lunch for the cyclone victims around Rangoon. At 1 p.m. I would go to the office and turn in my photos and information. After that, I went back to the village to prepare dinner for the cyclone victims.

If someone donated a bag of rice, I would cook it for the victims. They didn't have cooking supplies, so my friend and I cooked the rice and delivered it to them. Sometimes one of the children there would say he wanted chicken curry, because every day they ate rice and bean soup. So we would collect donations for the ingredients and prepare chicken curry for them. Sometimes dinner was good and sometimes it wasn't—it depended on the donations we received.

Some elderly people were very weak and couldn't eat. They needed medical treatment, so I asked one of my doctor friends to come and to bring an IV drip.

Some people still had houses but they didn't have food, so the donors would give extra bags of rice to them. But the donors couldn't donate every day—they could only donate once a week for each affected area. Some of the affected areas were flooded, so the donors couldn't reach the victims—we helped by taking bags of rice to those victims. Although the death toll in Rangoon was not as high as in the delta, the food crisis in Rangoon was really bad.

I WOULD FACE WHATEVER WAS BEFORE ME

Four weeks after Nargis, the government declared that there were no victims in the city of Rangoon. After the government made that declaration, the local authorities came to the small Buddhist temple where I had been volunteering and evicted all the refugees who had taken shelter there. The government didn't want victims gathering in the area, so they made them leave by force.

In June, I tried to help the cyclone victims get international attention. A plainclothes police officer saw what I was doing and yelled, "Who are you?" He searched me and the victims and abused us verbally. I got very angry.

"Why are you saying these things to the victims?" I yelled at him. Then he arrested me.

They brought me to the police station. At first, I was angry. Later, I began to worry, especially for my mother. I knew my parents would be so worried. But then I began thinking about what would happen to me, and I decided I would face whatever was ahead.

They put me in a small cell in the police station. I was mixed in with the regular criminals. I'd never experienced anything like this, and I felt sad for the first time. They kept me there for two nights. Then they blindfolded me and took me to the interrogation center. They put me in a room and took my blindfold off. The room was small, about six feet wide. The walls were solid except for one window, and through it I could see the policewomen changing guard every hour.

During my interrogation, I was asked who had donated money, their names and addresses, how I contacted them, who I went through, and what my connection to them was. They asked me about the intention of the donations my colleagues and I had been delivering. They asked me if I had a relationship with the exile media groups—that was the main question they asked.

The government sees everything from a political point of view, so they suspected the donors, international and local, of being their enemies. They are always suspicious. The police were watching the local donors to see who they were affiliated with and what their political intentions were. They were especially interested in the donors' relationships with the National League for Democracy. The government thought the donors were from anti-government organizations and from political organizations outside Burma. If we have connections to political organizations outside Burma, that violates Section 17-1.[8] Having relations, even through donations, with outlawed parties or outlawed organizations carries a sentence of around three years in jail.

---

[8] Section 17-1 is an article of the 1908 Unlawful Associations Act: "Whoever is a member of an unlawful association, or takes part in meetings of any such association, or contributes or receives or solicits any contribution for the purpose of any such association…"

Our government was suspicious of the international community, since all countries except China and North Korea criticized them. Based on that, they suspected journalists as well. When the police officers grabbed me, they first thought I was a donor or a social worker, but after they checked my documents and saw I was a journalist, they were even more suspicious.

The interrogators were from my country, from my people. Why were they doing this? The interrogators are not criminals, not monsters. Some are intellectual, some have degrees—they are knowledgeable people. Why do they do it? I think there are two kinds of people who do these things. Some are participating because they are ordered to do so, and some just misunderstand what they are doing. These people are bad for the country, for the state.

Towards the end of the interrogation, they told me, "If you say anything about this interrogation, you will be charged." So I signed a paper that promised I wouldn't tell anyone.

After that, they sent me to Insein Prison. I wasn't afraid. I'd made up my mind before any of this happened: as a journalist, I knew I could face arrest. That made the situation easier to bear.

MY FRIENDS SUPPORTED ME

The trial began two weeks after my arrest, but they didn't sentence me until five months later.

Some political prisoners after Nargis were charged with 17-1. They probably would have liked to charge many more people with this, but they couldn't find the connection to outside political organizations, so they charged most people with section 505-B, which carried a two-year sentence.[9] A 505-B charge meant that you had disgraced the state or that you had intentions to destroy the state. That's what they charged me with.

---

[9] 505-B is an article of Chapter XXII of the Burmese Penal Code forbidding "statements, rumors or reports" with "intent to cause fear or alarm in the public."

When my trial finished, my friends and family told me that people internationally were trying to help our cause. My friends supported me, but they felt very sorry and sad for me. My parents also felt sad.

INSEIN PRISON

I spent the first seven months in prison with the other prisoners in the hall. There were three or four hundred of us living there. In the main prisoner hall, there was a wooden floor and we slept side by side in a row. At the end of the rows where we slept, there were three toilets for fifty to eighty prisoners. For the political prisoners, they put in nicer toilets. I didn't mind being with the other criminals; being with other people made the time pass.

We didn't get breakfast. The prison provided hot water in the morning, so we could make tea. Our families brought us tea leaves, instant noodles, and other dried food. My family sent coffee mix.

Lunch was rice with sour leaf soup and fish paste. For dinner, political prisoners each got soup and one egg. The soup was so light, you could see through to the bottom. It was dirty, made only of salt and vegetable leaves. The non-political prisoners didn't get an egg, only soup and rice. Also, I don't know if the men were treated the same. We women asked for our rights, so we got an egg added to the normal dinner.

WE WERE STILL PROTESTING

After seven months in the prison, I was moved to solitary, where I was confined to a small room for eight months.

They put me in solitary confinement because I'd asked for prisoners' rights. When some high-up officials were visiting, the prison director wanted us to pretend that the hall where we slept was actually a workspace—the director wanted to show the officials that our prison was a working prison. The director told us to pretend to be working in the sleeping hall. She ordered us to pack our belongings and clear out, and we didn't like that. Some others and I refused. I was angry. Even though we were inside the prison, we were still protesting. Because I was asking for more rights, the prison director sent me to solitary confinement.

The solitary confinement room was eight by ten feet, with only one small window. From 6 a.m. to 6 p.m., we were able to go out one at a time—first for two hours and later for three hours. When one prisoner went out, the others had to return to solitary. When we went outside we walked and exercised in the sun. For example, I would go out from 6 a.m. to 8 a.m. Then I went inside and another prisoner went out until 12 p.m. From 12 p.m. to 2 p.m., everyone stayed in, and then at 2 p.m. I went out again. I felt lonely and missed my family, but I didn't regret what I had done.

There were only two other women in the solitary building, so we requested to have lunch and dinner together. They allowed this. Although there were only two other women in solitary confinement, there were around ten women political prisoners in the hall and many more male political prisoners. The other prisoners' families would pass information to us while we were inside.

I BEGAN MY JOURNALISM WORK AGAIN

My sentence was for two years, but I was released after a little more than a year.

The prison director came to my room and told me I was going to be released. I was on a list of prisoners who would be granted amnesty. I didn't expect to be on the list. It was 9 a.m. when she told me, and I was released at 11 a.m.

I didn't feel very happy, because I had about seven or eight months still left on my sentence, and I was sad to leave the other people in solitary confinement. They were serving long sentences for political activity.

After I was released, I rested at home for one month and then I began my journalism work again.

THEY NEVER GIVE US A REASON

My family had even stronger feelings against me being a journalist, but they still couldn't stop me because it was my ambition. They just advised me to be safe and not take risks. Now I do interviews and contribute to education magazines and local NGO news. I also work for the local news and weekly journals, writing about the economy and business. Before prison, I worked as a market reporter, but now I do political reporting because, given our country's current situation, I think politics are the most important thing to cover.

For about one or two months after my release, I felt that the authorities were watching me, but now I don't think they are, not much. The biggest challenge for journalists in Burma is the scrutiny board. The news I submit to my editor may or may not be allowed to print after the censorship board reviews it. Worrying about the censorship board is a daily concern. You can get around it by writing for the Burmese media based outside the country—the "exile media," as we call it. In Thailand, America, or Japan, you can write without scrutiny, without censorship. But people inside Burma cannot reach these websites. I like to focus on the local people, and the weekly paper is important for local people.

When I was a reporter at the weekly paper before my arrest, I would go to the market and talk to wholesale dealers and shop owners, and then bring information back to the office, where I wrote articles and submitted them to my editor. My editor would edit the articles and sometimes add background information or sources and then submit them to the scrutiny board. I had to submit about five stories per week, and sometimes only two or three stories would be approved by the board. Reporters don't normally go to the scrutiny board, so I never went, but the editors had to go every week.

So many news stories are not allowed, but since we already know about the censorship, we just don't write those stories. One of my news stories that the censorship board did not allow was a story about the price hike for rice. I talked to a wholesale rice dealer, a government official, and two or three other sources. The story was strong, but the censorship board didn't allow it. I think they didn't allow the story because it showed that the Burmese exchange rate is unstable. Rice is a very sensitive subject for the government—it affects their image.

We cannot ask the scrutiny board why they censor certain stories. They never give us a reason.

Also, for the upcoming November 2010 elections, the Burmese media was allowed to interview politicians applying for party registration, but the scrutiny board only allows opinions supporting the election to be published. This year, I think around 40 percent of the content and 40 percent of the interviews were removed by the board. Personally, I don't believe the upcoming elections will bring change, but for the sake of our country, I hope they will. I haven't decided yet if I will vote.

THIS COUNTRY NEEDS JOURNALISTS

As a journalist, I want freedom for our media. If we had a free press, we could cover more news stories on more topics. I want to write more freely; I want to write opinion pieces and news articles. People would become better educated, and maybe that would help develop our country.

My dream is to be a better journalist. As a reporter, I don't have much skill. I'm still trying to learn how to become a better writer, so I can develop my own style.

I've stopped using my real name, because I'm nervous the scrutiny board will ban my stories just because I wrote them. They might also put pressure on a newspaper that is using my stories. Despite all of the challenges, I don't want to work as a journalist outside Burma with the exile media. This country needs journalists even more than an open and democratic country does. If our country were a democracy, I might leave, but for now, this country needs more journalists.

Before 1988, the situation for political prisoners in Burma was worse that it is now; after the '88 uprising, political prisoners spoke up. Then the government was pressured from outside the country, and the situation seemed to improve. I have told you my story because we have to speak up to the international community about our current situation, so the next generation of political prisoners will see improvement in their conditions.

HOW SWEET THE FRUIT CAN BE

One day when I was a child, I was playing with some fruit. My mom had never let me eat this fruit before, because she was worried I would choke on the seeds. But I accidentally broke the fruit open and I saw it was ripe, so I tasted it. It was so sweet. The situation in Burma is like that. The people don't even know what that fruit is, but when they start to learn and become concerned about the issues in Burma, then they will start to understand how sweet that fruit can be.

YUN

16, sex worker

ETHNICITY: *Burman*

BIRTHPLACE: *Outskirts of Rangoon, Burma*

INTERVIEWED IN: *Rangoon, Burma*

We met Yun in a hotel room in Rangoon one afternoon. Her boss was under the impression that we had hired her for the day. Before we started to talk, we drew the curtains shut against the bright afternoon sun. Yun spoke slowly and softly about the circumstances that led to her becoming a sex worker, often pausing to reflect on her words before she continued. Yun's story reflects some of the major human rights crises in Burma today, including the HIV/AIDS pandemic, the healthcare crisis,[1] and the lack of access to education. The government's severe mismanagement of the economy has left the country with a GDP per capita of $1,100—though independent economists place the figure at under $600.[2] Such chronic poverty leaves many women like Yun vulnerable to the growing sex work industry.

If I could, I would rewind my life and start over again from the beginning.

---

[1] The SPDC invests 40 percent of their budget into the military and only 3 percent on healthcare.

[2] GDP per capita statistic of $1,100 is from the CIA *World Factbook*.

I wouldn't want my parents to die. I would like to get along with my great-aunt. I would try my hardest at school so I could become a doctor. That was my dream, but I don't think that's possible anymore.

I was born on the outskirts of Rangoon. I was four years old when my father died. I remember he was pressing the pump handle to get water from the well, and he said that he had abdominal pain. He went to see a doctor and the doctor gave him the wrong medicine. Just after taking the medicine, my father died.

My father loved me very much. He wanted me to study hard at school because he wanted me to become educated. Mathematics and Burmese language were my favorite subjects. I liked mathematics because I liked the sums, figures, and statistics. I liked Burmese language because it was easy to learn, since it is Myanmar's language. I always studied with my mother close by, and she would help me with my lessons.

My experience at school was both happy and sad. I was happy to study—learning, memorizing lessons, and taking exams. I had many friends, both boys and girls. To relax, we would play and jump rope in the road. But I was unhappy that some of the teachers and students discriminated against me and harassed me because I had only one parent.

I WANTED TO BE CLOSE TO HER

After my father died, our economic situation became very difficult. When I was eight years old, my mother started to do sex work. My grandmother—my mother's mother—was living with us and she forced my mother to do it. She suggested so many times that my mother do it that eventually, my mother couldn't bear it anymore. That's how it started.

Sometimes my mother would get called for a job; she didn't want to go, but my grandmother forced her to. When my mother left the house to work, I didn't know exactly what she was doing.

That year, my mother started to get sick. A friend of hers came to visit her, and my grandmother told her that my mother was infected with tuberculosis. Because of my grandmother, everyone found out that my mother had TB. After that, my friends stayed away from me because they thought maybe I would get TB too, and they were afraid they could get infected from me. I was very lonely and sad when they wouldn't play with me anymore. It wasn't fair. It had nothing to do with me. I was angry, and I hated those friends very much. Only one friend treated me kindly—her name is Lwe Lwe. She always encouraged me and made me feel better.

Although my mother was getting sicker and sicker, she still looked healthy until I was eleven years old. That year, she started to look very sick very quickly. At first she was getting thinner and thinner. Then her lips turned blue and she became hollow-eyed. She looked like a dead body. I was so sad to see her changing like this. I wished I could take her place. My mother couldn't work when she got so sick, so relatives from my father's side of the family supported us so we'd have enough money to eat.

When my mother became seriously ill, my grandmother told me for the first time that my mother had been working as a sex worker. She said this was how my mother got sick, but she didn't explain what a sex worker really was, so I still didn't know. My grandmother also revealed to me that the disease my mother had was HIV, not TB. My mother had been lying to me about her disease. At the time, I didn't know anything; I had no idea what HIV was. I saw my mother go to the doctor and get medical care, but I don't know if she got specific medications for HIV.

By that time, I wasn't talking to my grandmother anymore. We had a rocky relationship because of my mother's disease. I was angry at my grandmother for making my mother do the work that caused her to get sick. I didn't want to talk to her.

I spent a lot of time around my mother, but I couldn't help take care of her because she always told me to get away from her. She said I could get the disease from her, but I still wanted to be close to her—I wasn't worried about getting sick. But as the sickness got worse and worse, I had less and less chance to be near her.

Early one morning, I went to wake my mother up so she could take her medicine. I thought she was just sleeping at the time, but a few minutes passed and she still didn't wake up. I thought she had just lost consciousness, but in fact she had already passed away. I was thinking, *Now I have no parents. What should I do?*

My mother's funeral was a big gathering. So many people were there, including my father's relatives and people from the village. I was so sad, and I wanted to cry very much. I didn't go near my mother's coffin; I stayed at the back of the gathering with my friend Lwe Lwe.

As soon as the funeral was finished and my mother was taken for cremation, my father's relatives took me back to their house. They lived in another town close to Rangoon. My grandmother argued with my father's relatives because she didn't agree that I should live with them, but I was happy to go.

I WAS AN OUTSTANDING STUDENT

On the way to my relatives' house, I was thinking about how I would face a new life. I thought that in my new life I would have the opportunity to study more, and that I would try very hard and do my best to become an educated person. I wanted to study every subject, and I wanted to become a doctor one day. I wanted to take care of people and see them get better.

I lived with my grandfather—my father's father—and also my great-aunt, who was my grandfather's sister. They helped me study by paying my tuition and hiring a tutor for me. I was in eighth grade.

My new school was better than my last one. At the new school, my relatives were known to be rich, so the teachers took very good care of me and treated me very nicely. I tried hard and I was an outstanding student—I was happy when I got prizes for doing the best in my studies. I got so much support from my relatives. I also made new friends at the new school, both rich and poor. After school, we'd all eat our lunch and study together.

Living with my grandfather and my great-aunt, I felt like my life was very different from before. In my hometown, I was poor and I had to be satisfied with being an average student in the classroom. I never got the first prize. In my new life, my grandpa was very rich, so I could get and do whatever I wanted. My situation was better, but I missed my father and mother very much, especially when I got a prize for being outstanding at school.

But the problem was that my great-aunt didn't like me. She was very strict with me, no matter what I was doing. If I went somewhere, she would ask me where I was going and why I was going there. She was very cynical and always thought the worst about me. Sometimes, if I was sitting on a chair, she told me that chairs were only for adults or rich people, and that children had to sit on the floor. She would say that to me no matter where I was sitting, and I obeyed her. I didn't want to confront her because I was worried we'd get into a fight.

My grandfather and great-aunt often argued because my great-aunt wanted me to drop out of school. My great-aunt always failed to pick me up from school and my grandfather would get angry. She didn't want to see my grandfather use any more money to pay for things like my tuition and food.

I finally stopped going to school when I was thirteen because of her pressure. I was in ninth grade. Since our relationship wasn't good, I didn't want to stay with her and my grandfather anymore. I didn't want to see my great-aunt's face and I didn't want to speak with her. My grandfather tried to bar me from leaving their home, but I went to stay with my uncle on my mother's side of the family, who had agreed that I could go and live with them.

I HAD NO WAY TO REFUSE

My uncle and his wife stayed in another town, not far from Rangoon. At first I was happy to be there, but since my uncle was very poor, I didn't get to go back to school. He drove a school bus, and he didn't have enough money to pay the school fees for me, so I just stayed at home.

My aunt didn't want me to stay at her house without doing anything, so she decided to make me work. She told me she wanted me to be a sex worker, but I still didn't know what it was. All I was thinking was that she wanted me to die, because my mother died from a disease she got doing this work.

My aunt explained what sex was and then she tried to show me a video. It was the first time I learned anything about sex. I was really shy; I refused to watch the video and told my aunt that I didn't want to watch it. But she slapped me, so I had to watch. I didn't understand.

When I was very young, I thought my mother was doing her job because she liked it and was happy. I only came to understand what my mother had really been doing for work when my aunt showed me that video. When my aunt explained the job to me, my only response was, "I don't want to." But I thought about how I had nowhere else to go, so I decided to stay at the house.

The next day my aunt brought a man to our house. He was fat, and he looked Chinese; he was over fifty years old. When he first arrived, I didn't know what was going to happen. But a few minutes later she and my uncle made up a room and then my aunt told me to enter it. Then I understood. I started running around the house and I thought about jumping down from the veranda. My aunt said, "Oh no-no-no! I'll let you do as you wish. The guest will go back home." So I went back inside, but then they grabbed me and forced me to enter the room.

I knew they wanted me to do what I had seen in the video. I was thinking, *I will not do that!* But they locked the room from the outside and the man used force to take my clothes off. I can't remember very well if he said anything to me or not, but he hurt me. When I refused to do what he wanted, he beat me, pulled my hair and hit my face and ears. I just stayed silent because I knew I couldn't ask for help. I didn't like the situation, but I understood that I had to do this job. I had no way to refuse.

I don't remember exactly how long they locked me inside the room. After it was finished, the man informed my aunt that we were done and then he left. My aunt told me that she would buy me gold and new clothing, but later, when I asked her for it, she said she had no money. I understood then that she had cheated me and just wanted me to work for her.

I was fourteen years old when I lost my virginity. I felt afraid and shy. I didn't want to leave the house.

I CAN'T EVEN TRY TO ESCAPE

My aunt was the boss of a group of sex workers. She normally didn't keep the other girls in her house, but sometimes, if a guest made an appointment, she would call a girl and they would come to the house.

My aunt started sending me to other places to work. When she had clients, she would call for me to go to a hotel. My aunt's friend would pick me up and take me there. At that time, they called me about twice a month to go to hotels in our area. It went on like this, twice a month, for three or four months. I had nothing in my mind then except that I was angry with myself. I regretted that I had not been patient enough at my grandfather's house, and that I hadn't endured my great-aunt's scolding.

After three or four months, another friend of my aunt's took me to my current home, where I live and do sex work. The apartment is not so far from my first house. My aunt stopped being the boss of a group of sex workers; now she just collects money from me, and another woman, Khin Lay, is my boss.

There are three of us living together. There is another woman who is a sex worker for the same boss, and we're friends; she is twenty years old. There's also Auntie Mie, who's over forty years old; she works for the boss. She looks over us and treats us very well.

There are only two of us working at the apartment, so if more than two customers come, they order a woman from another house over the phone. The other girl who lives with me chose to come work here. There was another girl before, but Khin Lay, the boss, sent her back home. I don't know Khin Lay very well because she only comes to our apartment once a week. My aunt takes money from her once every ten days.

I meet customers at least twice a day. So many different men come to see me. Some are Chinese and Indian. Some are middle-class, but most of them are rich men. They pay my boss 25,000 or 30,000 kyats for two hours.[3]

---

[3] 25,000 kyats is approximately US$25; 30,000 kyats is approximately US$30.

When I am working, I can say no if a man wants me to do something that I don't want to. If a man doesn't want to use a condom, I apologize to him and tell him it's a rule, so they always use one. [4] We have condoms and gel, and I take birth control. I am able to get health checkups sometimes, and my boss explains to me how to protect myself from pregnancy and diseases like HIV. I'm not afraid anymore.

On a normal day, I get up at five o'clock in the morning and eat *mohinga*. Usually I have to go out to work at night, so after my breakfast I sleep again. After I wake up again, if I have a client, then I am brought to a hotel to work after taking my shower.

When I'm not working I have to ask permission to leave the house. When my boss Khin Lay isn't at the apartment, I have to stay inside because she locks the apartment from the outside. When she comes back, then I can go out to buy things.

I have never tried to escape from the apartment. I have never had the idea to leave this job because the situation is such that I can't even try to escape.

Sometimes I feel happy when I'm with Auntie Mie and the other girl. Together we chat about some of the experiences we have with the customers. We say whether they treat us roughly or if they're kind. If I'm faced with a customer who treats me roughly, I want my friend to know, and to be careful with this customer.

My aunt takes all of my money when I do a job. She'll come today to collect the money. Sometimes when I see her I ask her not to take the money so often, because I want to buy some gold jewelry for myself. Since my aunt takes all of my wages, I just rely on tips that the customers sometimes give me to buy clothes.

* * *

---

[4] A 2005 article in the *Journal of Sexual Health* estimated that there were between 5,000 and 10,000 sex workers in Rangoon. Half of those surveyed by the researchers reported using condoms all the time; the number was on the rise from an estimated 30 percent in 1998.

I PLAN TO LEAVE

I want other people to know about my life. I want people to know about what my uncle and aunt did to me. They make me do this work and they take all my money.

I think they did this to me because no one in my family has a good job, and the whole family relies on my wages. I think they made me become bad because this job gets more money than other jobs.

I do the job, but I hate it—this job caused my mother's death. I have found that there are so many women doing this kind of work in Rangoon. I think these other women's situations were like mine—they were poor— so they became like me. I think another job would be better for me because other jobs are honest. Other people do good things, the right things for their livelihood.

There is a customer named Aung Lwin who I think could maybe help me leave. He told me he has a place in Naypyidaw, the new government capital, where he will open up a new beauty salon. He asked me to manage it, so my plan is to go and work there.

I will do everything at the beauty salon—nail-cutting, haircuts. I am not sure that my aunt would allow this, but I will leave—I just won't say anything to her about my plan.

PHILIP

34, Shan State Army-South soldier, foreign relations officer
ETHNICITY: *Shan and Pa-O*
BIRTHPLACE: *Muang Kueng Township, Shan State, Burma*
INTERVIEWED IN: *Loi Tai Leng, SSA-S army base, Shan State, Burma*

We interviewed Philip on the front porch of his home in Loi Tai Leng, headquarters of the Shan State Army-South (SSA-S), as the rain pounded down on the roof and engulfed the verdant mountains surrounding us.[1] Philip is a soldier and foreign relations officer in the SSA-S, one of the ethnic armies still in active opposition to the State Peace and Development Council. Philip spent eighteen years living as a monk, but was unsatisfied with his capacity to work for an independent Shan State. The fighting between the SPDC and the armed opposition groups creates dangerous and unstable conditions for villagers living in areas where there are conflicts with non-state armed groups. As part of the war against opposition groups in Burma, the SPDC uses the notorious four-cuts counterinsurgency strategy, which aims to weaken the opposition armies by cutting off their supplies of food, funding,

---

[1] The Shan State Army South (SSA-South) is an armed opposition group in Burma's Shan State, with posts along the Burmese–Thai border. Unlike the Shan State Army-North (SSA-North), it has not signed a ceasefire agreement with the government and continues to seek Shan state autonomy though active armed resistance.

recruits, and information. They do this by forcibly relocating local populations, burning down houses and entire villages, detaining, torturing, and/or killing those suspected of having contact with opposition armies, and stealing or extorting food, crops, money, and livestock from villagers.[2]

According to estimates from the exile news organization Mizzima, there are twenty-four armed ethnic groups in Burma—nineteen have signed ceasefire agreements with the regime, while five remain in active opposition. Many of the ceasefires remain tenuous. Altogether, tens of thousands of armed opposition soldiers remain under arms.

I grew up in the center of Shan State, in Muang Kueng Township. The mountain there is very well known, because it's the second tallest mountain in Shan State—about 8,000 feet tall. My parents were farmers; we grew tea, rice, and vegetables. My father is Pa-O and my mother is Shan. Pa-O people are also from the mountains of Shan State.

The summer I was twelve, I came back to the village at five o'clock in the evening after taking care of my neighbor's buffaloes and cows, and I saw fire and smoke. I heard shooting noises and people screaming; the village was overwhelmed with the smell and crackling sound of burning houses.

I had no idea what to think. Whenever and wherever there was fighting between the Shan rebel soldiers and the Burmese soldiers, the villages would be burned. But usually when the Burmese government military burned villages, we had time to escape with a bag of clothes.[3]

This time, the Burmese soldiers had burned down the whole village.

Most of the people had gone into hiding for their safety. My family members were working on the farm, and when we went back to the village and saw that it had been burned, we ran into the jungle for safety

---

[2] From 1992 on, tens of thousands of civilians in ethnic minority villages along the Thailand–Burma border have been forced by the Burma army to relocate to army-controlled areas, with a significant increase in the scale of relocations after 1996.

[3] The military regime's four-cuts policy regularly removes inhabitants in border ethnic areas where the military regime has been at war with armed ethnic opposition groups. For more on the four-cuts policy, see appendix pages 461-462.

just like the others. We had to keep moving from place to place through the jungle, until we reached a place were we could establish a new village. My parents were really sad that we were not treated like human beings. This event had a big impact in my life—it made me care about human rights and want to fight for justice where there is injustice.

Three different villages I lived in were burned down, and my family had to run all three times. Most of the time, we would run straight to the jungle and then move to another village. The Burmese soldiers wouldn't tolerate a new village being set up in the same place.

I FIGHT FOR MY HOMELAND

I am a soldier in the Shan State Army because I want to work for my country, and because independence is the best way forward for the Shan people. English speakers call me Philip, but my Shan name is Yawd Muang. I don't fight for myself, or for my family—I fight for my homeland. I have been a soldier in the Shan State Army for ten years. Before that, I was a monk for eighteen years.

When people talk about Burma, normally they only talk about two things: first, democracy and Aung San Suu Kyi; and second, about the drugs and the Golden Triangle.[4] For international people to truly understand what the deep problems in Burma are, they have to come here and observe. In Shan State, everyone knows that Burmese soldiers go to the villages and commit human rights abuses. They take everything, rape girls and torture people. When the SPDC kills people, it's like they're killing mosquitoes. They don't care, they just want to keep their power.

Mahatma Gandhi fought the British by protesting only with his hands—no weapons, nothing. He went into the streets and boycotted everything, with millions of people in India supporting the fight for independence, until the British left. But if you oppose the SPDC, you

---

[4] The Golden Triangle is located in the mountainous region where the borders of Burma, Thailand, and Laos meet. It is one of the world's largest heroin production regions.

need to have a gun to protect yourself and protect your country. If not, they'll kill you. If they catch a monk with a flower in his hand saying "Please forgive me, please don't kill me!" they don't care—they will kill you. They have even tried to kill people like Aung San Suu Kyi, because she's very popular and the leader of democracy. They have guns; they have power.

We want the international community to know that here in Shan State, we have a country. We have over 60,000 square miles of land and millions of people here. The Shan people are the second largest population in Burma. We have the same religion as the Burmans, but a different culture and a different language. Before the Burmese occupation, we had our own king and our own land. The British occupied Burma for about sixty years, and after the British left, there was the Panglong Agreement in 1947.[5] The Burmese government made an agreement with Shan, Kachin, and Chin leaders to establish a federal union. They agreed that after ten years, the Shan people could decide whether to continue in the federal union or to have a separate government.

But then in 1962, General Ne Win took power in a coup d'état. He soon sent troops into Shan State. When they entered the villages, they beat villagers, forced porters to carry their belongings, arms, and ammunition. They stole rice, pigs, hens, and cows. They assassinated many Shan leaders or sent them to jail. Some were tortured and died in jail.

Since General Ne Win destroyed the Panglong Agreement by doing this, we should have automatically become independent in 1962.

We are fighting until the SPDC leaves. I believe we need to have our own country and our own government. I have told many people, "We have only two choices—you either become a servant of the enemy, or you become their leader and rule over the country. If you don't fight, you become a servant forever. You have to fight—we all have to fight."

---

[5] The Panglong Agreement was an agreement between Aung San's government and the Shan, Kachin, and Chin peoples on February 12, 1947. It granted autonomous administration in the ethnically controlled areas. See appendix IX for further detail.

I ONLY WENT TO SCHOOL ONCE

There were twelve children in my family—ten boys and only two girls. One of my brothers joined the army of the Communist Party of Burma (CPB) and two other brothers joined the Shan State Army-South.[6] One of them died fighting against the Burmese army.

When I was young, my family never had much time to stay at home in the village because of the fighting between the Burmese and the Shan. There were three groups fighting in Shan State when I was growing up— the Shan Army, the Burmese Army and the army of the Communist Party of Burma. Many times I saw the Burmese army, and the Shan army fighting inside and outside the village. When there was fighting, we had to run into the jungle for safety so that we wouldn't be arrested by SPDC soldiers or tortured and killed by them. It was horrible.

When I was six years old, I developed an illness that made me lose the ability to walk, so when there was fighting, my father would have to carry me into the jungle. I wasn't able to walk until I was ten or eleven years old. Since we lived in the jungle at the top of a mountain, there was no chance for me to go to the hospital or get medicine from a doctor. Two of my younger brothers died when they were young because they got sick but there was no hospital nearby.

I only went to school once, for two hours, and then I never went back again. I had to leave school after those two hours because my family had to work together. I had to take care of my younger sisters, take care of the buffaloes, and get rice and food. But I always wanted to study.

At twelve years old, Philip decided that he wanted an education. He was ordained as a novice monk during the Poy Sang Long festival, and then he went to study at a

---

[6] The Communist Party of Burma (CPB) emerged in the mid-1930s, among anti-British fervor and impoverished peasants who were hard-hit following the collapse of the international rice market and heavy taxes. Although banned by Ne Win's one-party state, the CPB controlled large swaths of land in north/northeastern Burma until an internal mutiny led to its collapse in April 1989.

NOWHERE TO BE HOME

monastery on the Thailand–Burma border.[7] Philip describes his time there as being "surrounded by the resistance," with Shan resistance soldiers always present and providing the monks with all their food. It was at this temple that Philip learned why the resistance soldiers were fighting the government army for an independent Shan State. After five years at that temple, Philip spent the next five years at a monastery in Bangkok, studying Pali and Thai language. He then spent a year studying at a monastery in Rangoon, and finally became fully ordained as a monk at twenty-one years old. Philip was a monk for eighteen years.

WE HAVE TO TAKE RISKS FOR OUR COUNTRY

It was around 1996 when I went from being a novice to becoming a monk. At that time, from 1996 to 1998, the situation in Shan State was especially bad for the people. There was forced relocation, villages being burned down—the four-cuts policy.

I decided to help the Shan State Army. As a monk, I started working more in politics so I could help the people, but I didn't think I would eventually become part of the army.

The Chairman of the SSA, Sao Yawd Serk, called for a gathering of Shan monks, civilians, and soldiers in 1997.[8] We gave the promise that we would not give up our responsibility to fight for our homeland. We had to end the conference when the Burmese army started an offensive in our area.

For the next six or seven years, I continued helping the SSA with diplomacy. I traveled around and attended meetings about forming a Shan government, and I worked with the Chairman and with the civilians. My family didn't know what I was doing at the time. But we have to take risks for the benefit of our country and future generations.

---

[7] Poy Sang Long is translated to the Crystal Sons Festival, a ceremony among the Shan people where young boys participate in a parade, take monastic vows, and study Buddhist texts for a period of a few weeks.

[8] Sao Yawd Serk is the leader of the Shan State Army-South and Chairman of the Restoration Council of the Shan State.

I DON'T WANT TO DIE TODAY

In 2000 I decided to officially join the SSA as a soldier instead of just helping as a monk. By that time, I had already worked with the SSA as a monk for six or seven years before I made the decision.

It was a personal choice to resign from being a monk to join the army. As a monk you cannot do anything about protecting yourself, so how can you protect your land? You are only speaking, meditating, and praying. I don't think that's enough, so I decided to work for the people. I don't support fighting, but I support defending our country. I don't want to die today; I want to die tomorrow.

The first year I joined the SSA, our headquarters was built in a place we call Loi Tai Leng—*loi* means "mountain," *tai* means "Shan," and *leng* means "life"—like "the mountain of progress." I lived there and I worked in diplomacy with the international media and the Thai media for the first few years. Then I went to the front line in 2003, for four years.

On the front line, we had to sleep, eat, and do everything in the jungle. We slept under trees, but once in a while, we could stay in a village. Whenever we encountered the Burmese army, we had to fight. We had to be careful all the time, because if you lose the game, you die. I stayed in the jungle four years. Sometimes we didn't see other people for two or three months.

I had to get up in the early morning, around four or five o'clock, and call all the soldiers to get up. Sometimes we didn't have time to take off our shoes for three or four days. Sometimes we had to go a day or two with no food to eat. When you're hungry, your stomach gets hot inside, so I would take a handkerchief, put it in water, and rub it on my stomach. That would stop the hunger a little bit. It's not easy in the jungle; you have no food, no bed, and no friends waiting for you, as you do in the village.

You had to carry your gun and always be listening. Every hour we had to figure out where the Burmese army was, where they were staying. We only had two choices: we fight or we move. If we thought we could win, okay, we decided to fight. But if there were more of them or the situation was not good, then we told our soldiers to split up or move far away from them.

I was in combat, but my main responsibility was to build good relationships with civilians, so that our people could understand how we could work together for freedom. I would tell the people that they did not need to be afraid of the Shan soldiers, as their duty is to protect our people and the country.

We call for the men in each family to join the Shan State Army, but some men come on their own, with their own heart and spirit. They have two choices: they can join for five years or forever. However, we cannot give a rank to a soldier who is staying only five years.

I came back to Loi Tai Leng in 2007 for a training. When the training finished, the chairman called me to work in the office here. Now I'm like the general secretary for foreign affairs. I'm working in diplomacy and on relations with the Thai and international media.

UNTIL WE HAVE OUR HOMELAND

I think the conflicts in Burma are increasing more and more—political conflict, economic crises, social crises, everything. The people are getting poorer and poorer, but the SPDC is getting rich because they have the power. The SPDC takes everything from our land—gemstones, gold, wood, and oil. They are developing their country by taking our resources. The SPDC also gets the benefit when foreign countries do business here; it's money in their pockets.

The Burmese army gave permission to businessmen to cut down the trees here. We couldn't protect our land, we could only get the tax. The SSA earns money from natural resources and from taxing foreign businesses that do business in Shan State. This is the system of every country; if I go to the United States to do business, then I have to pay taxes to you. If you come to our country to do business, you have to pay a tax to the SPDC and you also pay a tax to us. But this year we ordered our soldiers to stop the Burmese businessmen from taking wood from Shan State, because the people have been suffering from the land being destroyed. The benefit was only going to the foreign companies and the SPDC. What's more, the SPDC gets electricity for Rangoon and lower Burma from the hydropower projects in Shan State. But the local people in Shan State living near the dam can't afford any electricity—it's too expensive.

If you visit Burma, you can see in the villages and in the townships that people in Burma are very poor. The SPDC is developing Naypyidaw for themselves, with electricity and power lines, but people in the rest of the country don't even have candles for light.[9]

The SPDC is preparing for the 2010 elections, but it's an election only for themselves. Even if some civilians do support them, it's not from their spirit—it's by pressure, by the gun. They wrote the constitutional amendments alone—the people and the minority ethnic groups didn't have the chance to participate or give suggestions. The junta doesn't care. Their political road map is only in theory, not in practice.

Shan people have tried different things for political reconciliation. First, we have a political party, the Shan National League for Democracy, that was elected in 1990. But they never had a chance to work; they were arrested and put in jail.[10] Second, there is a ceasefire group, the Shan State Army-North (SSA-N).[11] They signed the ceasefire because they didn't want the people to suffer, but twenty years later they've never had any political benefits from the ceasefire. The ceasefire agreement may have lessened forced portering, forced relocation, and human rights abuses in the ceasefire-controlled area, but it has not eliminated them. The SSA-N now must either remain as a ceasefire group or be transformed into a home guard force or border guard force working for the SPDC. If the ceasefire

---

[9] Naypyidaw is 200 miles north of Rangoon, and has been Burma's new capital since March 2006, when the government built it specifically to serve that purpose.

[10] For more information, see the "1990: The Election" section of the "A Brief History of Burma" in the appendix, page 465.

[11] In the 1990s and 2000s, the Burmese government negotiated ceasefire agreements with the majority of the ethnic non-state armed groups.

groups don't accept to join the HGF or BGF, the SPDC will fight them.[12] Now the SPDC is sending reinforcement troops to the ceasefire areas and opposition areas. I'm sure that war will happen in Burma in the future.

We've sent many letters to General Than Shwe and the SPDC asking for negotiations and peace talks, but they reject our proposals and say we must surrender first. No, if we lay down our arms for them, then they will cut our necks—we can only have negotiations if it's even. I don't think the military is the best way to solve the problem because we'll have more people dying and the country suffering. But they rejected our proposal and they don't want to talk anymore, so this is our last resort. We have to fight.

The fact that the SSA wants independence doesn't conflict with the Burmese democracy movement. Once we get democracy, we can have discussions in the parliament, and there'll be no need for fighting in the jungle.

If we kick the SPDC out of Shan State, we will be independent and have our own government. Now it's time for the regime to be gone; I think their rule will end. In Shan State, we have Pa-O, Palaung, Lisu, Akha, Kokang, and Wa people—an independent Shan State would be for all of us. We have different cultures and different languages, but we stay together like one family. Only with unity can we work together and forgive each other.

I am sure we will win our independence because we are not fighting alone now. But whether or not we're fighting alone, this is our job—we have to fight until we get back our homeland and until all the Burmese soldiers leave our country. We need to have SSA soldiers. If a person has no bones, you cannot stand, you cannot walk, you cannot do anything. Soldiers protect the country and the land.

I want to see my country peacefully building a democracy. I will be in the SSA forever—until we get independence, or until I die.

---

[12] In preparation for the 2010 elections, the SPDC asked all ceasefire groups to incorporate into a Border Guard Force or Home Guard Force under SPDC leadership. Many of the groups have resisted this call, leading to rising tensions between ceasefire groups and the government.

USA

LAW EH SOE

39, photojournalist

ETHNICITY: *Karen*

BIRTHPLACE: *Pa'an, Karen State, Burma*

INTERVIEWED IN: *Buffalo, New York, USA*

We met Law in his apartment in Buffalo, New York, where he served us home-cooked Burmese food and showed us his small but growing library of books in Burmese and English. Dressed in a longyi, *Law sat on the couch and began telling his life story. His voice raised in excitement as he passionately recounted his journey to becoming a photojournalist. Law's determination to document the lives of everyday people in Burma was ignited when he shot his first roll of film during the '88 uprising.[1] During the 2007 Saffron Revolution, Law took photos of the SPDC's brutal crackdown on protesters. Law described how his ongoing commitment to capturing and sharing these images put his life in danger and forced him to leave Burma.*

In 2008, my family had our first Christmas together in twenty years. I hadn't seen my brother for twenty years, and my mom for almost six years. I arrived in the U.S. in March 2008, with only an IOM packet of

---

[1] In 1988, deteriorating economic conditions sparked nationwide protests against the ruling government. See appendix 463-465 for information about the uprising.

travel documents and my camera, the one I used in the 2007 uprising.[2]

My niece came to meet me at the airport too, but she didn't know who I was. So my mom and my brother's wife told her, "This is your uncle." She was scared of me, but it was a wonderful time. It's so very difficult to explain that kind of moment.

It's not only my family that's been separated—it happens to thousands of families from Burma. So that's why I made a decision when I graduated university. I wanted to do something meaningful and wonderful for my people, and also for my country. At the time, I was crazy about photography. So I made a firm decision: I will be a photojournalist. So many of my friends, they mocked me. It's a crazy thing, you know? Among our Karen people, there are no photojournalists. How could I compete? The people in the city, in Rangoon, they have thousands of good photographers there. In the villages we don't have enough training. Especially if you dream of working with an international news agency like AFP or AP[3]—it's 100 percent insane, you know?

It's almost impossible to work as a wire agency photographer in Burma. After 1962, the government did not allow the wire agencies to hire staff photographers in Burma. It's like an iron curtain in Burma; they want to block the world from seeing the country. I believe the government tries their best to stop any young photographers from rising in Burma. But for me, I decided, one day I will become a photojournalist. I didn't become a photojournalist because I was hard-working, I became a photojournalist because my heart was burning for it.

THE CAMERA STAYED IN MY HEART

I was born in 1971, in Pa'an, the capital city of Karen state. But I mostly grew up in a very simple village. My mother divorced my dad when I was

---

[2] The International Organization for Migration is an intergovernmental organization that helps organize the travel of migrants, including refugees, across borders.

[3] Agence France-Presse and Associated Press.

seventeen, and she had to raise her sons without enough income, even though she was working as a nurse at the same time she was raising us. She was a nurse for the government in Burma, and she earned less than ten dollars a month. She had to move around several villages in Karen state, so I grew up in a village without electricity, and then I finished my high school study in Pa'an. Pa'an is a small, beautiful city under the Zwegabin Hill.[4] There's a college, and also a high school. We have a wonderful Karen community there.

I first knew about photography because my dad is a freelance photographer for a newspaper in Burma. When I was a kid, I was so proud when he raised his camera before the people—I felt like he was my hero. I loved him so much. But in 1997, he divorced my mom and remarried. It made me so sad. I still have bitter memories about that, but maybe it was a good experience for me. Since my mom went to different villages for work, I had to stay with several families. Some of them were my friends and some were my mom's friends. I think only a broken family can understand this kind of situation. I love my dad, but I feel like we have different attitudes. He wasn't crazy about photography like I am. But the camera stayed in my heart.

I started to read magazines in English when I was young. Even though I wasn't good at English, I loved to read. I read *National Geographic*, some old *Life* magazines, and also *Time* and *Newsweek*. I would also compare the images with the photography in Burma. In Burma, photographers like my dad have to take photos of everything that's fine—beautiful smiles, wonderful landscapes, wonderful pagodas, people wearing traditional costumes in a ceremony. You see it in the newspapers, the magazines, and local media. But the people are different behind all that. As a villager, as a country boy, I know the people's heartbeat. I know they are suffering and I know what the reality is.

That's why even though I didn't have good instruction, I knew how

---

[4] The Zwegabin Hill is a mountain along the Thailand–Burma border, with a peak at 2,372 feet above sea level.

I should take photographs, like the kinds of photographs in *National Geographic* and *Time* magazine. The books and magazines were like my teachers. I also loved to watch movies, because I could learn English from reading the subtitles. But I didn't have a good education. Even when I graduated school in 1988, I had to wait three years to start university because all the universities were closed.[5] That made me see things differently. Actually, I shot my first images in the 1988 uprising.

MY ANONYMOUS HEROES

On August 8, 1988—8-8-88—I was in Rangoon. I had gone there in January and stayed eight months, because I wanted to see a very famous evangelist who was in Burma at the time. I was staying with a relative. Even though I went to Rangoon initially because I wanted to see the evangelist and to see what Rangoon was like, I'd also heard rumors that something was going to happen on 8-8-88. I had actually missed seeing the evangelist because when I arrived to Rangoon, he had already left and traveled to the U.S.—but I was there for 8-8-88. I saw the uprising.

On 8-8-88, I didn't march with the people who were protesting, but I was very excited and energized when I saw what they were doing. Thousands of people were shouting slogans against the government. It was my first experience ever seeing people dare to go against the government, to go against the Burma Socialist Programme Party—BSPP.[6]

People were just marching through the streets peacefully and shouting, but then the soldiers blocked the streets and started shooting. I saw from very far away what was happening. First I heard the shooting.

---

[5] After the 1988 uprising, the government closed all universities for three years to prevent further student uprisings.

[6] The Burma Socialist Programme Party was the only legal political party in Burma during the years 1962–1988. In 1971, the BSPP changed from a small cadre to a mass party with around 1 million members. The party congress met periodically and repeatedly "elected" Ne Win as its chairman. For more on the Burma Socialist Programme Party, see appendix pages 462-462.

I heard hundreds of shots being fired... *Doo doo doo doo doo doo!* And then I saw the military shooting and the people running. People were running for their lives. It is very difficult to run with rubber sandals, so thousands of sandals were left behind in the streets as the people ran away. I also had to run away, but I would have taken a picture of those thousands of sandals in the street if I could have.

At that time, all of the buses stopped running so I had to walk back from downtown Rangoon to where my relative lived. It was quite far, maybe seven or eight miles. I didn't see anyone die when I was running away, but I heard that many people were killed. I felt very bad.

People are used to seeing photos of some ruler, some leading figure. But I admire the anonymous heroes like the ones who were protesting that day. The anonymous heroes who are very dedicated, who are very brave—who give their own precious lives for the people. I always feel that they are my heroes. They make me feel humble.

WE WANTED JUSTICE

After that first crackdown in Rangoon, I went back to Pa'an. When I returned, everyone knew about what had happened. They had been following what the BBC and Voice of America were saying on the radio about the events in Rangoon. I told my close friends in high school all about what I had witnessed firsthand. We decided we had to take action with the university students against the government.

We were a group of young friends and also some university students. We had a meeting with some high school students and we decided to spark another uprising in Pa'an. The thing was, we knew all of the people were waiting to see who would ignite it, who would light the dynamite of protests again. So that's why we dared to do it, to start a protest. We knew the situation, how the people really felt. All of the people wanted to go against the Burma Socialist Programme Party, and it was very easy to spark a protest, especially with the high school students. It was very simple.

The young people wanted to see change. We wanted justice and peace in the country. Now I realize that back then we didn't really know much about politics, but we sincerely wanted to change the political system in our country for the benefit of our community, for the benefit of our people.

I personally wanted to spark another uprising in Pa'an because as a teenager, I knew that people in our country were suffering from poverty and injustice. I knew we needed change. I didn't want to see more bloodshed.

I've seen many horrors in my life—I saw persecution when I was young. When I was in the village, just twelve years old, the government soldiers shot a villager. They arrested him and loaded him on a truck to take him to do forced labor. And then he ran, and they shot him. I just heard the gun shot, but then I watched his last moments. I could see his last breath before me, beside his relative. It made me very sad—I then understood how our situation really was.

Around that time, from 1984 to 1986, the Burmese military and the Burma Socialist Programme Party had big, big operations into the KNU stronghold.[7] The BSPP said that the KNU was their enemy. Thousands of Burmese government soldiers in hundreds of military trucks would pass through our village. Usually they came through at nighttime. They would pass through our village around midnight especially, but sometimes they came during the day. We knew that they would go and fight. They would go and kill our own people or do miserable things to them. Even as a kid, you know these things because you're there, and you hear stories from the survivors.

I was around twelve or thirteen at the time of the big military operations. I remember the people would just run away from the battlefields in the nearby villages and say that the Burmese government soldiers had

---

[7] The Karen National Union (KNU) is an ethnic opposition organization formed just before Burmese independence, seeking autonomy for the Karen people. The KNU has an armed wing, the Karen National Liberation Army (KNLA). The war between the KNLA and Burma's military is the longest running of the post–WWII era, lasting from 1949 until today. See appendix pages 460-461 for further detail.

LAW EH SOE

been exchanging fire with the KNLA and that hundreds of villagers had died. They would tell us that their people were treated very inhumanely and killed by the Burmese soldiers. When the people ran away from the battlefield, they told us about how their people died from forced labor during the military operations. The Burmese used the villagers as human shields; the villagers were forced to stay in between the two groups that were fighting. They were just there between them, you know, without arms. They were also forced to clear the mines. Choppers would pass over our village, taking away the wounded Burmese soldiers from the battlefield.

It wasn't like what you see in a movie. Real fighting is miserable. In movies there is a main actor, a protagonist, but in real fighting, everyone is equal—everyone is in a dangerous and miserable situation. In the movies, there is a script. But in real war, there is no script.

WE WERE OVER THE MOON

So it was a funny experience, planning the uprising in Pa'an. Before we started the spark, we informed some senior people, like medical doctors and university students. We told them that we, the high school students, were planning to do something, and we asked them to please lead us. We said, "We need your instruction, your guidelines on how to do it." But they didn't dare do it. We felt a little upset, but we decided to do it anyway.

We planned the Pa'an uprising for about three days. My friends and I were very energetic. All of the students and people were waiting to see who would lead. If you dared, you could be a leader. It was very easy, very simple. The high school students gathered in Pa'an during the last week of August to protest. Then we ignited this "dynamite," and it happened—we just gathered and marched. But the funny thing is that once the uprising started, thousands of people joined, and then the cowardly people who didn't dare join us at first took the leadership roles. I thought, Oh! This is politics! It was my first experience like that. When they took the leading roles, I prayed for them.

There were thousands of people there at the protests. Everyone had sunburns even if they walked under their umbrellas, but we didn't care. We were over the moon; our spirits were very high.

We were wearing armbands and ties on our head, and we were carrying flags with a fighting peacock on them. The fighting peacock is a symbol of freedom in Burma and is used by the NLD.[8] It was so hot and crowded, and everyone was chanting. It was very loud, thousands and thousands of people were chanting, saying we wanted change, we wanted democracy. It was like thunder.

During the protests, I took on the simple role of photographer.

At the time, my dad was not in Pa'an, but he had left a camera in the house there. This was the first time I rebelled against him. I knew that my dad locked his camera in a box, and I just broke the box and took the camera out. It surprised me that I dared to take it, because I was so afraid of my father. I usually didn't dare to even look at him in the eye. I still remember, it was a Yashica MG-1 camera. But I didn't know how to use it, so I ran to see my dad's close friend and I asked him to teach me. He explained to me about the viewfinder and showed me, "You need to focus and then just hold the film like this." So I learned within five minutes.

The next day, I rushed to the scene of the uprising. I just started shooting images. Even now, I can never forget that day. My first roll of film. I was holding the camera with one hand, and shouting and raising my fist with the other hand. It was an amazing moment to me. I was among the people!

I went to the photo lab and said, "Please develop this for me." It was

---

[8] The National League for Democracy is a political party in Burma formed in the aftermath of the 1988 pro-democracy uprising, and headed by General Secretary Aung San Suu Kyi. The party was the decisive winner of the 1990 elections. See appendix pages 465-468 for further detail. The image of the peacock has been used on flags as an emblem of Burmese nationality throughout Burma's modern history. The National League for Democracy's flag which displays the peacock in a fighting stance, was first used by student activists against British colonial rule.

the most excited I'd ever been in my life. The man at the lab knew that I didn't even know how to hold the camera before, but now I had shot this film of a historical movement in our country.

"Okay," he said, "don't worry."

It was like being a new father, waiting for the first-born child, staying in the delivery room. I was very excited. I was just walking around the room, thinking, *Wow. What will my pictures be like?* It was a very exciting moment. After a little while, he showed me the negatives. I checked them and thought, *Oh, that's not too bad*—it made me excited. Even now, I'm always excited for my picture results. I never changed in that way. I did the same thing later, taking pictures during the Saffron Revolution in 2007. I was so excited then, and it is the same now. Whenever I hold the camera, I forget everything.

We marched for around ten days in Pa'an. That was my first experience in politics. I didn't know about politics, I simply knew we needed change. I wanted to see our ordinary people have a better life. Maybe you can label this as politics. For me, no, it's just simple—we need change. And then we need to be dedicated and commit to it. That's all.

But the sad thing was when the military took power on September 18, 1988.[9] That November I went to visit one of my friends who was with the KNLA. I met with him in the Thailand–Burma border area because I wanted to see the conditions in that area.

My friend had joined the KNLA that year because he wanted to see change, and he wanted to fight back against the government. He and the other soldiers took arms because they thought they could reach some resolution in this way. My friend was just a regular soldier. I think at that time, almost all of the young Karen people had the same dream about joining the KNLA. The KNLA had a great influence over all of the young

---

[9] On September 18, 1988, a group of generals calling themselves the State Law and Order Restoration Council—SLORC—overthrew the Burma Socialist Programme Party in a coup d'état. The SLORC immediately deployed the army to violently suppress the uprising.

people. When we were young, all of the Karen people saw injustice, we saw civil war. We saw the KNLA fighting back against the government and we hated the government. Some decided to join the KNLA, but I think that no parent would want to see their son in the battlefield.

While I was at the border, I observed the situation. Only two things were in my mind while I was there. First, I thought about how that environment was not safe for me. Second, I thought about how I would love to go to Rangoon University. For those two simple reasons, I decided to go back home.

After two months staying with my friend and observing the situation there, I told him that I needed to go back to study in Rangoon. So I went back home. My mom had been worried that they would raid the house because I'd taken pictures of the uprising, so she had burned all my pictures. But it was like a seed, and then the seed became a small plant. That's what first made me a photographer.

YOU MUST RESPECT YOUR CONSCIENCE

I loved that Yashica MG-1. I started taking pictures of church events, like weddings and ceremonies. So after those first years, I really knew how to use the camera. One day, my very respected Christian minister came to discuss cameras with me. He told me, "I have committed to go in a few days to the Naga Hills as a missionary. I will stay there for over five years, and I need to document it with a camera."

Then I thought of something. I told him, "You take my camera. Yeah, you take my camera."

"But why? Do you have an extra camera? How will you take photos?"

"No, you take it. God will provide for me." He was surprised, but it made me feel wonderful. It was my only camera, but ten years later, I had three or four cameras. But I'll never forget that, because you always have to give the best of what you have.

From 1991 to 1996, I was at Rangoon University, studying law. When I graduated in 1996, my friends were trying to become lawyers and judges. My father came and told me that it was also time for me to become a lawyer or a judge, but I refused and said I wanted to become a photojournalist. Angrily, he told me that I was selfish. But I just said to myself, *No. I will do the thing I should do and also the thing I want to do.* That's why I chose to be a photojournalist. My dad didn't speak to me for almost a year.

From 1996 to 1998, I worked as an apprentice for a camera crew. It's a funny thing, you know, working without payment, but I did it for almost two years. Even though they used a TV camera, I could learn from them—how to do research for a story, how to chase the news, and how to do an interview. And then from 1998 to 2002, I worked for a rich Karen businessman as his personal photographer. The first payment for me was the equivalent of five dollars for one month. I never cared about the money, but as a human being you do need it. But my burning desire kept me alive; I was still dreaming that one day I'd become a staff photographer for a wire agency.

THE ONLY PLACE WHERE YOU CAN FIND TRUTH

I later did photo projects about daily life in Rangoon and the villagers living beside the Salween River. In 2001, I took my first trip outside Burma, to Thailand. That's where I first used the Internet. In 2003, I started sending my images from inside Burma, by Internet. It was very difficult. Sometimes we had to wait an hour or more to send just one or to two pictures. I think the government has a machine that combs through everything and delays pictures from being sent outside of Burma. But the wonderful thing was that I had very good friends in Rangoon who are very skillful with the Internet and computers, so they helped me.

There are many kinds of photos that the government does not want other countries to see. The government does not like photos of people's daily life, of the villages, etcetera. If they see that you are taking these kinds of photos, they will be angry. But I don't want to just take pictures of very famous people, like political leaders and military generals—I want to focus on daily lives of the ordinary people. I want to focus on the people who are the victims of politics, the victims of the system. People like my family and others. But I have to be careful when taking the pictures.

If you want to know the situation of another country other than Burma, you can just pick up a daily newspaper. But in the daily newspaper in Burma, you just see the government's picture of the country. You see development and advanced technologies—about their opening ceremony for a new bridge, or for a new hydropower project. Everything looks like it's wonderful. The daily newspaper in Burma is full of propaganda; the only place where you can find 100 percent truth in the newspaper is in the obituaries.

When I was in Chiang Mai, Thailand, I heard that an organization was looking for a photojournalist from inside Burma to train. They approached me about the training and introduced me to a gentleman named Jack Picone. Jack is a journalist from Australia, and he was my trainer for five days in 2000 or 2001. He became my mentor, as well as a very good friend. Jack trained me in Jakarta, too, in the first World Press workshop in Jakarta, for Southeast Asian photographers in 2002.

Jack taught me photography and about journalism. He taught me to respect all my subjects because they each have their own dignity. So many photographers take the images of their subjects for themselves—they lack respect for them. As a photographer, you have to respect your conscience. That's all. Jack taught me how to become a photographer with a wonderful heart. This lesson is the most wonderful thing he taught me.

From 2002 to 2003, I was hired to do some projects for groups in Thailand—some NGOs and magazines. For my security, I used different names. I was very proud of the work. I had one project where I covered the current life of people inside Burma and also in refugee camps in Thailand. And then in 2003, I was hired by AFP. In less than ten years, I'd achieved what I wanted to do.

But the most wonderful thing that happened to me in my life was when one day my dad came and met me in Rangoon, because he was living near the Thailand–Burma border. And he said, "Son, I'm very proud of you because I saw your pictures in the *Bangkok Post.*" It was the most amazing thing in my life. It was 2003, and I was living in Rangoon, working as a staff photographer for AFP. I was the first photojournalist for the Karen people. Maybe in America, in the UK, or in France, they will get thousands of photojournalists. But for me, among my people, I was the first one. Even if I don't have great photography skills, I can show something.

WITH MY CAMERA, I CAN CARRY
A MESSAGE FROM THE PEOPLE

In Burma, it's very difficult to become an accredited journalist for the foreign press. You have to have a special license to be employed by a foreign agency. I had to wait over three years to be accredited. It was tougher for me because I am an ethnic Karen; the government doesn't trust ethnic people, especially the Karen. There were only twenty-one journalists accredited as working for a foreign news agency when I got accredited. They knew us very well, and they can take action against you if you photograph something they don't want you to.

The government in Burma hates journalists; it's very difficult to get a passport in Burma if you are a journalist. But Burmese people love photographers and welcome me because they know that the picture will go to the outside world. They know that through my lens the people outside of Burma will see who we are and what our difficulties are. With my camera, I can carry a message from the people. So that's why they love me. That's all. It's very simple.

When you are with the people, they will protect you. But with the government, you have to be very careful. We know we're taking a risk. I knew what could happen if the government got me. But my passion kept me alive.

THE OLD WOUNDS ARE STILL BLEEDING

In 2007, they tried to arrest me two times, when I shot photos of the monk uprising, and also when they tried to arrest the activist Su Su Nway.[10] When they make arrests, they drag people like animals, so I shot photos of that. After, they tried to chase me. The government people were in plainclothes, but we knew. Everyone simply ran. Run, run, run. By then I didn't dare sleep at my apartment, so I had to move around several times. They tried to raid my apartment, but I was already staying somewhere else.

As a photographer, you're just crazy for it—you don't care what's happening. I know there are hundreds of people beside me, but I just take the picture. And then when my blood cools off, I think, "Oh, they might come and arrest me."

During the marches, I thought two things. First, when I saw thousands of monks peacefully marching on the street in protest, I thought there would be big change. And also I thought that the army would never shoot these very reverent monks. But they did it. They killed monks.

And the second thing I thought: by 2007, the government thought that the people had already forgotten about the 1988 uprising. No, the old wounds are still bleeding. The 2007 uprising shocked the government. Four generations of students were united: 1962, 1974, 1988, and 2007.[11] They did it together.

I just ran, did my pictures, and gave them to my friends. They went to separate Internet cafés and sent them to the European Pressphoto Agency (EPA). Maybe you saw the picture of a young monk— he's shouting and holding his bowl upside down. It's from the 2007 uprising. I took that picture.

I was at the same location as Kenji Nagai, the Japanese photographer. I tried to remind Nagai that the SPDC soldiers would shoot soon, because

---

[10] Su Su Nway is a labor rights activist who was arrested for putting up anti-government billboards in Rangoon during the Saffron Revolution. She was sentenced to twelve and a half years in prison.

[11] 1962, 1974, 1988, and 2007 were all years when there were relatively large-scale student demonstrations against the military.

I could sense they would do something, but when I tried to approach him, I think he maybe thought that I was his rival or something. I just reminded him and two Western photographers. I just said, "They will shoot soon." And they did. I ran away just before they shot him. When they started shooting, I just ran. And then, in the evening, I heard that Nagai had been killed.[12] And then I saw that, accidentally, I had taken his picture when he was taking a photo of the monks. So he was in my camera, just a few minutes before he died.

After Kenji Nagai was shot and killed, I was worried because I was like a living witness for the shooting. I think the Burmese government decided to kill him because he was a dear friend of the Burmese people. In Rangoon, very few men wear shorts, but Nagai was wearing shorts; it was easy to identify him and see that he was a foreigner.

I was also worried because I had such close connections to the opposition leaders. I thought that the Burmese military would catch me and try to do something to me. I thought the government might give me serious trouble. If I had been arrested, I bet they would have locked me up. U Win Tin, a journalist and one of our country's heroes, was just released after nineteen years in prison. People like him are our heroes. One of my very close friends who is a journalist was arrested and is still being held in Insein Prison right now.

I knew the government was looking for me because just after I left, they raided my friend's house where I had been hiding for a week. I only stayed in Rangoon for two days. Then I left and went to the border area. I stayed on the Burma side of the border, because I had a good relationship with some people there. So this time, when I was in trouble, they helped me out. It's like a movie—but it's not like Hollywood.

When I got to the border area, I received help from some friends. When I was there, a man I knew from before gave me a satellite phone.

---

[12] Kenji Nagai was a well-known Japanese photojournalist. While covering pro-democracy protests in September 2007, he was shot dead at point-blank range by a Burmese soldier who subsequently confiscated his camera.

"You can call anytime you want." He brought a TV from the city and he set it up for me with a satellite dish so I could see what was happening in Rangoon.

And then, for the first time in my life, I saw that CNN, the BBC, and Al Jazeera had all used my picture. This was the most wonderful thing in my life, I was so proud. I can't compare my skills with many other photographers—I'm not a good photographer, but I can do something. In the 1988 uprising, mostly Westerners came and took photos inside Rangoon. In 2007, this was my time. Also, I saw that in Norway, some people were protesting Burma's government because they were shooting and killing the monks. A few countries went to protest before the Burmese Embassy, and they were using the photo I took. I thought, *Yeah, this is wonderful! That's my picture!* I was very proud of it.

I stayed inside Burma by the border for almost two months, and then my friends told me to leave the border and go immediately to Mae Sot—they said there was someone there who could help me. My friends paid money to take me over the border crossing. I was shedding tears in the car as I went toward the border. I asked myself so many questions. I thought maybe I was being a coward, running to another country. But the thing was, before I left for the border, monks came and they prayed for me. They told me very simply, "Law, please never feel sad. Please go to where you need to. You have done enough here, so please go forward. Please go to America because God will use you there."

Soon after I arrived in Thailand, a gentleman called me and said his organization wanted to help. He asked, "Where are you now? Are you safe?" He said to me, "We will pick you up and take you to Bangkok."

"Sir, I do not have a passport because I just ran from the border crossing," I said to him.

"You don't need a passport," he told me.

"I deeply appreciate this," I said. "I deeply thank you for your help to me."

And then—I will never forget this until my last breath—he said to me: "We will never ignore the people who help us."

It was wonderful. So maybe a week later, the U.N. processor came. Within a month, I got into the United States resettlement program. That was January 2008.

I ALWAYS SEE IT AS HALF FULL

On March 18, I had to leave Thailand. I reached America on March 19, 2008. It was my birthday. Before the plane landed at JFK airport, I was still thinking about how I spent those two months in a remote area in Burma, and then now, I could see the Statue of Liberty. It was a wonderful moment. But the very simple thing was that my mom wanted to see me. My mother had been resettled to Buffalo in 2005, with my youngest brother. It had been almost six years since the last time I saw her. Like many people in Karen State, my family was suspected of supporting the KNU. Because of this, my mother and brother had to flee to the Nu Po refugee camp. My other brother fled even earlier and was resettled in 2000.

I had to sleep one night in New York. It was like another planet. But the thing is, it wasn't a big culture shock for me because I read the newspaper and magazines, and I watch TV. I thought, *So now I'm in the land of opportunities.*

When I was in Burma, I'd never been cold. But here I've been in the cold many times. In Buffalo, I worked in a communication product company for a month. After only one month there, the refugee agency came and said, "We need you." So that's why I went to work with them, and I've been there for almost nine months already. Working as an interpreter is a wonderful experience. I've been to schools, the hospital, the clinic, police stations—several places. I interpret for people from Burma: Karen, Burmese, Chin, and Arakanese. Also, I'm going to college now. I'm studying social sciences in Buffalo. Classes are wonderful, but I hate math. It's awful for me and I'm not interested in it. I started writing some essays that I sent in to a Burmese website.

I'm living with my mother, my two younger brothers, their wives, and my niece. Buffalo is like the unofficial capital of refugees in New York. Resettled refugees have a wonderful life here. In every place, every corner of the world, they have different kinds of opportunities. But at the same time, there are challenges. For older people, the language barrier is a challenge. Also, culture shock. Young people adapt easily and quickly—it's both a good thing and a bad thing.

Sometimes it makes me sad. One day, I went with a refugee woman to the clinic. While we were waiting at the clinic, we had a conversation. She said, "Yeah, we have a good life. Good social services. But the thing is, I miss my mountains, my river." She just said it simply, you know. But it made me sad. Nothing is like home—for me too. But in life, almost 75 percent of what happens, you never expect. The thing is how you deal with the challenges. You can see the cup is half empty, or you can have a half full cup. I always see it as half full.

I want to stay low profile, so I don't usually want to do interviews. But a journalist came from the *Buffalo News* to interview me, and they published an article about me. So that's why when I go to the store or the clinic, they know that I'm a journalist. I think the people should know, so that the next generation knows what we have come through.

In America, I get $10 an hour. In a month, that's 2,000-something dollars. Maybe for American people, it's very little money. For me, it's more than enough. I have a wonderful life. I just share my payment with my mom, and buy food. I only save some money to buy books. People told me I should go to the library, but although I love to read, I love to underline books too. I want to set up a library. One day when I go back to Burma, I will ship all my English books to Burma and I will leave the Burmese books here.

So many Karen people are stateless, but at least now I can apply for permanent residence. At least here we belong to some country. I love Buffalo—we are already Buffalonian. My mom has a wonderful life here, after suffering for almost thirty years.

But just a month ago, my mother was diagnosed with colon cancer. She is going to have a major operation on July 22. It's like God's timing because she kept praying to see me, and now I'm by her side, you know? She'll have her operation in a few days.

The thing is, life is like that. Nothing is permanent under the sun, my friend. I feel sad sometimes to have left Burma, but now I'm beside my mom. I'm very close to her, you know, so she is very happy that I am here. I have two brothers who are both married and have families now. But I've stayed single, so I can be beside my mom. She's very happy. It's God's timing. Simple faith is the most important thing I've learned from my mother.

PHOTOGRAPHY IS IN MY HEART

So this is the biggest puzzle of my life. I was crazy for photography—it was almost fifteen years of my life. I got some achievements in Burma. My pictures were published in *Time* magazine, *Newsweek,* and also CNN and BBC. I was very proud of it. I have very good connections in Burma. But now I'm here in the United States, and almost all the people in my pictures are in prison. It makes me feel sick.

So that's why it's a very sad thing for me now. Sometimes I don't want to hold the camera, because photography isn't my job—it's my heart, it's my art. It's very difficult now. Here, and even in Thailand, people came and asked me, "Please take our picture." I don't want to take the picture, but I have to. Here in the Burmese community, they come and ask me because they know that I'm a photographer. I should not deny them, because I'm the only one here. But today, I don't want to take pictures.

When the *Buffalo News* came to meet me last month, they looked at my pictures, the ones used by CNN and the BBC. They told me, "You should take some more pictures."

"No," I said. When I was asleep that night, I had a dream that I was running around shooting pictures with two cameras. And shooting, shooting more, taking many pictures. Then I just ran. And when I woke up, I cried bitterly.

For me, being a journalist is the same as being a pure historian. That's why I chose to work the way I did. I have a plan. I want to document the first generation of Karen Burmese in Buffalo, and people's lives on the borders of Burma. I also have a dream to publish a book of photos about Karen people's lives in different places—inside Burma, in the battlefield, in the conflict areas, the refugee camps, and also America or Canada.

To be honest, when I read the first draft of my story for this book, I cried because I recalled all of the memories. I suffered trauma—that's why I took a break from my work. Sometimes I don't want to speak about everything that happened. But I recall everything, and the people should know. It has changed me. I don't know why, but now I would love to go back to the Burma border. I will try to go there next year.

I would like to go to journalism school because I want to improve my technique. I have been mostly self-taught. Then I want to go to the Thailand–Burma border and share my knowledge with the next young generation of photographers from Burma. That's why I truly believe that God sent me here to the United States to come and get an experience that I can bring back to Burma.

When I see the images of the refugees, especially of the IDPs (internally displaced people), it makes me want to cry. When I was like twenty-five or thirty years old, I felt very tough. I very rarely shed a tear. I thought I was very strong, but I was blocking the feelings inside my heart. When I did these interviews with you for this book, I didn't answer with my lips. I answered your questions with my heart. So that's how it is different, my friend. I used to sell my photos for money, but now I just want to contribute them toward some meaningful mission.

The 2010 elections? One hundred percent dishonesty. They're already set up. They already have a script. So now all the ethnic armies are ready to fight for everything—Kachin, Kayan, Wa, Shan—they are ready now. Now the SPDC faces a terrible internal situation with the ethnic people. There's also the international pressure. So we'll wait and see.

But we will need to do something. As Mother Teresa said, "We cannot do great things. We can only do little things with great love." When

I was a teenager until I was twenty-three or twenty-four, I admired Che Guevara. And now in my thirties, I admire Mahatma Gandhi and Mother Teresa and the way they see the world. They live very simply. They act very simply. And also they did great things with big hearts. It's wonderful.

U AGGA NYA NA

28, monk

ETHNICITY: *Burman*

BIRTHPLACE: *Kyaukpadaung Township, Mandalay Division, Burma*

INTERVIEWED IN: *Utica & Brookyn, New York, USA*

U Agga is an activist monk whom we first met in Utica, New York, where he lived with three other Burmese monks in exile. Several months later, he welcomed us to the Brooklyn brownstone to which he and the other monks had moved, in order to be closer to the network of people working for human rights in Burma. The brownstone was simply furnished, and now serves as a monastery as well as an office for the All Burma Monks' Alliance. The monks, wearing their traditional saffron-colored robes, were busily walking in and out of the house and meeting with friends, in preparation for their monastery's opening ceremony later that week.

In 2007, U Agga marched in the Saffron Revolution, a monk-led uprising against the policies and oppression of the SPDC. The marches were the largest anti-government demonstrations in Burma in almost twenty years. When protests intensified in Rangoon, with tens of thousands of people marching, U Agga found himself in the middle of the military government's brutal crackdown.

The first time I marched in protests was in the uprising in 1988. I was six years old. Almost the whole country came onto the streets to march. Even in small villages, they went to see the march, to make demands of Burma's military regime.

I was with some other kids in my village, and we saw some students and adults holding up the portrait of Daw Aung San Suu Kyi wearing a farmer's hat. We tried to find out who she was, and we wanted to learn the political slogans they were saying. Some students explained to us that she was the daughter of General Aung San, the revolutionary who freed Burma from the British. The protests first started after the government made some currency notes worthless. People got very upset and took to the streets, and they started to demand democracy.

My older brothers, who were eighteen and twenty-five years old, got in a truck to go to the demonstrations in Kyaukpadaung town, which was very close to our village. Some student leaders had come to our village in trucks to take villagers to the demonstrations in town. But my brothers didn't allow me to go with them—so I waited and got in the next truck with some of my young friends. My parents didn't know.

I was originally marching with university and high school students, and then other ordinary civilians—all kinds of people—marched in the protests. I was so happy to march with everyone; it was fun, and I was happy to see all the people and monks marching harmoniously in the streets. At the time, I didn't know the meaning of democracy, but I knew about the brutality of the military dictatorship.

But then many people were killed in cities like Rangoon or Mandalay, because the army just started shooting people with their guns. Thousands of people died from the shootings in the 1988 uprising. Not so many people died in my hometown. When they started shooting, we all ran to hide in the houses. All the students were running away, and some people took me to a house to rescue me. I was very afraid.

There's no justice or freedom in Burma. Even when I was very young, I knew the government ruled the people very brutally. I saw the military regime make people in my village do forced labor to build a railroad. If they couldn't do forced labor, they had to pay money. I would also listen during student meetings at the monastery—they talked to each other about the brutality of the military regime and how it oppresses the people. They talked about people who were arrested for writing about politics or human rights. They also talked about Daw Aung San Suu Kyi and the 1990 elections. The NLD—Daw Aung San Suu Kyi's party—was the most popular party, but after they won the national election, the military government didn't allow the elected people to hold office. It was listening to people talk about the 1990 elections that first got me interested in politics.

I WANTED TO TRAVEL OUTSIDE BURMA AND SEE OTHER PARTS OF THE WORLD ONE DAY

I became a novice monk in 1992, when I was ten years old and living in my hometown, a small village in Kyaukpadaung Township. After the popular uprising in 1988, the government closed all of the schools and universities throughout Burma, so I decided at the time to go to the monastery to study Buddhist religion and writing. When I first moved to the monastery when I was ten, I only intended to live in the monastery for about a week or ten days or so. But after a week, I changed my mind and decided to stay there for longer so that I could study Buddhism and meditation.

I stayed in my village at the monastery for three years as a novice. After I left my village I moved to a monastery in the region to study Buddhism and Sanskrit scriptures. My routine there was to wake up early in the morning, at about four o'clock, and then to pray, meditate, and chant with all of the other monks—sending our loving-kindness prayers.[1] After that we would all eat breakfast together, and then we'd study the scriptures. I was fully ordained as a monk when I was twenty.

After I lived in that monastery for seven years, I moved to Rangoon so that I could study English—it's the best place in Burma to be educated in other languages. I had realized that English is the universal language,

---

[1] From the Theravada Buddhist *Metta Sutra*, chanting loving-kindness is a form of meditation directed toward others.

and I wanted to be able to communicate with many different kinds of people. I wanted to travel outside of Burma and see other parts of the world one day. In Burma, most monks cannot speak English or are very weak in it because their monasteries don't allow them to learn it—they say it takes time away from the monks' study of Sanskrit and Buddhist scriptures. This is why it took me a really long time to find a monastery that would allow me to focus on the English language.

I studied English in a monastery that was a language center. The monastery taught seven languages—English, Chinese, Japanese, German, Italian, Thai, and Korean. Students could study whichever language they wanted, so I chose English. English is the most popular one these days. There were 100 monks in the monastery—they came from different small villages and cities in all of the different states of Burma. In truth, it was very difficult for us all to get along in the very beginning because we were from many different parts of Burma, but after only five days, we were all friendly with each other.

Living in Rangoon, I would usually go to Shwedagon Pagoda on Saturdays and Sundays. On those days I would practice my English with foreign tourists. Shwedagon Pagoda is the most important religious site in Burma. Many people go there after they finish working for the day to relax, pray, visit with their friends or family, things like that. It is a very peaceful place, and it is very quiet. It is also an interesting place to go and see many different kinds of people together at once.

It was a risk to talk about politics and human rights abuses with the tourists in Burma, but whenever I met tourists who were interested, I tried to talk to them. Young students were especially interested in learning about Burma. The tourists would show me what their guidebooks said about Aung San Suu Kyi, and I would be really interested in speaking with them about her. I'd explain more about her and about my country's political situation.

The tourists were surprised that I talked about politics with them; they didn't know anyone else who would talk about politics in Burma in public. But I could not control myself—sometimes, if people wanted to hear even more, I would take them to places where there were no people and talk to them secretly.

WE CANNOT JUST WATCH

In our country, there are not even basic human rights. The military regime oppresses the people as they wish, and there is no rule of law. We cannot express our own views, so that's why I work with other monks, trying to get democracy for Burma, trying to change our government.

Monks are normal civilians, but I think they have a very special status in our country since most people are Buddhist. The monks are revered by the people. On a regular day, most monks go from house to house collecting alms—the laypeople treat the monks well, offering rice and dishes of food. If the monks need clothing or funding for their education, the people will support them. Most monks have to rely on the laypeople in Burma, so when the people are experiencing hardship, the monks cannot just watch. When the students took to the streets before the Saffron Revolution, many of them were arrested and put in jail.[2] When the monks heard about these brutalities, we could not ignore it—that's why we decided to march against the military regime.

Monks have influence on the people because many people respect the monks, and throughout many generations, monks have become involved in politics. So if we want to organize politically, for example, it's easier for us than for laypeople to organize the people and the students.

Our organization is the All Burma Monks' Alliance. During the Saffron Revolution in 2007, we organized and inspired students and laypeople to join the demonstrations together. We had to travel to many different cities and organize many monks to become involved in the Saffron Revolution. Then we had to send out many letters and organize students

---

[2] On August 19, student activists from the '88 Generation Student group led a protest in Rangoon against the regime's removal of fuel subsidies. It was one of the protests that started the nationwide Saffron Revolution.

from different universities. In our country, it is very dangerous to work in politics, so we have to do political work very carefully. Anybody who is involved in politics can be arrested and harassed at any time. The Saffron Revolution was my first time doing a big protest; well, my first time was in 1988, but I was a kid and I didn't understand very well what was happening. But when the Saffron Revolution broke out in 2007, I understood our country's terrible situation and the brutal regime very well. By then, I had already been a monk for about thirteen years.

The Saffron Revolution started because the military regime heavily increased the price of fuel and basic commodities in August of 2007. The military regime sells our natural gas to countries like China, India, and Thailand, so fuel is very expensive in Burma, even though we have a lot of natural gas. Most people in Burma cannot pay such high prices. Most people cannot even get enough electricity—in most cities, even big cities like Rangoon, the electricity goes out almost every day. People get electricity for just a few hours each day—sometimes the lights come on in the early morning, or when people are sleeping, but after maybe three hours, they go out again. People living in the countryside can't get any electricity at all. It's difficult for people to work with the electricity shortage, and most people were very angry about the situation in 2007.

Another reason for the Saffron Revolution was that the military regime was spending a lot of money to build their new capital, Naypyidaw. They built so many buildings for no reason. They didn't need to build a new capital. We already had a capital—Rangoon. When they built this new capital, they took a lot of land from farmers without giving them compensation.[3] A lot of the farmers were in trouble because they lost their livelihood. The construction of Naypyidaw also made the prices of fuel and basic commodities become much higher than before. So one of our demands in the peaceful protest was to decrease fuel prices.

---

[3] Approximately 7,000 square km of land were confiscated from landowners to create Naypyidaw. In 2005, the International Labor Organization received 2,800 reports of cases of forced labor in the construction of the new city.

Another way the government oppresses the people is by making it difficult to get cell phones. Most people in Burma don't have cell phones because they're very expensive and very difficult to get. Even if someone can afford it, it's very complicated to submit an application for cellular service to the government. It's especially difficult for political activists to get cell phones because the military government is worried it will make it easier for them to organize a political movement. The government especially watches former political prisoners. That's why most former political prisoners decide to leave Burma, because it's like they're still in prison. They have to report everything they do and they are watched all the time.

The government only spends money to expand its army. They're spending the money just for warfare and for their own families. They're also trying to build a nuclear reactor because they have connections with North Korea.[4] The military dictatorship bullies the people because they don't care about them.

Because of the high fuel and commodity prices, about 500 monks in Pakokku decided to do a peaceful march, chanting loving-kindness. But military soldiers brutally cracked down on all those monks who were marching peacefully. When we heard this news, the All Burma Monks' Alliance issued a statement calling for all monks in Burma to march peacefully. Burmese monks made four demands: number one, the regime must apologize for cracking down on the monks; number two, all political prisoners, including Daw Aung San Suu Kyi, must be released;[5] number three, the price of fuel and basic commodities must be lowered; and number four, the regime must have dialogue with Daw Aung San Suu Kyi, our national leader, and the rest of the democratic opposition. But the military didn't comply with our demands.[6]

---

[4] Defectors from Burma's military state that the regime turned to North Korea to build nuclear facilities in the Naung Laing Mountains of central Burma.

[5] As of November 2010, it was estimated by the Association for the Assistance of Political Prisoners (Burma) that around 2,203 political prisoners are held in jails throughout Burma.

[6] For more on this, see the Saffron Revolution section of the appendix, pages 468.

SEPTEMBER 20 AND 21

Some monks began marching on September 18, 2007, but there was heavy rain on the 18th and 19th, so I could not get to the protests because of flooding. I was also finishing an exam at my monastery, but my mind was on the protests—I was eager to go. I joined on September 20. We marched in our saffron-colored robes, holding the alms bowls upside-down, which meant we were excommunicating the Burmese military regime from Buddhism. If someone is removed from the Buddhist religion, it's a very strong symbol. That's why when the monks held the alms bowls upside down to excommunicate the Tatmadaw, it was a very serious message.[7] The students and civilians encouraged us while we were marching—they were clapping, shouting, and paying their respects to the monks, and they offered us water, medicine, candy, and some donations of money.

Many students and civilians joined us, and some watched from their apartments or from the sidewalk. The students wore white shirts and *longyis* while they marched alongside us. Although we marched all day, we were not tired; the students and civilians inspired us to keep marching for justice in Burma. I had never seen so many monks outside—I think there were at least 50,000 monks marching in Rangoon.[8] It was a very good opportunity for the monks and students to march together in harmony. Monks have a very close relationship with students, because whenever we do peaceful protests, we organize with each other—not only in 2007, but throughout history.

Some monks brought religious flags from their pagodas. The religious flag represented the unity of Burmese monks. We were just chanting the *Metta Sutra*, loving-kindness, chanting and singing along the way. We didn't recite any political slogan as we marched, we were just praying:

---

[7] Burma's armed forces, the Tatmadaw, was founded by General Aung San to fight the British. Since 1962 Burma has been ruled by its military.

[8] Estimates for the final days of the demonstrations range as high as 100,000 protesters.

May all human beings be free and happy; may all human beings be free from danger; may all human beings be free from physical suffering and mental suffering; may all human beings be free from fear and anger.

We marched with all the monks together in the middle and the students and civilians surrounding us. The students and civilians marched in two lines on either side of us, to protect the monks in case the security forces attacked us. In the beginning, not so many people joined, but after about two days, we kept marching and it built up more and more. It became very crowded—the streets and sidewalks were full of people. It was especially crowded when we made a speech near Sule Pagoda, in the area by City Hall.[9]

SEPTEMBER 22

Before I left my monastery to continue marching on September 22, I heard that monks and students would march in front of Daw Aung San Suu Kyi's house that day. I was confused and I thought it must be just a rumor, because it's very dangerous for monks or students to march in front of her house—there are always many security forces there. I didn't think they would allow us to march there, because the military government never allows anyone to meet with Daw Aung San Suu Kyi. But after we marched to Shwedagon Pagoda that day, we all decided to march in front of her house.

The military government is so afraid of Daw Aung San Suu Kyi, because she is powerful. Her party won the 1990 election, and most people love her as the true leader of Burma. If someone wears a T-shirt with her photo on it, that person will be watched and probably arrested. The military government tries to make the people forget her, they try to cut her off from the people, but she is always in their hearts.

When we arrived near Aung San Suu Kyi's house, the soldiers and riot police would not allow us to continue. Some of the monk leaders

---

[9] Sule Pagoda is located in the center of Rangoon and was used as a central rallying point for both the '88 demonstrations and 2007 Saffron Revolution.

tried to negotiate with the soldiers, and then one soldier went to speak with a senior general to get permission for us to march. The monks promised the soldiers that we would not do anything violent, that we would just march and pray and chant the *Metta Sutra*. After we negotiated with them, they decided to let us march in front of her house.

It was drizzling that day. When we began to march by her house, most of the monks and students began chanting more loudly. We were praying for her, praying that she would be well and happy and have a long life. I think Aung San Suu Kyi heard our chanting, because she came out to the street and stood at the gate of her house. She put her palms together and paid respect to the monks at the gate of her house. Many students bowed to show their respect for her. The leading monks tried to speak with her, but they weren't able to because there were many soldiers surrounding her. I couldn't see her very clearly because the riot police were standing around her, but I could see her face and hands very clearly.

I felt sad when I saw her, because she has been under house arrest for such a long time without having committed any crime. We stayed for about ten minutes to chant and pray in front of her house. Seeing Aung San Suu Kyi that day is the most wonderful memory I have. Since 1988, I had heard so many students and people talk about her reputation, about how she sacrifices her life for the people of Burma. I had learned about her in the foreign media, and I heard that she won the Nobel Peace Prize in 1991. I had seen Aung San Suu Kyi's photo before—I remember in 1988 when the students were demanding democracy and they held up her portrait. But it's very rare to see a photo of her. Because of all of these things, I was always interested to know more about her. So when I saw her in person for the first time, I was so surprised and happy; I was so emotional. Not only me—most of the monks felt the same way. When we returned to our monastery after marching that whole day, we weren't even tired; we talked to each other about how we felt when we saw Daw Aung San Suu Kyi.

IT WAS DIFFICULT TO KNOW FOR SURE IF SOMEONE WAS MILITARY INTELLIGENCE

I didn't see journalists during the first few days of the marches, but then I saw a lot of them around September 23, 24, and 25. In the beginning, the monks didn't allow journalists to take photos or video, because they were worried about military intelligence. But then they decided it was important to let the world know why they were marching, so they allowed journalists to document the marches.

I saw many Burmese and foreign photographers and journalists when I was marching. At first they were shooting video covertly, but after a few days they were shooting more openly. Toward the last days of our protest, I was even interviewed by a video journalist and a photographer from the U.S. It seemed like they were looking for a monk who could speak English, so I talked with them a bit about my experience and feelings during our protest. They also asked for my address, but I couldn't give it to them because it would have been a security risk—it was difficult to know for sure if someone was military intelligence, or was connected to them.

It was easy for journalists to take photos during that time, but it became very dangerous for them when the crackdown began—this happened after almost a week of peaceful protests.

SEPTEMBER 26

The military regime imposed a curfew on the night of September 25. They announced on the state-run television station that they would arrest or shoot anyone who marched anywhere in the city. They said they would take action on anyone gathered in groups of five or more. They also made the announcement that night from military truck loudspeakers going through the streets of Rangoon. But even though they imposed the curfew, more and more monks and students came out the next day.

On the morning of September 26, I went with many monks to Shwedagon Pagoda. The pagoda looks like a big golden mountain. As well as being the most important religious site in Burma, it is also the most famous place for political rallies, because in 1988 Aung San Suu Kyi made a speech to a big crowd at the west gate of Shwedagon Pagoda. Her father, General Aung San, also made a speech at Shwedagon Pagoda when he was struggling for independence.

We arrived at Shwedagon Pagoda around 10:30 a.m. When we arrived at the east gate, I saw the soldiers there, pointing their guns at the protesters. There were soldiers stationed everywhere around the pagoda. Many rows of soldiers were blocking the main road to the pagoda, and they had weapons. About two hundred soldiers stood in front of a blockade made of iron and wood, as well as a fence made of tin. When I saw the military blockades, I felt that things would be very tense—I thought they were ready to crack down. At the time, there were probably around 250 monks, and about 500 students and civilians were standing and sitting behind us.

When we reached the military soldiers, they said that nobody could go to the pagoda and nobody could march that day because a curfew had been put into effect. When we confronted the soldiers, they told us they already had the order to shoot anyone who marched that day. We responded, "We came here just to pray and chant very peacefully. We will not harm anybody. We will just go and pray in this pagoda. We are not breaking any laws; we have the right to pray."

Then they asked us, "Will you go back to the monastery or will you go to prison?"

"We will not go back to the monastery and we will not go to prison," we said. "If you want to shoot, you can shoot, but we will not go back to our monastery." And then they started getting very aggressive with us. We tried to negotiate with them for nearly forty minutes, to convince them not to crack down on the march. Many students and people were surrounding the monks, so I didn't feel scared when I was talking with the soldiers and police officers. Actually, I felt very happy that we could talk directly with them, to tell them that the reason we went there was to develop our country—I was happy to try to solve this in a peaceful way.

I spoke to the soldiers with other monks, including U Gawsita, who is now my friend; we requested that they didn't use violence. We said, "In our country, all people—including soldiers like you—have many problems. There are people with political problems, or people with economic problems. Our people are oppressed by this military regime in many ways. People are starving, there's the economic crisis and many other kinds of problems. This is because of the military dictatorship system." Some of the soldiers were listening to us, and they seemed to accept this explanation. However, they could not avoid their orders from the senior military leaders. If the soldiers didn't obey their orders, I'm sure they would also be imprisoned or punished.

The students and civilians were sitting around the monks while we were trying to negotiate. While someone was explaining why we were there, an officer from the security force came and said, "No, don't talk politics, don't talk politics!" We said, "We are not talking politics, we are telling the truth about what will happen in our country." But we couldn't negotiate with them. "If you do not go back to your monastery, we will have to take you to prison or the detention center," they said. At that time, some monks were asking the students and civilians not to react to the soldiers violently—we were worried for their security.

Some of the monks from my monastery tried to negotiate by sitting down in front of the soldiers and praying. We thought that if we sat and prayed in front of them, they would not crack down; we wanted to show loving kindness for the welfare of the people, and we expected it could help solve the problem in a peaceful way. While we sat in front of the soldiers, some leaders from different monasteries were trying to talk with the soldiers, and other leaders tried to enter Shwedagon Pagoda through a different way. But then the soldiers started to crack down, and we were trapped between two groups of soldiers.

The soldiers brutally cracked down on our group. They used so much tear gas to disperse the crowd that I couldn't see Shwedagon Pagoda. It hurt our skin, especially our faces—it burned. After the tear gas, the soldiers started beating the protesters. Many of the monks were in the middle of the crowd when they started to crack down, but I climbed over the monastery wall. I could clearly see soldiers beating the monks with bamboo sticks and batons—they were beating their backs, their hands, their legs, and especially their heads. The civilians were so angry and upset because they'd never seen anyone beat a monk before. They were shouting loudly and angrily at the soldiers, and some people were throwing stones at them. At that moment I thought about how brutal the military leaders are, and how they are not real Buddhists—they are only Buddhists for name's sake, to get support from the people—they're just pretending. If they were real Buddhists, they would not beat or arrest monks. The military regime is overwhelmed by their power.

I saw many monks who were wounded—some were bleeding from their heads—but we couldn't take them to the hospital. The military regime had ordered the hospitals not to treat any monks or students who were wounded during the protests. Soldiers were dragging monks through the streets and arresting them. I saw them taking monks and putting them into a military truck—I saw about seventy monks and students being put into trucks that day.

I was hiding for about twenty or thirty minutes after they cracked down with beatings and tear gas, and then a group of us—monks and students who escaped from the crackdown—gathered near Kandawgyi Lake to prepare to march in the downtown city center of Rangoon.[10] At Kandawgyi Lake, people gave us drinking water to wash our faces because the tear gas made our faces sting. Five or six people also brought us masks to protect us from tear gas, in case the soldiers dispersed us again. They were ordinary masks, like the kind people use to protect themselves from pollution.

We rallied outside of Kandawgi Lake, in a street near a bus stop. There were so many monks and students that cars couldn't pass. We discussed where we would march and how we would avoid the military soldiers and the tear gas. Since all the monks and students had come out

---

[10] Kandawgi Lake is located just east of Shwedagon Pagoda in southern Rangoon.

that day, we were not willing to go back home or back to the monastery without marching; everyone was willing to march for the whole day. We also discussed how we would respond if the soldiers shot at us. Then our group marched to the downtown area, near Sule Pagoda. Even more monks and students came out to join us after the crackdown. They came by bus and truck, more and more of them. I was not scared to march again, although we were worried that more monks would be arrested. We wore the masks to protect us from the tear gas, and we gave the students some masks too. The soldiers tried to block us while we were marching, but the crowd was too big for them to block us. If they blocked one way, we would march another way to avoid them.

We marched near Shwedagon Pagoda again after the crackdown, and some soldiers started shooting up toward the buildings, to threaten the protesters. They didn't shoot directly at the protesters that day, but the next day they started shooting directly at the crowds. I was already in hiding that day—not many monks were out on the 27th, because the military had already started raiding monasteries. By that time, it was mostly students and civilians marching in the streets.

THEY COULDN'T AVOID ORDERS

I think some of the soldiers didn't want to crack down on the protesters, but they had to obey the orders from the senior officer or else they would be punished and maybe even sent to prison. When I looked at some of their faces, they seemed sad. They knew it was a bad deed to hurt a monk. But I saw the senior officers ordering the young soldiers to crack down. One of my monk friends was trying to talk to a soldier before the crackdown, and the soldier said he didn't want to do it but he couldn't avoid the general's orders.

Not enough people are joining the army, so the army doesn't allow soldiers to leave until they are very old. The army also uses many child soldiers—some of them are very young. If they didn't recruit children, the army would become very weak. It's very difficult for a soldier to leave the army, but some soldiers do manage to run away to Thailand and other countries.

Most of the soldiers involved in the crackdown were from rural areas. Many people saw military trucks coming from outside of the city into Rangoon at midnight during the protests. Many of these trucks were near Shwedagon Pagoda and Sule Pagoda, and also blocking other main streets. The military arranged for these military trucks to come from remote areas for the crackdown. Even if soldiers are stationed in other areas, it is their duty to go to Rangoon to crack down on any protest breaking out. When we confronted the soldiers in front of Shwedagon Pagoda, some of them couldn't speak Burmese, because they're from different ethnic groups.

THEY RAIDED THE MONASTERIES

After the crackdown on September 26, I went back to my monastery. I had already expected that the soldiers might arrest or even shoot the monks, but I didn't expect that they would raid the monasteries in the middle of the night. About one week after we first started marching in the peaceful protests, the SPDC soldiers started to raid monasteries in Rangoon every night. Many of the monks in Rangoon couldn't sleep— they stayed up in fear every night. The military soldiers targeted the bigger monasteries, where many monks live.

At midnight on September 26, they raided my friend's monastery, the Ngwe Kyar Yan monastery in South Okkalapa Township, Rangoon. He was a friend from my village. The soldiers left their truck far away from the monastery and approached by foot so that the engine wouldn't wake up the monks.

During the raid, people were woken up by the sound of monks shouting and screaming for help. But even though people wanted to go to the monastery, they had to stay inside their houses because of the curfew. After the soldiers raided my friend's monastery, the news spread throughout the whole city.

As soon as I heard, I went to my friend's monastery to see if he was okay. I wanted to find out if he had escaped or not. But when I got there, I couldn't enter because there were many soldiers surrounding the monastery. There were many civilians nearby too—a lot of people were looking angrily at the soldiers. There were no monks inside. I returned to my monastery and discussed with my monk friends where we could run or hide. There were many trucks patrolling around Rangoon, and we didn't know if they would raid our monastery or not.

Someone from my friend's monastery later told me that soldiers had arrested and imprisoned many of the two hundred monks there, and that some of them had been tortured and killed. People had gone inside the monastery and seen a lot of blood and bamboo sticks left by the soldiers. The military targeted monks who were leaders in organizing the protests, and they tortured them. Some monks escaped from the monastery that night by climbing over the wall, but I never found out what happened to my friend that night.

The next day, on September 27, people living near the monastery told us our monastery would be raided that night. They told us as soon as they saw the military trucks in the area. The army left the military trucks far away from the monastery because they didn't want us to find out about the mission and run away. All the people around my monastery were worried that the monks would be arrested. Many of these people invited us to hide in their houses, but we refused their invitations because we were worried they would get in trouble just because of us. So the people told us to run away or to hide in a safe place. Some monks went to hide in the bushes and in a big tree near my monastery. Other monks hid in the ceiling of the monastery or on the roof.

As for me, I was hiding with four other monks in the bushes near my monastery for the whole night. I couldn't sleep. It was a very full moon that night, so I saw the soldiers coming very clearly. There were about twenty of them, and we were about 100 monks. I was so scared that the soldiers would find me, because nobody would witness if we were arrested or tortured, or taken away.

I could clearly see the soldiers patrolling around the monastery. I was so scared and so focused on the soldiers that night that I didn't notice the mosquitoes biting me or the leeches on my legs until the morning. They searched our monastery for about twenty-five minutes. They didn't find any monks, so I think they thought we had all left the city.

The military did monastery raids at nighttime, around midnight. They never came to arrest and do raids during the day, because there would be many witnesses to the torture and arrest of the monks. So when they raided the monasteries at night, nobody could witness it or tell the international community. When we marched in the Saffron Revolution, many people would see what happened, so we were not afraid to confront the security forces and the soldiers. But when they tried to raid our monasteries, all the monks were afraid.

I KNEW I COULDN'T GO BACK

The morning after I hid in the bushes, I had to prepare to run away. No monks could stay at our monastery anymore, so I went into hiding around Rangoon. I realized it wasn't safe to hide there for a long time, so some people helped me change into civilian clothes, because the soldiers would interrogate any monk they saw. I hid for several nights in people's houses, and then after about one week, I decided to run away to a small village in Kayin State.[11] I hid there for one month.

I stayed in the monastery of one of my friends who is from Kayin State. We had lived in the same monastery before the Saffron Revolution, and now he was living at the monastery in his village. Even when I was hiding there, I couldn't go anywhere in the daytime, so I stayed inside the monastery. If I heard a dog barking when I was asleep at night, I would feel a little scared. I didn't have any family in Kayin State—my family was in central Burma. I tried to wait until the situation for monks in

---

[11] Kayin State (or Karen State) is a state in southwestern Burma that borders Thailand.

Burma got better, but it just got worse and worse, and I couldn't go back to my monastery in Rangoon or to my village. One of my monk friends in Kayin State told me it would be better in Mae Sot, Thailand, a town on the border with Burma. He and many of his friends often went there, and he knew about the refugee camps there. He said I would be safer there, so I decided to run away to Mae Sot.[12]

I took a bus to a village in Myawaddy Township, then I crossed over the river and into Thailand on a raft. We couldn't cross the border using the Friendship Bridge, so I crossed with other people by raft.[13] We each had to pay 1,000 kyats.[14] It was three o'clock in the afternoon when I crossed, and I was worried about getting caught.

After crossing the river, I took a small bus with about fifteen other people from the bridge to the Mae Sot market. I met some Burmese monks who were visiting from the refugee camps, so I asked them about how I could go to the camp. But after I talked to them about that, I met a Burmese lady who knew a lot about Mae Sot and all the political groups there, and she told me not to go to the refugee camps because they had bad living conditions. She told me to stay at a safehouse in Mae Sot, because they helped all of the monks and students who had fled to Mae Sot after the Saffron Revolution. A Burmese reporter took me to live at a safehouse, where I stayed for a month with two other monks and about fifteen students who'd also escaped. When I first arrived in Thailand, I felt hopeless for my future because we had to live in Thailand illegally, so we couldn't just go anywhere as we wished. After one month staying there, I moved to a Thai monastery.

---

[12] Mae Sot is a town on the Thailand–Burma border, across from the Burmese town of Myawaddy. Mae Sot is known as a hub for political and social organizations working for change in Burma as well as working to help the refugees and migrant workers in Thailand.

[13] Located in a "special economic zone" between Burma and Thailand, the Friendship Bridge connects the two countries with an overpass across the Moei Tributary. It is the official entry point, but people who do not want to or cannot cross officially find other ways.

[14] Approximately US$1.

One of my friends, another monk named U Gawsita whom I met at the protests in Burma, also fled from Burma and had been hiding in the forest near his village for over one month. After a month, he decided to flee to Mae Sot as well, but he encountered many difficulties along the way. He crossed over from Burma to Thailand in a boat, and just about five or ten minutes after he crossed, he was arrested by the Thai police because he had no passport or other documents to show.

U Gawsita arrived just after we had started a monk group in Mae Sot. At the time there were eight monks in our group, and we just called ourselves the Saffron Revolution Monks. When we heard that U Gawsita had been arrested by the Thai police, we tried to find a way to save him. We spoke with many Burmese reporters to ask them for advice on how we could rescue U Gawsita. The reporters are very skillful in dealing with the Thai police, so they went to arrange for his release. After two days, we collected enough money to help pay for his release.

If we had been unable to rescue U Gawsita from the Thai police, it would have meant a death sentence for him for sure. U Gawsita is a very well-known leader from the Saffron Revolution. You can see his face and his picture everywhere in the media—the picture is of him holding a megaphone in front of the group of monks marching. It would be very bad if he was deported to Burma, and we were very worried for him. U Gawsita was very worried too; while he was in detention, he decided that if he was going to be deported back to Burma he would jump in front of a train rather than go back. Thankfully, we were able to have him released.[15]

When I decided to go to Mae Sot, I expected that I wouldn't return to Burma until we got freedom. As soon as I arrived in Thailand, many big media groups came to interview me, and I told them everything I saw during the protests. I understood that I definitely wouldn't be able to go back to Burma after interviewing with those big media groups, because the regime already had my information and had seen my face. But I knew

[15] U Gawsita currently lives with U Agga in Brooklyn, NY.

I couldn't go back to Burma anyway, because they were trying to arrest any monk who had been involved in the protests. That's why I decided to do interviews about what I saw—because I knew I couldn't go back.

Then some congressmen came from America, and they were interested in learning more about our Saffron Revolution. They invited me and the monks I was living with to testify to a delegation of congressmen. After we testified, we were determined to be refugees and were soon told that we would be resettled to the United States. But I had to stay in Mae Sot for ten more months because I found out that I had tuberculosis, so I didn't pass my medical tests.[16] I was sad to stay in Mae Sot longer. U Gawsita and one other monk arrived in Utica, New York in March, and one other monk was sent to California.

I was happy that I found out about the tuberculosis early, because it was easy to treat. I didn't even feel bad at the time, I actually felt healthy. I had to take medicine for six months, and then I left for the U.S. ten months after the other monks. I didn't know much about the U.S., but I was interested in living there, learning more English, and also studying there.

I HAD NEVER SEEN SNOW IN MY COUNTRY

I arrived in America in January 2009; it was a very long journey. It was my first time on a plane, so I was very excited. Some staff from the International Organization for Migration were at the Bangkok airport to show me where I had to go, and then two more IOM staff members were at the airport in South Korea to help me change planes.[17] I arrived in New York City and some IOM staff were waiting at JFK

---

[16] As mandated by the Centers for Disease Control, refugees testing positive for communicable diseases such as tuberculosis must be treated in their country of temporary refuge before entering the United States. Ailments or diseases sometimes delay the resettlement process but do not necessarily exclude a refugee from leaving the country.

[17] The International Organization for Migration is an intergovernmental organization that helps organize the travel of migrants, including refugees, across borders.

Airport to help me. At JFK, I transferred to another plane and flew to the Syracuse airport. I spoke to the lady who sat next me on the flight; she was a traveler from Syracuse. When we got off the plane, she was joking with me and saying I wasn't wearing good enough shoes—she said I needed to buy snow boots in Utica. I was just in simple sandals, and I was surprised to see many people wearing big snow boots when I got off the airplane!

I was surprised to feel the very cold weather and to see the snow. I'd never seen snow in my country. When I arrived in Syracuse, my monk friends were at the airport and we drove directly to Utica. I was so happy to see them and to be with them again.

The first difference I noticed was the really cold weather. I was really afraid to go outside in the winter; I wanted to stay inside all the time. But I had to go to English class every day, and some people helped me get warm clothes and snow boots.

My daily routine when I lived in Utica was to wake up at about five o'clock to pray and meditate for about forty-five minutes. Then I studied English and listened to public radio in English to practice my listening skills. I would go to my ESL class at the refugee center from eighty-thirty a.m. to 11 a.m., and then come back home for lunch. I would go back to my ESL class, then come back home to study again. The other students were also refugees—they were from Burma, Somalia, Kenya, and many other countries. It was difficult for me to understand them because we spoke with different accents.

I lived with three other monks in Utica. I talked with some American people in my neighborhood about our country, our political situation, and the military dictatorship.

There were some Burmese families who had been living in Utica for maybe five years already, so we had a small community here. Even though we were living in America, we still lived Burmese-style—we had Burmese celebrations and we celebrated Buddhist ceremonies like in Burma.

WE ARE STILL HOPING

We moved to Brooklyn on August 9, 2010. The main reason we moved here was for work, because in Utica there weren't so many Burma activists. Here, there is much more political activity, so it's much easier to meet with many different political activists and work with the movement.

Brooklyn is much busier and more crowded than Utica. So far, I like it here. I'm still learning how to take the subway. We are renting this house to use as our monastery for a very cheap price from our friend's family. Our friend's wife is from Burma, and they helped us move here. We are also supported by the Burmese community here. This won't be our permanent place; we intend to reside here for two years, and then we will find a permanent place either in New York or in Washington, D.C.

We get invited to talk about Burma at many different universities, such as Columbia, American University, and UCLA. It's usually the students who invite us to educate them about our country, so we talk about justice and our country's human rights abuses, about the military that rules our country, and about how they oppress the people. We tell the students about our experiences. Some students ask about the current situation inside Burma, or about U.S. policy. Some students also ask what kind of results we got from the 2007 Saffron Revolution. I tell them I feel our peaceful protest was successful because many people in the international community are now much more aware of the Burmese military regime's brutality. I also tell them we are not so satisfied with U.S. policy. We're frustrated because their engagement policy doesn't work.[18] When the students ask us what they can do, we tell them to contact our organization, the All Burma Monks' Alliance, to find out how they can help.

I'm used to speaking now, so it's not difficult. It's important to raise awareness about our country, because many people don't know about

---

[18] Under the Obama Administration, U.S. foreign policy with Burma was expanded to include senior-level dialogue with Burmese officials while upholding sanctions. This was part of a wider attempt to shift U.S. foreign policy.

Burma. It's also important that we do what we can for our country while we're living in exile. I need to keep working for democracy until our country's government changes.

If Aung San Suu Kyi had the chance to run in the 2010 elections, the government would change for sure. She would have a resounding win. But the military is not allowing her to run—it's just a fake election, and the military leaders will arrange the results as they wish. Actually, Aung San Suu Kyi's NLD Party already won an election in 1990, but the junta ignored the results of that election and they didn't hand over their power. The military regime knows that she would win if she ran in the 2010 election, so that's why they keep finding reasons to keep her under house arrest.

The American government should increase the sanctions as long as the military regime does not release Aung San Suu Kyi and the other political prisoners.[19] They should pressure the military regime and give them a timeframe for releasing Aung San Suu Kyi and the political prisoners. I really hope Burma will become free and that we will get democracy. Even though the military regime is trying to hold a sham election, we are still hoping.

I still think about going back to Thailand and Burma. When our government changes, when we get democracy—then I'll go back to my country. I really hope I can go back to Burma because I get very homesick. I haven't had contact with my family since I left Burma. My family lives in a small village that, like most villages in Burma, has no phone or Internet, so it's very difficult to contact them. Even if I got the chance to contact them, it would be hard to talk because the military government might find out they talked to me, and then they might punish my family.

One of my American friends whom I met in 2006 at Shwedagon Pagoda went back to Burma last April. He visited my family to explain

---

[19] The U.S. has implemented three rounds of sanctions, in 1997, 2003, and 2010, banning imports, new investment, and travel for military generals, and extended the U.S.A. Patriot Act powers to implement financial sanctions.

my situation and gave them a photo of me. That's the hardest thing for me about being here—being so far away from my family and having difficulty contacting them. They don't know about what is happening with me, and I don't know how they're doing. What I also really miss about Burma is the New Year water festival, which is so popular in Burma. So when it's that time of year, we try to listen to Burmese New Year songs here and whatever we can to celebrate.

I like being in America. I'm trying to learn English right now, and I intend to study political science. I'd like to study at a university in the future. Now that I'm outside of Burma, I try to read as much as I can about history and politics. I would also like to study Buddhism in English. Right now I prefer to continue living as a monk, but I don't know how it will be in the future. I can't see the future yet.

So far, I haven't found anything I don't like in America. Here, we can express our own views and talk about politics. We can talk anywhere. It's surprising for me to have freedom of speech, and to write and talk openly about our experiences. We feel free.

THE BEGINNING OF UNDERSTANDING

by K'pru Taw

K'pru is the associate editor of Nowhere to Be Home. *He conducted, interpreted, translated, and transcribed numerous interviews for this book. K'pru is a twenty-one-year-old Karen man who grew up in Mon State, Burma. He is one of thousands of young people from Burma living on the Thailand side of the Thai–Burmese border in order to take advantage of educational and work opportunities. Like so many of his peers, K'Pru struggles through the daily challenge of living on his own and without legal status. Though he only started his study of English five years ago, he has worked as a teacher at a school for migrant children, as a language tutor, and in training and documentation with several nonprofit organizations. He dreams of attending university and then going back to Burma one day to work as a diplomat or peace negotiator. K'pru stresses that while he was inside Burma it was like he was "blind," which he contrasts with the critical thinking-based education he's received while living in Thailand. We also interviewed K'pru for this collection, and following are some of his reflections on working on this book, as well as on the situation in Burma.*

I started working on this Voice of Witness project because I believe the information in the book can be very helpful for anyone who reads it. The more interviews I did, the more open I became—the more I wanted to listen. Now when I hear what another person is saying, even if I haven't experienced the same situation myself, I can feel it.

Whenever I have free time, I read books and I try to understand other people's lives. If I read about refugees in Sudan (*Out of Exile*) or about other migrant people, then I try to connect it with my experiences. I read the Voice of Witness book about Hurricane Katrina (*Voices from the Storm*); the people faced a lot of difficulties during the flooding. I remember how in my village we also had a flood and we lost all of our rice paddies. It made our lives even more difficult. I try to connect all of the Voice of Witness stories to my own life, and that is when and how I begin to understand new things.

When I lived in Burma, we only knew we were struggling, in the field, in the village. We didn't think about our circumstances, because we didn't know how to compare them to anything else. In school, I just finished my work because if I didn't the teacher would beat me, and I didn't want to be shamed in front of the other students. Critical thinking was discouraged—if we learned to think, then we might start criticizing the government.

The government publishes a newspaper, but they only include the good things they do, like building bridges and roads. We read that every day, but it didn't make any sense: we were still struggling. We didn't see good or bad, we only saw our own lives—the government bans all information from the outside world. Most people in Burma cannot judge the government and say what is right or wrong—they haven't seen other ways of life, so they have no idea. We had brains, but we couldn't think.

I left my village when I was sixteen because I heard that I could continue my education in a refugee camp. My friend's brother, who used to be a

KNLA (Karen National Liberation Army) soldier, came to our village, and he said young people like me could continue their schooling in the refugee camps in Thailand, where you could get support from an organization. He said I could even study to become a doctor or a medic.

I was very inspired; I wanted the chance to gain an education, then go back to my village and help people.

When I saw the refugee camp, I felt there was hope and that my dreams could begin.

It was the first time I saw many different ethnicities and religions from Burma together in one place. People were speaking different languages, and they had different ideas. It was very confusing for me at the time. At first, I hated some of the people who were different than me, but then I slowly started to understand other people, and then we were working together, eating together—living peacefully together.

For example, I became friends with people at the camp who support the KNLA, because I wanted to understand their feelings. They had these feelings because of their experiences with oppression and torture in their lives, so they wanted revenge against the SPDC. Now I understand why they want to support those fighting the SPDC. Since my village was a white zone for most of my life, the SPDC wasn't killing villagers or doing anything severe. But in the black zones, the SPDC kills people—they're not just doing forced labor and taking money from people. They oppress people everywhere in Burma, but they have different strategies in different areas. It made me very sad and very angry at the SPDC when I heard these things.

For the 2010 election, Than Shwe has already chosen who will be the president, but he would like to hold the election to show the international community. The SPDC always does that. They make a referendum or a conference, and they call ethnic groups to come and participate. But they never use the ethnic people's ideas. They just call them to come so they can say to the international community, "Oh, ethnic people are coming to our conference. They are participating." So it's similar. They will just hold their election but they will control everything.

I want to live in a country where we have lot of ethnicities, with a government that gives power to every ethnicity. I don't want to just have a free, separate Karen State or Mon State. I just want to have one government that shares power with the different ethnicities.

In my opinion, democracy is still far away in Burma. I think the people who have suffered in Burma need to forgive others. If you are able to forgive, the situation changes. If we are divided and in conflict with each other, then the government can control us easily—it is all part of the SPDC strategy.

You know, there are a lot of young people in the Burmese military. I would like to meet them and talk to them. I would like to be friends with them. Because one day, as the older generation passes, the young people of Burma will join together. I think the new generation will take the lead in bringing change to Burma. The ethnic minority youth as well as young Burmans, young people in the army, and young religious people will work together. They will think about all of the negative impacts that SPDC rule had on the people, and they will not just work for their own benefit. The young people will share their ideas and have common goals. I think peace is when the majority of people understand each other.

If Burmese people read this book, then they will know they are not alone in their struggles. For example, readers from another part of Burma can see that people in Karen State also encounter many difficulties, many atrocities—and see how they are the same. People in Burma should read this book because although they have their own difficulties, they often don't know about other people's hardship. When people read this book, I want them to learn to be tolerant, to forgive people, to learn about other people before judging them, and to try to be understanding. I just want them to be positive. I think it's very important to have hope, because then you are determined to go onward until the end of the journey.

If people from around the world do more to help Burmese people, help them gain more education and encourage them, it will be good for Burma. It might take a long time, but I believe that through teaching the young people critical thinking, we could overthrow the government.

APPENDICES

I. ACRONYMS

List of Common Burma Acronyms

AAPP(B) Assistance Association for Political Prisoners (Burma)

ABFSU All Burma Federated Student Union

ABSDF All Burma Student Democratic Front

BBC British Broadcasting Corporation

BCMF Burma Children Medical Fund

BCP Burma Communist Party (same as CPB)

BDB Border Guard Force of Bangladesh

BSPP Burma Socialist Programme Party

CNA Chin National Army

CNF Chin National Front

CPB Communist Party of Burma (same as BCP)

DKBA Democratic Karen Buddhist Army

DVB Democratic Voice of Burma

ESL English as a Second Language

IOM International Organization for Migration

KDA Kachin Defense Army

KIA Kachin Independence Army

KIO Kachin Independence Organization

KMT Kuomintang, Chinese Nationalist armed group

KNDO Karen National Defense Organization

KNLA Karen National Liberation Army

KNU Karen National Union

KWAT Kachin Women's Association of Thailand

LGBT Lesbian, Gay, Bisexual, and Transgender

NGO Non-Governmental Organization

NLD National League for Democracy

MSF Médecins Sans Frontières, a.k.a. Doctors Without Borders

PPP People's Patriotic Party

SLORC State Law and Order Restoration Council

SPDC State Peace and Development Council

SSA-N Shan State Army-North

SSA-S Shan State Army-South

UNDP United Nations Development Program

UNHCR United Nations High Commissioner for Refugees

VCC Village Councilor Chairman

VOA Voice of America

VPDC Village Peace and Development Council

II. GLOSSARY

All Burma Student Democratic Front (ABSDF)—Student guerilla army founded after the 1988 uprising. The ABSDF fought against the Tatmadaw alongside the Karen National Liberation Army, the New Mon State Party, and non-state armed groups. The ABSDF was primarily active from 1988 until 1995, when the Tatmadaw seized their base in Manerplaw.

Aung San—General Aung San was the architect of Burmese independence. He founded the Burmese army (the Tatmadaw) and the Anti-Facist People's Freedom League. He was assassinated in July 1947, six months before the end of colonial rule. He is also the father of Aung San Suu Kyi.

Aung San Suu Kyi—1991 Nobel Peace Prize Laureate Daw Aung San Suu Kyi has become an icon for democracy and human rights around the world. The party she leads, the National League for Democracy, was the decisive winner in Burma's 1990 elections, however the military junta that controls the country never allowed her party to govern.

British Broadcasting Corporation (BBC), Burmese Language Service—Radio and television news service headquartered in London. The BBC's radio programs are picked up by millions of Burmese inside the country and provide Burmese people with access to news that is censored in the state media outlets. Aung San Suu Kyi was able to receive their signal during her years under house arrest.

Burmese Names—Burmese do not have first and last names. They only have one name that usually consists of two, three, or four syllables. Names are not based on lineage, so one cannot determine genealogy simply by looking at the names.

Burma Socialist Programme Party (BSPP)—The only legal political party in Burma during the years 1962–1988. The party congress met periodically, and repeatedly "elected" Ne Win as its chairman.

Cheroot—A cheap form of cigar made popular by the British during colonization.

Communist Party of Burma (CPB), also Burma Communist Party (BCP)—Although banned by Ne Win's one-party state, the CPB controlled large swaths of land in north/ northeastern Burma until an internal mutiny led to its collapse in April 1989. The CPB emerged in the mid-1930s, among anti-British fervor and impoverished peasants who were hard-hit following the collapse of the international rice market and heavy taxes.

Daw—Daw is added as a prefix to Burmese names as an indication of respect for an older woman. For example, many refer to Aung San Suu Kyi as Daw Aung San Suu Kyi.

Democratic Karen Buddhist Army (DKBA)—The DKBA broke with the Karen National Union and signed a ceasefire agreement with the government in 1994. The leaders of the group complained that as Buddhists they did not have enough of a voice in the Christian-dominated Karen National Union.

Democratic Voice of Burma—Funded by the Norwegian government, the Democratic Voice of Burma brings news and commentary to people in Burma via satellite TV.

Forced Labor—Compulsory, unpaid labor. The SPDC imposes forced labor on citizens throughout Burma, in areas such as cultivation, infrastructure projects (including building roads, railways, and dams), municipal work, and in war zones. Portering is a specific type of forced labor that entails carrying rations, supplies, and weaponry for the military; porters are frequently used as minesweepers as well.

Kachin Independence Organization (KIO)—Founded in 1961, the KIO is a political organization that sought to create an independent Kachinland. Its armed wing, the KIA, was one of the most well-organized and effective non-state armed groups fighting in Burma in the 1960s, 1970s, and 1980s. In 1994, it signed a ceasefire agreement with the national government.

Karen National Union (KNU)—Established in 1946 after negotiations with the British failed to secure the Karen their own country, the Karen National Union fights for the autonomy of the Karen people within a federated Burma. The war between the KNU's armed wing, the Karen National Liberation Army (KNLA), and the Burmese government is the longest-running war of the post–World War II era, lasting from 1949 through to the present day. There are no indications that it will end soon.

Longyi—A cylindrically sewn cloth sheet worn throughout Burma. It drapes from the waist to the feet, and is worn by both men and women.

National League for Democracy (NLD)—A political party in Burma formed in the aftermath of the 1988 pro-democracy uprising, and headed by General Secretary Aung San Suu Kyi. In the 1990 general elections, the party garnered 59 percent of the general vote and 80 percent of the parliamentary seats, but the military junta never ceded power to them. In 2010 the military declared the party to be illegal.

Ne Win—Commander-in-Chief of Burma's armed forces from 1949 to 1972, Ne Win led the country during the caretaker government (1958–1960) and through the Burma Socialist Programme Party (1962–1988).

Pagoda—Usually bell-shaped structures built of bricks or stone and painted white or gold. They are holy Buddhist symbols and are used in religious practice.

Panglong Agreement—An agreement formed between Aung San's government and the Shan, Kachin, and Chin peoples on February 12, 1947. It granted partial autonomous administration in the ethnically controlled areas.

Shan State Army-North (SSA-North)—An armed opposition group in Burma's Shan state. It signed a ceasefire agreement with the SPDC in 1996.

Shan State Army-South (SSA-South)—An armed opposition group in Burma's Shan state. Unlike the Shan State Army North (SSA-North), it has not signed a ceasefire agreement with the government, and continues to seek Shan autonomy through active armed resistance.

Shwedagon Pagoda—Located in the northern part of Rangoon, the Shwedagon Pagoda is one of the oldest and most sacred pagodas in Burma. It has functioned as the stage for many political activities and events.

State Law and Order Restoration Council (SLORC)—Framed as a caretaker government, the SLORC has remained in power since the 1988 coup. In 1997, they changed their named to the State Peace and Development Council.

State Peace and Development Council (SPDC)—The military junta that has ruled Burma since 1988. In 1997, the military regime changed its name from the State Peace and Law Order Restoration Council (SLORC) to the SPDC.

Tatmadaw—Burma's armed forces, founded by Aung San to fight for independence against the British. The Tatmadaw has ruled the country since 1962, when, under the leadership of General Ne Win, it overthrew Burma's post-independence system of parliamentary democracy.

Thingyan—The Burmese New Year water festival that usually falls in April. During the five-day festival, people throw water on each other to wash off the previous year's sins and start the new year off fresh.

Than Shwe—General Than Shwe serves as Commander-in-Chief of the Myanmar Armed Forces and chairman of the State Peace and Development Council (SPDC). He also heads the Union Solidarity and Development Association (USDA), a mass organization that coordinates government at the local level. The amalgamation of positions means that Than Shwe is the effective leader of Myanmar's ruling military junta.

U—U is added to the front of Burmese names as an indication of respect for an older man. For example, retired general-turned-democracy activist Tin Oo is often referred to as U Tin Oo.

United Wa State Army—The United Wa State Army emerged in 1989 in the wake of the communist party's fall. At the beginning of the twenty-first century, the United Wa State Army made an estimated $550 million a year from the sale of opium, heroin, and amphetamines. It continues to be the most powerful of the non-state armed groups.

Voice of America (VOA), Burmese Language Service—Radio and television news service headquartered in Washington, D.C., Voice of America's radio programs are picked up by millions of Burmese inside the country, providing Burmese people with access to news that is censored in the state media outlets.

III. NAME CHANGES, BURMA VS. MYANMAR

In 1989, Burma's ruling junta, the State Law and Order Restoration Council (SLORC), changed the romanization of many place names in the country. The transliteration of the then–capital city's name was changed from Rangoon to Yangon, and the major river delta in the south of the country was changed from Irrawaddy to Ayeyarwady. The old names had been transliterated by the British, and the SLORC regime stated that their English adaptations were far from the Burmese pronunciations.

The SLORC also changed the name of the country from Burma to Myanmar. This, the junta claimed, was a move toward more ethnic inclusivity. The name Burma was adopted by the British in reference to the Burman, the majority ethnic group in the country. However, Myanmar is the name for the country in the majority ethnic group's language—so, in reality, neither name is particularly ethnically neutral.

Arguments over the name change have become symbolic of the long standoff between the regime and the democracy movement. The democracy movement's supporters around the world argue that SLORC was not a legitimate government and therefore had no right to change the country's name, so they continue to recognize the country as Burma.

Internationally, the use of the name is mixed. The UN officially recognizes the country as Myanmar, as do most Asian countries, while the U.S. State Department and United Kingdom still refer to it as Burma.

In this book, we left it up to the narrators to choose. If the narrator (or interpreter) switched back and forth between terms, we used Burma. We also chose to use the old transliterations.

OLD	NEW	OLD	NEW
Burman	Myanmar	Karen State	Kayin State
Irrawaddy	Ayeyarwady	Karenni State	Kayah State
Pegu	Bago	Burman	Bamar
Rangoon	Yangon	Arakan State	Rakhine State
Arakan	Rakhine	Tenasserim	Tanintharyi
Karen	Kayin	Karenni	Kayah

There have also been some more recent name changes. For example, the regime recently started using the term "region" for the areas in central Burma previously referred to as divisions.

IV. GEOGRAPHY

A mix of mountains, hills, and valleys, geography has had a profound effect on Burma's history.

Burma is located in Southeast Asia, on the Bay of Bengal. It shares long expanses of its border with India, China, and Thailand, as well as shorter stretches of land along the borders of Bangladesh and Laos. The Irrawaddy River Valley runs through central Burma, which is surrounded by a horseshoe-shaped mountain range. The first civilizations in Burma were established in valleys along waterways. Later, hill dwellers created decentralized networks of clans and principalities.

Most people in Burma today are farmers. Agriculture accounts for half of the country's GDP and two-thirds of its labor force. Rice is the primary crop, with wet rice cultivation practiced in the valleys and dry rice cultivation in the hills. Valley and hill communities generally live under different political atmospheres. In the hills, military rule is met by over two dozen armed opposition groups, some of which control significant pieces of territory. In other parts of the hills, the government resembles a military occupation, where checkpoints restrict people's travel. In urban valleys, the military has become an everyday part of life. One vivid example of this is an act that requires people to register all house guests with the military—though it should be noted that this law is inconsistently enforced.

V. ETHNICITY

Burma's hills and mountains are extremely diverse. Anthropologists have identified over 130 distinct ethnicities. The Burmese government recognizes eight major ethnic groups, each associated with an ethnic state: Chin, Kachin, Karen (or Kayin), Karenni (or Kayah), Mon, Rakhine (or Arakan), and Shan. The ethnic states form a horseshoe around seven lowland divisions (now officially called regions). These divisions are dominated by the majority Burman ethnic group.

All estimates of the populations of Burma's ethnic groups are highly contentious; differing estimates cannot be reconciled. Below are two sets of estimates, one from Burma's ethnic leaders, and one that combines the percentages from the government's 1983 census with the regime's 2008 population count.

Ethnic Group	Location	Primary Religion	Population (reported by Ethnic National Parties, 1991)	Population (according to 1983 census and 2008 official figure)
Burman	Central valleys	Buddhism	-	40 million
Karen	Northeastern Hills and Irrawaddy Delta	Christianity, Buddhism, and Animism share equal following	3-7 million	3.8 million
Shan	Northeastern Hills	Buddhism	4 million	4.9 million
The Mon	Southeastern	Buddhism	4 million	1.4 million
Rakhine	Western Burma	Buddhism	2.5 million	2.6 million
Chin	Northwestern Hills	Christianity	2-3 million	.2 million
Rohingya	Western	Islam	2 million	-
Wa	Northeastern Hills	Buddhism	1–2 million	-
Kachin	Northern-central Hills	Christianity	1.5 million	.9 million

Other groups include Chinese, Pakistani, Indian (once 7 percent of the population, now around 1 percent), and Bangladeshi, among other minorities.

VI. HISTORY OF BURMA: TIMELINE

563 BCE–483 BCE—Buddha's lifetime. Burmese legend holds that the Buddha witnessed the construction of Shwedagon Pagoda, located in modern-day Rangoon.

1044–1287—Pagan Dynasty. United upper and lower Burma, and in its time saw the growth of Buddhism. The dynasty started a relationship between the monks and the state that has continued, in varying forms, throughout Burma's history.

—The fall of the Pagan Dynasty ushered in a period of small kingdoms, including the Shan (Tai) rulers who founded Keng Tung, a Burman-dominated Ava-based kingdom, the Mon-dominated Hathawaddy Pegu kingdom, and the Arakan kingdom.

1486–1752—Toungoo Dynasty. Again united upper and lower Burma. Territory spanned parts of present-day Burma, Thailand, and Laos.

1752–1885—Konbang Dynasty. Last dynasty to rule much of the area that would become Burma. The rulers embarked on an ambitious modernization plan, but soon lost the country to Great Britain.

1825—First Anglo-Burmese War. Konbang Kingdom loses Rangoon and other coastal towns to Great Britain.

1860—Second Anglo-Burmese War.

1885—Third Anglo-Burmese War. Burma's modern borders formed. Colonial Burma was governed by the British through their Viceroy in Calcutta, India.

1937—Burma is granted its "independence" from India, but remains a colony of Great Britain.

1942—Word War II breaks out. General Aung San and Burma's independence fighters back the Japanese, while many ethnic nationalities, including the Karen, Kachin, Shan, and Rohingya, back the British.

1945—Aung San's Anti-Fascist People's Freedom League switches sides, joining the British against the Japanese.

1947—General Aung San's liberation movement signs the Panglong Agreement with the Shan, Karen, and Kachin ethnic groups.

—General Aung San assassinated.

1948—Burma gains independence from the British.

1949—U.S.-backed Chinese Nationalist Kuomintang (KMT) non-state armed group enters Shan State.

1958—Prime Minister U Nu temporarily surrenders power to the military.

1960—U Nu again elected prime minister.

1962—Military coup overthrows democratically elected U Nu, citing concerns over negotiations for ethnic autonomy. New prime minister Ne Win deports all Indians, whose legacy he associates with colonialism.

1967—Burma Army institutes four-cuts policy to rout out non-state armed groups by cutting off food, recruits, money and intelligence.

1974—Alliance is formed between nine ethnically based armed groups, including Karen National Union, Kachin Independence Organization, and the New Mon State Party, all fighting against the state.

1985—Regime announces first currency demonetization to curb black market spending. The results are disastrous, with people losing much of their cash savings.

1987—Burma declared a Least Developed Country by the UN. A second demonetization in 1987 would be the spark for the 1988 uprising.

1988—Nationwide pro-democracy demonstrations by workers and students force the resignation of three successive prime ministers. Demonstrations are brutally suppressed, leaving an estimated 3,000 dead. U.S. and other Western governments withdraw support for the regime.

1990—Regime holds election. Aung San Suu Kyi's National League for Democracy wins 59 percent of the vote and 80 percent of the parliamentary seats. (Aung San Suu Kyi and many party members were either under house arrest or in prison at that time.) Military junta does not cede power.

1995—Aung San Suu Kyi freed from house arrest.

1996—Students again protest the government in Rangoon.

2000—Aung San Suu Kyi placed back under house arrest.

2002—Aung San Suu Kyi again released from house arrest.

2003—At Depayin, Aung San Suu Kyi's convoy is attacked and scores of her supporters are killed. She is again placed under house arrest.

2004—General Khin Nyunt deposed by fellow junta leaders. (Khin Nyunt was the head of Burma's Military Intelligence and had negotiated ceasefire agreements with many of the non-state ethnic militaries.)

2007—Nationwide uprising of Buddhist monks, dubbed the Saffron Revolution. Regime brutally cracks down on the demonstration, beating, arresting, and killing some of the monk participants. Three years after the demonstration, approximately 1,000 monks and laypeople remain in jail for their participation.

2008—Regime drafts constitution, which is then approved in a fraudulent referendum.

Cyclone Nargis hits Burma's Irrawaddy Delta, leaving 140,000 dead.

November 2010—First national elections in twenty years are held on November 7.

—**Day of Election:** Fighting breaks out in eastern Burma's border areas in Myawaddy and Three Pagodas Pass. A splinter group of the Democratic Karen Buddhist Army (DKBA) seizes police stations, citing the government's unfair election practices as their reason for revolt.

—**November 13:** Aung San Suu Kyi released from house arrest for the first time in over seven years.

—**November 17:** The government's Union Solidarity and Development Party declares victory.

VII. NON-STATE ARMED GROUPS

NON-CEASEFIRE GROUPS

—Arakan Liberation Party (ALP) / Arakan Liberation Army (ALA)
—Chin National Front (CNF) / Chin National Army (CNA)
—Karen National Union (KNU) / Karen National Liberation Army (KNLA)
—Karenni National Progressive Party (KNPP)
—Shan State Army-South (SSA-S)

CEASEFIRE GROUPS

—Myanmar National Democracy Alliance Army (MND/AA)
—United Wa State Army (UWSA)
—National Democratic Alliance Army (NDAA)
—Shan State Army-North (SSA-N)
—New Democratic Army, Kachin (NDA-K)
—Kachin Defense Army (KDA)
—Pa-O National Organization (PNO)
—Palaung State Liberation Front (PSLF)
—Kayan National Guard (KNG), a breakaway group from KNLP
—Kachin Independence Organization (KIO)
—Karenni State Nationalities People's
—Liberation Front (KNPLF)
—Kayan New Land Party (KNLP)
—Shan State Nationalities People's Liberation
—Organization (SSNP LO)
—New Mon State Party (NMSP)
—Democratic Karen Buddhist Army (DKBA)
—Shan State National Army
—Karenni National Defense Army, a breakaway group from KNPP
—Karen Peace Force (formerly KNU 6th Battalion)
—KNU/KNLA Peace Council (7th Battalion KNU)

VIII. A BRIEF HISTORY OF BURMA

PRE-COLONIAL KINGDOMS – PRESENT

1500s–1825: Burma's Kingdoms—*Burma's current military leaders claim to be building a modern nation inspired by images of the pre-colonial Burmese kingdoms. But unlike today's country, those kingdoms were marked by highly changeable ethnic identities and shifting borders.*

Fluid ethnicities and ever-changing borders distinguished Burma's early kingdoms. The king's territory changed with the season, shrinking almost to the palace walls during rainy season and expanding during the dry season when servants of the court could travel easily. In the valleys, society was stratified. Nobles staffed government positions, collected taxes, and financed the king's projects. Monks brought the concerns of common people to the king. Noble status was both inherited and merit-based.

Much to the confusion of the British, hill dwellers' ethnicities were modifiable. One could be born a Kachin villager, captured and made a slave by a Tai, then earn one's freedom, incorporate into the Tai village, earn noble status, and ultimately die a Tai noble. These shifting identities perplexed British census takers who, frustrated by their inability to place Burma's people into neat boxes, noted an "extreme instability of language and racial distinctions in Burma."

1825–1885: Modernization—*In the nineteenth century, Burma's kingdom implemented economic reforms in an attempt to "modernize," hoping to ward off Western invasion. During the same period, hill-based ethnic groups began to develop nationalist identities.*

In 1825, British soldiers seized pieces of lower Burma in what was later dubbed the First Anglo-Burmese War. Alarmed by these events, the Burmese kings set out to create development schemes, hoping to build economic strength and prevent further invasion.

However, the kings' development plans inadvertently laid the foundation for British colonial rule. In order to develop, the king encouraged farms across the country to switch from growing rice for domestic consumption to growing cotton and teak wood for export. While trade flourished, the kingdom became dependent on imported rice from the British territories. In the 1870s and 1880s, a global recession caused the price of cotton and teak wood to drop. Without the profits from this trade, independent Burma couldn't afford rice from the British territories—the king lost his tax base and a number of uprisings ensued. Thibaw, Burma's last king, was unable to maintain control over the countryside. In 1885, the British took advantage of this instability and sailed gunboats up the Irrawaddy River to annex independent Burma.

A few years before the gunboats arrived in Mandalay, missionaries had introduced Western religion, education, and notions of immutable racial identities to the hill peoples. The British recruited soldiers from the hills and used them to suppress uprisings in the valleys. These experiences helped create Burma's modern ethnic nationalism. An

American missionary named Dr. Vinton celebrated the Karen minority's alliance with the imperial army against the Burman majority, saying, "I never saw the Karen so anxious for a fight... This whole thing is doing them good... From a loose aggregation of clans we shall weld them into a nation yet." Once characterized by fluid identities, the hill dwellers began to commit to over 100 more inflexible ethnic identities. However, not all hill people would immediately side with the British. The imperial occupation also met a number of hill-based insurgencies.

1885–1942: The British in Burma—*In the valleys, the British broke the backbone of the Burman noble class, leaving industries in the hands of Indian merchants. In the hills, existing hierarchies were reinforced and new ones created.*

"The people of this country have not, as was expected, greeted us as deliverers from Tyranny," read a telegram sent in 1886 by the British Secretary for Upper Burma. The British did not enjoy the "consent of the governed," but maintained their occupation by capitalizing on and instigating divisions in the country.

Different policies were established for Burma's hills and valleys. In the valleys, Burmese society was completely uprooted; the British dismantled the king's court, abolished the monks' role of relaying commoners' grievances, and created a legal code that allowed occupying soldiers to recruit Burmese for forced labor. The Burman hierarchy was replaced by Indians and British who reported to the colonial viceroy.

In the hills, the British allied themselves with village heads, simultaneously reinforcing and creating new "tribal" hierarchies. Separate governing councils were established for particular ethnic groups. They recruited soldiers from the ethnic minority areas to fight in the colonial army.

The face of Burma changed during colonialism. Rangoon became populated by Indian traders and businessmen. Many Chinese immigrated and set up small businesses. The economy flourished, but the recent immigrants enjoyed the most wealth—a grievance that helped fuel Burma's independence movement.

In the 1930s, Aung San, the father of Burma's modern nationhood, began organizing for independence as a student at Rangoon University. He called for a modern nation with equal rights among citizens, and for a social welfare system. As the world braced for World War II, Aung San recognized the conflict between Britain and Japan and saw the tumult as an opportunity for political movement.

1942–1945: World War II—*World War II elevated Burma's independence movement. However, the influx of arms intensified the conflict between General Aung San and ethnically-based opposition groups.*

During World War II, hill ethnic groups generally sided with the British. Aung San and his fellow independence fighters sided with the Japanese in 1942, but in 1945 he switched over to support the British.

The influx of weapons had a profound effect on Burma's politics. The Allies left the hill peoples heavily armed, with populations that strongly supported their militaries. The Japanese left stockpiles of weapons that were picked up by both Aung San's militias and rival anti-colonial groups. Ethnic nationalist groups, in particular the Karen, would later highlight Japanese and Burman practices of sacking villages during the war to justify their demands for independence from Burma.

1945–1948: Independence and the Panglong Agreement—*A conference on the eve of independence promised inter-ethnic cooperation and foreshadowed post-colonial divisions.*

In the city of Panglong, Aung San's nascent government—which at the time represented the people in the Burman valleys and Rakhine and Mon minority regions—gathered with Shan, Chin, and Kachin ethnic leaders to sign the Panglong Agreement. The agreement promised that Burma's diverse ethnic groups would form a union but retain state sovereignty. The Shan noted that the agreement gave them the right to hold a referendum on separating from the union after ten years. The Karen participated in the Panglong meeting as observers but did not sign. The Muslim Rohingya and the Naga Hill people were not present at all.

The Panglong Agreement brought hope for a united independent Burma. But communication between ethnic groups deteriorated after Aung San, who had chaired the meeting, was assassinated. Burma's first ethnic uprisings would be led by the groups that did not sign at Panglong.

1948–1962: The Cold War Comes to Burma—*Despite efforts to avoid the Cold War, democratically elected prime minister U Nu lost his authority to militant groups sponsored by competing world powers.*

In 1948, U Nu took office as the first prime minister of independent Burma. His platform combined Buddhist teachings with social democratic ideals. Internationally, he was a leader in the Non-Aligned Movement, an attempt by newly independent countries to remain neutral in the Cold War. He helped organize the 1955 Afro-Asian Solidarity conference to unite the world's newly independent countries, securing aid and diplomatic support from his neighbors.

U Nu entered office amid religious and political turmoil. Many among the non-Buddhist ethnic groups were angered by his emphasis on Buddhism as the country's guiding light. A group of Muslims from Arakan State was already in rebellion and seeking their own state. The Communist Party of Burma (CPB) likewise started to rebel, frustrated that U Nu was not doing enough to reverse the country's colonial legacy. Not even a year had passed when fighting between the army, the Karen National Defense Organization (KNDO), and Chinese Nationalist Kuomintang troops (KMT) began to destabilize the fragile young democracy.

Britain gave vocal support to their old allies, the Karen nationalists, in their struggle to secede from the union. In response to a group of army mutineers who entered Karen Christian churches on Christmas Eve 1948 and slaughtered eighty Karen village

APPENDICES

people, Karen leaders and missionaries began rallying villagers around the cause of Karen nationalism. American Baptist churches in Karen State preached exodus, portraying the Karen as Moses' tribe. The British, agitated by U Nu's non-aligned stance, promised to support Karen independence. The KNDO rose up, and within months Karen infantry had captured fifteen cities in central Burma and began shelling Rangoon. Burma's army retaliated, securing the capital city and beginning the longest-running civil war of the post–World War II era, lasting over sixty years, from 1949 until today.

Meanwhile, KMT troops started flowing over the border into Shan State, after their defeat in China to Mao Zedong. Low on funds, the KMT began stealing farm supplies and growing opium to finance its activities. Advisors for the U.S. Central Intelligence Agency (CIA) soon came to the aid of the KMT, assisting them in sabotage missions against communist China.

Burma's democratic government felt threatened by the actions of the CIA–KMT alliance and sought intervention from the United Nations. Through the UN, U Nu asked the U.S. to pressure Taiwan to withdraw the KMT troops. The U.S. agreed, and in 1953 worked with the KMT to evacuate 2,000 troops from Burma to Taiwan. By 1954, a force of around 6,000 remained in Burma, and reinforcements continued to be sent from Taiwan. U Nu saw this withdrawal as a farce, and in protest refused aid money from the U.S.

Shan leaders became increasingly frustrated with the fighting that surrounded the military's counterinsurgency efforts against the KMT in Shan State. In November of 1959, Shan rebels seized the town of Tangyan. Other ethnic groups began to voice their growing frustrations with the central government. A year and a half after the uprising in Shan State, the Kachin Independence Organization (KIO) was formed. The KIO was partly a response to concerns among the mostly Christian Kachin people regarding a 1961 law that made Buddhism the official state religion. In 1961, a number of mainstream Shan leaders brought together leaders from other ethnic minorities to propose some constitutional amendments to address the ethnic groups' calls for autonomy. Prime Minister U Nu endorsed and attended these meetings. However, their vision would never be put into practice.

In the 1950s and early 1960s, the country's instability was met by increased militarization. The civilian government had difficulty controlling many basic state functions, and the military took over law enforcement, tax collection, food distribution and even magazine printing. Curfews and forced labor policies developed for control during colonialism were again enforced.

Overwhelmed, U Nu ceded power in 1958 to a military caretaker government. In the 1960 elections, U Nu won the election and reassumed his duties as Prime Minister. However, just two years later a coup d'état put the military in power once again. The orchestrators of the coup cited concerns that U Nu was negotiating to grant greater autonomy to the Shan and Karenni States, which the generals feared could lead to their eventual independence.

1962–1980s: Armed Resistance and Counterinsurgency—*Modeled on the United States' efforts in Vietnam and the British anti-communist strategy in Malaysia, coup leader General Ne Win's counterinsurgency campaign proved to be a failure.*

461

Unlike U Nu, Ne Win—who had seized power in the 1962 coup d'état—was a staunch nationalist. Instead of reaching out to the UN and the Non-Aligned Movement for vision and leadership, Ne Win sought to "develop [Burma's] own ways and means to progress" and violently rid the country of its colonial legacies of foreign rule and divided ethnicities. Soon after taking office, he ordered the expulsion of all Indians whose families had immigrated to Burma after 1825, the year that the British seized the first pieces of Burmese territory. This decision crippled Burma's economy. Many Indians were at the center of Burma's financial operations, serving both as the bankers who helped finance businesses and the owners of the teak and rice farms that dominated Burma's exports.

In 1967, Ne Win instituted the four-cuts policy, modeled after the British anti-communist efforts in Malaysia and the U.S. strategy in Vietnam. The regime aimed to cut off armed groups from food, recruits, money, and intelligence. It set up strategic villages in the midst of areas with armed opposition groups. Forcibly moving villagers into these new villages, the army designated the old locations "free-fire zones" to rout out the non-state armed groups. Widespread human rights abuses occurred as a result of the relocations. For many countries, this was the popular counterinsurgecy tactic of the time. Mao Zedong had said the guerilla must "swim with the people like a fish swims in the sea," to which the U.S.-led response was often summarized as "drain the swamp to catch the fish."

The world powers backed Ne Win. The United States provided military training for high-level officials, the Soviet Union provided strategic advice, Israel designed the agricultural systems for some military villages, China provided diplomatic support, and countries from both the communist and capitalist blocs sold weapons to the regime. Despite such impressive opposition, the non-state armies actually multiplied in number.

Ne Win's decision to abolish the constitution that promised autonomy for Burma's ethnic groups intensified ethnic leaders' opposition to his regime. In 1976, a coalition formed of nine ethnically based political organizations with armed wings. This included the Karen National Union (KNU), the New Mon State Party (NMSP), and the Kachin Independence Organization (KIO). Together with the Burmese Communist Party, these groups controlled a significant amount of Burma's territory and continued to resist the central government throughout the 1970s and 1980s.

1971: First Congress of the Burma Socialist Programme Party—*The Burma Socialist Programme Party was transformed from a small cadre to a mass party.*

At the time of Ne Win's coup, the Burma Socialist Programme Party consisted of a small cadre of generals, the Revolutionary Council that had seized power in 1962. The leadership sought to expand their members throughout the country. By 1972, they had 73,369 full members, half of whom came from the military or police. By 1985, 2.5 million people attended regular party cell meetings, while a much larger group participated in grass roots groups for workers and peasants.

Regional representatives to the national congress were chosen by the party and elected by an up or down vote from the citizens. Although the candidates ran unopposed, there were some instances when the party chose new candidates in response to popular pressure. The representatives themselves had very little power, one of their major duties being to report back from the congresses at community meetings. Decisions in the party were made though a system of "democratic centralism," with the central executive committee in charge of most decisions. General Ne Win remained the chairman of the party from 1962 until 1987.

1974: Labor and Democratic Uprisings—*Worker and student demonstrations in 1974 contested military rule. Their actions went on to inspire dissidents for decades.*

In 1974, inflation and rice shortages caused the regime to cut workers' rations in half. Tensions boiled over that May. Walking out of state-owned factories, workers demanded better pay and more subsidized rice. In Rangoon, around forty factories were shut down. The number of workers in the streets grew each day, until June 6, 1974, when the regime opened fire on the crowds to disperse them. Official records state that twenty-two demonstrators were killed, but the actual number may have been in the hundreds.

Later that year, students called for Ne Win's resignation after the regime refused to hold a state funeral for national icon U Thant, the former Secretary-General of the United Nations. Enraged students seized U Thant's body and constructed their own mausoleum. Symbolically, the students built the mausoleum in front of the former student union at Rangoon University, which the military government had demolished in 1962 to curb radical student activity. Thousands gathered to hear anti-BSPP speeches. Declaring martial law, the police stormed the campus at night and arrested nearly 3,000 people. Despite the risks, resistance to military rule continued.

Students and workers joined together in a march to commemorate the one-year anniversary of the 1974 workers' strike. This demonstration was again crushed by soldiers, and as a response, the regime closed the universities. The military increased its surveillance of students for years to come, and threatened to fire professors who did not report their students' anti-government activity. Thirteen years later, an alliance between students and workers would temporarily overthrow the regime.

1985–1988: The 8-8-88 Uprising—*Economic stagnation sparked a student and worker uprising, which temporarily overthrew military rule.*

In 1988, economic stagnation had pushed many over the edge. Students marched down the streets of major cities shouting democracy slogans, workers held strikes, and revolutionary politics were discussed in tea shops across the country. For six weeks, the military did not silence dissent.

Two demonetizations had caused a recession in 1987 and 1988. Three years earlier, the regime had taken a number of bank notes out of circulation in order to check black market speculation and curb the rising price of food. The measure was not successful. The regime continued to print money, and the inflation rate rose to 14.7 percent. In 1987, Ne Win again chose to combat inflation by taking bank notes out of circulation. This time, when the old notes were liquidated, Ne Win offered no exchange of old bills for new. Families were devastated to lose their cash savings overnight.

Anti-regime activists attempted to capitalize on the public outrage and organized demonstrations on college campuses in September 1987. But the demonstrations were small and the military moved quickly to shut down the offending universities. Two months later, the universities were re-opened for exams. The semester ended quietly.

In March 1988, demonstrations again took place on college campuses. On March 16, a group of students staged a march between Rangoon's two major universities, Rangoon University and the Rangoon Institute of Technology. The police and military cornered the demonstrators between high walls on one side and a lake on the other, and then attacked the students. Some students fled down alleys, others scaled the large walls, and others fled into the lake, where some were beaten unconscious and left to drown. Around 100 students were killed and hundreds more were arrested. Forty-one students suffocated to death in a police van parked outside of Insein Prison in Rangoon.

Furious over the violent crackdown, more and more students took to the streets. The universities were again closed, but students continued organizing. They circulated a letter by a former general named Aung Gyi that warned Ne Win of violent uprisings if he did not fix Burma's economy.

On July 23, General Ne Win resigned, reportedly because of the demonstrations. He called for a referendum to be held on the issue of multi-party elections. General Sein Lwin, head of the riot police, was selected to succeed Ne Win. The protests intensified.

In August, students and workers united in a general strike that temporarily paralyzed the government. The strike started on August 8 (8-8-88), when dock workers in Rangoon walked out on their shifts. Impromptu unions and strike committees were formed around the country. Groups of teachers, health workers, and lawyers joined the strike.

Although the soldiers continued to crack down on demonstrators, even firing on and killing some, the protests spread nationwide. Reacting to the state's violence, mobs of villagers raided police stations and captured weapons. The crowds lashed out, beating soldiers, policemen, and suspected spies, shooting some of them with slingshots and homemade bows and arrows.

The general strike was followed by a temporary end to the military crackdowns. Sein Lwin was pushed from power. His replacement, Dr. Maung Maung, pulled the troops back to their barracks as the demonstrations spread. On August 26, Daw Aung San Suu Kyi— the daughter of Burma's independence hero General Aung San—addressed a crowd of several hundred thousand in front of the Shwedagon Pagoda in Rangoon. She proclaimed, "Our purpose is to show that the entire people entertain the keenest desire for a multi-party democratic system of government." She also called for the demonstrators to uphold a commitment to nonviolence. In September, 968 of the 1,080 members of the Burma Socialist Programme Party congress voted to hold multi-party elections.

Elections seemed imminent. Daw Aung San Suu Kyi, former general Aung Gyi, former Prime Minister U Nu, former army chief of staff U Tin Oo, and independence hero Bo Yan Naing began talks to plan for the transition. Students had been gaining support for an interim government from embassies, including the United States, Germany, Japan, and Australia. U Nu wanted the others to join an interim government that he had formed, but they were distrustful of U Nu's leadership abilities. Student leaders appealed to the politicians to form a government within forty-eight hours, but an agreement could not be reached. The political deadlock left a power vacuum that the military quickly filled.

On the morning of September 18, the military staged a coup against the ruling Burma Socialist Programme Party. The new military government named itself the State Law and Order Restoration Council (SLORC). By the afternoon, soldiers had been deployed across the country, breaking up strike centers and blockades. Anyone who resisted was shot. After two days, hundreds were killed and the uprising was crushed. The total number of killings during the crackdowns is estimated at around 3,000, though some put the number at 10,000.

In the aftermath, thousands of mostly Burman students fled to the jungles and formed student guerilla armies, including the All Burma Student Democratic Front (ABSDF), that fought alongside the Mon and Karen rebels. The unity of the groups was noteworthy—they were able to overcome the legacies of British divide and rule, and the subsequent divisive policies of the military government which had exaggerated and solidified ethnic differences.

1990: The Election—*The 8-8-88 uprising led to an election during which the National League for Democracy, under the leadership of Aung San Suu Kyi, won 80 percent of the parliamentary seats.*

Days after the crackdown, the SLORC announced that political parties could register for the first time since 1964. Daw Aung San Suu Kyi traveled across the country, giving speeches in ethnic minority villages and wearing various traditional ethnic dress as a display of solidarity. Her tour was reminiscent of her father's work to secure ethnic rights via the Panglong Agreement. The more popular she became with the people of Burma, the more threatening she became to the regime. Aung San Suu Kyi's willingness to work with the rebellious students and ethnic groups motivated the military to detain her under house arrest in 1989.

Aung San Suu Kyi's party continued to campaign despite her detention. Elections were held in May of 1990, and her party won 59 percent of the popular vote and 80 percent of the seats. From the beginning, the SLORC had been vague about what the elections were meant to decide, but it was widely believed that they were to form a transitional government. Yet after the results were revealed, the regime claimed that the purpose of the elections was to select delegates for seats at a constitutional drafting assembly. The regime would not surrender power until a new constitution was created. Aung San Suu Kyi and many NLD members remained imprisoned.

1991–2007 (Part I): Ceasefire Agreements—*During the 1990s and 2000s, the regime signed ceasefire agreements with numerous non-state armed groups.*

In the 1990s, the regime redoubled its efforts against the armed groups. This included the splintering of the Karen National Union. One branch, the Democratic Karen Buddhist Army (DKBA), split from the KNU and signed a ceasefire agreement. This allowed Burma's army to seize the city of Manerplaw, which had served as a stronghold for the KNU and fighters from the ABSDF, the majority lowland Burman student resistance group. The regime continued its advances, fighting battles and signing ceasefire agreements with the United Wa State Army, the Kachin Independence Army, the Shan State Army-North, and fourteen other ethnic armed groups. By 1998, for the first time since the early days of independence, the vast majority of Burma's territory was controlled by either the national government or a ceasefire group.

The government's counterinsurgency efforts were marked by excessive violence and human rights abuses. The Thailand-based Thailand–Burma Border Consortium estimates that the military destroyed 3,500 villages between 1996 and 2009. Rape by Burmese soldiers, the kidnapping of villagers for use as porters or to act as human minesweepers, widespread use of forced labor, and extra judicial killings have all been documented by myriad human rights reports. Although less well documented, human rights abuses also occurred within the ranks of the ethnic armies, particularly the recruitment of child soldiers and extra judicial killings. Burma has frequently been cited as having the most child soldiers of any country in the world, with tens of thousands of child soldiers in Burma's army and the ethnic militias.

As a result of the fighting, 250,000 Muslims fled Arakan State for Bangladesh, hundreds of thousands of Karen, Shan, and Mon relocated to Thailand to escape the fighting, and tens of thousands of Chin sought safety in India. During this period, many villagers suffered internal displacement as their villages were destroyed.

1996: Protests and the continued suppression of the democracy movement—*Despite draconian laws, the democracy movement in Burma has persevered from the 1990s to the present day.*

In 1995, the regime released Aung San Suu Kyi from house arrest. She immediately resumed her political work, giving talks to crowds of thousands in front of her lake-side home. Her house also became an organizing base for the National League for Democracy.

Students were energized by Aung San Suu Kyi's release. In 1995 and 1996, students came to classes dressed in black to commemorate the anniversary of the first student killed in the '88 uprising. In October, a few students from the Rangoon Institute of Technology got into a quarrel with auxiliary policemen at a local restaurant. The policemen beat and arrested several students. Protests broke out, demanding the release of the students and an end to police brutality. The students were released, but the victory was short-lived. More students were detained. In response, students gathered in the center of Rangoon to listen to speeches on the history of student activism in Burma. Late in the night, with speeches still going on, riot police scattered the group, beating and arresting those who remained.

After the 1996 demonstrations, the universities were again closed; most did not reopen until 2000. Although little changed, the demonstrations served an important role in sustaining the spirit of the democracy movement.

In 2000, the regime again placed Aung San Suu Kyi under house arrest. She was freed in 2002 and embarked on a tour around the country, delivering speeches in Rangoon and visiting the rural ethnic nationality areas. Everywhere she traveled, large crowds gathered to hear her speak. In 2003, her motorcade was attacked by a government-sponsored mob in an incident known as the Depayin Massacre. Aung San Suu Kyi's driver managed to protect her, but dozens of her supporters were killed. She was placed back under house arrest soon after the event. Nobody was ever convicted for the attack.

1991–2007 (Part II): The Globalization of Burma—*Both the regime and the democracy movement, led by Aung San Suu Kyi, took advantage of the rapidly growing global economy and information networks.*

After the 1990 election, the regime began courting foreign investment, most notably by inviting foreign investors to create apparel factories for export to Western markets, and by signing natural gas pipeline deals with U.S.-owned Unocal and French-owned Total. During the years immediately following the '88 uprising, the government struggled to pay its civil servants and solicited business deals with the West for money.

The democracy movement organized to cut off the military's new revenue sources. Following the model of Nelson Mandela's African National Congress that brought an end to white minority rule in South Africa, Aung San Suu Kyi and the NLD reached out to activists in the West to block the regime's financial lifelines. In a 1997 *New York Times* op-ed, Aung San Suu Kyi wrote, "...[investment] only goes to enrich an already wealthy elite bent on monopolizing both economic and political power... Take a principled stand against companies that are doing business with the Burmese military regime." Solidarity groups began to emerge around the Western world.

The U.S.-based Free Burma Coalition, founded in 1995 by a PhD candidate named Zarni, used boycotts to pressure American multinationals. They organized a vast decentralized network of activists to hold demonstrations at college campuses and shopping malls. The movement experienced its first victory when Pepsi agreed to cut its relations with Burma's regime after college students across the U.S. convinced their schools to end contracts with the company in protest of their business with Buma's regime. Levi-Strauss, May department stores, and scores of additional U.S. companies followed suit. After nearly all American companies had cut business ties with the military regime, activists pressured Congress to make sourcing from Burma illegal for all U.S. businesses, which became law in the 2003 Burmese Freedom and Democracy Act. Burma Campaign UK and other European Burma campaigns experienced many similar successes.

In the early 1990s, a recent graduate from University of Virginia Law School, Katie Redford, teamed up with a Karen activist, Ka Hsaw Wa, to use the law to target the regime's financiers. In 2005, U.S.-owned Unocal settled out of court on a lawsuit that accused the company of using forced labor to build a pipeline in Karen State. The activists had resurrected a 1789 statute, which stipulates that U.S. companies can be sued for violations of the "Laws of Nations." That same year Unocal sold their shares of the pipeline to Chevron, which still operates in Burma due to an exemption in the 2003 U.S. sanctions.

The regime's base of support shifted with changes in the world economy. Throughout the 1990s, the regime financed its military with Western natural gas projects. As the Asian economies grew and globalized, more Asian companies joined their Western counterparts. Korean-owned Daewoo signed on to explore the Shwe Gas fields in 2004, and in 2008, the China National Petroleum Corporation (CNPC) signed a deal for the sale and transport of Shwe Gas to China via an overland pipeline.

In 2003, Zarni of the Free Burma Coalition participated in a joint study with other exiles, which concluded that the Western boycott could not bring an end to military rule in Burma while Thailand, India, and China continued to support the regime. Solidarity activists began to look for other strategies of influence. The plan formulated in 1990 had relied on a world in which the United States and Western Europe were the only major powers. By the mid-2000s, Western governments would have to find ways to work with Asian governments to exert influence on Burma's ruling junta.

Global Burma solidarity groups increasingly took their work to the level of the United Nations. In 2008, the solidarity groups launched a campaign to bring Burma's generals before the International Criminal Court (ICC) for their human rights violations in ethnic nationality areas. As of August 2010, the United States, the United Kingdom, Australia, and the Czech Republic have endorsed this call.

2007: Saffron Revolution—*A new generation of activists enter Burma's political arena.*

In September 2007, tens of thousands of monks marched down the streets of Burma's major cities. They called for dialogue between the military government and the democracy movement, as well as an end to a price hike that was wreaking havoc on Burma's poor.

In mid-August, the regime had unexpectedly increased diesel and compressed natural gas prices. Food and transportation costs rose, putting strains on Burma's people. Students from the newly formed '88 Student Group—activists who had participated in the 1988 uprising nearly nineteen years before—began marching in Rangoon, demanding a drop in fuel costs. The regime quickly arrested many of the demonstrators.

After the arrest of the '88 Student Group students, a group of monks took over the protests. They marched through the streets of Sittwe and Rangoon, chanting the *Metta Sutra* prayer of loving-kindness and calling for the regime to lower prices. The monk demonstration took place in several cities. It was a huge public relations liability to the regime, which partly claims its legitimacy from being "good Buddhists." On September 5, the authorities in Pakokku reacted harshly, tying up and beating some of the monks. News about the beatings spread quickly. Up until that point, the monk demonstrations had remained relatively small, but the authorities' actions provoked many monks and laypeople alike.

On September 10, a newly formed group called the All Burma Monks' Alliance (ABMA) issued a statement calling for the regime to apologize to the monks, reduce fuel and food prices, release all political prisoners, and begin dialogue with the democracy movement—or face a countrywide religious boycott where monks would refuse to provide their services to the military.

Eight days later, tens of thousands of monks marched down the streets of Rangoon, Mandalay, Sittwe, and other towns and cities across the country. Monks marched with their alms bowl upside down, symbolizing that they were refusing to take offerings from the military. The protests grew. Laypeople formed human chains around the monks. On September 22, the monks marched by the house of Aung San Suu Kyi, where she remained under house arrest. She paid the monks respect from behind the gates of her compound.

On September 24, the state-appointed monastic council, the Sangha Maha Nayaka, warned monks not to engage in secular affairs. The protesting monks did not submit to the warning and again gathered by the thousands in the street, singing the *Metta Sutra* prayer of loving kindness. Soldiers and military trucks were deployed in downtown Rangoon in front of Shwedagon Pagoda, Burma's most famous religious site, which the monks were using as a base for their demonstrations. Commentators had been speculating for days about whether the soldiers would fire into a crowd of monks.

In front of the pagoda, the soldiers gave the monks one last warning to disperse. The monks stood fast and asked the soldiers to drop their weapons and join them. The soldiers refused, and instead began beating and arresting monks, firing tear gas, rubber bullets and—later that day—live rounds at the monks. Across the country the protests were broken up in the same way.

After cracking down on the protests, the regime cracked down on the monasteries. Many of the activists involved in the uprising were given long jail sentences of up to sixty-five years in prison; in the months following the demonstration, the number of political prisoners in Burma doubled to nearly 2,100. Monasteries were raided and some left nearly deserted as monks were either imprisoned or fled to the jungle or to neighboring countries. However, many hold that the demonstration was not a failure.

The uprising gave rise to a new generation of activist groups, such as Generation Wave, which uses hip-hop and graffiti to spread anti-junta messages. Perhaps most significantly, the uprising destroyed any public image of the "consent of the governed." Images of soldiers beating monks on the street quickly shattered the regime's claim of being "good Buddhists."

2008: Constitution and Referendum—Five months after cracking down on the monks' protests, the regime announced it had finished the constitutional drafting process that it embarked upon in 1991. The new constitution was "approved" by the people of Burma in a process that Burma experts consider fraudulent. According to the government, the popular referendum on the constitution was approved by 92.5 percent of voters, with a 98.1 percent voter turnout.

Many of the provisions in the constitution have caused uproar among Burma's democratic forces, ethnic minority groups, and the international community. Some of the key grievances include the following:

—The constitution requires all ceasefire groups to consolidate into a Border Guard Force/Home Guard Force under the supervision of the national government—a request which has proven to be unrealistic.

—It provides no civilian oversight of the military.

—It specifies that those married to foreigners are not able to run for political office, thus barring Aung San Suu Kyi from the political process.

—25 percent of the seats in parliament are reserved for the military. A 75 percent vote is needed to reform the constitution.

—The military is allowed to dissolve the parliament to maintain the peace.

Despite these criticisms, those who believe that the constitution may be a small step in the right direction point out that:

—The new parliament is partly federated, with seven ethnic states and seven Burman-dominated regions in central Burma all represented.

—The new parliament will give a new venue for people to publicly air grievances.

—The constitution also sets up regional parliaments, which, some argue, will make regional government more accountable.

May 2008: Cyclone Nargis—*The deadliest storm in Burma's recorded history shed light on the regime's relationship to the international community, as well as its lack of strong institutions for handling emergencies.*

When Cyclone Nargis ripped through the wooden homes and rice paddies of Burma's Irrawaddy Delta in 2008, some 140,000 people were left dead. Below is a timeline of the events surrounding the storm:

May 2

—Evening, storm makes landfall on the mouth of the Irrawaddy River.

May 3

—Cyclone Nargis sweeps through Irrawaddy Delta with winds of up to 132 miles per hour and a storm surge of twelve feet.

May 4

—The regime reports 20,000 homes destroyed and 90,000 people made homeless. Early death estimates are in the hundreds but are expected to rise.

—The World Food Program and other aid agencies already on the ground in Burma are able to attend to some of the victims, but are unable to approach the worst affected areas.

May 5

—The official death toll reaches almost 15,000.

—The regime issues a rare appeal for foreign aid, provided the government be allowed to supervise its distribution.

—French President Sarkozy denounces this condition of aid transfer as unacceptable. That same day, U.S. First Lady Laura Bush takes the opportunity to lambaste the regime for a litany of failings, including failure to issue a storm warning, proceeding with plans for a constitutional referendum scheduled for May 10, and continuing to hold political prisoners.

—Aid groups criticize Bush, warning that a staunch political stance may increase the regime's reluctance to accept aid workers.

—At the same time, the U.S. gives a quarter of a million dollars in aid to be distributed by the regime.

—Regime announces it will go forward with the referendum scheduled for May 10.

May 6

—With global attention focused on Burma, the U.S. House of Representatives passes a resolution condemning the regime for a number of its undemocratic actions, starting with Ne Win's 1974 creation of the Burmese Socialist Party and ending with the referendum scheduled to take place on the May 10. The members of Congress state their hope for the resolution to dissuade the regime from holding the referendum.

May 7

—Indian and Bangledeshi airplanes land in Rangoon with aid for the delta.

—The regime accepts the aid but refuses to grant visas to aid workers.

—France calls for an international humanitarian intervention.

—France's request for a UN Security Council–led discussion on intervention is vetoed by permanent members China and Russia. The countries accuse France of making a dangerous attempt to expand the council's mandate.

May 9

—The regime states that it will allow aid supplies and money, but not aid workers.

May 10

—The regime holds a referendum on the 2008 constitution in all but the hardest-hit areas.

May 14

—Neoconservative thinker Robert Kagan publishes an article in the *New York Times* calling for armed intervention, which he openly hopes will lead to regime change.

May 15

—The regime grants visas to aid workers from countries in the Association of South East Asian Nations (ASEAN), but not to Western aid workers.

—Forty-three members of the U.S. Congress send a letter to President Bush calling for a humanitarian intervention into Burma's sovereignty.

May 16

—Burma's state television counts 77,738 dead and 55, 917 missing.

May 23

—Regime pledges to allow aid workers from all nations access to the delta.

Following months

—Debate rages in Western donor countries about the effectiveness of the aid given to Burma for the cyclone survivors.

—Humanitarian aid groups working in the disaster zone note the growth of civil society as Burmese citizens mobilize their own networks to deliver aid. These breakthroughs are documented in reports by Refugees International and other humanitarian aid organizations.

—Workers providing aid are subject to crackdowns by the military government. A report released jointly by Johns Hopkins University's Bloomberg School of Public Health's Human Rights Clinic and the Thailand–Burma border based Emergency Assistance Team Burma (EAT Burma) documents multiple human rights abuses, including forced relocations and ethnic discrimination in aid distribution.

IX. THE THREE PRIMARY ACTORS:

THE NATIONAL LEAGUE FOR DEMOCRACY
THE NON-STATE ARMED GROUPS
THE MILITARY GOVERNMENT

Burma's democracy activists and solidarity groups call for "genuine tripartite dialogue," or a discussion between the three primary actors in Burma's politics: the democracy movement, the ethnically based armed groups, and the military. Below is a brief sketch of these actors.

The National League for Democracy (NLD) and Aung San Suu Kyi—*The decisive winner of the 1990 elections, the National League for Democracy seeks national reconciliation.*

Although the party is dominated by the valley-dwelling Burman majority, their leader, Aung San Suu Kyi, has made strides toward gaining the trust of Burma's many ethnic groups. She is considered a national icon, as was her father General Aung San, the hero of Burma's independence movement. Many inside Burma and around the world hope that, if she remains free, she can help build trust between Burma's majority Burman population and the groups of ethnic minorities that have been at war with the central state for decades. She was released from her term under house arrest on November 13 2010. She has stated that her first step is to "listen to the people."

The NLD had operated legally in Burma since the 1990 election, with NLD offices serving as hubs of anti-dictatorship speech despite the regime's continued crackdown against its members. The party was officially banned and its offices closed in May 2010, after the NLD's Central Executive Committee voted to boycott the 2010 elections. This boycott was in response to the regime's refusal to allow political prisoners to run for election. This left the NLD, whose key leaders are often in and out of prison, in a difficult position. The NLD also wanted changes to be made to the 2008 constitution before they would run in the election that was to put the constitution into practice. Some have speculated that the NLD's newly banned status will re-invigorate their underground organizing efforts.

Aung San Suu Kyi, the NLD's General Secretary, was awarded the Nobel Peace Prize in 1991 and is an international icon for peace and democracy. The National League for Democracy has enjoyed strong support from Western governments, with the United States as one of its strongest backers. Aung San Suu Kyi's name has been mentioned over 1,000 times on the floor of the U.S. Congress, and she is the recipient of the Congressional Medal of Honor—the highest award Congress can bestow on any civilian. The U.S. has also helped to keep Burma on the international agenda in the UN and other international venues, such as US-ASEAN summits. Numerous countries in Europe, the United States, Canada, Australia, and New Zealand, as well as Western donors, aid refugees and political dissidents on the Thailand–Burma border. The voices of exiled members of Burma's democracy movement are broadcast into the country over Western-funded Burmese-language radio services such as Voice of America, Radio Free Asia, and the British Broadcasting Corporation, which reach millions of listeners.

The Ethnic Armed Groups—*Both ceasefire and resistance ethnic nationality movements are concerned about autonomy.*

Most of Burma's major ethnic groups have at some time since independence been organized around armed resistance movements. In general, the leaders of these movements seek autonomy within a federated, democratic Burma. However, many of the groups have their roots in secessionist struggles, and independence sentiment remains strong within their ranks.

Mizzima, a Burmese exile media outlet, identifies nineteen major ethnic nationality armies, all of whom signed ceasefire agreements with the regime between 1990 and 1995. These groups include the Shan State Army-North, United Wa State Army, and Democratic Karen Buddhist Army. Mizzima also identifies five non-state armed groups who are still fighting today: the Shan State Army-South, the Karen National Liberation Army, the Arakan Liberation Army, the Karenni Army, and the Chin Liberation Front.

The government has called for the armed groups to reconstitute themselves into Border Guard Forces and Home Guard Forces under the command of the Burmese military. As of November 2010, only a handful have complied with this order. This situation has led to high-profile standoffs between some of the ethnic groups' militaries, particularly the Kachin and the Wa. Some analysts have questioned what this will mean for the long-term stability of the ceasefire agreements.

The Military Regime—*The military regime seeks to consolidate its power over all of Burma.*

Burma has been ruled by its military since 1962. It has one of the largest armed forces in the world. The state spends about 40 percent of its budget on the military and less then 3 percent on healthcare in a country where an estimated 32 percent of children are born moderately or severely underweight. The World Health Organization ranks Burma's healthcare system 190 out of 191. Rampant human rights abuses, such as extrajudicial killings, arbitrary incarceration, impunity for rape, the use of child soldiers, and forced relocations have all been well documented by human rights groups.

A few years after Burma's independence in 1948, the country was destabilized by non-state armed groups and divided leadership in the central government. Many of the armed groups, such as the KMT, the Karen National Defence Organization, and the Red Flag Communists, were in some way supported by foreign powers (the United States, the United Kingdom, and the People's Republic of China, respectively). Burma's ruling generals began their military careers fighting in Burma's jungles against these non-state armed groups. Battles raged though the 1950s, '60s, '70s, and '80s. It was not until the 1990s that the regime signed ceasefire agreements. The current government sees this as its accomplishment, one that it believes is secured with force. The military also claims success in improving the government's financial stability though natural gas extraction.

Some have speculated that in the wake of the 2010 election, new political groups will emerge and Burma watchers will need to reconceptualize Burma's primary actors. Since *Nowhere to Be Home* is going to press only shortly after the elections, it is still too soon for this book to discuss whether this will be the case.

X. BURMESE IN THAILAND

MIGRANTS FROM BURMA IN THAILAND
by Soe Lin Aung, MAP Foundation

Some 2–4 million migrants from all over Burma have chosen to live and work in Thailand, their migration rooted in decades of political and economic stagnation inside Burma. In a range of sectors and occupations, and in many different parts of Thailand, migrant communities help drive the country's economy, and in many places have become part of the fabric of everyday life. Thailand's export industries, long the cornerstone of the Thai economy, feature high concentrations of migrants from Burma, especially in factory-based garment and textile manufacturing. Many migrants also work in construction and agriculture, in domestic work, in the sex and entertainment industries, on plantations, in the seafood industry, in small-scale shops and marketplaces, and as restaurant workers and waste-pickers. While Thailand has sought to increase migrant registration and formalize migration channels in recent years, these attempts have seen only limited success; the vast majority of migrants remain undocumented, with restricted access to healthcare, education, and legal justice. Working conditions, labor rights, and wages are substandard in many migrant communities, while the constant threat of arrest, detention, deportation, and extortion serves to compound the challenges migrants face every day. Still, migrants and their families have drawn on strong community networks to maintain a resilient sense of social dignity and cultural pride, thereby challenging their victimization and making progress in their communities.

BURMESE POLITICAL GROUPS IN THAILAND
by Thelma Young

After the fall of the armed resistance headquarters of Manerplaw in 1995, many people from Burma working for democratic change began to set up offices along the Thailand–Burma border. The Thai town of Mae Sot holds the greatest number of organizations and offices. Other ethnic democratic and social organizations opened offices in Mae Hong Son, Mae Sariang, and Sangklaburi, where they are geographically closer to their ethnic communities in Burma. These organizations, if based in Burma, would face severe oppression and debilitating restrictions. Even operating in Thailand, they have to maintain a low presence and work below the radar for their security, so as not to garner attention that would impact Thailand–Burma relations.

The network of Burmese human rights and democracy organizations along the Thailand–Burma border, as well as on the China, India, and Bangladesh borders with Burma, constitute an extensive and developed underground civil society. There are a significant number of organizations; most ethnic groups have at least a youth group, a women's organization, a political organization, and other social development organizations.

Though their offices are based on the Thailand–Burma border, these organizations do substantial and covert work inside Burma. They help their communities inside run social and democratic programs, and share information that would otherwise be completely blocked. Though the border organizations are widespread and diverse, almost all share the common goal of bringing democratic change and national reconciliation to Burma, and in recent years there have been extensive efforts from organizations to cooperate more toward these goals.

BURMESE REFUGEES IN THAILAND

There are approximately 150,000 refugees from Burma living in nine official refugee camps on the Thailand–Burma border. Refugees living in the camps are supplied with basic housing and food rations, as well as access to education. However, the refugees are not given freedom of movement. They are "warehoused," meaning they are not permitted to leave the camp they live in. Some refugees have been born inside the camps, never allowed to leave, or have otherwise been kept inside for up to twenty years. The United States has started an ambitious resettlement program which resettled nearly 17,000 refugees from Burma in 2010 alone. However, resettlement does not necessarily mean a decrease in the refugee camp population; conflict in eastern Burma is ongoing, and the possibility of resettlement may attract refugees to live in the camp as opposed to other options like migrant work. Thailand—along with Malaysia, Bangladesh, and the United States—is not one of the 141 nations that signed the 1951 refugee convention.

XI. MAE TAO CLINIC

In the narrative that appears on pages 87 to 93, Naw Moe Wai describes her experience being helped by a free clinic called the Mae Tao Clinic, and a special program set up through the clinic called the Burma Children Medical Fund (BCMF). To find out more about the vital work of these two organizations, please see: www.maetaoclinic.org and www.burmachildren.com.

Naw Moe Wai is one of many people who, due to lack of access to adequate healthcare inside Burma, go to the Mae Tao Clinic each month for free or greatly reduced treatment expenses. The Mae Tao Clinic was established in Mae Sot, Thailand in 1989 to meet the needs of Burmese migrants in Thailand and internally displaced people in Burma. Its founder is Dr. Cynthia Maung, a Karen doctor who fled Burma along with many of her compatriots in 1988. According to the Mae Tao Clinic's 2009 Annual Report, the clinic saw 75,210 total patients in 2009 and had 153,703 total visits to the clinic within the year. In 2009, the Mae Tao Clinic's caseload experienced a 24 percent increase from the previous year, and it only continues to grow.

Because the Mae Tao Clinic does not have the funding or resources to perform major surgeries, Naw Moe Wai's daughter Phyu Phyu is currently receiving treatment through the Burma Children Medical Fund (BCMF). The BCMF was set up in response to the increasing number of children at Mae Tao Clinic who require surgery that neither the clinic nor Mae Sot Hospital can provide. Often the only chance these children have to undergo surgery is to be referred to Chiang Mai Hospital or another major hospital.

XII. THE ROHINGYA: STATELESS PEOPLE

by Chris Lewa

Adapted from an article titled "North Arakan: An Open prison for the Rohingya" that appeared in Forced Migration Review *issue 32, online at: www.fmreview.org/statelessness.htm.*

Many minorities, including the Rohingya of Burma, are persecuted by being rendered stateless.

Hundreds of thousands of Rohingya people have fled to Bangladesh and farther afield to escape oppression or in order to survive. There were mass exoduses to Bangladesh in 1978 and again in 1991–92. Each time, international pressure persuaded Burma to accept them back and repatriation followed, often under coercion. But the outflow continues.

The Rohingya are an ethnic, linguistic, and religious minority group mainly concentrated in North Arakan (or "Rakhine") State in Burma, adjacent to Bangladesh, where their number is estimated at 725,000. Of South Asian descent, they are related to the Chittagonian Bengalis just across the border in Bangladesh, whose language is also related. They profess Sunni Islam and are distinct from the majority Burmese population who are of East Asian stock and mostly Buddhists. Since Burma's independence in 1948, the Rohingya have gradually been excluded from the process of nation-building.

The 1982 Citizenship Law

In 1982, Burma's military rulers brought in a new Citizenship Law which deprived most people of Indian and Chinese descent of citizenship. However, the timing of its promulgation, shortly after the refugee repatriation of 1979, strongly suggests that it was specifically designed to exclude the Rohingya. Unlike the preceding 1948 Citizenship Act, the 1982 law is essentially based on the principle of *jus sanguinis* and identifies three categories of citizens: full, associate, and naturalized.

Full citizens are those belonging to one of 135 "national races" settled in Burma before 1823, the start of the British colonization of Arakan. The Rohingyas do not appear in this list and the government does not recognise the term "Rohingya." Associate citizenship was only granted to those whose application for citizenship under the 1948 act was pending on the date the act came into force. Naturalized citizenship could only be granted to those who could furnish "conclusive evidence" of entry and residence before Burma's Independence on January 4, 1948, who could speak one of the national languages well, and whose children were born in Burma. Very few Rohingyas could fulfil these requirements. Moreover, the wide powers assigned to a government-controlled "Central Body" to decide on matters pertaining to citizenship mean that, in practice, the Rohingyas' entitlement to citizenship would not be recognized.

In 1989, color-coded Citizens Scrutiny Cards (CRCs) were introduced: pink cards for full citizens, blue for associate citizens, and green for naturalized citizens. The Rohingya were not issued any cards. In 1995, in response to the UNHCR's intensive advocacy efforts to document the Rohingyas, the Burmese authorities started issuing them a Temporary Registration Card (TRC), a white card, pursuant to the 1949 Residents of Burma Registration Act. The TRC does not mention the bearer's place of birth and cannot be used to claim citizenship. The family list, which every family residing in Burma possesses, only records family members and their date of birth. It does not indicate the place of birth and therefore provides no official evidence of birth in Burma—and so perpetuates the Rohingyas' statelessness.

The Rohingya are recognized neither as citizens nor as foreigners. The Burmese government also objects to them being described as stateless persons but appears to have created a special category for them: "Myanmar residents," which is not a legal status. However, on more than one occasion, government officials have described them as "illegal immigrants from Bangladesh." In 1998, in a letter to the UNHCR, Burma's then–Prime Minister General Khin Nyunt wrote: "These people are not originally from Myanmar but have illegally migrated to Myanmar because of population pressures in their own country." And a February 2009 article in the government-owned *New Light of Myanmar* newspaper stated that, "In Myanmar there is no national race by the name of Rohinja."

Deprivation of citizenship has served as a key strategy to justify arbitrary treatment and discriminatory policies against the Rohingya. Severe restrictions on their movements are increasingly applied. They are banned from employment in the civil service, including in the education and health sectors. In 1994, the authorities stopped issuing Rohingya children with birth certificates. By the late 1990s, official marriage authorizations were made mandatory. Infringement of these stringent rules can result in long prison sentences. Other coercive measures, such as forced labor, arbitrary taxation, and confiscation of land, also practiced elsewhere in Burma, are imposed on the Rohingya population in a disproportionate manner.

RESTRICTIONS OF MOVEMENT

The Rohingya are virtually confined to their village tracts. They need to apply and pay for a travel pass even to visit a neighboring village. Travel is strictly restricted to North Arakan. Even Sittwe, the state capital, has been declared off-limits for them. Their lack of mobility has devastating consequences, limiting their access to markets, employment opportunities, health facilities, and higher education. Those who overstay the time allowed by their travel pass are prevented from returning to their village as their names are deleted from their family list. They are then obliterated administratively and compelled to leave Burma. Some Rohingyas have been prosecuted under national security legislation for traveling without permission.

Rohingyas are also forbidden to travel to Bangladesh, although in practice obtaining a travel pass to a border village and then crossing clandestinely into Bangladesh has proved easier than reaching Sittwe. But, similarly, those caught doing so could face a jail sentence there for illegal entry. Many people, including patients who sought medical treatment in Bangladesh, were unable to return home when, during their absence, their names were cancelled on their family list. Once outside Burma, Rohingyas are systematically denied the right to return to their country.

MARRIAGE AUTHORIZATIONS

In the late 1990s, a local order was issued in North Arakan, applying exclusively to the Muslim population, requiring couples planning to marry to obtain official permission from the local authorities—usually the NaSaKa, Burma's Border Security Force. Marriage authorizations are granted on the payment of fees and bribes and can take up to several years to obtain. This is beyond the means of the poorest. This local order also prohibits any cohabitation or sexual contact outside wedlock. It is not backed by any domestic legislation, but breaching it can lead to prosecution, punishable by up to ten years imprisonment.

In 2005, as the NaSaKa was reshuffled following the ousting of General Khin Nyunt, marriage authorizations were completely suspended for several months. When they restarted issuing them in late 2005, additional conditions were attached, including the stipulation that couples have to sign an undertaking not to have more than two children. The amount of bribes and time involved in securing a marriage permit keeps increasing year after year.

The consequences have been dramatic, particularly on women. Rohingya women who become pregnant without official marriage authorization often resort to backstreet abortions, an illegal practice in Burma, which has resulted in many maternal deaths. Others register their newborn child with another legally married couple, sometimes their own parents. Some deliver the baby secretly in Bangladesh and abandon the baby there. Many children are reportedly unregistered. Many young couples, unable to obtain permission to marry, flee to Bangladesh in order to live together.

EDUCATION AND HEALTH CARE

As non-citizens, the Rohingya are excluded from government employment in health and education, and those public services are appallingly neglected in North Arakan. Schools and clinics are mostly attended by Rakhine or Burmese staff who are unable to communicate in the local language and who often treat Rohingyas with contempt. International humanitarian agencies are not allowed to train Muslim health workers, not even auxiliary midwives. Some Rohingya teach in government schools, and are paid in rice-paddies under a food-for-work program, as they cannot hold an official, remunerated teacher's post.

Restrictions of movement have a serious impact on access to health and education. Even in emergencies, Rohingyas must apply for travel permission to reach the poorly equipped local hospital. Access to better medical facilities in Sittwe hospital is denied. Referral of critically ill patients is practically impossible. Consequently, patients who can afford it have sought medical treatment in Bangladesh but are sometimes unable to return to their village. Likewise, there are few secondary schools in North Arakan and pupils need travel permission to study outside their village. The only university is in Sittwe. After 2001, most students could no longer attend classes and had to rely on distance learning, only being allowed to travel to Sittwe to sit examinations. Since 2005, however, even that has been prohibited.

Not surprisingly, illiteracy among the Rohingya is high, estimated at 80 percent.
For the Rohingya, the compounded effect of these various forms of persecution has driven many into dire poverty, and their degrading conditions have caused mental distress, pushing them to flee across the border to Bangladesh.

In Exile

In Bangladesh, the 28,000 Rohingyas still remaining in two camps are recognized as refugees and benefit from limited protection and assistance by the UNHCR, but it is estimated that up to 200,000 more live outside the camps. Bangladesh considers them irregular migrants and they have no access to official protection.

The combination of their lack of status in Bangladesh and their statelessness in Burma puts them at risk of indefinite detention. Several hundred Rohingyas are currently languishing in Bangladeshi jails, arrested for illegal entry. Most are still awaiting trial, sometimes for years. Dozens have completed their sentences but remain in jail—called "released prisoners"—as they cannot be officially released and deported, since Burma refuses to re-admit them.

Tens of thousands of Rohingyas have sought opportunities overseas, in the Middle East and increasingly in Malaysia, using Bangladesh and Thailand as transit countries. Stateless and undocumented, they have no other option than relying on unsafe illegal migration channels, falling prey to unscrupulous smugglers and traffickers, or undertaking risky journeys on boats.

In December 2008, Thailand started implementing a new policy of pushing Rohingya boat people back to the high seas. In at least three separate incidents, 1,200 boat people were handed over to the Thai military on a deserted island off the Thai coast and ill-treated before being towed out to sea on boats without an engine and with little food and water. After drifting for up to two weeks, three boats were finally rescued in the Andaman and Nicobar Islands of India, and two boats in the Aceh province of Indonesia. More than 300 boat people are reportedly missing, believed to have drowned.

The issuing of a TRC to Rohingyas has been praised as "a first step towards citizenship." On May 10, 2008, the Rohingya were allowed to vote in the constitutional referendum, but the new constitution, which was approved, does not contain any provisions granting them citizenship rights. Although they were also permitted to participate in the controversial general elections on November 7, 2010, there is no political will for the Rohingya to be accepted as Burmese citizens in the foreseeable future.

> *"We, Rohingyas, are like birds in a cage. However, caged birds are fed*
> *while we have to struggle alone to feed ourselves."*
> *—A Rohingya villager from Maungdaw, North Arakan*

Chris Lewa is coordinator of the Arakan Project, a local NGO primarily dedicated to the protection and promotion of human rights for the Rohingya minority of Burma, through documentation (including first-hand testimonies) and research-based advocacy.

NOWHERE TO BE HOME

XIII. REFUGEE RESETTLEMENT TO THE UNITED STATES

The United States accepts more Burmese refugees than any other country. Other countries to which Burmese refugees are resettled include Australia, Canada, New Zealand, and the Nordic countries. Unlike Finland, Norway, and Canada, which seek the most trained and educated refugees and rank applicants according to integration potential, the United States does not rank refugees based on their level of education and professional potential. According to UNHCR guidelines, refugees are not able to choose the country to which they will be resettled.

The United States has implemented an ambitious resettlement program; the number of Burmese refugees resettled to the United States has increased exponentially since 2006. In 2006, approximately 1,000 people were resettled from Burma. In 2007, the number was increased to 13,000. The total number of Burmese refugees resettled to the U.S. in 2010 was 16,693. In 2011, the U.S. plans to admit 18,500 refugees from Burma.

In order to qualify for resettlement in the U.S., a refugee must a) belong to an ethnicity considered a priority for resettlement by the United States, b) be referred by a U.S. embassy, the UNHCR, or another non-governmental organization, c) meet the U.S. definition of a refugee as determined by the U.S. Department of Homeland Security (DHS) / U.S. Citizen and Immigration Services (USCIS), and d) not possess a number of criteria for exclusion. A refugee must also have access to a U.S. refugee processing post or USCIS/DHS officer and not already be resettled in another country.

The U.S. has a system for ranking importance for resettlement. Those who have been identified by the UNHCR, an NGO, or an embassy as individuals who do not have other safe options are put in the first priority group. The second priority group, referred to as "P2 groups," is for entire groups of people that the U.S. has identified as particularly vulnerable. From Burma, ethnic minorities that live in Thailand's refugee camps and ethnic minorities that are currently in Malaysia are both classified as P2 groups. The third grouping is focused on family reunification (spouses, unmarried children under twenty-one, or parents); the application for resettlement must be initiated by a family member living in the U.S., and is only open to certain nationalities.

The U.S. identifies a number of grounds for exclusion: health-related grounds (certain communicable diseases or mental and physical disorders), criminal/moral grounds (persons convicted of multiple serious crimes, drug trafficking, or prostitution), and security grounds. Waivers can be used to circumvent grounds of exclusion, except in the case of participation in genocide, conviction of a serious crime, membership in the Nazi party, and drug trafficking.

As of May 31, 2010, over 6,200 Burmese refugees successfully used waivers to be cleared of terrorist-based exclusion. Many of Burma's non-state armed groups fit the U.S. definition of terrorist groups, and many individuals among the ethnic groups seeking to be resettled have engaged in acts that the U.S. defines as providing "material support" to terrorists. These offenses range from acts as small as providing a member of an armed group with food or a place to stay, to more significant connections, such as membership in one of the armed groups.

When refugees arrive in the United States, they are placed with private and state agencies (known as VOLAGS, or "Voluntary Agencies") that have signed cooperative agreements with the State Department to provide services to the refugees for the first ninety days they are in the U.S. The organizations (which include the International Rescue Committee and Lutheran Immigration and Refugee Services, among others) often work with refugees' relatives who have filed sponsorship papers. For refugees without friends or family, an agency often contacts an individual, church, or outside group for additional sponsorship.

Refugees are eligible for a number of benefits upon arrival. They are granted eligibility for Welfare and Medicaid programs for the first eight months after they arrive, at the discretion of the state in which the refugee is a resident. After seven years, refugees become ineligible for most benefits if they do not acquire citizenship. Refugees are also able to attend public schools, but must pay tuition charges for most public universities. They are also granted employment benefits, but cannot work for the federal government until they are granted citizenship. Refugees can apply for a refugee travel document which allows them to leave the U.S. for up to one year. One year after arrival, refugees are eligible to adjust their status to permanent resident; five years after arrival, they can petition for naturalization.

Overseas Processing Entities (OPEs) handle refugee cases and facilitate aspects of U.S. refugee processing, specifically ensuring that refugees fit within the United States' processing priorities and are from a designated nationality accepted by the United States. OPEs assist refugees in their interviews with the DHS/USCIS, and after DHS/USCIS approval, OPEs work to arrange medical exams and transport to the U.S., as well as coordinating with a VOLAG about resettlement. The International Rescue Committee operates the OPE in Bangkok, Thailand which processes Burmese refugees from Thailand.

XIV. BURMESE REFUGEES IN MALAYSIA

by James Meisenheimer

Burmese refugees have been seeking safety within Malaysian borders for much of the past two decades. However, in recent years, the number of refugees fleeing to Malaysia has increased dramatically. The UNHCR officially recognizes that there are some 83,000 Burmese refugees and asylum seekers currently living in Malaysia. However, it is estimated that there are an additional 200,000 to 500,000 refugees in Malaysia who remain outside of the UNHCR's protection.

The vast majority of Burmese refugees enter Malaysia by land through its northern border with Thailand. Having come without passports, visas, or any other form of documentation, they often pay exorbitant sums of money to be smuggled into the country. Once they enter Malaysia, the refugees scatter to various parts of the country, mostly relying on networks of friends or relatives to find accommodation and employment. Unlike Thailand, there are no refugee camps in Malaysia. Multiple families often share single-room apartments in Malaysia's capital city, Kuala Lumpur. Living without documentation, Burmese refugees in Malaysia face constant security threats including arrest, detention in abject conditions, and deportation; they therefore must keep as low a profile as possible, in some cases rarely leaving their living quarters.

IMMIGRATION LAW ENFORCEMENT IN MALAYSIA

Despite persistent advocacy by Malaysian NGOs and international organizations, the Malaysian government has yet to ratify the 1951 UN Convention relating to the status of refugees and its 1967 Protocol. The Burmese who flee to Malaysia are classified as undocumented. The number of undocumented migrants in Malaysia has swelled to between 2 and 4 million as the country's economic growth has spurred increased demand for workers in the construction, manufacturing, fishing and service industries.

In 2009, the Malaysian government arrested 26,545 individuals for illegal entry into the country. The autonomy of the Malaysian police, immigration, and enforcement agencies has resulted in extensive abuses during the arrest operations of refugees. Instances of physical and verbal abuses, as well as monetary demands, are commonly reported, regardless of which agency is administering the arrest. The agencies are also able to determine procedures that follow after an arrest.

While Malaysian law requires that all individuals be brought to court, many are immediately brought to one of Malaysia's Immigration Detention Centers (IDCs). Forgoing the legal process makes it more difficult for the UNHCR and refugee community organizations to track and help individuals who are arrested. If a refugee is brought before a court, they are usually charged and found guilty of illegal entry and unlawful presence in Malaysia under the 1959/63 Immigration Act. This offense is punishable by a sentence of up to, but not exceeding, five years of imprisonment, six strokes of cane, and a fine of

10,000 MYR ($3,300 USD). In June 2009 the Malaysian government announced that they had sentenced 47,914 migrants—including both men and women—to be caned since the amendments took effect in 2002.

PROLONGED DETENTIONS, DIFFICULT CIRCUMSTANCES

Malaysia's immigration policy uses the fear of arrest, detention, and deportation as a deterrent to undocumented migration. The biggest fear for refugees in Malaysia is a prolonged sentence of detention in one of Malaysia's seventeen Immigration Detention Centers.

Until 2009, detainees were commonly trafficked to the Thai–Malay border, where they were either sold to human traffickers in Thailand or had to buy their freedom for 1,200–1,800 Malaysian rinngits ($400–600 USD). But after international criticism escalated, including the release of a report by the United States Senate Committee on Foreign Relations, trafficking practices have decreased. Unfortunately, this has led to an increase in lengths of detention to an average of six months, as well as greater overcrowding of IDCs.

Increased detention in substandard conditions has led to more deaths in detention centers. In 2009, it was reported that around 1,300 migrants and refugees had died while detained in IDCs since 2006.

The deaths of detainees in IDCs are directly linked to overcrowding, lack of medical access, and inadequate standards of accommodation, nutrition, and cleanliness. The duration of detention varies according to the ability of the UNHCR to interview and identify individuals who may be considered refugees. The more refugees are detained in IDCs, the harder it becomes for the UNHCR to conduct interviews quickly. In July 2009, there were 2,765 Burmese nationals held in Malaysian IDCs. For almost all of these individuals, the UNHCR offers their only hope of release.

REFUGEE COMMUNITY ORGANIZATIONS

Refugees in Malaysia are not allowed to work legally, travel freely or obtain access to healthcare and education. The UNHCR helps those who are registered under its protection in some of these regards, but for the other 200,000–500,000 refugees there is little they can do. Filling this void are a number of refugee community organizations that provide shelter, education, health access, and a loose network of employment. The organizations are divided along ethnic lines, with each ethnic group having one or more representative organizations, but most—with the exception of the Rohingya—are unified in the Coalition of Burmese Ethnics in Malaysia (COBEM). The refugee organizations are almost entirely self-sufficient and funded by the communities themselves.

By virtue of these organizations' existence, thousands of refugees have been resettled to third countries, and and thousands more have been able to survive in a country which deprives them of many human rights.

During 2009 and 2010, James Meisenheimer worked closely with the Arakan refugee community in Malaysia, documenting abuses and helping find legal assistance for refugees detained in Immigration Detention Centers.

XV. EDITOR'S NOTE FROM
LAW EH SOE'S STORY

Law Eh Soe's story raises larger questions and concerns about freedom of the press in Burma. Reporters Without Borders ranked Burma 171st out of 175 nations in their latest worldwide press freedom index, and reported that there are currently twelve journalists imprisoned in Burma. Freedom House gave Burma and North Korea the two worst ratings in their report "Freedom of the Press 2010," and wrote of the ten worst-rated countries: "In these states, which are scattered around the globe, independent media are either nonexistent or barely able to operate. The press acts as a mouthpiece for the regime, citizens' access to unbiased information is severely limited, and dissent is crushed through imprisonment, torture, and other forms of repression." The report also stated that "the Burmese junta was continuing to monitor internet cafes and that at least seventeen journalists were arrested and imprisoned by the end of last year [2009]." The military-run Press Scrutiny Board wields a heavy hand in censoring all publications, creating an environment in which many journalists censor themselves.

XVI. LEARN MORE ABOUT BURMA

NON-FICTION

—Christina Fink, *Living Silence: Burma Under Military Rule*

—Pascal Khoo Thwe, *From the Land of Green Ghosts: A Burmese Odyssey*

—Aung San Suu Kyi, *Freedom from Fear*

—Emma Larkin, *Finding George Orwell in Burma*

—Bertil Lintner, *Burma in Revolt: Opium and Insurgency Since 1948*

—Thant Myint-U, *The Making of Modern Burma*

—James C. Scott, *The Art of Not Being Governed*

—Martin Smith, *Burma: Insurgency and the Politics of Ethnicity*

—David Steinberg, *Burma / Myanmar: What Everyone Needs to Know*

—Sean Turnell, *Fiery Dragons: Banks, Money Lenders and Microfinance in Burma*

FICTION

—Amitav Ghosh, *The Glass Palace*

—George Orwell, *Burmese Days*

BURMESE LANGUAGE

—*Burmese By Ear* by John Okell, the world's leading Burma language instructor, course available for free download: http://www.soas.ac.uk/bbe/

The VOICE OF WITNESS SERIES

Voice of Witness is a nonprofit book series, published by McSweeney's, that empowers those most closely affected by contemporary social injustice. Using oral history as a foundation, the series depicts human rights crises in the United States and around the world. There are currently six books in the series, including:

SURVIVING JUSTICE
America's Wrongfully Convicted and Exonerated
Edited by Lola Vollen and Dave Eggers   Foreword by Scott Turow

These oral histories prove that the problem of wrongful conviction is far-reaching and very real. Through a series of all-too-common circumstances—eyewitness misidentification, inept defense lawyers, coercive interrogation—the lives of these men and women of all different backgrounds were irreversibly disrupted. In *Surviving Justice*, thirteen exonerees describe their experiences—the events that led to their convictions, their years in prison, and the process of adjusting to their new lives outside.

ISBN: 978-1-934781-25-8   469 pages   Paperback

VOICES FROM THE STORM
The People of New Orleans on Hurricane Katrina and Its Aftermath
Edited by Chris Ying and Lola Vollen

The second book in the McSweeney's Voice of Witness series, *Voices from the Storm* is a chronological account of the worst natural disaster in modern American history. Thirteen New Orleanians describe the days leading up to Hurricane Katrina, the storm itself, and the harrowing confusion of the days and months afterward. Their stories weave and intersect, ultimately creating an eye-opening portrait of courage in the face of terror, and of hope amid nearly complete devastation..

ISBN: 978-1-932416-68-8   320 pages   Paperback

UNDERGROUND AMERICA
Narratives of Undocumented Lives
Edited by Peter Orner   Foreword by Luis Alberto Urrea

They arrive from around the world for countless reasons. Many come simply to make a living. Others are fleeing persecution in their native countries. But by living and working in the U.S. without legal status, millions of immigrants risk deportation and imprisonment. They live underground, with little protection from exploitation at the hands of human smugglers, employers, or law enforcement. *Underground America* presents the remarkable oral histories of men and women struggling to carve a life for themselves in the United States.

ISBN: 978-1-934781-15-9   379 pages   Hardcover and paperback

OUT OF EXILE
The Abducted and Displaced People of Sudan
Edited by Craig Walzer
Additional interviews and an introduction by Dave Eggers
and Valentino Achak Deng

Millions of people have fled from conflicts and persecution in all parts of Sudan, and many thousands more have been enslaved as human spoils of war. In *Out of Exile*, refugees and abductees recount their escapes from the wars in Darfur and South Sudan, from political and religious persecution, and from abduction by militias. They tell of life before the war, and of the hope that they might someday find peace again.

ISBN: 978-1-934781-13-5   465 pages   Hardcover and paperback

HOPE DEFERRED
Narratives of Zimbabwean Lives
Edited by Peter Orner and Annie Holmes

The fifth volume in the Voice of Witness series presents the narratives of Zimbabweans whose lives have been affected by the country's political, economic, and human rights crises. This book asks the question: How did a country with so much promise—a stellar education system, a growing middle class of professionals, a sophisticated economic infrastructure, a liberal constitution, and an independent judiciary—go so wrong?

ISBN: 978-1-934781-94-4   304 pages   Hardcover and Paperback

Thanks to the generosity and assistance of many donors and volunteers, Voice of Witness is currently at work collecting oral histories for a variety of new projects around the world. For more information about the series, or to find out how you can help or donate to the cause, visit the Voice of Witness website:

VOICEOFWITNESS.ORG

ACKNOWLEDGEMENTS

We would like to express our deep gratitude to the narrators, who devoted an enormous amount of time and careful reflection in sharing their stories; the trust and courage they embody is an inspiration to us.

We thank all of our loved ones for their boundless support and encouragement throughout the process of compiling this volume, especially Susan, Gary, John, Jeannie, Dora, Lisa, Marc, Kika, and James. And for their commitment to social justice, we honor Eve, Dena, and Andrew; three friends whose lives continue to be measured in impact, not years.

We thank our Associate Editor, K'pru Taw; this book would have never come to fruition without his incredible commitment and his kind and sensitive way of engaging everyone he meets. We are deeply thankful to Michael Haack for giving so much of his time and detailed attention to the appendices as well as to each story. We are grateful to Emily Hong, Thelma Young, Debbie Landis, Cindy Choung and Soe Ling Aung for contributing their energy and vision to this project and supporting us in crucial ways, at critical times.

We are grateful to Amazon, the Open Society Institute, and Not On Our Watch, without whose support this project would not have been possible.

We thank the following experts for their continuous guidance throughout the process of compiling this book. Their advice and feedback played a critical role in shaping this project: David Scott Mathieson, Amy Alexander, Matthew Smith, The Arakan Project, Mike Paller, Josh Machleder, Christina Fink, Patrick Pierce, and Liz Tydeman.

We are extremely grateful to the following people for their support and generous assistance: mimi lok, Chris Ying, Juliana Sloane, James Robert Fuller, Min Zin, Ari Schindle, Ashin Sopaka, Greg Constantine, Alec Knuerr, Kim Jolliffe, Bill Berkeley, Po Po, Win Win, Jack Healey, Annie Tritt, Katrina Jorene Maliamauv, Professor David Steinberg, Professor John Dale, Casey McNeill, Brianna Townsend, Jared Hall, Marisa, Patrick Cook-Deegan, Nadi Hlaing, Molly Norris, K2, Khine Pray Thein, Latheefa Koya, Kanchana Thornton, Katie Camarena and Michele Bohana.

We are also indebted to all of the community and political organizations that took the time to advise us, guide our interviewee selection, and offer their support and encouragement. The interpreters deserve special thanks in particular for being consistently patient and gracious, and generously volunteering their time to support this project. Their work was critical to the completion of this book.

In particular, we would like to thank the people at EarthRights International, the Chin Refugee Center, the member groups of Coalition of Burma Ethnics–Malaysia, the Chin Human Rights Organization, Tenaganita, the US Campaign for Burma, Grassroots Human Rights Education and Development, the International Burmese Monks Organization, the All Burma Monks' Alliance, Generation Wave, Burma Children Medical Fund, Assistance Association for Political Prisoners (Burma), Zomi Service Center, the Network for Documentation–Burma, the National League for Democracy–Liberated Areas, Democratic Party for a New Society, and Burma Refugee Organization.

Although the information contained in the section introductions, the footnotes, the glossary, and the appendices has all been fact-checked to the best of our ability, please be aware that the situation in Burma and among the diaspora changes very quickly. As for Burma's history and politics, much of it, like all history and politics, is often subject to individual interpretation. Any and all errors are the responsibility of the editors and not those who graciously assisted the making of this book.

About THE EDITORS

MAGGIE LEMERE has traveled and worked in Asia, Africa, and Latin America. She holds an MA in international peace and conflict resolution from American University in Washington, D.C. Maggie focuses her writing and photography projects on issues of human rights and social concern.

ZOË WEST is a writer whose work investigates social issues and cultural exchange. Zoë grew up in the United States and has since lived and worked in Southeast Asia, Europe, and Central America. She is pursuing graduate studies in social anthropology at the University of Oxford.